# Site Development Foundations:
## Academic Student Guide

*President and COO*

Debra Hoopes

*Senior Vice President*

James Stanger, Ph.D.

*Vice President, Publishing*

Todd Hopkins

*Senior Content Developer*

Kenneth A. Kozakis

*Managing Editor*

Susan M. Lane

*Editor*

Sarah Skodak

*Project Manager/Publisher*

Tina Strong

Customer Service     ComputerPREP
Certification Partners, LLC
1230 W. Washington St., Ste. 111
Tempe, AZ 85281
(602) 275-7700

# Site Development Foundations

## Developers

James Stanger, Ph.D., and Kenneth A. Kozakis

## Contributors

Chris Rossi, Patrick T. Lane and Irina Heer

## Editor

Susan M. Lane

## Publisher

Tina Strong

## Project Managers

Todd Hopkins and Tina Strong

## Trademarks

## Disclaimer

## Copyright Information

# Table of Contents

## List of Labs

## List of Figures

## List of Tables

# Course Description

*Site Development Foundations* teaches you essential Web page development skills. You will learn to develop Web sites using Hypertext Markup Language (HTML) and Extensible HTML (XHTML). You will learn to write code manually, as well as use graphical user interface (GUI) authoring tools. You will also learn to insert images, create hyperlinks, and add tables, forms and frames to your Web pages.

In addition to learning about XHTML and HTML coding, you will learn about CGI and use it to connect Web pages to databases. Other topics include validating your XHTML code, recognizing the importance of Internet marketing and search engine optimization, using style sheets to format Web page content, and implementing fundamental design concepts. Throughout the course, you will learn how Web sites are developed as managed projects. You will also identify e-commerce solutions and relate Web site development to business goals.

*Site Development Foundations* provides an introduction to tasks, job roles and careers in Web development. This course will teach you to work as a productive part of a Web site development team. Hands-on labs include real-world scenarios based on a previously live version of the Habitat For Humanity site. Note that students will build prototype pages using Habitat For Humanity content. This content is provided by Habitat For Humanity with permission to use it in labs teaching site development skills. The prototype pages that students build do not necessarily represent, duplicate or simulate the current live Habitat For Humanity Web site, which can be visited at *www.habitat.org.*

All CIW Foundations courses offer Case Studies for class discussion about real-world skills applications, and job-related topics such as project management and the relationship between technology and business operations. Guided, step-by-step labs provide opportunities to practice new skills. You can challenge yourself and review your skills after each lesson in the Lesson Summary and Lesson Review sections. Additional skill reinforcement is provided in Activities, Optional Labs, Lesson Quizzes and a Course Assessment that are available from your instructor.

This coursebook includes a supplemental CD-ROM containing the lab files used in class. To practice the skills presented in class or to perform any labs that were not completed, refer to the Classroom Setup section for information about system requirements and using the lab files.

The CIW Foundations courses prepare students to take the CIW Foundations certification exam.

## Series

*Site Development Foundations* is the second course in the CIW Foundations series. CIW Foundations consists of the following courses:

- Internet Business Foundations

- *Site Development Foundations*

- Network Technology Foundations

## Prerequisites

No prior experience using the Internet, developing Web pages or configuring networks is necessary. However, students should be familiar with an operating system such as Microsoft Windows Vista before taking this course. The CIW Foundations courseware does not provide entry-level computer literacy. Rather, it builds upon computer literacy training and certifications such as Microsoft Office Specialist (*www.microsoft.com*) and IC[3] (*www.certiport.com*).

## Certification

The CIW Foundations series of courses prepares students to take the high-stakes CIW Foundations certification exam. Those who pass the CIW Foundations exam earn the highly respected CIW Associate certification, which is recognized throughout the industry as validating essential Internet skills for the workplace. The CIW Associate certification proves that an individual has evolved from being an Internet consumer to an Internet producer, capable of producing real-world Internet applications. A CIW Associate certificant can use common Internet-ready applications, can create properly formed HTML/XHTML documents, knows database essentials, understands project management concepts and can troubleshoot networks. For information about taking the CIW Foundations exam, visit *www.CIW-certified.com*.

# Courseware

This coursebook was developed for instructor-led training and will assist you during class. Along with comprehensive instructional text and objectives checklists, this coursebook provides easy-to-follow hands-on labs and a glossary of course-specific terms. It also provides Internet addresses needed to complete some labs, although due to the constantly changing nature of the Internet, some addresses may no longer be valid.

The student coursebook is organized in the following manner:

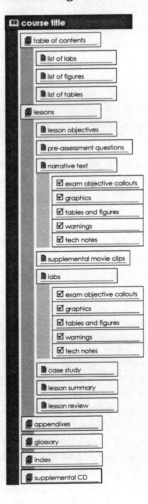

When you return to your home or office, you will find this coursebook to be a valuable resource for reviewing labs and applying the skills you have learned. Each lesson concludes with questions that review the material. Lesson review questions are provided as a study resource only and in no way guarantee a passing score on the CIW Foundations certification exam.

## Coursebook versions

The CIW Foundations courseware is designed for various classroom environments: academic, learning center and corporate. These coursebooks are available in both instructor and student versions. Student versions are available for both the academic environment and the learning center/corporate environment. Check your book to verify which version you have.

- **Instructor (Academic, Learning Center and Corporate)** — Example syllabi for 10-week and 16-week instruction periods are included on the instructor supplemental CD-ROM. Learning centers can teach this series at an accelerated pace; consult the implementation tables on the supplemental CD-ROM. The supplemental CD-ROM also includes an appendix listing the CIW Foundations certification exam objectives and locations of corresponding material in the coursebook. The instructor version of this book includes Instructor Notes in the margin, which provide additional tips and commentary for the instructor to supplement course narrative. Margin callouts also direct instructors to material that relates directly to specified CIW Foundations objectives. The instructor book and supplemental CD-ROM contain all answers to Activities (pen-and-paper-based), Optional Labs (computer-based), Lesson Quizzes and the Course Assessment. This book also includes handout versions of all Activities, Optional Labs, Lesson Quizzes and the Course Assessment, which the instructor can photocopy and assign during class or as homework. Lesson Quizzes and Course Assessments are provided as study and course-grading resources only; success on these materials in no way guarantees a passing score on the CIW Foundations certification exam. The movies provide supplementary instruction in a multimedia format, and enhance the coursebook narrative and labs. However, movie content does not comprehensively address CIW Foundations exam objectives and is not intended to replace coursebook content.

- **Student (Academic)** — The student book and supplemental CD-ROM include Pre-Assessment and Lesson Review questions for each lesson. However, the student book does not provide answers to these questions. It also does not include any Activities, Optional Labs, Quizzes or the Course Assessment. Students can obtain these elements and answers only from the instructor. The student supplemental CD-ROM contains appendixes and files used to perform many of the labs in the coursebook. The supplemental CD-ROM also includes an appendix listing the CIW Foundations certification exam objectives and locations of corresponding material in the coursebook. Lesson Quizzes and Course Assessments are provided as study and course-grading resources only; success on these materials in no way guarantees a passing score on the CIW Foundations certification exam. The movies provide supplementary instruction in a multimedia format, and enhance the coursebook narrative and labs. However, movie content does not comprehensively address CIW Foundations exam objectives and is not intended to replace coursebook content.

- **Student (Learning Center/Corporate)** — Designed for the learning center/corporate environment, this student book includes Pre-Assessment and Lesson Review questions. The student supplemental CD-ROM contains appendixes; files used to perform many of the labs in the coursebook; and answers to the Pre-Assessment Questions, Lesson Review Questions, Course Assessment, Activities, Optional Labs and Lesson Quizzes. The supplemental CD-ROM also includes an appendix listing the CIW Foundations certification exam objectives and locations of corresponding material in the coursebook. Lesson Quizzes and Course Assessments are provided as study and course-grading resources only; success on these materials in no way guarantees a passing score on the CIW Foundations certification exam. The movies provide supplementary instruction in a multimedia format, and enhance the coursebook narrative and labs. However, movie content does not comprehensively address CIW Foundations exam objectives and is not intended to replace coursebook content.

## Additional online resources

In addition to the material found in the coursebooks, students can visit CIW Online at *www.certification-partners.com/cciivv/CIW-Online/index.html* to help them prepare for the CIW Foundations certification exam. CIW Online provides a variety of online tools students can use to supplement the Official CIW Courseware, including:

- **Practice Exam questions** — The CIW Certification Practice Exams help measure proficiency on specific topics or the full range of CIW skills objectives. With nearly 700 exam questions, this powerful tool can be used to pre-assess certification aptitude, to prepare for the high-stakes exam environment, and to identify skills gaps and additional study needs. Visit *www.CIW-certified.com/training/practice-exams.asp* or call 602-275-7700 for product and purchase information about currently available CIW Certification Practice Exams.

- **Course review questions** — More than 1,300 course review questions that can be used for quizzes, tests and other class assignments. The multiple-choice questions cover numerous topics throughout the Foundations course material, not just those topics addressed by the CIW exam objectives. The questions are completely integrated with material from the book and can be used to assess students' understanding of the course material.

- **Interactive exercises** — Student activities that consist of fill-in-the-blank, true-or-false, categorizing, matching and crossword puzzle exercises. The self-testing exercises provide immediate scoring and feedback after completion, allowing students to focus on topics that require additional study. The exercises are based on Foundations content and prepare students to excel in tests and quizzes that feature multiple-choice questions.

- **Online flashcards** — Over 400 glossary flashcards that test students' vocabulary of important Foundations terms. The interactive flashcards show a vocabulary term on one side and the definition on the other. Students may move through the flashcards as necessary for extra review.

# Course Objectives

After completing this course, you will be able to:

- Discuss the importance of a business Web site that complements your organization.

- Identify front-end and back-end Web page design issues, demonstrate knowledge of Web site development principles, and define the concepts of creative design and branding standards.

- Discuss the history of markup languages, and identify markup language standards and the organizations that define them.

- Define markup and document structure tags, and use Cascading Style Sheets (CSS) and markup tags to apply formatting to Web pages.

- Use both a text editor and a GUI markup language editor to create XHTML pages.

- Create HTML and XHTML pages with horizontal rules, images, browser-safe colors, hyperlinks, tables, Web forms, client-side image maps and frames.

- Test processing of Web forms using a public test engine, and validate your HTML and XHTML code to W3C standards.

- Identify requirements for Web site publishing, identify uses for client-side and server-side Web technologies and languages, and connect Web pages to databases.

- Identify the benefits of Dynamic HTML (DHTML) and the Document Object Model (DOM).

- Identify Web page development techniques for PDAs and smart clients, use Web application frameworks to create and manage dynamic Web sites, and use TinyURL to create short aliases for long URLs.

- Use advanced Web 2.0 technologies to customize your Web pages.

  ✧  Compare using a service provider to hosting your own Web server.

  ✧  Compare e-commerce to traditional commerce, and identify e-commerce payment models.

  ✧  Discuss Internet marketing issues and search engine optimization (SEO), and their effects on the content and performance of your Web site.

  ✧  Identify issues related to working in a global environment.

# Classroom Setup

Your instructor has probably set up the classroom computers based on the system requirements listed in the following sections. Most software configurations on your computer are identical to those on your instructor's computer. However, your instructor may use additional software to demonstrate network interaction or related technologies.

# System Requirements

This section lists the hardware, software and connectivity requirements to implement this course.

## Hardware

Each classroom should be equipped with an individual computer workstation for each student and the instructor. The following table summarizes the hardware requirements for all courses in the CIW program.

*Note: The CIW hardware requirements are similar to the minimum system requirements for Microsoft Windows Vista Business implementation.*

| Hardware Specifications | Minimum Requirements |
|---|---|
| Processor | 1 GHz 32-bit (x86) or 64-bit (x64) processor |
| L2 cache | 256 KB |
| Hard disk | 40 GB with at least 15 GB of available space |
| RAM | At least 1 GB |
| CD-RW | 32X |
| Network interface card (NIC) | 10BaseT or 100BaseTX (10 or 100 Mbps) |
| Sound card/speakers | Required for instructor station, optional for student stations |
| Video adapter | Support for DirectX9 graphics with:<br>• WDDM Driver<br>• At least 128 MB of graphics memory<br>• Pixel Shader 2.0 in hardware<br>• 32 bits per pixel |
| Network hubs | Enough 10-port 10BaseT or 100BaseTX (10 or 100 Mbps) hubs to allow classroom computers to communicate |
| Monitor | Super VGA (1024 x 768) |

## Software

If you are teaching all three CIW Foundations courses sequentially, there is no need to reformat your computers for each course. The recommended software configurations for computers used to complete the labs in this book series are as follows.

## Internet Business Foundations

To be installed before class:

- **Microsoft Windows Vista Business** (typical installation)
- **Microsoft Internet Explorer 8.0** (typical installation)

To be installed by students during course labs:

- **Firefox 3.0.5** (binary provided in the C:\CIW\Internet\Lab Files\Lesson03 folder)
- **Google Chrome 1.0** (binary provided in the C:\CIW\Internet\Lab Files\Lesson03 folder)
- **Ogg Codecs** (binary provided in the C:\CIW\Internet\Lab Files\Lesson04 folder)
- **Aethera** (binary provided in the C:\CIW\Internet\Lab Files\Lesson06 folder)
- **Thunderbird 2.0** (binary provided in the C:\CIW\Internet\Lab Files\Lesson06 folder)
- **TightVNC, Bzip2 and Bunzip2** (binaries provided in the C:\CIW\Internet\Lab Files\Lesson07 folder)
- **Audacity and Windows Live Messenger** (binaries provided in the C:\CIW\Internet\Lab Files\Lesson08 folder)
- **Ad-AwareAE** (binary provided in the C:\CIW\Internet\Lab Files\Lesson09 folder)
- **GanttProject** (binary provided in the C:\CIW\Internet\Lab Files\Lesson10 folder)

## Site Development Foundations

To be installed before class:

- **Microsoft Windows Vista Business** (typical installation)
- **Microsoft Internet Explorer 8.0** (typical installation)
- **Firefox 3.0.5** (typical installation)

To be installed by students during course labs:

- **Lynx** (binary provided in the C:\CIW\Site_Dev\Lab Files\Lesson01\Lab_1-2\Lynx folder)
- **FormMail** (binary provided in the C:\CIW\Site_Dev\Lab Files\Lesson07\FormMail folder)
- **KompoZer** (binary provided in the C:\CIW\Site_Dev\Lab Files\Lesson10 folder)
- **Audacity** (binary provided in the C:\CIW\Site_Dev\Lab Files\Lesson11 folder)

To be installed by instructor for instructor-led demonstration in Lab 11-1:

- **XAMPP** (binary provided in the C:\CIW\Site_Dev\Lab Files\Lesson11\Lab_11-1\XAMPP folder)

## Network Technology Foundations

To be installed before class:

- **Microsoft Windows Vista Business** (typical installation)
- **Microsoft Internet Explorer 8.0** (typical installation)
- **Firefox 3.0.5** (typical installation)

To be installed by students during course labs:

- **uTorrent** (binary provided in the C:\CIW\Network\Lab Files\Lesson01 folder)
- **FileZilla_v3.0.2.1** (torrent file provided in the C:\CIW\Network\Lab Files\Lesson01 folder)

- **7-Zip** (binary provided in the C:\CIW\Network\Lab Files\Lesson01 folder)

- **FineCrypt 10.1** (binary provided in the C:\CIW\Network\Lab Files\Lesson05 folder)

To be installed by instructor for instructor-led demonstration in Lab 1-4 (any one of the three):

- **VMware** (*www.vmware.com*)

- **Parallels** (*www.parallels.com*)

- **VirtualBox** (*www.virtualbox.org*)

Create a virtual machine using an operating system other than Windows Vista; Mac OS X or Ubuntu Linux, for example. Load an application or two for that operating system so you can demonstrate to students the benefits of using a virtual machine.

## Connectivity

Internet connectivity is required for this course. You will experience optimal performance with a dedicated Internet connection (e.g., a cable/DSL modem or a T1 line). However, you can teach the course using slower connections (e.g., 56-Kbps modem).

## CIW Master Supplemental CD-ROM

Each coursebook includes a supplemental CD-ROM. The files on the CD-ROM are referenced and used throughout the course.

When you insert the CIW Master Supplemental CD-ROM, you will see a list of courses. Select the appropriate course, and you will be prompted to unzip an executable file. This executable file will create a directory of all supplemental materials for the course. You can choose to download the directory to the default location, which is C:\CIW\[*Course_Title*]. Optionally, you can select another location. After you choose the location and unzip the file, a directory will be created on your hard drive. All supplemental files for the course will be downloaded to this directory. You can then create a shortcut to this directory on your Desktop. As you conduct the course labs, you can use this shortcut to access your lab files quickly.

## CIW v5 Foundations Movies

The CIW Foundations courses offer movie files from LearnKey that discuss selected technology topics. To view the movies, log on to the CIW Online Campus at *http://www.certification-partners.com/ciw-online/*. Use the coupon provided with your instructor materials to register for the movies and view them online. If you have any questions, please contact Product Support at (866) 370-3511 or support@certification-partners.com.

To view the movies, you need the following programs:

- Microsoft Internet Explorer 5.5 (or later) browser (*www.microsoft.com*), or Mozilla Firefox 3.0 (or later) browser (*www.mozilla.com*)

- Windows Media Player 9 (or later) and all necessary codecs

- Windows Update, to obtain the latest updates for the versions of Internet Explorer and Media Player you have installed on your computer

*Note that students will install Windows Media Player and Mozilla Firefox software on their systems during labs in the Internet Business Foundations course.*

Consider the following points about the CIW v5 Foundations Movies:

- The movies provide supplementary instruction in a multimedia format, and enhance the coursebook narrative and labs. However, movie content does not comprehensively address CIW Foundations exam objectives and is not intended to replace coursebook content.

- CIW Foundations coursebooks include a Movie Time appendix that indicates appropriate points at which to view the supplemental movies.

- Instructors in a classroom environment are strongly encouraged to present movies to the entire class using a computer screen projector. Group presentations enable instructors to present and discuss movie content when appropriate. Controlling the presentation of movies also minimizes distractions from course material and essential lecture or lab time.

- Students are strongly encouraged to watch the movie clips on their own if they are unable to view them in class. Each student is provided access to the CIW Online Campus to view the movies.

- The coupon provided allows instructors and students to view the movies. Do not distribute the coupon to unauthorized users.

# Conventions and Graphics Used in This Book

The following conventions are used in these coursebooks.

**Terms**  Technology terms defined in the margins are indicated in **bold type** the first time they appear in the text. However, not every word in bold type is a term requiring definition.

**Lab Text**  Text that you enter during a lab appears in ***italic bold type***. Names of components that you access or change in a lab appear in **bold type**.

**Notations**  *Notations or comments regarding screenshots, labs or other text are indicated in italic type.*

**Program Code or Commands**  Text used in program code or operating system commands appears in the Lucida Sans Typewriter font.

The following graphics are used in these coursebooks.

 *Tech Notes* point out exceptions or special circumstances that you may find when working with a particular procedure. Tech Notes that occur within a lab are displayed without the graphic.

 *Tech Tips* offer special-interest information about the current subject.

 *Warnings* alert you about cautions to observe or actions to avoid.

 This graphic signals the start of a lab or other hands-on activity.

 The *Movie Time* graphic signals appropriate points in the course at which to view movie clips. All movie clips are © 2009 LearnKey, Inc.

 Each lesson summary includes an *Application Project*. This project is designed to provoke interest and apply the skills taught in the lesson to your daily activities.

 Each lesson concludes with a summary of the skills and objectives taught in that lesson. You can use the *Skills Review* checklist to evaluate what you have learned.

 This graphic indicates a line of code that is completed on the following line.

# Lesson 1: Introduction to Web Site Development

## Objectives

By the end of this lesson, you will be able to:

⟡ 2.7.3: Verify compliance with government and industry accessibility standards, including W3C Web Accessibility Initiative (WAI), U.S. Government Section 508, Americans with Disabilities Act (ADA).

⟡ 2.10.1: Identify the uses and benefits of various document and multimedia file formats, including PDF, RTF, PostScript, EPS, MOV, MPEG, streaming media, non-streaming media.

⟡ 2.10.2: Define the following Web-related mechanisms for audience development (i.e., attracting and retaining an audience): push technology, pull technology, visitor tracking.

⟡ 2.10.3: Identify common proprietary Web site and page enhancement elements, including Adobe Flash and Microsoft Silverlight.

⟡ 2.10.4: Evaluate the benefits and drawbacks of proprietary technologies such as Flash, Shockwave, movie formats.

⟡ 2.12.1: Test and validate Web documents.

⟡ 2.12.2: Estimate download time for Web pages.

⟡ 2.12.4: Document results of Web site functionality testing.

⟡ 2.16.6: Identify the importance of online indexing and cataloging.

⟡ 2.17.2: Define Common Gateway Interface (CGI) methods, including .Net, Django, Python, JavaServer Pages (JSP), Server-Side JavaScript (SSJS), Active Server Pages (ASP), PHP Hypertext Preprocessor (PHP), Ajax.

⟡ 2.17.3: Define database connectivity technologies (e.g., Open Database Connectivity [ODBC], Java Database Connectivity [JDBC]), and demonstrate the ability to connect databases with Web sites and other Internet-based services.

⟡ 2.17.4: Identify basic SQL commands for querying remote databases.

↪   2.19.2: Manage branding issues when developing a site (e.g., logo placement and sizing).

↪   2.21.4: Consult respected Web development resources, including books, trade journals, online sources, qualified individuals, user groups.

# Pre-Assessment Questions

1. What language is considered to be the *de facto* standard for creating Web sites?

   _____

   _____

2. You are designing a Web site for a client. The site must be attractive, uncluttered and easy to navigate. These requirements are considered what type of Web site design issues?

   a. Back-end issues
   b. Programming issues
   c. Database issues
   d. Front-end issues

3. Which term is used to describe the rate of data transfer over a network connection, measured in bits per second?

   a. Accessibility
   b. Download
   c. Bandwidth
   d. Spam

# Developing a Business Web Site

The Web is the primary medium that many customers (and potential customers) use to find information about the products or services they want. And therefore, all, or certainly most, businesses have their own Web sites. Providing a Web site is an essential step for any business today, and the Web site can serve as the business's primary means of advertising and marketing. It is your responsibility to ensure that the Web presence you are creating complements your organization.

A business that is just starting up, or one that is changing or expanding its offerings, must perform some key steps:

- Identify a market need or opportunity.

- Identify a unique product or service to address that need or opportunity.

- Define the target market.

- Determine how the business can best communicate with the target market.

- Establish a brand for the product or service.

- Determine how to advertise the product or service, including developing a Web site.

Once the business has completed the first four steps, establishing a brand for the product or service and creating a Web site are key steps to building and maintaining demand for the product or service, and helping the business to succeed.

Whether you become a Web developer or not, you can help any business that you work for, start up or acquire by understanding the importance of the business's branding, marketing and Web site.

## Branding concepts

**OBJECTIVE**
2.19.2: Branding
issues

**brand**
A concept or
collection of
symbols associated
with a product,
service or person.

A **brand** is a concept or collection of symbols associated with a product, service or person. Brands can be expressed in the form of pictures, icons, logos and other graphical representations of the item that the brand is intended to represent. The brand that a business establishes for itself can be extremely helpful in increasing the public's awareness of its product or service, and can help sustain and increase the growth of the business.

Branding is the process by which a business uses its brand to enable people to remember its product or service over a competitor's product or service.

Following are some branding concepts to consider when deciding on a brand:

- **The brand should be simple** — Easy-to-remember logos or graphics make very good brands. People tend to remember simple things and ignore or forget complex things.

- **The brand should be different** — A business's brand will be easier to recollect if it is different from those of competing products or services.

- **The brand should be safe** — A business must ensure that its logo, icon or picture does not inadvertently offend its target market. Decision-makers must be aware of cultural, regional or national attitudes before deciding on a particular brand.

- **The brand should make a promise** — The brand needs to clearly express to customers the most important benefits of the business's product or service.

- **The brand should reflect the company's attributes** — The brand needs to describe what the customer will experience when he or she buys that business's product or service (e.g., quality, a unique experience, customer service and so forth).

- **The brand should reflect the company's personality** — The brand needs to reflect the way the customer will feel when they purchase that business's product or service. The customer's emotional connection to the business's brand is a critical component to establishing repeat business.

Branding standards and creative design will be discussed in more detail later in this lesson and course.

*You must first have a clearly established brand before you can begin to create a compelling Web page. Consider this before you try to choose colors, determine a navigation scheme, etc. You may want to rush right into a discussion of search engine optimization (SEO), but first you must focus on the company brand. You will study SEO — which is the practice of modifying a Web page's content so it ranks highly in search engine results — later in this course.*

## Developing a Web site

**OBJECTIVE**
2.21.4: Respected Web development resources

The purpose of a Web site is to provide a way for a business's customers to find that business over the Internet. If you are involved in developing a business's Web site, there are many resources available to help you. You can find Web development training, tips, tricks and advice from various resources, including courses such as the one you are taking, online tutorials, user groups, professional trade journals, scholarly writings, reference books and so forth.

A Web site is part of a business's marketing effort and is the company's first form of advertising. Marketing is essentially presenting the business's product to potential customers in such a way that they want to buy it, and they want to buy it from that company instead of from someone else.

### Sample resources

Selected resources to consider as you learn more about Web design and development include the following:

- **Design & Publishing** (*www.graphic-design.com*)

- **CIW Community** (*www.ciwcommunity.org*)

- **A List Apart** (*www.alistapart.com*)

- **CYMK Magazine** (*www.cmykmag.com*)

- **Computer Graphics World** (*www.cgw.com*)

- **Web Designer Magazine** (*www.webdesignermag.co.uk*)

- **Layers Magazine** (*www.layersmagazine.com*)

- **WebDevForums.com** (*www.webdevforums.com*)

- **W3Schools** (*www.w3schools.com*)

As you review resources, use the following questions to help determine whether the site is reputable:

- Has the site been updated recently? Is the magazine still in publication?

- Is the site or magazine created by people who are recognized experts? Find out the names of contributors and editors, then conduct additional searches.

- Does the resource tend to push one product over all others? In some cases, vendor-specific sites may be excellent resources; but always be careful to temper vendor-specific solutions with skills-based approaches to Web design.

### *Effective Web page design for businesses*

Visitors do not read Web pages — they scan them, picking out individual words and phrases. To help visitors find information quickly, you should structure page text so that it is easy for visitors to scan. Highlighted keywords, meaningful subheadings and bulleted lists are ways to capture visitors' attention and help them find the information they are seeking.

To capture a visitor's interest, you should convey the business's central message in the first two paragraphs of the page, and makes sure that all subheadings, paragraphs and bullet points start with appropriate keywords that users will notice as they scan the page.

Effectively designed pages:

- Feature crisp, concise text (limiting the word count to half of what would be used in conventional writing).

- Include one idea per paragraph.

- Include search engine keywords in the main portions of text.

- Convey the central message using the inverted-pyramid writing style (i.e., the conclusion is presented at the top of the page, followed by supporting information).

Although a stunning Web site may attract visitors initially, a Web site that is simple to use will keep visitors coming back. Navigating a Web site should be easy. Each page should include a navigation bar directing visitors to major parts of the site. The site should provide multiple ways to navigate back to the home page so that visitors can start over if they get lost.

The rest of this course will teach you the basic concepts of designing, developing and modifying Web pages and sites using various Web development techniques.

# Creating Web Pages

Since the World Wide Web's popularity has increased the Internet's prevalence, the skills of Web page creation have become vital to many careers. You are likely to need skills with Web-based technologies for various job-related tasks, including:

- Informing colleagues about progress on team projects.

- Using or contributing to the company intranet.

- Working with customers online.

- Posting or retrieving résumés.

You may also want to work as a Web developer or site designer, with responsibility for the Web pages of an entire company or organization. Whatever job role you choose, this course will teach you how to create Web pages using text editors and graphical development applications. Each tool creates similar pages, but the creation processes are quite different.

**markup language**
A series of commands used to format, organize and describe information on a Web page.

It is important to understand that Web pages are no longer viewed only through standard Web browsers. Your mobile phone, Personal Digital Assistant (PDA) and digital camera are all capable of reading **markup languages**. In fact, many Web design professionals refer to HTML or XHTML as "markup," simply because many of their pages will be viewed using applications other than Web browsers. Because markup languages are becoming more common in the workplace, it is important for you to understand how to use them.

Web page creation by any method requires a working knowledge of at least two markup languages:

**Hypertext Markup Language (HTML)**
The traditional authoring language used to develop Web pages for many applications.

- **Hypertext Markup Language (HTML)** — traditionally the standard markup language on the Web, and in other settings. HTML is standardized by an organization called the World Wide Web Consortium (W3C). You can learn more about the W3C at *www.w3.org*.

**Extensible Hypertext Markup Language (XHTML)**
The current standard authoring language used to develop Web pages and other electronically displayed documents. XHTML requires stricter code syntax than HTML.

- **Extensible Hypertext Markup Language (XHTML)** — effectively the next version of HTML. The W3C also oversees the development of XHTML.

HTML and XHTML are markup languages that define page layouts, hyperlinks, fonts, graphics and more to enable pages to render in Web browsers and other devices. You will learn about both languages in detail throughout this course. You can type HTML or XHTML code manually into a text editor, use a graphical user interface (GUI) editor program to create the code automatically (by pointing and clicking your mouse), or combine both methods.

*In this course, the term HTML will sometimes apply to XHTML, and vice versa, except where major differences exist. You will learn about the history of markup languages in a future lesson.*

## Additional Web page elements

Web pages can incorporate more than just HTML or XHTML. You can use other languages to enhance a page, such as JavaScript, JScript and VBScript. You can also enhance Web pages by inserting specialized content created with programs and technologies such as Flash (*www.adobe.com/products/flash/*), Java (*www.java.com*), ActiveX (*www.microsoft.com*) and Microsoft Silverlight (*www.microsoft.com/silverlight/*). You will learn about all these technologies later in this course.

**OBJECTIVE**
2.17.2: CGI methods

### Databases and Web pages

Web sites can use databases to store information about the products a company is ready to sell. These databases can be connected to Web pages so that employees can readily check on company inventory. Web pages can also be used to obtain information from end users and store it in databases. To accomplish this, you can use XHTML code to create a user-input form.

A form allows end users to enter information into a Web page that sends the information to an organization or business. There are various types of forms. When an end user enters information into a form and clicks OK or Send, the page sends the user's information to a database in which the information can be processed. Information might include opinions or user preferences, bids in eBay auctions (*www.ebay.com*), or credit card information to make purchases from a company such as Amazon.com (*www.amazon.com*).

## Web pages and CGI

**OBJECTIVE**
2.17.2: CGI methods

A user-input form must contain code that references a Web server. This code is called an application, or a Web server application. This application helps convey the information provided by the end user to the Web server, or to a database server that can store and/or process the information. Such applications are called Common Gateway Interface (CGI) applications because they enable information to pass in and out of a server. Various CGI implementations exist. CGI implementations use various computer languages and technologies, including those discussed in Table 1-1.

*Table 1-1: Popular CGI technologies*

| CGI Technology | Description | Additional Information |
|---|---|---|
| **Perl** | A traditional CGI technology that is platform-independent (i.e., you can install it on any server-based operating system). Once you install the Perl interpreter on the system, you can use Perl-based CGI applications. Available at *www.cpan.org* and *www.activestate.com.* | Because of its relative longevity, Perl is well known and is supported by many operating systems. It is renowned for creating stable applications. As a universal technology, you can install the Perl interpreter on almost any operating system (e.g., Linux, Solaris, Windows). |
| **PHP Hypertext Preprocessor (PHP)** | A newer CGI technology that will run on multiple platforms. Once you install the PHP interpreter on the system, you can create applications. Available at *www.php.org.* | Although it is a newer technology, PHP has become quite popular due to its relative simplicity and ability to create powerful applications. A universal technology. |
| **Active Server Pages (ASP)** | An older, proprietary CGI technology available only on Microsoft-specific systems or systems with a special interpreter installed (e.g., the ChiliSoft ASP interpreter). The ASP interpreter is installed on all Microsoft Internet Information Services (IIS) systems. Developers can create ASP scripts using VBScript or JavaScript. To learn more about ASP, visit *www.microsoft.com.* | ASP is powerful because it is specially designed to work with the underlying operating system. ASP requires developers to learn VBScript and/or JavaScript. |
| **.NET** | Microsoft's standard development platform. A proprietary set of technologies and languages available mostly on Windows systems and installed on all IIS systems. .NET allows you to use various languages, including C# (a replacement for Java), JavaScript, VBScript or Visual Basic. To learn more about .NET, visit *www.microsoft.com.* | .NET is Microsoft's latest effort to interconnect all Internet-based servers. A more powerful option than the older ASP approach. .NET provides additional database connectivity, and allows you to use more powerful languages (e.g., C#), although C# is more difficult to learn than VBScript, Perl or PHP. |
| **JavaServer Pages (JSP)** | A universal CGI technology that uses the Java interpreter, allowing developers to create CGI using the Java language. Download Java at *www.java.com.* To learn more about JSP, visit *http://java.sun.com/.* | Like Perl and PHP, JSP is a universal technology. Although Java is more difficult to learn than PHP or Perl, it is also a more powerful language and creates more stable applications. |
| **ColdFusion** | A proprietary CGI technology designed to be easier to install and use than other interpreters and languages. To learn more about ColdFusion, visit *www.adobe.com/products/coldfusion/.* | ColdFusion purportedly does more work using less code, which generally makes your applications easier to develop and use. Although ColdFusion is a proprietary technology, you can install it on various operating systems (e.g., Linux, Windows, Solaris). |

*Table 1-1: Popular CGI technologies (cont'd)*

| CGI Technology | Description | Additional Information |
|---|---|---|
| **Python** | An open-source CGI technology that emphasizes code readability by employing minimalistic code syntax and semantics. Python is an object-oriented programming language that can be easily integrated with other languages. To learn more about Python, visit *www.python.org*. | Python runs on Windows, Linux/UNIX, Mac OS X, OS/2, Amiga, palm handhelds and Nokia mobile phones. Python has also been ported to the Java and .NET virtual machines. Python uses white space as block delimiters, which is unusual among popular programming languages. |
| **Django** | An open-source Web framework written to help developers use the Python language. To learn more about Django, visit *www.djangoproject.com*. | Django makes the creation of complex, database-driven Web sites easier by emphasizing the use of components that can be reused. It also emphasizes the DRY (Don't Repeat Yourself) principle, which seeks to eliminate any duplication so that modifying an element of a program will not affect other logically unrelated elements. |
| **Ajax** | A CGI programming methodology that enables Web applications to interact with users in much the same way they do with desktop applications. You can use Ajax to create dynamic and interactive Web pages without the need to refresh or reload the page. To learn more about Ajax, visit *www.asp.net/ajax/*. | Ajax uses a number of existing technologies together (XHTML, CSS, the Document Object Model [DOM], JavaScript and XMLHttpRequest), and enables Web applications to make incremental updates to the user interface without the need to reload the page in the browser. |
| **Ruby** | An object-oriented programming language based on Perl and **Smalltalk**. It has powerful capabilities, but is easier to use than many other languages, including Java and C#.<br><br>To learn more about Ruby, visit *www.ruby-lang.org*. | Includes the Ruby On Rails framework, which makes it possible to use Ruby to rapidly develop applications. |

**Smalltalk**
A programming language that pioneered object-oriented programming. Not popularly used in Web development.

**Tech Tip**

*Other CGI technologies are also available. You do not need to understand the details of these technologies for the CIW Foundations exam, but know that CGI is necessary to enable a Web form for communication between an end user and a Web server.*

## Markup languages and Wireless Application Protocol (WAP)

**Wireless Application Protocol (WAP)**
A standard protocol that wireless devices use to access the Internet.

**Wireless Markup Language (WML)**
A markup language that presents the text portions of Web pages to wireless devices.

Wireless handheld devices, such as mobile phones and Personal Digital Assistants (PDAs), access Web pages using **Wireless Application Protocol (WAP)**. WAP provides text-based Web browsing and secure e-mail to wireless handheld devices. Instead of using HTML to present Web pages, WAP-enabled Web pages use **Wireless Markup Language (WML)**, which presents only the text portion of Web pages. This course does not discuss WML further, but you should be aware of this emerging technology.

## Optimizing the impact of the Web page

The practice of search engine optimization (SEO) involves making changes to a Web site's content so that the site ranks as highly as possible in search engine results. A high ranking on a search engine results page can help increase the number of visits (i.e., hits) per month, ensuring more visibility for your product or page.

SEO techniques are designed to get Web pages to conform to the expectations of search engine applications. These applications, often called bots, automatically scan Web pages and index them. Search engine companies then analyze these Web pages and rank them according to relevance.

When a Web user visits Google or Yahoo!, these search engines are supposed to return the most relevant Web pages for the user's search. Search engine companies consider many factors, including but not limited to:

- How many hyperlinks from other sites point to a page.
- How informative a page is.
- How well a page's code is structured.

Throughout this course, you will learn about foundational techniques for creating sound Web pages. You will learn about consistently using words — called keywords — that search engines deem important. You will learn how to use them not only in the Web page text content, but also as you name pages and images. You will also learn about many other techniques that may appear to be completely unrelated to SEO, but are in fact foundational for anyone conducting search engine optimization. Such activities include:

- Using properly validated X/HTML code.
- Applying Cascading Style Sheets (CSS).
- Structuring pages correctly.

## Text Editors and Markup Languages

You do not need to use a special editor application to create markup language code (e.g., XHTML or HTML). You can use a simple text editor. A text editor is any program that allows you to type simple text and edit it, such as Microsoft Notepad and WordPad, or UNIX-based programs such as Vi and Pico. However, you must save your code files as plain text. Any formatting instructions embedded in a file by a word-processing program, for example, can prevent the file from functioning properly.

**Multipurpose Internet Mail Extensions (MIME)**
A protocol that enables operating systems to map file name extensions to corresponding applications. Also used by applications to automatically process files downloaded from the Internet.

After you save the Web page code as a text file, you should save it with the .htm or .html file name extension. Many operating systems and Web browsers are configured with **Multipurpose Internet Mail Extensions (MIME)** to automatically process files with these extensions. Figure 1-1 shows a text editor with HTML code. You will use Notepad as your HTML text editor in the first part of this course. You will then use a simple GUI-based editor application later in the course.

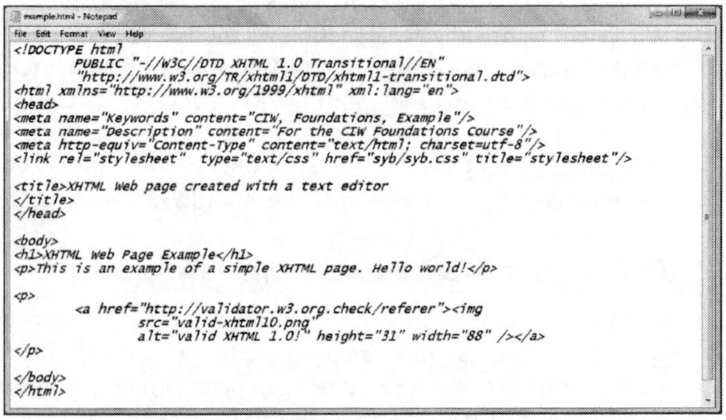


```
<!DOCTYPE html
        PUBLIC "-//W3C//DTD XHTML 1.0 Transitional//EN"
        "http://www.w3.org/TR/xhtml1/DTD/xhtml1-transitional.dtd">
<html xmlns="http://www.w3.org/1999/xhtml" xml:lang="en">
<head>
<meta name="Keywords" content="CIW, Foundations, Example"/>
<meta name="Description" content="For the CIW Foundations Course"/>
<meta http-equiv="Content-Type" content="text/html; charset=utf-8"/>
<link rel="stylesheet"  type="text/css" href="syb/syb.css" title="stylesheet"/>

<title>XHTML Web page created with a text editor
</title>
</head>

<body>
<h1>XHTML Web Page Example</h1>
<p>This is an example of a simple XHTML page. Hello world!</p>

<p>
        <a href="http://validator.w3.org.check/referer"><img
                src="valid-xhtml10.png"
                alt="valid XHTML 1.0!" height="31" width="88" /></a>
</p>

</body>
</html>
```

Figure 1-1: XHTML code in text editor

Many text editors exist, all with more capability than Microsoft Notepad. Open-source examples you may want to use include:

- Notepad++ (*http://notepad-plus.sourceforge.net*).
- jEdit (*www.jedit.org*).
- Vim (*www.vim.org*).
- Cream (*http://cream.sourceforge.net*).
- Emacs (*www.gnu.org/software/emacs*).

Most of these products have versions that will run on multiple operating systems.

# Graphical User Interface (GUI) Editors

**graphical user interface (GUI)**
A program that provides visual navigation with menus and screen icons, and performs automated functions when users click command buttons.

GUI markup editor applications place markup instructions into files for you, so you need not know HTML to use GUI editors. Many GUI HTML editors still do not produce valid XHTML. Nevertheless, such editors provide a **graphical user interface (GUI)** that makes it easy for you to create HTML pages without writing any code manually. You simply point and click with your mouse, and the code is generated by the program. Commands are displayed on the graphical user interface as they will appear in a browser, thus the programs are often called WYSIWYG (What You See Is What You Get) editors. Some developers feel that using a GUI editor application saves time. Others feel that GUI editors create confused HTML code and do not provide true flexibility.

Popular GUI HTML editors include Adobe (formerly Macromedia) Dreamweaver, Microsoft Expression Web (formerly FrontPage), Mozilla SeaMonkey and Adobe GoLive. In this course, you will use the KompoZer GUI editor, shown in Figure 1-2.

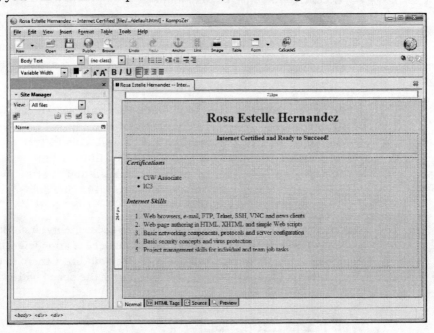

*Figure 1-2: KompoZer GUI markup editor*

## Why learn markup languages?

As already mentioned, most GUI HTML editor applications have not kept pace with the evolution of HTML and XHTML, and do not provide options for more recent markup standards. However, many of these GUI programs allow you to modify your HTML code manually from the GUI. If you know HTML, you can maximize the benefit of these programs by manually adding code that the GUI editor does not. Further, if you are considering learning any scripting or programming languages, such as JavaScript, VBScript or Java, you *must* learn how to write code manually.

Learning to write your own markup code in a text editor will enable you to create highly attractive, functional XHTML and HTML documents, regardless of any other available software. Another reason to use a text editor is so you can learn the fundamentals of markup languages, then update a page to the latest standard or recommendation. You will learn about markup language standards later in this course.

# Front-End Issues

Front-end issues are essentially interface issues. A Web page acts as an interface for information. You can structure the information in tables, forms and other less-formal ways. A properly created Web page should:

- Be accessible by all users, including those with disabilities (e.g., hearing or sight impairment).

- Incorporate attractive images and graphical elements.

- Contain constantly updated hyperlinks and content.

- Use tables wisely (ideally, tables should be used to place information in tabular format, not to structure entire Web pages).

- Present carefully designed forms.

- Securely attach pages to databases.

- Use the most current technologies appropriate for the page.

- Use images sparingly. Images can clutter the page and create bandwidth problems. You will learn more about bandwidth shortly.

- Be easily navigable and without dead ends.

**image map**
A Web page image with clickable regions that are defined as "hot spot" hyperlinks to other pages or page sections.

- Include alternative navigation links. For example, when defining an **image map** for a Web site (image maps are discussed later in this course), you should provide standard hypertext links to the site as well. This feature helps accommodate visitors who have deactivated image downloading in their browsers. Also, many developers use image maps to define an entire page. Although attractive, this strategy can effectively exclude such a page from search engine spiders unless you provide alternative text information.

The Web presents several obstacles to user accessibility, including the fact that you have no control over the ways in which users will access and view your pages. You do not know which browsers they will use, nor can you direct them to certain areas of the pages or site. Furthermore, you have no control over the speed with which users will be downloading your pages.

## Web page accessibility

When you create a Web page, you must ensure accessibility to make your pages available to all visitors of your site. For example, consider that the baby-boomer generation (anyone born between 1946 and roughly 1964) commands an enormous amount of income. As this generation ages, its members will develop sight, hearing and cognitive challenges. Ignoring these common disabilities in your design means that you will exclude this group of individuals. As a result, you will not have as popular or as lucrative a site as you may like.

An accessible Web page has two characteristics:

- A user-friendly and accessible front end

- Server resources that process and store user input, also known as the back end

## Front end and accessibility

First, an accessible Web page has a user-friendly interface, or front end. This includes interesting graphics and well-structured information so that readers can gain the maximum benefit from your content as quickly as possible. It also includes content that can be accessed easily by users who have disabilities and other more-common challenges. For example, consider using fonts that can be resized and color schemes that do not interfere with reading the content on the page.

The W3C estimates that up to 10 percent of the world's population has disabilities that, if not accommodated by Web sites, can cause companies to lose significant amounts of revenue (*www.w3.org/Talks/WAI-Intro/slide7-0.html*). To ensure accessibility in your Web pages, you have several options:

- Follow government-mandated standards.

- Follow standards developed by the industry, including the W3C. For example, the XHTML standard helps ensure that Web pages are accessible. A great advantage of XHTML is that if you follow the standard and validate your pages to it, your pages will be more accessible.

- Follow standards developed by your particular business or organization.

Accessibility standards may include statements such as the following:

- All information in the site must be accessible via a text-based browser or a browser on which image viewing is deactivated.

- The site must include accommodations for screen-reader technology, which is any technology that renders text-based pages in audio. This technology ensures that users with impaired vision can still obtain information from Web sites, and is often called "Web-aware." Screen-reader technology reads pages much like a text-based browser. Information on a Web page that is accessible only via an image will not be presented to some visitors, because screen-reader technology will simply report images as images; it will not report information displayed in them. This type of exclusion could potentially expose your site to a lawsuit. The Window-Eyes Screen Reader application provides an example of screen-reader technology (*www.synapseadaptive.com/syn/pro/soft/blindness.htm*).

## Back end and accessibility

Secondly, your Web page should download easily to your visitors' computers and connect properly to databases. This ability depends on the Web server and the network, also known as the back end. Your Web pages should accommodate limitations presented by the Internet. For example, many users download pages at slow modem speeds and may not use the most recent browser versions.

As you will see, careful design enables you to inform and please as many visitors as possible. Following are discussions of accessibility, front-end and back-end issues that you must consider before designing Web pages.

OBJECTIVE
2.7.3: Accessibility
standards and
compliance

## Americans with Disabilities Act (ADA)

The Americans with Disabilities Act (ADA) was enacted in 1990 to protect the civil rights of disabled people. This law has many sections, and includes mandates for equal employment opportunities and public accommodations for disabled people. It also includes mandates that electronic information be accessible to disabled people. Significant compliance failures are subject to financial penalties.

According to the U.S. Justice Department, the ADA also applies to cyberspace communications. In an opinion letter dated September 9, 1996 (*www.usdoj.gov/crt/foia/cltr204.txt*), the U.S. Department of Justice stated the following:

> *"Covered entities under the ADA are required to provide effective communication, regardless of whether they generally communicate through print media, audio media, or computerized media such as the Internet. Covered entities that use the Internet for communications regarding their programs, goods or services must be prepared to offer those communications through accessible means as well."*

Because it is an active law, the ADA is relevant to anyone designing pages in the United States, and anyone creating sites that will be visited by users who live in the United States. The standards are officially known as the U.S. Department of Justice ADA Standards for Accessible Design. A judiciary hearing was held regarding ADA and private Internet sites. You can read more about these findings at *www.tracecenter.org/docs/ada_internet_hearing*.

Any penalties are the result of prosecution brought by the U.S. Justice Department; lawsuits from individuals and class action suits are not possible. The Justice Department tries to determine good-faith efforts before bringing lawsuits, and generally punishes only violators who exhibit long-term, wanton disregard for the standards. To learn facts and myths about ADA, visit *www.usdoj.gov/crt/ada/pubs/mythfct.txt*.

As a Web designer, your job is to create what the Department of Justice calls "reasonable accommodation" in your Web sites for people with various disabilities. You must make reasonable accommodations if you are a covered entity, which according to ADA is any "private employers, state and local governments, employment agencies and labor unions" (*http://www.eeoc.gov/types/ada.html*). Critical ADA compliance factors to consider when creating reasonable accommodations in your Web sites include:

- Ensuring that all images have text-based descriptions so that sight-impaired visitors can access sites through screen-reader technology.

- Providing text-based alternatives to all non-text content (e.g., Java applets).

- Providing forms that are easily read by screen-reading technology.

**Tech Tip** *Video is not ADA-compliant because sight-impaired visitors cannot see it. Video with audio but no alternative text support is a problem because hearing-impaired visitors cannot hear it.*

For more information about ADA, visit the following sites:

- The ADA Home Page (*www.ada.gov*)

- A paper that summarizes ADA from a legal perspective, "Applying the ADA to the Internet: A Web Accessibility Standard" by Cynthia D. Waddell, J.D. (*http://people.rit.edu/easi/law/weblaw1.htm*)

- Usability.gov, which is a U.S. Department of Health and Human Services site (*www.usability.gov*)

- An accessibility article on the All Things Web site (*www.pantos.org/atw/35588.html*)

- Current Web design articles in About.com's Web Design/HTML section (*http://webdesign.about.com/od/accessibilityvalidators/a/use_acces_valid.htm*)

### Additional disabilities acts and initiatives

Following is a partial list of disabilities acts and initiatives for various nations:

- Canada's Common Look and Feel Standards for the Internet page (www.tbs-sct.gc.ca/clf-nsi/index_e.asp)

- The Australian Government's Guide to Minimum Web Site Standards — Accessibility page (www.agimo.gov.au/practice/mws/accessibility)

- India's Maharashtra Right to Information Act (www.geocities.com/mahadhikar/act.html)

- The e-Japan Priority Policy Program (www.kantei.go.jp/foreign/it/network/priority-all/index.html)

- The United Kingdom's Disability Discrimination Act of 1995, Part III (www.opsi.gov.uk/acts/acts1995/1995050.htm )

Additional information about various national laws and standards is available on the W3C at *www.w3.org/WAI/Policy.*

### Web Content Accessibility Guidelines (WCAG)

Web pages should be accessible to all people, including those with disabilities. To assist in this mission, the W3C has created the Web Accessibility Initiative (WAI). The WAI has developed the Web Content Accessibility Guidelines (WCAG) to provide a universal set of standards promoting accessibility. According to the WAI, the Web's full potential can only be realized by "promoting a high degree of usability for people with disabilities." The WAI works with worldwide organizations in five main areas: technology, guidelines, tools, education and outreach, and research and development.

 *The European Union uses mostly the WCAG standards.*

WAI aims to ensure that core technologies used on the Web, such as HTML, Cascading Style Sheets (CSS), Extensible Markup Language (XML) and the Document Object Model (DOM), are equally accessible to all users, including those with physical, visual, hearing and cognitive disabilities. (You will learn more about these technologies later in the course.) For example, a person with a visual disability may be unable to view a multimedia presentation on the Web. One way to solve this problem is to include text equivalents of the presentation in the code. The multimedia player, such as RealNetworks RealPlayer or Microsoft Windows Media Player, could then access the text equivalent and present it to the user in Braille or as speech.

The WAI works with numerous W3C Working Groups to ensure that the standards for various W3C technologies include accessibility options. For example, the HTML standard supports improved navigation, extended descriptions of complex graphics, and multimedia captions. It also supports device-independent user interface descriptions that allow users to interact with Web pages using mouse, keyboard or voice input.

You can visit the following Web sites to learn more about Web page accessibility for disabled people:

- Web Accessibility Initiative (WAI) (*www.w3.org/WAI*)

- Web Content Accessibility Guidelines (WCAG) Recommendation (*www.w3.org/TR/WCAG10*)

- The WAI Policies page (*www.w3.org/WAI/Policy*)

- The WAI Evaluation page (*www.w3.org/WAI/eval*)

- The WCAG fact sheet (*www.w3.org/1999/05/WCAG-REC-fact*)

- Curriculum for Web Content Accessibility Guidelines 1.0 (*www.w3.org/WAI/wcag-curric*)

Following are additional WAI concerns and standards:

**user agent**
Any application, such as a Web browser, mobile phone, PDA or help engine, that renders HTML for display to users.

- **User agent accessibility** — A **user agent** is any device used to view an HTML/XHTML page. The most common user agent is a Web browser. Additional user agents include mobile phones, e-mail applications and various applications on PDAs. The W3C User Agent Accessibility Guidelines document is available at *www.w3.org/TR/UAAG10*.

- **WCAG checklist** — A checklist for the accessibility guidelines detailed in the WCAG is available at *www.w3.org/TR/WAI-WEBCONTENT/full-checklist.html*.

- **Accessibility for developers** — The W3C also addresses ways to ensure that development tools can be used by disabled people. For more information, read the W3C Authoring Tool Accessibility Guidelines at *www.w3.org/TR/WAI-AUTOOLS*.

Accessibility extensions include the following:

- You can obtain accessibility plug-ins for creating Web pages with Adobe Dreamweaver at *www.adobe.com/products/dreamweaver*.

- You can obtain accessibility extensions for Adobe Flash that help you develop and also read the output at *www.adobe.com/products/flash/*.

- Microsoft provides extensive information about accessibility features for all of its operating systems and products at *www.microsoft.com/enable/training/default.aspx*.

## WCAG conformance requirements

The WAI Web Content Accessibility Guidelines 1.0 specification divides conformance requirements into a hierarchy with three levels. Note that in accordance with accessibility guidelines, conformance level names are spelled out in text so they can be understood when rendered to speech. The conformance levels are defined as follows:

- **Conformance Level "A"** — All Priority 1 checkpoints are satisfied.

- **Conformance Level "Double-A"** — All Priority 1 and 2 checkpoints are satisfied.

- **Conformance Level "Triple-A"** — All Priority 1, 2 and 3 checkpoints are satisfied.

Each level of conformance encompasses a specific set of checkpoints, each with an assigned priority level. The WAI defines the three priority levels of checkpoints as follows:

- **Priority 1** — A Web content developer *must* satisfy this checkpoint to provide accessibility for all users. If a Priority 1 checkpoint is not satisfied, then one or more groups of users will be unable to access information in the Web document. This checkpoint is a basic requirement for some groups to access Web documents.

- **Priority 2** — A Web content developer *should* satisfy this checkpoint. If a Priority 2 checkpoint is not satisfied, then one or more groups of users will have difficulty accessing information in the Web document. This checkpoint removes significant barriers to accessing Web documents.

- **Priority 3** — A Web content developer *may* address this checkpoint. If a Priority 3 checkpoint is not satisfied, then one or more groups will have some difficulty accessing information in the document. This checkpoint improves access to Web documents.

All checkpoints are organized under 14 specific guidelines. The guidelines are developed with consideration for groups of users with specified disabilities or needs. The WAI defines the 14 guidelines as follows:

1. Provide equivalent alternatives to auditory and visual content.

2. Do not rely on color alone.

3. Use markup and style sheets properly.

4. Clarify natural language usage.

5. Create tables that transform gracefully.

6. Ensure that pages featuring new technologies transform gracefully.

7. Ensure user control of time-sensitive content changes.

8. Ensure direct accessibility of embedded user interfaces.

9. Design for device-independence.

10. Use interim solutions.

11. Use W3C technologies and guidelines.

12. Provide context and orientation information.

13. Provide clear navigation mechanisms.

14. Ensure that documents are clear and simple.

Although different situations should be considered when designing Web documents, each accessible design choice generally benefits several disability groups, and the Web community as a whole. For more detailed information, you can read the WAI specification at *www.w3.org/TR/WAI-WEBCONTENT/*.

## Section 508 of the Rehabilitation Act

On June 21, 2001, the U.S. government implemented Section 508 of the Rehabilitation Act: Electronic and Information Technology Accessibility Standards. Section 508 requires that all electronic and information technology developed, procured, maintained or used by federal agencies be comparably accessible to users with disabilities. Section 508 is based on the Priority 1 and 2 checkpoints of the W3C's WAI Web Content Accessibility Guidelines 1.0. You can learn more about Section 508 by visiting the following URLs:

- Federal Information Technology Accessibility Initiative, Section 508 home page (*www.section508.gov*)

- U.S. Access Board, Section 508 of the Rehabilitation Act (*www.access-board.gov/508.htm*)

The chief purpose of Section 508 is to ensure that disabled individuals have a comparable level of access to information. Each standard aims to ensure that Web page design and other computer-based elements do not limit access to information by disabled users. Section 508 specifies the following standards for Web sites:

- All non-text elements must have a text-based equivalent.

- If using multimedia, all equivalent information must be properly synchronized with the multimedia so that disabled persons are not at a disadvantage.

- Information must be equally available in color and without color.

- Documents must be made available without requiring an associated style sheet.

- Text descriptions must be made available for all image maps.

- Client-side image maps should not be used because they cannot be properly presented to visually impaired users.

- If using tables for data, you must identify all row and column headers.

- If a table has two or more rows or columns, you must use row and column headers.

- Sites that use frames must have titles that easily enable alternative browsers to navigate through each frame.

- Pages must not contain designs and/or technology that cause perceptible screen flicker. Screens must not flicker at a frequency between 2 Hz and 55 Hz because such flicker can cause some people to have epileptic seizures.

- If necessary, a separate text-only site should be made available to ensure access.

- When scripting technology is used to enable a site feature (e.g., a form), a plaintext alternative must be available that allows an assistant application to read the feature.

- When using active content such as an applet, a link must be provided that complies with these standards.

- All forms must enable users to complete and submit forms using disability-assistance technologies. The pages must also contain text or alternative help methods for disabled users.

- Pages must contain ways to skip repetitive links, which are links repeated throughout site pages to aid navigation. Repetitive links can interfere with assistance technology such as voice-enabled browser.

- If a page requires input from a user within a certain period of time, the page must alert the user when time is going to expire. Sufficient time must then be given to the user so that he or she can respond.

You can visit *www.section508.gov/index.cfm?FuseAction=Content&ID=12#Web* to read the Section 508 standards.

In the following lab, you will visit sites that post accessibility standards. Suppose you belong to a Web development team. Your project manager approaches you and asks about common Web accessibility standards. She has a half-hour available for you to show her some resources on the Web. What sites would you visit?

## Lab 1-1: Viewing accessibility standards sites

In this lab, you will view sites devoted to Web accessibility standards.

1.  Open a Web browser.

2.  Visit the following sites:

    - The W3C Web Content Accessibility Guidelines (WCAG) site at **www.w3.org/TR/WCAG10**

    - The Section 508 site at **www.section508.gov**

    - Canada's Common Look and Feel Standards for the Internet site at **www.tbs-sct.gc.ca/clf-nsi/index_e.asp**

3.  Read some information at each site you visit. How does each site define accessibility? How are the standards similar and different among sites? Can you see the ways in which accessibility standards are applied to these sites?

4.  Conduct searches on the Internet for additional accessibility standards relevant to your particular situation. What other standards can you find?

In this lab, you viewed sites devoted to Web accessibility standards.

## Child Online Protection Act (COPA)

The Child Online Protection Act (COPA) was passed in 1998 to help reduce the possibility that minors will be exposed to harmful material. Section 231, paragraph 1 of the COPA states the following:

> *Whoever knowingly and with knowledge of the character of the material, in interstate or foreign commerce by means of the World Wide Web, makes any communication for commercial purposes that is available to any minor and that includes any material that is harmful to minors shall be fined not more than $50,000, imprisoned not more than 6 months, or both.*

The document also discusses harmful material, prohibited conduct, child-protective technologies and law enforcement. You can learn more about COPA by visiting the following sites:

- The COPA Commission Home Page (*www.copacommission.org*)

- The COPA original statute (*www.copacommission.org/commission/original.shtml*)

As you develop Web pages, make sure that you do not engage in activities that might violate COPA or similar acts.

**OBJECTIVE**
2.12.1: Validating
Web documents

## Verifying Web page accessibility

You can manually verify Web page accessibility, but it is much quicker to use automated accessibility validators. Table 1-2 describes some of the most common tools.

*Table 1-2: Accessibility validators*

| Validator Tool | Description | Web-Based or Stand-Alone Tool? | URL |
|---|---|---|---|
| **W3C Page Validator** | Powerful HTML and XHTML validator | Web-based and Firefox add-on | *http://validator.w3.org* *https://addons.mozilla. org/en-US/firefox/ addon/2250* |
| **Total Validator** | Powerful HTML and XHTML validator | Firefox add-on | *https://addons.mozilla. org/en-US/firefox/ addon/2318* |
| **Cynthia Says** | A free site devoted to the W3C Web Content Accessibility Guidelines (WCAG) | Web-based | *www.cynthiasays.com* |
| **STEP508** | A free, dedicated verification engine designed to validate sites for Section 508 compliance | Stand-alone | *www.section508.gov* |
| **Vischeck** | A free service that simulates how a site will appear to color-blind users | Web-based | *www.vischeck.com/vis check* |
| **MAGpie** | A free application that validates Web sites, and creates audio captions and multimedia descriptions | Stand-alone | *http://ncam.wgbh.org/ webaccess/magpie* |

Tech Tip

*Partial color blindness is much more widespread than commonly realized. If your target audience is the entire world, read about color blindness to determine which color combinations are most easily read by the largest number of people. For information, color deficiency simulations and links to color-blindness tests, visit www.visibone.com/colorblind.*

Additional Web page accessibility validation tools are available at *www.w3.org/WAI/ER/ tools/*. It is important to understand that these automatic validators may not find issues related to the latest accessibility standards. Manual validation is generally the most thorough approach.

## General Web page accessibility considerations

You have now learned about many accessibility standards, guidelines and validation tools. The following sections discuss common Web page challenges and resolutions.

### Addressing visual challenges

Following are some common challenges and solutions for accommodating Web users with vision impairment:

• **Text readability** — Make sure that fonts used are the correct size.

• **Text support for images** — All images must be described in text using special HTML code.

• **Screen-reader support** — Ensure that all pages and page elements can be rendered by audio screen readers.

### Addressing audio challenges

Following are some common challenges and solutions for accommodating Web users with hearing impairment:

- **Alternative audio support** — If you include audio content on a page, make sure that a text-based equivalent is readily available for hearing-impaired users.

- **Alternative speech input** — If your site includes the ability for speech input, make sure that an equivalent keyboard entry mechanism is available.

- **Text support for audio elements** — Make sure that any audio elements are clearly marked with alternative text so that readers can obtain the information.

### Addressing cognitive and technical challenges

Following are some common challenges and solutions for accommodating Web users with cognitive impairment or equipment limitations:

- **Page content that flashes, flickers or strobes** — Such content may cause problems for those with neurological disorders.

- **Alternative navigation** — Navigation aids should be provided to help those with lower cognitive skills.

- **Audio support** — Audio transcriptions of text-based content may help users with reading disabilities such as dyslexia.

- **Low-resolution alternatives** — Design Web pages so that they do not require large, expensive screen resolutions, or provide low-resolution alternatives.

In the following lab, you will use a Web page accessibility-testing strategy. Suppose your Web development team has created a site following the WCAG standards. You are assigned to validate the site. One step you would perform in this validation process is ensuring that the site can be easily browsed by a text-based editor.

 **Lab 1-2: Using a text-only browser to evaluate accessibility**

In this lab, you will conduct a partial validation test to determine the accessibility of a site for users employing voice-recognition software. Sight-impaired Web users often use voice-recognition software to augment or replace their limited ability to view a Web page. Voice-recognition software is capable of reading text, but not images, on a Web page. You can use a text-based browser to determine how well a site uses text to describe its images.

1.  Verify that you have created the **C:\CIW\Site_Dev\Lab Files\** directory on your computer, and that the **Lab Files\** folder contains subfolders and student files for all lessons in this course. If this directory does not exist, insert your student supplemental CD-ROM in your CD drive now, and extract the files for the **Site Development Foundations** course.

    *Note: Instructions for using the CIW Master Supplemental CD-ROM are provided in the front matter section of this book.*

2.  Open **Windows Explorer** and navigate to the directory **C:\CIW\Site_Dev\Lab Files\ Lesson01\Lab_1-2\**. Copy the **Lynx\** directory to your Desktop.

*Note: If you cannot obtain the Lynx\ directory, use a Web browser to access a Win32 version of Lynx from www.fdisk.com/doslynx/lynxport.htm, then follow the remaining steps in this lab.*

3. Once you have copied the Lynx application to your Desktop, open a command prompt and change to the Desktop\Lynx\ directory using the following command:

**cd desktop\lynx**

4. Launch the Lynx text-only browser by entering the following command in the command prompt:

**lynx http://www.usdoj.gov/crt/ada/adahom1.htm**

5. You will see the ADA Home Page appear in the Lynx browser, as shown in Figure 1-3.

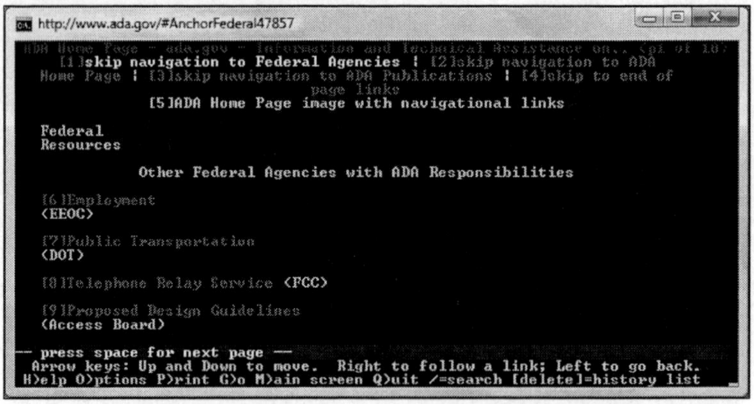

*Figure 1-3: Official ADA home page in Lynx Web browser*

6. You cannot use your mouse to navigate through Lynx. Following are common Lynx commands you can use to navigate:

- **G** — allows you to specify a URL (precede all URLs with *http://* or *https://*)

- **H** — summons the Help page, if present

- **UP ARROW key** — moves to the top of the page

- **DOWN ARROW key** — moves to the bottom of the page, by link

- **RIGHT ARROW key** — moves to the next page

- **LEFT ARROW key** — moves to the previous page

- **Q** — quits Lynx (by first pressing Q, then pressing Y)

7. Review the ADA guidelines discussed previously in this lesson.

8. Navigate through the official ADA home page. How well are the images described when viewing this page in a text-only format? Does this page follow its own guidelines?

9. Visit the following page, and consider how this page follows ADA guidelines:

**http://people.rit.edu/easi/law/weblaw1.htm**

**10.** Visit additional sites, including the following:

- Amazon.com (***www.amazon.com***)

- CNN (***www.cnn.com***)

- BBC (***www.bbc.co.uk***)

**11.** How well are images described when viewing these pages in text-only format? Do these pages follow other accessibility guidelines?

**12.** When you are finished viewing these sites, press **Q** then press **Y** to quit Lynx, then type ***Exit*** and press **ENTER** to close the command prompt.

**13.** As a class, discuss how these sites follow or do not follow ADA guidelines.

In this lab, you considered user disabilities in regards to Web page creation.

In the preceding lab, you used Lynx to test Web-accessibility standards. Lynx is a free, open-source, text-only browser. Lynx supports the HTTP, HTTPS, FTP and NNTP protocols. Users with disabilities, especially visually impaired people, often use text-based browsers to view the Web. In some cases, users may elect to disable graphics to view Web pages more quickly than if the graphics were visible. You can use Lynx to view your Web page to see how understandable your Web page is when the graphics are eliminated.

Many spider programs view your Web page the same way Lynx does. By using Lynx to test your Web pages for accessibility, you may be able to make appropriate changes to allow your site to score higher in Web search engine search results, thereby increasing your exposure.

> **OBJECTIVE**
> 2.12.4:
> Documenting test results

## Documenting changes

As you make changes to your Web site, make sure that you keep a written record of all changes. The practice of documenting changes to a site is called change management. Documenting change is essential because it allows you to:

- Remember which changes have been made to the HTML code and/or pages on the site.

- Ensure that you publish all security updates to the Web server.

- Provide evidence of good-faith efforts to ensure accessibility.

- Verify that you have fulfilled requests from departments in your organization.

## Site maps

A site map can be an important part of Web page accessibility. It allows visitors to view a summary of your Web site's structure. A site map should show the locations of all site sections, usually beginning with the index page on top. Useful site maps include the following:

- **Topical hierarchy** — A site map should clearly outline the site's sections in a visual, hierarchical format. However, do not provide only a graphic as a site map. Alternative browsers may not render the graphic, and alternative image text may not describe the graphic's content adequately for users who cannot see it.

- **Aptly named site sections** — Make sure that each section of your site is named accurately to enable users to find the pages they need.

- **Search capability** — Visitors might not find the exact information they seek even after consulting your site map. You can include a search engine text box on the site map page (or a link to your site's search engine) so that visitors can search for the resource they want.

A useful site map is the product of proper site planning. If you begin creating your site map after you have finished creating the site, then you have skipped some steps in proper site planning.

**OBJECTIVE**
2.19.2: Branding
issues

## Creative design and branding standards

A Web page is often part of a larger marketing and sales strategy. In fact, Web sites have become a means for creating and ensuring brand recognition and mind share. In short, Web sites have become an important marketing tool. You must design your Web pages according to marketing demands. To do this, you should understand the motivations of a marketing specialist.

A marketing specialist's primary goal is to establish name and brand recognition. For example, many people can immediately identify the hood ornament symbol of a Mercedes-Benz, and many people are equally familiar with the McDonald's "golden arches." Both are examples of name and brand recognition. You were introduced to branding at the beginning of this lesson.

A term closely related to name recognition is mind share. One way for an organization or company to increase business and gain recognition is to adopt catch words, phrases and other sound bites that help the general public identify a product, person or service. Examples of mind share include Intel Corporation's "Intel Inside" and Microsoft Corporation's "Where do you want to go today?" Such commercial phrases help to keep a company's name in the minds of the public. The Habitat For Humanity Web site (*www.habitat.org*), shown in Figure 1-4, was created with name recognition in mind.

*Figure 1-4: Habitat For Humanity home page*

The primary way to achieve such recognition is to clearly define and execute a branding standard, which is a set of comprehensive marketing goals and strategies. Most organizations devise a branding standard through well-coordinated meetings and carefully devised plans.

The primary goal of a Web developer is to help the company reinforce its branding standard. As you design page layout and create graphical content, remember that your site is part of a larger context. The look and feel of your Web site should be consistent with the design principles, color schemes, graphics and logos found in existing company stationery, posters and advertisements. If your company uses a particular sound bite or catch phrase, find a way to cleverly incorporate it into your site. If you can apply effective design principles to your company's marketing strategy, your site will be more successful.

## Design and branding standards meetings

You will probably need to meet with various departments and individuals to ensure that your Web site complements the company's branding strategy as effectively as possible. Such meetings generally focus on the following:

- Target markets
- Market messages
- Media choices
- Color combinations
- Sales strategies
- Technologies you want to use

A thorough discussion of the ways that your Web pages fulfill branding standards is beyond the scope of this course. However, you should understand that as you write HTML code, you will probably do so to fulfill very specific organizational goals.

## Audience development techniques

**OBJECTIVE**
2.10.2: Audience development mechanisms

You may be asked for your input regarding ways to develop an audience for your Web site. You might discuss the following methods:

**OBJECTIVE**
2.10.3: Proprietary technologies

- Providing standard Web site features, including properly placed video, audio and active content (e.g., Adobe Flash programs, Microsoft Silverlight applications, Java applets).

- Providing unique Web site features, which include ideas generated by you and your Web team, and input from other areas of the company (marketing, sales, upper management).

- Using logos and other images traditionally used by the company.

- Coordinating your efforts with traditional marketing strategies. You should work with the marketing department to ensure that your Web site's look and feel complements the company's marketing slicks and traditional paper items (e.g., letterhead, envelopes, notepads).

- Tracking user visits, which can indicate the popular parts of your site, and can help you to improve the unpopular parts.

- Analyzing and interpreting statistics to help increase Web site efficiency. For example, consider ways to increase visitor time at site locations where revenue is generated.

- Working with the sales and marketing teams to obtain input from customers about desired Web site features.

Table 1-3 explains additional techniques that can help develop your audience.

**mailing list server**
An e-mail server that regularly sends e-mail messages to a specified list of users.

**spam**
Unsolicited and unwanted e-mail messages; the online equivalent of junk mail.

**cookie**
A text file that contains information sent between a server and a client to help maintain state and track user activities. Cookies can reside in memory or on a hard drive.

*Table 1-3: Audience development techniques*

| Technique | Description | Benefit |
|---|---|---|
| **Push technology** | Any technology that automatically provides information to a customer list. In legitimate cases, the customer initially makes a request to be placed on the list. Customers receive information until they ask to be removed. One example of push technology is a **mailing list server**. Illegitimate examples of push technology include **spam**. | Customers automatically receive new information about a product or service. This technique is often sales-based and marketing-based because many organizations push information to customers and potential customers. |
| **Pull technology** | Any technology that provides information to a customer only upon request. A more standard way to disseminate information from a server. For example, whenever you download a file from a Web site or collect your e-mail, you are using pull technology. | Because the customer asks for information and content, this technique is demand-based and immediate. |
| **Visitor tracking** | Any technology that provides the following information:<br>-The number of visitors that connected to the site or specific pages<br>-The length of time visitors remained at the site or specific pages<br>-The frequency with which a specific visitor returns to the site<br>For example, Web sites use **cookies** to help determine how often end users visit the site. You can also track users by viewing log files. | This technique provides feedback that you can use to update site content, revise site navigation, review product offerings, market to all or specific customers, and so forth. |

## Portals

A portal is a Web site that acts as a centralized access point for other sites. There are two types of portal: vertical and horizontal.

- **Vertical** — a portal dedicated to one specific interest or field (e.g., women's health, network security, sports or politics), also called a "vortal." Each linked site on a vertical portal maintains a topical focus. Examples include CNET (*www.cnet.com*), Slashdot (*http://slashdot.org/*) and RealEstate.com (*www.realestate.com*). Intranets and extranets are also examples of vertical portals because they provide links to external sites and are dedicated to a specific topic: the businesses that host them. Intranets are sometimes known as corporate portals.

- **Horizontal** — a portal that provides links to various Web sites with no particular focus. Examples include Yahoo! (*www.yahoo.com*), Google (*www.google.com*) and AOL (*www.aol.com*). Each of these sites contains links to other sites, but linked sites represent diverse interests (e.g., travel, news, shopping), rather than one focus.

Portals can provide various services, including e-mail accounts, chat services, message forums, stock information and access to newsgroups. Many portals also provide search engines.

 *A portal is also known as a gateway.*

### Portal benefits

A portal can benefit both end users and businesses. A portal benefits end users because it directs them to the best sites for a particular topic, and helps users find information and products faster. A portal benefits businesses because it can create a stream of customers who generate revenue. A business can also use a portal to help position its brand, improve brand recognition in a market, and strengthen the brand by comparing it with competitors.

## Wiki sites

A wiki is a Web site that allows all visitors to collaborate in its construction. You can use a wiki to create an information repository or portal. A wiki uses specialized Web-based software (called wiki software) that allows any visitor to update the site using a Web browser.

 *The word wiki is coined from the Hawaiian phrase "wiki wiki," which means "very quick."*

Wiki software cooperates with a Web server to generate pages in HTML or XHTML so that a Web browser can render them. However, most wiki pages are written in simplified markup language called LaTeX (*www.latex-project.org*) that accommodates the fast-paced nature of a wiki site.

Specific pages of a wiki can be locked down while leaving others available for public or permitted editing. The first wiki ever established was the Portland Pattern Repository (*http://c2.com/ppr*). Following are examples of current wiki sites:

- Wikipedia (*www.wikipedia.org*)

- LinuxQuestions.org (*http://wiki.linuxquestions.org/wiki/Main_Page*)

- BerliOS (*http://en.wikipedia.org/wiki/BerliOS*)

- MemoryAlpha (*http://en.wikipedia.org/wiki/Memory_Alpha*)

Many purveyors of wiki software exist, including the following:

- Wiki Base (*http://c2.com/cgi/wiki?WikiBase*)

- Wiki Choicetree (*http://c2.com/cgi/wiki?WikiChoicetree*)

- JSPWiki (*www.jspwiki.org*)

## File formats and active content

**OBJECTIVE**
2.10.1: Document and multimedia file formats

Web servers provide more than just pages created in markup languages. You will populate your pages with various content formats, including Portable Document Format (PDF) documents, images and media files.

### Common file formats and MIME types

All of the file formats you will use on your Web pages have a specific MIME type. The Internet Assigned Numbers Authority (IANA) is responsible for standardizing MIME types. Table 1-4 lists common file formats used in Web pages.

*Table 1-4: Common file formats*

| File Format | File Name Extension | Description | MIME Type |
|---|---|---|---|
| **HTML** | .html or .htm | HTML files. | text/html |
| **XHTML** | .html or .htm | XHTML files. | application/xhtml+html |
| **Joint Photographic Experts Group (JPEG)** | .jpeg or .jpg | A standard Web page image format. Provides variable image quality and compression algorithms to help reduce file size. | image/jpeg |
| **Graphics Interchange Format (GIF)** | .gif | A standard Web page image format. Does not provide native compression. Two types of GIF exist: <br>-GIF87a (standard) <br>-GIF89a (animated GIF) <br>Animated GIFs show a series of embedded images, simulating motion. GIF files can also be interlaced for gradual display during a slow download. | image/gif |
| **Portable Network Graphics (PNG)** | .png | The newest standard Web page image format. Supports compression, and various quality levels and file sizes (the higher the image quality, the larger the file size). PNGs can also be animated. | image/png |
| **Text** | .txt | Standard (ASCII) text files. | text/plain |
| **Cascading Style Sheets (CSS)** | .css | CSS formatting is defined in text files, which can be attached to HTML documents to apply the defined styles. | text/css |
| **Rich Text Format (RTF)** | .rtf | Documents that contain simple formatting (e.g., underlining, bold, and font faces and sizes). | text/rtf |
| **PostScript** | .ps | A language designed to describe page formatting for text and graphics. Developed by Adobe, but has become an open standard. | application/postscript |
| **Portable Document Format (PDF)** | .pdf | Adobe Acrobat proprietary format, based on PostScript technology. Can retain sophisticated formatting and graphics. | application/pdf |
| **Zip** | .zip | Files compressed using the zip/unzip family of file applications. | application/zip |
| **Pretty Good Privacy (PGP) / GNU Privacy Guard (GPG)** | .pgp <br><br> .gpg | Files encrypted by PGP/GPG. | application/pgp-encrypted <br><br> application/gpg-encrypted |

Table 1-4: Common file formats (cont'd)

| File Format | File Name Extension | Description | MIME Type |
|---|---|---|---|
| Moving Pictures Experts Group (MPEG) – audio | .mpeg | MPEG streaming audio. | audio/mpeg |
| MPEG – video | .mpeg | MPEG streaming video. | video/mpeg |
| MPEG Audio Layer 3 (MP3) | .mp3 | MP3 audio file format. | audio/mp3 |
| Ogg-Vorbis | .ogg | Ogg-Vorbis audio file format. | application/ogg |
| WAV | .wav | Native digital audio format of Windows operating systems. | audio/wav audio/x-wav |
| RealPlayer | .ram, .ra | Audio and video files in the RealPlayer format (*www.real.com*). | audio/ram audio/pn-realaudio ram audio/x-realaudio ra |
| Word | .doc | Microsoft Word documents. | application/msword |
| Excel | .xls | Microsoft Excel documents (spreadsheets). | application/vnd.ms-excel |
| PowerPoint | .ppt | Microsoft PowerPoint documents (presentation slide shows). | application/vnd.ms-powerpoint |
| Unrecognized images | N/A | For any images and streaming media not currently standardized by IANA. | application/octet-stream |

For a full list of MIME types from the official source, visit the IANA site at *www.iana.org/assignments/media-types*.

## Proprietary formats and evaluating their use

Many of the file types previously discussed are standard and do not require your system to have special plug-ins. Proprietary formats may require special plug-ins, but can enhance the look and feel of your Web site. Table 1-5 provides an overview of drawbacks to consider in relation to proprietary file formats.

OBJECTIVE
2.10.4: Evaluating proprietary technologies

Table 1-5: Issues with proprietary file formats

| Issue | Description |
|---|---|
| Difficulty/ inconvenience | Some plug-ins and software may be unduly difficult to obtain. If your development team agrees that a required plug-in or software is not too difficult for end users to obtain, then you can proceed using a proprietary technology without impacting your pages' accessibility and potential audience. |
| Cost | Some proprietary file formats (e.g., Microsoft Word) require software that must be purchased. You should consider free or open-source alternatives for file formats. |
| Audience limitation | As previously discussed, some formats limit a disabled person's ability to obtain information. For example, if you plan on posting essential information in a PDF document, you should provide equivalent information in standard text format elsewhere on the site because sight-assistance tools may not be able to convert the PDF document to audible content. |

# Back-End Issues

Server resources that process and store user input are referred to as the back end of a Web site. Because you are using your Web documents to communicate over a network, you should ensure that they operate as efficiently as possible. You have already learned the importance of the front-end interface. Now, you should consider some back-end issues.

## Database connectivity

Most Web sites do more than simply present text, a few image files and a couple documents. Fully functional Web sites also include database connectivity. Databases provide the ability to:

- Present stored information to customers, and allow them to search and retrieve.

- Receive information from customers and save it for later retrieval.

Many companies use database-enabled sites. Amazon.com, eBay and IBM are only a few examples.

### Types of databases

There are several database types:

- **Flat file** — Information is stored in a single table, often in a simple text file. The Windows registry is an example of a flat-file database.

- **Non-relational** — Information is stored statically. Information can be searched, but cannot be reorganized or placed into another database.

- **Relational** — Information can be sorted, altered and placed into other databases for retrieval.

- **Object-oriented** — A newer form with the capabilities of a relational database, plus greater storage and search efficiency.

This section will focus on relational databases because they are the most common.

### Relational databases

A relational database stores information in tables. These tables contain fields that allow data in the tables to be cross-referenced and joined in various ways. You or your database administrators define the categories and descriptions in the tables. Information in these tables can also be updated (e.g., added to or deleted). When you conduct a search in a site such as eBay to retrieve information about a type of item you want to buy, for example, you are using a Web-enabled relational database.

A relational database can consist of a single file or it can be distributed among several database servers. After you have organized a database, you can access its information in various ways. For example, if you have a database of employee information, you can query the database for an alphabetical list of employee names, or you can sort the employees by age, employee number, date of hire and so forth.

### Creating relational databases

Once you have created a category for information in a database, you create a table that has columns and rows. Each row contains an individual represented entity, such as an employee. As you read across the row, you see attributes of that entity, such as employee name, employee ID number or hire date. Each attribute type is specified in a column heading.

## Relational database vendors

Table 1-6 lists examples of relational database vendors.

Table 1-6: Relational database vendors

| Vendor | Description |
| --- | --- |
| Oracle | You can learn more about the latest Oracle products at *www.oracle.com*. |
| IBM | IBM's database product is called DB2. You can learn more about IBM products at *www.ibm.com*. |
| Microsoft | Microsoft offers a database server product called SQL Server. You can learn more about Microsoft products at *www.microsoft.com*. |
| MySQL | MySQL is an open-source database that will run on UNIX and Windows systems. You can learn more about MySQL at *www.mysql.com*. |
| PostgreSQL | PostgreSQL is another open-source database product that is often considered to be more powerful and stable. You can learn more about PostgreSQL at *www.postgresql.org*. |

**OBJECTIVE**
2.17.4: SQL for remote databases

**Structured Query Language (SQL)**
A language used to create and maintain professional, high-performance corporate databases.

## Databases, Web servers and SQL

After you have created several data tables, you can query them to glean information. Generally, if you want to query a relational database, you use **Structured Query Language (SQL)**. For example, using SQL, you can allow end users to determine the number of projects that Sandi Stanger finished by a certain date. You can also obtain a record that provides this information along with her employee ID number and hire date.

You should note that relational databases always separate the data you want (such as the information about Juan, Sandi or Sven) from the way you retrieve the data (i.e., the SQL logic itself).

You can also create a Web page that allows end users to conduct these queries through the page. You simply program the Web server pages to access server-side applications. These applications can receive parameters provided by end users, then use these parameters to query databases so that the end users obtain the information they want.

## Relational database manipulation terminology

Table 1-7 provides a summary of common relational database terms.

Table 1-7: Common relational database terms

| Term | Description |
| --- | --- |
| Join | The combination of two database tables to create a new table. |
| Table | A database topic that contains rows (records) and columns (fields or attributes). A table can be created from information initially or from tables through a join operation. |
| Record | One row of a relational database table. A record represents an entity. |
| Field | One column of a relational database table. A field represents a category of attributes. |
| Entity (i.e., record) | A person, place or thing represented in a database table row. All entities have attributes. Also known as a record. |

*Table 1-7: Common relational database terms (cont'd)*

| Term | Description |
|---|---|
| **Attribute (i.e., field or element)** | A specific category of information that relates to an entity. Attributes (i.e., fields) vary depending upon the nature of the entity. Attributes for a person in a database might include the person's name, phone number and e-mail address. Also known as a field or element. |
| **Linking attribute** | A common attribute between tables that allows a join to take place. |
| **Relation** | A link generated between two entities. |
| **Tuple** | A description of two or more entities that are currently linked by a relation. |
| **Query** | The process of searching a database, or the search command sent to a database. Also the process of combining databases. |

A relational database must treat all tables as if they could be connected, or joined, at various places. In a join, existing tabular data is manipulated to create a new table. It is possible to join tables from any part of a table. For example, you can join the left column of the table to the right column of the table. You can also connect tables from the inner or outer columns. The two main types of join are:

- **Inner join** — results in a new table in which the information in one column of the first table is combined with a column of the second table. An inner join is used when tables being joined have all values entered. Also known as a natural join, this is the most common type of join.

- **Outer join** — used to combine tables when one column of a table contains an empty, or null, value.

**OBJECTIVE**
2.17.4: SQL for remote databases

## SQL commands

SQL is an advanced, powerful language. Not all of the commands can be explained here, but following are some of the most common:

- **SELECT** — requests data from a particular table or table row

- **FROM** — delimits the beginning search point in a table or table row

- **WHERE** — delimits the ending search point in a table or table row

- **JOIN** — creates a new table from selected data

- **GROUP** — organizes results by a parameter, including an attribute name

- **SUM** — adds numerical information within records

## Accessing and updating databases

There are several ways to access a database file, including:

- **Locally** — You can access a database using programs installed on the same system as the database. Such applications (e.g., Microsoft Access) are usually provided by the database vendor.

- **Over the LAN from a share you establish** — Clients use a program such as Microsoft Access. Using such an application, you can form SQL queries that allow you to obtain information. You can also use this application to restrict access to database files.

- **Via the Web through a Web application** — As previously mentioned, you can use a CGI application created in one of various languages, including PHP, Perl, Microsoft C#, JSP, ColdFusion or ASP. If the Web page is configured correctly, you can use a simple Web browser to conduct queries. For example, whenever you conduct a Web search using Google or AltaVista, you are using a database.

## Database connection methods: Open Database Connectivity (ODBC)

You can also update database files by using the Microsoft Open Database Connectivity (ODBC) interface or its Java counterpart, Java Database Connectivity (JDBC). ODBC's primary purpose is to allow an operating system to register a database. ODBC supports SQL and all major database vendors. Once the database is registered, the operating system and its components (such as a Web server) can easily read and update the database. Figure 1-5 shows the ODBC window for Windows Vista.

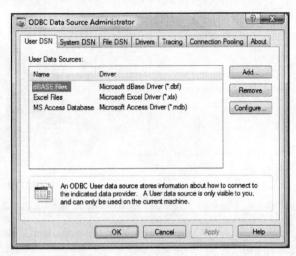

*Figure 1-5: Windows Vista Data Sources (ODBC) snap-in*

From this window, you can provide information that allows your system to recognize databases. Information can include:

- **Database drivers** — software that reads databases from various vendors

- **Database names** — information that allows easy retrieval of data

ODBC was developed by Microsoft and is proprietary to Windows-based operating systems.

## Java Database Connectivity (JDBC)

Java Database Connectivity (JDBC) was developed by Sun Microsystems. Unlike ODBC, JDBC is not limited to Microsoft operating systems. Like ODBC, JDBC supports major vendors (e.g., IBM and Oracle), and it also supports SQL. JDBC can be run on various systems, including Windows and UNIX. For more information, visit the JDBC home page at *http://java.sun.com/javase/technologies/database/index.jsp*.

To use JDBC, you must take the following steps:

- Install the Java environment, available at *http://java.sun.com* and *www.java.com*.

- Create an application (i.e., a program) that uses JDBC to access information. Applications can be written in various languages, including Java, JavaScript, PHP and Perl.

- Install JDBC-appropriate drivers for the database.

## Indexing and cataloging

**OBJECTIVE**
2.16.6: Online
indexing and
catalogs

Another Web site feature related to databases is the ability to index and catalog a site. More complex sites provide an internal search engine that allows visitors to conduct searches for site elements. Most Web servers, including Apache Server (*www.apache.org*) and Microsoft Internet Information Services (IIS) provide indexing features.

## Bandwidth and download time

**OBJECTIVE**
2.12.2: Estimating
download times

HTML pages require a relatively small amount of space on a hard drive. Because their file size is small, they are also easy to download over a network. However, as suggested by Figure 1-6, when you download an HTML page that refers to several graphics, you will generally download each graphic as well.

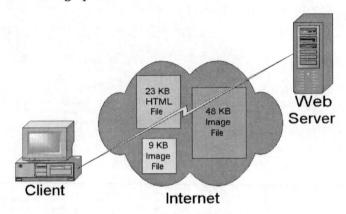

*Figure 1-6: Web page files downloading over network*

Image files can be quite large. For example, a simple JPEG image of your house or apartment could easily exceed 1 MB. A file this large usually takes some time to download over a network.

**bandwidth**
The amount of
information,
sometimes called
traffic, that can be
carried on a
network at one
time. The total
capacity of a line.
Also, the rate of
data transfer over a
network
connection;
measured in bits per
second.

Although both JPEG and GIF image formats support compression, remember that any file downloaded over a network requires **bandwidth**. To download a large file in a short amount of time, you need more bandwidth. If you cannot get more bandwidth, you need more time to download the file.

A graphic that accompanies an HTML page can take an unacceptably long time to finish downloading, especially if the user has a 33.6-Kbps or 56-Kbps modem. Even at **T1** speeds, a large file or graphic can cause a frustrating wait.

**T1**
A digital carrier that
transmits data at a
speed of 1.544
Mbps.

Therefore, make sure that your Web pages do not reference several large files. You should also avoid using too many small image files. It is difficult to determine an acceptable download size for files associated with an HTML page. However, you must consider the total size of your page, including all images, plug-ins and other programs. As a general rule, your pages should not exceed 100 KB without a very good reason.

### Determining download time for a Web page

To calculate download time for a Web page, follow these steps.

Step 1:   Check the size of the HTML file and any associated images, files or programs. For example, your page may consist of 11 files that total 84 kilobytes (KB).

Step 2:   Determine the speed of your network connection, which is generally measured in kilobits per second (Kbps). Some of the more common connection speeds are:

- 14.4 Kbps (slow modem speed).

- 28.8 Kbps (typical modem speed).

- 33.6 Kbps (typical modem speed).

- 56 Kbps (typical modem speed).

- 128 Kbps (upper-limit speed of ISDN connection).

- 512 Kbps (typical DSL and cable modem speed).

- 1.544 Mbps (full T1, enterprise-grade network line).

For this example, we will use 56 Kbps.

Step 3:   The connection speed and the file size must be converted into a common unit of measure for division: either bytes or bits. Consider that 1 byte equals 8 bits. The connection speed is already defined in bits: 56 kilobits = 56,000 bits. To convert the file size into bits, you should first convert it into bytes (84 kilobytes = 84,000 bytes). Then convert the bytes into bits by multiplying 84,000 by 8 (1 byte = 8 bits), which results in 672,000 bits.

Step 4:   Divide the file size (672,000 bits) by the connection speed (56,000 bits per second). The bits cancel out, and the result is 12 seconds. This result is the amount of time theoretically required to download the Web page.

Remember that the result derived from these four steps is a theoretical measurement. It does not consider certain factors, such as the fact that 56-Kbps modems rarely operate above 50 Kbps. Nor does it consider network overhead, noisy phone lines or network congestion. Therefore, the best way to determine how quickly users can download your HTML pages is to test them in real-world settings. For example, test your Web site by accessing it through a dial-up (i.e., telephone-line modem) connection. This method will provide a much more reliable estimate.

*Some sources refer to "bits per second" as "characters per second," although these terms are not technically equivalent. It is recommended that you use bits/kilobits/megabits/gigabits per second as the units of measure when discussing bandwidth and connection speeds.*

## Naming Web page files

As you create your Web pages, you may need to restrict the length of file names. You should also consider naming your HTML pages to correspond to their content. For example, if the page is a sales form, you could name it *salesform.htm*.

You can give your Web page files (i.e., HTML files) any name you want. However, you must identify each file as the appropriate file type by appending either the *.htm* or *.html* extension to the end of the file name. Some server administrators prefer that you use the .html file name extension. Others may prefer the .htm extension. When in doubt, ask your service provider or Web server administrator which standard you should follow.

More technologically complex pages may require file name extensions other than .htm or .html. For example, Active Server Pages (ASP) files require the .asp extension, and JavaServer Pages (JSP) files require the .jsp extension.

### Default files and the HTTP server

You should remember that your pages will probably reside on a Web server (also called an HTTP server). Usually, an HTTP server looks for a default page, which is a specially named file. The server will present this page automatically each time a user enters the minimum amount of information required to connect to the site. Rather than having to enter the page address *www.company.com/index.html*, a user need only enter *www.company.com*. The server supplies the default page *index.html* automatically.

Default document names differ from server to server. Microsoft Internet Information Services (IIS) looks for the *default.htm* file. Apache HTTP server looks for the *index.html* file. You can change the name of the default document, but you should be aware that every Web server is preconfigured to a default document name. Following are some common default page names:

| | | | |
|---|---|---|---|
| • index.htm | • default.htm | • welcome.htm | • home.htm |
| • index.html | • default.html | • welcome.html | • home.html |
| • index.asp | • default.asp | • welcome.asp | • home.asp |
| • index.jsp | • default.jsp | • welcome.jsp | • home.jsp |

Consult the Web server documentation, your site administrator or your Internet Service Provider (ISP) to ensure that your default file name functions properly on your Web server.

### HTTP 404 – File Not Found error

An HTTP 404 – File Not Found error indicates that you have requested a file that does not exist on the specified Web server. This server-generated error indicates that the server is functioning, but the specific file you requested from that server cannot be located because the file may have been renamed or removed from the site.

You will also receive this error if you request a site's default document by the wrong name. For example, the default document name for the Yahoo! Web site is *www.yahoo.com/index.html*. If you request *www.yahoo.com/default.html*, you will receive a 404 error.

Many Web browsers, including Microsoft Internet Explorer, will automatically generate a custom page when an end user requests a non-existent page. Increasingly, Web site administrators create a custom page that will appear whenever a user requests a non-existent page. Figure 1-7 shows a custom 404 error page.

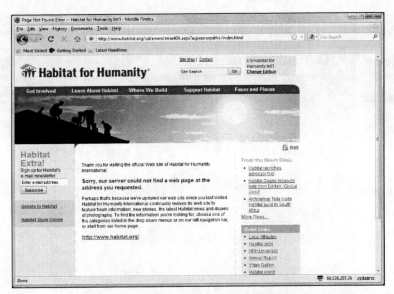

Figure 1-7: HTTP 404 – File Not Found error

Now that you understand the front-end and back-end issues involved in Web site creation, you will learn how to create Web pages using HTML.

# The Habitat For Humanity Web Site

Habitat For Humanity (also known simply as Habitat) is a not-for-profit, volunteer-driven organization that builds and sells homes for families across the world. The potential homeowner becomes a partner in building the home, and contributes to the actual building process as much as possible. This practice is called "sweat equity." Volunteers also help build the home. For years, Habitat has specialized in helping young people across the world contribute their time to help others obtain decent housing.

Habitat For Humanity has built more than 150,000 homes across the world. Habitat also arranges no-interest mortgages and reasonable payment schedules for the homeowner, in cooperation with businesses and charitable organizations.

*Habitat For Humanity has allowed CIW to use an earlier prototype version of its Web site as an example of a commercial-grade site. This permission is in no way an endorsement of CIW or Certification Partners. Habitat's permission to use portions of its site in labs teaching site development skills does not represent any sort of alliance or partnership. Students will build prototype pages using Habitat For Humanity content, which is owned and copyrighted by Habitat For Humanity. The prototype pages that students build do not necessarily represent, duplicate or simulate the current live Habitat For Humanity Web site, which can be visited at www.habitat.org.*

Visit the current live version of the Habitat Web site at *www.habitat.org*. As you review the Habitat site, evaluate the site's ability to convey Habitat's message and achieve its goals. As you do so, consider the following questions:

- What strategies does the Habitat site adopt to obtain volunteers for building homes?

- What technologies (e.g., search engines, PDF documents) are used on this site to help achieve its goals?

- What front-end issues should be considered for this site?

- Review the site for offered features. What back-end technologies will be required to fulfill the offered features?

# Planning the Site at Both Ends

Puja is part of a Web development team. Planning so far has focused on the "look and feel" of the Web site, and has included discussions about color schemes and image choices. Puja makes the following list of additional items that need to be discussed in relation to the site:

- Accessibility standards

- Markup languages to use (e.g., XHTML Transitional, XHTML Strict)

- Development environments to use (e.g., simple text editor, GUI editors such as Dreamweaver)

- CGI choices

- Database connectivity

- Now, Puja has been asked to determine the ideal Web server platform for this site. She has been given the following information:

- Her company uses Sun Solaris almost exclusively. Sun Solaris is a version of UNIX. UNIX systems have supported languages such as Java and Perl for years.

- The company has a team of developers who know scripting languages such as JavaScript and Perl.

- Several of the developers are accustomed to using Apache Server, an open-source Web server that can run on any operating system but is traditionally used on UNIX.

After considering this information, Puja decides to use Apache Server, which supports Perl.

\*　　　\*　　　\*

As a class, discuss the factors that you should consider when choosing a server platform, including:

- Existing operating systems.

- Development resources.

- Cost of operating systems and/or Web server software.

## Lesson Summary

### Application project

Calculate the amount of time it will take a user to download a 70-KB home page if he or she is using a 56-Kbps modem. Do you think this time requirement is acceptable to a waiting user?

Now consider the usefulness of databases to your Web site. To learn more about ODBC, visit the Microsoft Web site and conduct searches. The following URLs also contain helpful information:

> *http://dev.mysql.com/doc/refman/5.0/en/myodbc-connector.html*
>
> *www.oracle.com/technology/docs/tech/windows/odbc/htdocs/817help/ sqoraWhat_is_ODBC.htm*

You can also visit the unixODBC project at *www.odbc.org*, which aims to port Microsoft ODBC to non-Windows systems.

To learn more about JDBC, visit the following URL:

> *http://java.sun.com/javase/technologies/database/index.jsp*

### Skills review

In this lesson, you learned that you can create Web pages in two ways: with a simple text editor or a GUI editor application. This course will teach you the basics of both methods.

You also learned the fundamentals of Web page design by studying front-end and back-end issues. You now understand how to help ensure Web site accessibility. You also know that Web pages are connected to databases using technologies such as CGI and ODBC. Before you develop a Web page or site, you must consider important variables such as the interface, business considerations, bandwidth and the names of your Web page files.

Now that you have completed this lesson, you should be able to:

✓ 2.7.3: Verify compliance with government and industry accessibility standards, including W3C Web Accessibility Initiative (WAI), U.S. Government Section 508, Americans with Disabilities Act (ADA).

✓ 2.10.1: Identify the uses and benefits of various document and multimedia file formats, including PDF, RTF, PostScript, EPS, MOV, MPEG, streaming media, non-streaming media.

✓ 2.10.2: Define the following Web-related mechanisms for audience development (i.e., attracting and retaining an audience): push technology, pull technology, visitor tracking.

✓ 2.10.3: Identify common proprietary Web site and page enhancement elements, including Adobe Flash and Microsoft Silverlight.

✓ 2.10.4: Evaluate the benefits and drawbacks of proprietary technologies such as Flash, Shockwave, movie formats.

✓ 2.12.1: Test and validate Web documents.

✓ 2.12.2: Estimate download time for Web pages.

✓ 2.12.4: Document results of Web site functionality testing.

✓ 2.16.6: Identify the importance of online indexing and cataloging.

✓ 2.17.2: Define Common Gateway Interface (CGI) methods, including .Net, Django, Python, JavaServer Pages (JSP), Server-Side JavaScript (SSJS), Active Server Pages (ASP), PHP Hypertext Preprocessor (PHP), Ajax.

✓ 2.17.3: Define database connectivity technologies (e.g., Open Database Connectivity [ODBC], Java Database Connectivity [JDBC]), and demonstrate the ability to connect databases with Web sites and other Internet-based services.

✓ 2.17.4: Identify basic SQL commands for querying remote databases.

✓ 2.19.2: Manage branding issues when developing a site (e.g., logo placement and sizing).

✓ 2.21.4: Consult respected Web development resources, including books, trade journals, online sources, qualified individuals, user groups.

# Lesson 1 Review

1. User-friendly Web page interfaces, such as a pleasing layout and accessible navigation, are considered to be what type of issues?

   _____

2. Calculate the time required, in seconds, to download a 14,000-byte Web page using a 56-Kbps modem.

   _____ 4 Sec. _____

   _____

3. If you request a file that does not exist on a Web server, what types of messages will you receive? (Name or describe at least two.)

   _____ File not found 404 + 401 _____

   _____

   _____

4. What W3C project promotes Web page access for disabled Web users?

   _____

   _____

5. What technology provides text-based Web browsing and secure e-mail to wireless handheld devices?

   _____

# Lesson 2: Markup Language and Site Development Essentials

## Objectives

By the end of this lesson, you will be able to:

✿ 2.1.1: Relate the history of markup languages to current techniques and technologies, including Standard Generalized Markup Language (SGML), previous versions of Hypertext Markup Language (HTML).

✿ 2.1.2: Identify the format and various versions of HTML, including HTML 4.01, Extensible HTML (XHTML).

✿ 2.1.8: Explain the importance of consistently developing to a single W3C standard (e.g., XHTML 1.0 Transitional).

✿ 2.6.1: Describe the functionality of XML.

✿ 2.7.1: Obtain input from stakeholders about acceptable technologies and color combinations.

✿ 2.7.2: Create an initial Web site diagram (i.e., a story board or prototype), and translate it into a site map.

✿ 2.7.4: Validate Web page design according to technical and audience standards adopted by employers.

✿ 2.7.5: Verify Web site usability, viewability and browser compatibility.

✿ 2.12.3: Test Web pages in multiple browsers.

✿ 2.13.1: Work as a team member to develop pages and sites.

✿ 2.13.2: Collaborate with technical (e.g., IT) and non-technical (e.g., marketing) members of the organization to ensure sites meet requirements.

✿ 2.13.3: Determine information and audience requirements for a site, including stakeholders such as customers, employees, shareholders, suppliers.

- ➴ 2.13.4: Document a Web site plan.

- ➴ 2.13.5: Communicate the Web site plan effectively, both orally and in writing.

- ➴ 2.13.6: Obtain and document feedback, then improve the site, including working closely with sales and marketing to evaluate site effectiveness.

- ➴ 2.14.1: Define legal issues related to a Web site, including trademarking, licensing, copyrighting, licensing copyrighted materials, scope of copyright, reach of copyright, copyrighting process, copyright infringement and consequences.

- ➴ 2.14.2: Identify fundamentals of project management, including major stages of a Web design/development project cycle.

- ➴ 2.14.3: Identify processes of pre-launch site/application functionality testing, including checking links, testing with various browsers, testing against corruption of your e-commerce site, load testing, access to the site, testing with various speed connections.

- ➴ 2.14.4: Manage existing sites (e.g., remove dead links and/or upgrade connectivity when necessary).

- ➴ 2.14.5: Remove old sites and pages.

- ➴ 2.15.1: Identify ways to elicit useful feedback from management and customers.

- ➴ 2.15.2: Use presentation aids and support material, including charts, tables, figures, written content, overhead projection.

- ➴ 2.15.3: Use presentation software (e.g., slide-based software).

- ➴ 2.15.4: Clarify technical concepts for a non-technical audience, and use strategies to retain listener interest.

- ➴ 2.15.5: Interpret verbal, non-verbal and written feedback.

- ➴ 2.15.6: Address diversity and corporate/organizational culture when communicating your message by customizing meeting and message delivery, and listening for responses.

- ➴ 2.15.7: Identify ways to lead meetings (e.g., make introductions, invite questions, set time frames, set action times, monitor time, ensure proper discussion focus, publish minutes).

- ➴ 2.19.3: Consider corporate/organizational culture when designing page layout.

- ➴ 2.19.4: Demonstrate sensitivity to ethnic and cultural issues in page layout and design.

- ➴ 2.20.1: Obtain proper permissions from developers when repurposing content (e.g., other developers' code, images, concepts).

- ➴ 2.20.2: Create and sign a Non-Disclosure Agreement (NDA) when necessary.

- ➴ 2.20.3: Identify situations in which it is necessary to consult with a legal team.

- ➴ 2.20.4: Identify ethical concerns when developing a Web site.

# Pre-Assessment Questions

1.  Which language allows you to use certain deprecated tags to alter text formatting on a page?

    a.  XHTML Strict
    b.  XHTML Transitional
    c.  SGML
    d.  XML

2.  Which of the following is an example of an HTML/XHTML markup interpreter?

    a.  CD-ROM
    b.  Proxy server
    c.  XHTML tag
    d.  E-mail program

3.  What are the three flavors of XHTML?

_____

# History of Markup Languages

**OBJECTIVE**
2.1.1: History of
markup languages

In this lesson, you will learn about the types of markup languages available to you for creating online documents. You will also learn about essential site development concepts.

## Standard Generalized Markup Language (SGML)

**Standard Generalized Markup Language (SGML)**
A metalanguage used to create other languages, including HTML and XHTML.

**metalanguage**
A language used for defining other languages.

**Standard Generalized Markup Language (SGML)** is a **metalanguage**, which means that it is used to create other languages, including HTML and XHTML. SGML was originally created by IBM and was standardized in 1986 by the International Organization for Standardization (ISO). SGML is a powerful markup language that describes documents by organizing concepts separately from their visual presentation. However, it is also very complex and difficult to learn.

SGML was not IBM's first metalanguage. IBM created the Generalized Markup Language (GML) in the late 1960s as a way to use formatted documents across different computer platforms. GML then evolved into SGML.

SGML's purpose was to describe only the information within a document, not the formatting of it. With SGML, you can describe how data elements in the document relate to each other. SGML was not designed to format the data's appearance on the page.

**Document Type Definition (DTD)**
A set of rules contained in a simple text file that defines the structure, syntax and vocabulary as it relates to tags and attributes for a corresponding document.

SGML essentially requires that you create, or define, your own document language rules. This set of language rules is called the **Document Type Definition (DTD)**. The DTD is generally specified in a separate file, which you reference, or declare, at the beginning of each document that you want to conform to the rules. Once the DTD is established, then all elements in the document must conform to it. You will learn more about DTDs and how to declare them later.

## Hypertext Markup Language (HTML)

Tim Berners-Lee of MIT invented Hypertext Markup Language (HTML) with colleagues from CERN (the European Particle Physics Laboratory) as a means of distributing non-linear text, called hypertext, to multiple points across the Internet. Berners-Lee felt that SGML and other languages were needlessly complex and did not suit the need for a cross-platform language that helped format documents.

**hyperlinks**
Embedded instructions within a text file that link it to another point in the file or to a separate file.

In HTML, one document links to another via pointers called **hyperlinks**. Hyperlinks are embedded instructions within a text file that call another location in the file or a separate file when the link is accessed, usually by a click of a mouse. The global set of linked documents across the existing Internet framework grew into the World Wide Web.

### Hypertext and hypermedia
Hypermedia is an extension of hypertext. It includes images, video, audio, animation and other multimedia data types, which can be incorporated into HTML documents. The Web can accurately be described as a hypermedia system.

Hypertext was first conceived by Ted Nelson in 1965. The first widely commercialized hypertext product was HyperCard, conceived by Bill Atkinson and introduced by Apple Computer in 1987. It incorporated many hypertext and hypermedia concepts, but was a proprietary system that worked only on Macintosh computers.

By contrast, HTML is a cross-platform language that works on Windows, Macintosh and UNIX platforms. In addition, HTML and the Web are client/server systems, whereas HyperCard works only on stand-alone Macintosh computers.

### HTML vs. SGML

Like SGML, HTML facilitates data exchange through a common document format across different types of computer systems and networks on the Web. However, HTML does not allow you to define a DTD and has fewer language elements than SGML. As a result, HTML is easier to use and has become the standard method of encoding information for Web documents.

### Markup languages

A markup language is very different from a programming language. Programming languages such as C, C++, Java and C# must be compiled before they are used. Applications that are compiled have separate program files and data files. In a markup language, the instructions and the data generally reside in the same file. Some instructions may reside in separate files (e.g., the DTD and style sheets), but markup languages generally do not require complex supporting libraries. Markup languages do not need to be compiled. In addition, HTML does not provide data structures or internal logic, as do procedural programming languages such as C and Pascal.

**tags**
Pieces of code, enclosed in angle brackets, that tell the HTML interpreter how to process or display text.

Whereas SGML is used specifically to define context as opposed to appearance, HTML has evolved into both a contextual and a formatting language. For example, by applying a heading style to text using HTML, you are marking the text contextually as an important topic that begins a new section, and you are also applying the visual formatting elements of bold type and a larger font size. HTML files are plain text files that have been "marked up" with special language elements called **tags**, which are embedded in the text.

Tags are pieces of text, enclosed in angle brackets (or "wickets"), that provide instructions to programs designed to interpret HTML. For example, you may want to change the color of some text in your file. You can apply this formatting by embedding opening and closing tags around the text that you want colored. If you want an image to appear in your document, you can use a tag to specify the source and placement of the image.

### Interpreters

HTML interpreters are programs that process HTML pages and render them to the user as text pages formatted in accordance with the embedded instructions. Examples of HTML interpreters are Web browsers, such as Opera, Lynx, Mozilla Firefox and Microsoft Internet Explorer.

HTML interpreters are not limited to browsers. Many programs on the market include HTML reading, exporting and creation capabilities as built-in features. For example, Mozilla Thunderbird, Microsoft Outlook and Windows Mail allow you to send and receive HTML e-mail messages, and to post fully formatted HTML messages to newsgroups. PDAs, digital cameras, DVD players and many other devices are also capable of reading markup.

Although HTML was specifically designed for use on the World Wide Web, many businesses are finding uses for HTML documents that have little or nothing to do with the Web. HTML files are very small and extremely portable, making this format an ideal choice when exchanging documents across any type of network.

### HTML 3.2 standard and HTML 4.01

**OBJECTIVE**
2.1.2: HTML and XHTML

HTML 3.2 is an older but still fully functional HTML standard. Many Web pages and HTML editors still use the 3.2 standard. This standard is quite universal because many people surf the Web using older Web browsers that cannot process all the elements required by the newer HTML 4.01 Recommendation.

The HTML 4.01 Recommendation was released in December 1999 and contains the latest specifications. You can access it at *www.w3.org/TR/html4/*. The 4.01 specification includes minor modifications to the 4.0 specification. Throughout this course, the HTML specification will be referred to as both HTML 4.0 and 4.01.

HTML allows you to use Cascading Style Sheets (CSS) and supports multiple spoken languages. For example, HTML 4.01 allows you to create Web pages that read languages such as Hebrew from right to left. HTML 4.01 also allows you to create ambitious tables and forms, as well as incorporate scripting languages. You will learn more about scripting solutions, such as DHTML, later in the course.

 *The W3C regulates the development of CSS standards.*

### HTML 4.01 flavors

As you develop Web pages in HTML 4.01, you should understand that it has three distinct variants, or "flavors." The HTML 4.01 flavors ensure that you can use the latest specification, yet remain backward-compatible with older Web browsers. Following is a short description of each flavor.

- **HTML 4.01 Transitional** — allows developers to insert formatting using either CSS or traditional layout instructions (e.g., HTML font, color and phrase elements). This version will render in browsers that do not support HTML 4.01 features such as CSS. This version also allows tags that the W3C considers to be less useful, known as "deprecated tags."

- **HTML 4.01 Strict** — requires the exclusive use of CSS when defining layout instructions. Deprecated tags are not allowed and will generate errors.

- **HTML 4.01 Frameset** — required for pages that use HTML frames, which place Web pages inside each other to create separate panes in the browser window. Some feel that frames provide additional functionality or enhance a site's look and feel.

 *You specify the flavor of HTML by using a document type declaration (<!DOCTYPE>) tag. You will learn more about the <!DOCTYPE> in this and later lessons.*

Many Web pages are written to versions of HTML 4.01. In this course, however, you will create pages using XHTML, which will be discussed shortly. To understand XHTML, you must first learn about XML.

## Extensible Markup Language (XML)

OBJECTIVE
2.6.1: XML
functionality

**Extensible Markup
Language (XML)**
A markup language
that describes
document content
instead of adding
structure or
formatting to
document content.
A simplified version
of SGML.

**Extensible Markup Language (XML)** is a language used to describe data elements on a Web page. It is not used to format the page's appearance. Businesses are rapidly embracing XML because of its potential to transform the way data is interchanged with all types of applications.

The Internet is a massive collection of data that is disparate and unstructured. XML is the technology that will enhance structure and navigation. This transformation will take years. However, it will replace the information overload with dynamic, targeted and personal information design.

Some of the quickest advances will occur with intranets and extranets because these systems tend to focus mostly on sophisticated personal and business transactions. These types of transactions require the elements that XML offers.

XML documents can be formatted into print documents, Web documents, PDF documents, comma-separated values (CSV), Wireless Application Protocol (WAP), Braille, text-to-speech and many other formats. This versatility allows XML to easily format wireless device content, for example, which is then sent using WAP. Because the documents are well-formed and define only the content, changes can occur on the fly (i.e., dynamically or without interruption), without administrators or programmers manually reformatting the content before transmission. You will learn about well-formed documents later in this lesson.

Because it is relatively new to the Web, XML is somewhat misunderstood. Many people think XML is just another set of markup used to format Web pages. This assumption is incorrect. In fact, XML is not used to format Web pages, but to describe the data from which Web pages are created. For example, you might use the following HTML tags to display a heading level in a Web page:

```
<h1>...</h1>
```

XML has no corresponding tags to emulate the same type of display in the browser.

 *Technically, you do not use XML to describe the meaning of information in your document. You use it to create your own language that in turn describes the meaning of information in your document. In this sense, XML is a metalanguage — a language used to create languages — just like SGML. Any tags you define yourself are said to extend XML.*

## *Purpose of XML*

If XML does not format content in a Web page, then what does it do with the data? The answer lies in XML's ability to make data and content meaningful to machines. HTML does very little to describe the content of a Web page to a computer or application. Consider again the heading level example, used as follows:

```
<h1> Tiger Woods </h1>
```

To a computer, the content between the two tags has no meaning; it simply is designated to the browser for display as a large, bold heading.

Now consider XML. Its extensibility means that XML can be used to assign specific meaning to the content between the tags, thus allowing it to be used by machines (specifically, applications). In the following example, notice that the content begins to develop meaning because the XML tag is more defined:

```
<golfer> Tiger Woods </golfer>
```

The XML tag makes the content between the tags more meaningful than does the HTML heading level. Further, XML can be as specific as needed, hence its extensibility. Consider the following example:

```
<golfer tour="U.S. Open"> Tiger Woods </golfer>

<golfer tour="U.S. Open" year="2008"> Tiger Woods </golfer>

<golfer tour="U.S. Open" year="2008" Ranking="#1"> Tiger Woods </golfer>
```

As you can see, each example is progressively more descriptive of the content. Now, the content between the tags (Tiger Woods) has defined meaning that can be understood by a computer or application. This is XML's power. XML is described as logical structure, which means that more importance is placed on the way in which descriptive data elements relate to each other in the hierarchy, than on the actual data itself.

In many ways, XML is a reduced version of SGML because it allows you to declare your own tags without SGML's complexity. The W3C governs the development of XML.

### Tree structure of a well-formed XML document

An XML document has two characteristics:

- It must be well-formed.

- It must be valid.

In XML, you must create what is called a "well-formed" document. For a document to be well-formed, it must contain a DTD and a root element, and have properly declared tags. You will learn about the XML DTD shortly. A root element is a container tag that encompasses all other elements in the document, similar to the <html> tag in an HTML document. In XML, all properly declared tags must nest in the correct order.

The primary characteristic of a well-formed document is that it forms a tree-like structure that stems from the root. Figure 2-1 demonstrates one way in which you could represent this tree structure visually. The root element in this example is CATALOG.

*Figure 2-1: Tree structure of elements in XML document*

### Example of a well-formed XML document

Following is an example of a document patterned after the hierarchy illustrated in the preceding figure.

```
<?xml version="1.0"?>
<catalog>
    <book>
            <title>A Certain Justice</title>
            <author>P.D. James</author>
            <year-published>2002</year-published>
            <isbn>0375401091</isbn>
    </book>
    <book>
            <title>Ashworth Hall</title>
            <author>Anne Perry</author>
            <year-published>2000</year-published>
            <isbn>0449908445</isbn>
    </book>
    <book>
            <title>L.A. Confidential</title>
            <author>James Ellroy</author>
            <year-published>2002</year-published>
            <isbn>0446674249</isbn>
    </book>
    <book>
            <title>Shadow Woman</title>
            <author>Thomas Perry</author>
            <year-published>2001</year-published>
            <isbn>0679453024</isbn>
```

```
            </book>
          </catalog>
```

This XML document is well-formed, but it is not yet valid. To create a valid XML document, you must declare a DTD.

### XML and valid documents: The DTD

Like SGML documents (and unlike HTML), an XML document must include a Document Type Definition (DTD), often of the document author's creation. The DTD defines the validity of all subsequent tags. If an XML document does not have a DTD, it will not render.

*Do not confuse the XML Document Type Definition (DTD) with the document type declaration or <!DOCTYPE> tag used at the beginning of HTML and XML files for identification purposes. You will learn about the <!DOCTYPE> tag in the next lesson.*

The XML DTD is necessary because you must define the meanings and structure of all XML tags. Remember that XML allows you to create a language that describes your text. XML is not a specified language, like HTML. Therefore, you must think ahead and define every element. In many ways, the DTD is the most important part of an XML document because it provides the rules, or grammar, for the descriptive tags. Specifically, it defines the syntax, structure and vocabulary of the XML document.

Generally, you place the DTD in a separate text file, but you can include it within the XML document if you prefer.

### XML and style sheets

**Extensible Stylesheet Language (XSL)**
A style language that provides formatting instructions for XML documents.

Because XML does not provide formatting instructions like HTML does, you must use a style sheet to format an XML document. You can use either CSS or **Extensible Stylesheet Language (XSL)**. One of the benefits of XSL is document transformation: With XSL, you can translate (i.e., transform) an XML page into an HTML page so that a browser can render it. You can also use XSL and CSS together. For more information about XSL, consult the W3C site at *www.w3.org/Style/XSL/*.

### From HTML to XML

**client**
An individual computer connected to a network. Also, a system or application (such as a Web browser or user agent) that requests a service from another computer (the server) and is used to access files or documents.

Because the requirements for XML and HTML are dramatically different, the developers of XHTML aimed to create a medium that would merge the two with enough forethought to make the transition from HTML to XML, yet without making all existing HTML documents unusable in XML **clients**. These requirements meant that XHTML could not completely depart from HTML 4, nor could it be patterned completely after XML. XHTML documents are not required to render correctly in standard clients, but will have little if any difficulty. For a more detailed discussion about compatibility issues, visit the W3C site at the following URI:

*www.w3.org/TR/2002/REC-xhtml1-20020801/#guidelines*

*When you use XML, the term Uniform Resource Identifier (URI) is preferred over the standard HTML term Uniform Resource Locator (URL).*

## Extensible Hypertext Markup Language (XHTML)

Extensible Hypertext Markup Language (XHTML) is the latest formulation of HTML. XHTML combines HTML with XML. The W3C specification defines XHTML as "a reformulation of HTML 4 as an XML 1.0 application, and three DTDs corresponding to the ones defined by HTML 4." You can read the W3C's XHTML specification at *www.w3.org/TR/xhtml1*.

As you have learned, HTML describes only a document's visual layout, and XML allows you to describe the function and context of the information contained in a document. XHTML allows HTML to become XML-compliant. Thus XHTML 1.0 extends HTML by allowing the convergence of HTML documents with XML structure, creating forward-compatibility for documents. For more information about how XHTML, XML and HTML work together, visit *www.w3.org/MarkUp*.

*XHTML is based specifically on the HTML 4.01 Recommendation, which repairs the "bugs" of HTML 4.0.*

HTML has been considered responsible for organizing data and formatting it properly on a Web page. XHTML separates these two responsibilities between HTML and XML. Thus, XHTML uses XML to organize the data in a page, which allows the data to become searchable. XHTML uses HTML to format the page's appearance in the Web browser. It is important to distinguish between the responsibilities of XML and HTML within XHTML. XML focuses solely on organizing data, whereas HTML focuses solely on the page's appearance. XHTML is more flexible than HTML, its predecessor.

### XHTML flavors

Like HTML 4.01, there are three flavors of XHTML:

- **XHTML Transitional** — allows formatting to be specified inside the document, although CSS is preferred. Also allows deprecated tags (e.g., the <font> tag and the *align* attribute). XHTML Transitional is the most popular version of XHTML.

- **XHTML Strict** — requires the exclusive use of CSS for all formatting elements. No deprecated tags are allowed.

- **XHTML Frameset** — required for pages that use frames, which place Web pages inside each other to create separate panes in the browser window.

OBJECTIVE
2.1.8: Using a single
W3C standard

### Choosing and applying a language standard consistently

This course focuses on the XHTML Transitional standard. Whether you develop your own Web pages using HTML 4.01 or XHTML 1.0 Transitional, or any other flavor of either markup language, it is important that you adopt a single W3C standard and apply it consistently throughout your document, Web pages or site. Otherwise, your pages may have difficulty rendering properly in user agents. This best practice also applies when you are using other types of languages in your online documents and sites, including CSS, scripting languages such as JavaScript, programming languages and so forth.

### Markup code validation

It is possible to validate all markup code automatically. Many validators exist, but the most authoritative is the W3C Markup Validation Service (*http://validator.w3.org*).

Using this service, you can upload local HTML files for validation, or provide the URL of a Web page to validate it. In this course, you will use the W3C validation service to validate your XHTML Transitional code. However, it is important to note that this validator reads the DOCTYPE declaration on an HTML page and validates according to the specified DTD. So, if your document references an HTML 4.01 Strict DTD, then the validator will validate code according to the HTML 4.01 Strict specifications.

To reiterate, make sure you adopt a single W3C standard and apply it consistently so that when you validate your markup code, the code and your specified DTD will match, and the results of the validation process will be legitimate.

Validating your markup code is worthwhile because validated code is most likely to be interpreted accurately by the majority of user agents. As a result, your pages will render as you expect and will be available to a larger audience.

Following are some tips to consider when validating your markup code:

- Do not be discouraged when you see multiple problems reported for a page. Sometimes one small flaw can cause the remaining code on the page to fail validation, even if the remaining code is actually valid.

- When errors are reported, search through the code carefully to find the true problem. Sometimes when a validation program finds a problem, it does not report the correct cause or it may not report the cause clearly.

- Make sure that you are validating the correct file.

## Universal markup creation

Good Web page coding generally involves ensuring that the content is rendered appropriately regardless of the browser used to render it. To ensure this type of consistent, or universal, rendering, Web page developers can apply certain practices to their coding that result in universal markup:

- Follow W3C standards carefully.

- Choose one standard version and flavor of any given language you use, and apply that standard consistently throughout your document, pages or site.

Creating universal markup code is important for several reasons:

- Your pages will be ensured to render in future versions of most browsers.

- Your pages will be more scalable. This means that as you add more sophisticated content, make pages searchable or use the content in ways you have not yet imagined, you can still use markup you created without having to revise the code extensively.

- Your pages will be more accessible to disabled users. You will be able to more easily make your pages compliant so that your site is available to the widest possible audience and does not present a liability to your organization.

In some situations you may find that universal markup seems unnecessary. For example, if you are writing markup code for a page for your company's intranet, and all employees use the same browser, you can feel comfortable using proprietary language extensions and technology. In this case, you can be relatively sure that your XHTML code will render consistently in that browser every time. But suppose the company's browser choice changes. Most situations call for pages that can be viewed in a variety of browsers, so creating universal markup is always good coding practice.

*Consistent use of an HTML standard — such as HTML 4.01 or XHTML 1.0, for example — will improve your page's ability to rank higher in a search engine results page.*

In the following lab, you will visit the W3C Web site to learn more about commonly used markup languages. Suppose your project manager has asked you to research current Web standards. She has heard that HTML is common but that newer standards exist, and she wants to know the best sources for this type of information. What Web pages would you research or recommend to explain Web standards?

## Lab 2-1: Reviewing W3C standards

In this lab, you will visit the W3C Web site to learn more about commonly used markup languages.

1.  First, you will learn more about the HTML 4.01 standard. Open a browser and visit ***www.w3.org/TR/html4***. Scroll through the specification to learn more about HTML's relationship to SGML, as well as HTML elements.

2.  Next, learn more about XML by visiting ***www.w3.org/XML***.

3.  Visit ***www.w3.org/MarkUp*** to learn more about XHTML.

4.  Now, visit the W3C home page at ***www.w3.org***. Review the mission of the W3C, then browse through the site.

5.  Visit the W3C Markup Validation Service at ***http://validator.w3.org*** and learn more about this service.

**OBJECTIVE**
2.1.2: HTML and
XHTML

6.  Further familiarize yourself with HTML, XML and XHTML by accessing Google, AltaVista or another search engine, and entering search strings such as the following: **"HTML versus XHTML"**

7.  Consider the sources presented in your search results. Link to some that look reliable, and read the various explanations that you find to better understand the differences between HTML and XHTML.

In this lab, you visited the W3C Web site and other sites to learn more about HTML, XML and XHTML.

# Web Site Development Principles

You need more than knowledge of markup languages and talent for design to contribute to a successful Web development team. You also need to understand the business concerns and issues associated with Web development, from copyright issues to site development planning. The following sections discuss many responsibilities of a Web project manager. You may have a different role on a Web development team, but understanding project management makes you a stronger and more valuable team member.

## Project management and the Web development project cycle

**OBJECTIVE**
2.14.2: Web project management fundamentals

Creating a Web site requires you to work closely with individuals and teams of individuals. To work smoothly with other teams, you must carefully outline and communicate the project's steps. While you may not manage the project, at the very least you will be part of it. So you must understand the typical Web development project cycle. Consider the following steps:

- Create and document an initial Web site plan.

- Obtain relevant input from stakeholders.

- Communicate the Web site plan.

- Consider technical and non-technical concerns.

- Develop the site.

- Publish the site.

- Manage the site.

Each step is discussed in the following sections.

 *Part of the management cycle is optimizing pages so that they rank highly in search engine results pages.*

## Creating and documenting an initial Web site plan

Before you can create any XHTML markup code, you must first create a plan for the site. This plan has several names, including:

- Site diagram.

**OBJECTIVE**
2.7.2: Web site diagram

- Storyboard.

Regardless of the name you use, this plan must include the following:

**OBJECTIVE**
2.13.4: Web site plan documentation

- A statement discussing the purpose and intended audience for the site. This statement may evolve over time, but it is important to begin with this statement to remind everyone involved why the site is being developed and to steer all efforts in the proper direction.

- A rough outline of the pages needed, including:

  — The default page (e.g., index.html), also called the home page.

  — Sections of the site (e.g., products, sales, international, contacts).

  — An estimate of the technologies required (e.g., databases, CGI, search capability, indexes).

Your Web team cannot create this plan in isolation. You must obtain input from stakeholders.

### Determining the audience and message

**OBJECTIVE**
2.13.3: Stakeholder and audience requirements

Successful Web sites have a strong, central theme aimed at a distinct audience. They have the ability to support this theme by providing clear explanations and related services. You must start with a strong message, then consider how this message will be presented. Even the best looking Web page or site will fail in its purpose if it does not have a clear message.

As you determine your audience, consider eliciting input from various parties, including:

- **Customer representatives** — Organizations often have important customers attend meetings and provide input. Customer representatives can teach you about the various types of messages that appeal most to potential customers. For example, some may want to focus on the value of a particular product, regardless of cost. In other instances, customers may help you focus on a message that shows your products to be inexpensive. Once you have surveyed customers to determine what the market wants, you can begin to craft Web pages that clearly convey your company's message to its intended customers.

- **Suppliers** — If you are planning for large sales as a result of your Web effort, make sure that your product suppliers are ready for this. Otherwise, you could damage the company's reputation by making promises that cannot be kept. Even though a Web authoring team works mostly on creating markup pages, your Web site's ability to communicate with the public means that such business concerns are essential for the overall success of the project.

- **Shareholders** — If your organization is publicly owned, you may need to obtain input from shareholders about the look and feel of the site.

## Validating design issues

OBJECTIVE
2.7.4: Technical and
audience standards

The design elements with which you display information on your site can be just as important as the information itself. As previously discussed, the front end you present to users may determine whether users remain at and return to your site. Consider the following design concepts:

- **Message** — Deliver a coherent message for each page. Information that is not relevant or otherwise distracts readers from a well-conceived central idea should be placed on another page or eliminated.

- **Fonts** — If specifying fonts, make sure that you use common ones so that browsers do not have difficulty rendering them. Use proper sizes; small fonts are difficult to read.

- **Images** — Make sure that all images used on a page contribute to either the page's navigability or its message.

- **Color** — Take time to consider color combinations so that your pages are as attractive and readable as possible.

Validation should occur on a regular basis as the site is being developed. Although a final validation is necessary, the final validation should not be the only one. As you validate design issues, consider the following:

OBJECTIVE
2.15.6: Diversity and
corporate culture

- **Organizational design standards** — You have already learned about the importance of branding standards. As you help develop Web pages, make sure that you are following developed rules and advice from your department and others. Such standards help support decisions concerning your organization's branding and marketing standards.

OBJECTIVE
2.19.4: Ethnic and
cultural issues

- **Ethnic diversity** — You may be asked to tailor messages to particular cultures and ethnicities. Project management will ensure that such needs are considered and recommended during planning meetings. It is your responsibility as a designer to create pages that implement all recommendations.

Your development team will also want to consider demographic and cultural issues, including:

- **Language choice** — Some organizations will need to use only one language for their sites, such as English. Others may need to create multiple sites in various languages to accommodate an international audience. Still others may offer an immediate choice of one or two languages because the government of the country in which they reside demands such accommodations, for example.

- **Common color schemes** — Preferences for color combinations differ from one culture to the next. Remain sensitive to and informed about such preferences.

- **Messages that appeal to customers** — You may need to alter your message about a particular product or activity if you present it to another culture. Consider the expectations and preferences of specific cultures so that your message is as clear and appealing as possible.

**OBJECTIVE**
2.19.3: Corporate culture

In the following lab, you will review Web sites from major manufacturers to learn how they address different cultures. Suppose your project manager has asked you to research sites that address cultural diversity, including sites that target populations using different languages. Consider the types and sources of examples that you could provide.

 | **Lab 2-2: Researching ways that Web sites address cultural diversity**

In this lab, you will review Web sites from major manufacturers to learn how they address different cultures.

1. Open your Web browser. Visit and compare the following sites:

    ***www.toyota.com***
    ***www.toyota.ru***
    ***www.toyota.ca***

2. After you have reviewed these sites, answer the following questions:

    - What language choices were offered at the *www.toyota.com* site? Why?

    _____

    - What language choices were offered at the *www.toyota.ca* site? Why?

    _____

    - What differences in color schemes exist? Why?

    _____

3. Compare the following Web sites from Ford Motor Company:

    ***www.ford.com***
    ***www.ford.ru***

4. After you have reviewed these sites, discuss the following questions as a class:

    - What differences exist in the color schemes? Why?

- Review the images and technologies used. Which site uses more active content?

- Does one site offer more car models than the other?

- What audience does the *www.ford.com* site seem to consider the most?

5. Visit additional sites and compare color schemes, languages and message approaches. Use a search engine to help you find examples of multicultural international approaches. What types of businesses tend to be most accommodating?

In this lab, you reviewed Web sites of major manufacturers to see how they tailor their company messages to various cultures.

## Obtaining relevant input from stakeholders

**OBJECTIVE**
2.7.1: Stakeholder input

When creating a Web site, stakeholders are relevant organization employees or contributors who can provide or help determine the following information:

- The purpose of the Web site.

- The site's look and feel.

- The services that the audience requires from the site.

- Funds available to develop the site.

- Development timelines. Although your team will largely determine how long it will take to create the site, your team will also have to coordinate with other departments in the organization. For example, the sales and marketing teams are likely to have important input about when the site is published, as well as its look and feel.

**OBJECTIVE**
2.13.2: Company site requirements and collaboration

As you work with your stakeholders, remember the following:

- People who will approve your project often have no technical expertise in your field. Nevertheless, remember that they are essential to the success of your project.

- Be prepared to explain non-technical needs to a technical audience. In other words, make sure that you can present business concerns to IT professionals in ways that will help ensure that your needs are met.

**OBJECTIVE**
2.13.1: Site development teamwork

Your site development team can consist of diverse professionals whose focuses and concerns will differ. However, each will have valuable contributions, and you must be able to communicate effectively with all of them. Following are some examples of team members who might collaborate with you on a Web development project:

- A representative from marketing to help guide branding issues

- An IT worker responsible for configuring servers and network access

- A representative from sales who can provide additional information about specific customer needs

- Members of the Web development team who will use Web technology to create the best site for the organization's needs

Once you have obtained all essential input, you can create your initial storyboard. Figure 2-2 shows a sample storyboard for a relatively simple site.

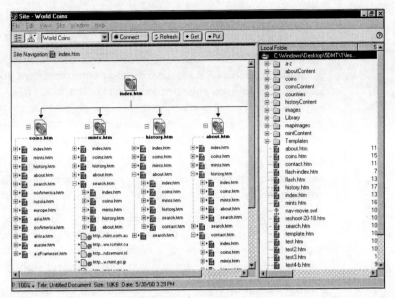

*Figure 2-2: Sample storyboard*

**site map**
A brief, hierarchical representation of a Web site that enables visitors to quickly identify areas of the site and navigate to them.

You and your team will develop this initial storyboard into a completed Web site. The storyboard also provides a **site map** to help visitors quickly find resources on your site.

### Documenting and communicating the plan

**OBJECTIVE**
2.13.4: Web site plan documentation

In addition to creating a site storyboard, you must also document decisions made in all meetings. All plans must be distributed and approved. Any decisions involving changes in dates and allocations of funds may require further approval from the organization.

As the plan moves toward finalization, you must communicate it effectively using at least some of the following strategies:

- Calling relevant parties to ensure that everyone is satisfied

- Sending e-mail messages

- Sending postal ("snail mail") messages if necessary

- Sending fax messages

A telephone call is appropriate at times, but because phone calls are not usually recorded, they cannot be readily recalled and referenced. E-mail and paper-based transmissions can be stored for later retrieval, and used for reference and accountability.

## Communicating the Web site plan

As you communicate the Web site plan, you will make oral and written presentations. Following are some typical strategies to consider.

### Oral presentations and presentation aids

**OBJECTIVE**
2.13.5: Web site plan communication

As you give oral presentations about your Web site plan, use presentation aids and tools to help illustrate your plan:

**OBJECTIVE**
2.15.3: Presentation software

- **Presentation software** — Slide-based software, such as Microsoft PowerPoint and StarOffice Star Impress, is common and user-friendly. Presentation software creates a sense of professionalism.

- **Overhead projection** — You may need to create transparencies of statistics and marketing ideas. Be prepared to bring an overhead projector.

- **Whiteboards** — You can bring your own whiteboard or use one that is already in the presentation room. A whiteboard helps you to present your ideas as well as write ideas gathered from your audience. You should always take your own set of notes during a team presentation, but you can also use a whiteboard or poster paper to record open discussions (often called brainstorming). Such discussions are very helpful because they show that you are listening to ideas.

- **Easel and poster paper** — If a whiteboard is not available, bring an easel and poster paper so you can take notes for everyone to see. Because an easel and poster paper are portable, you can keep this record of audience feedback.

- **Charts** — Pie charts graphically present information about a topic, showing the relative percentages of all constituent elements. For example, a pie chart can help you show the size of a particular market niche you are targeting. Bar charts are helpful for showing trends or a particular project's progress.

- **Published handouts** — Your audience can use handouts as notes from the meeting. If you want to emphasize a particular portion of a presentation, back it up with a handout.

Presentation tools help you convey information, and also prove that you have properly prepared for a meeting and are not wasting your audience's time.

## Leading discussions

Project managers generally lead and moderate meetings related to a Web development project. Consider the following strategies that you can use to effectively take the lead during a meeting:

- **Make introductions** — As you introduce people, explain their roles on the team.

- **Recall past business** — Make sure that each team builds on past decisions and considers past discussions in a meaningful way. At all times, try to make any repeated discussions culminate in a decision that allows the group to show progress on the project.

- **Create a list of action items, including timelines** — A list will help you communicate your team's progress.

- **Monitor time** — Even if important information is imparted in your meetings, if they are too long then important participants may not want to attend again.

- **Ensure proper discussion focus** — Provide an agenda of meeting topics so participants come prepared and expecting to discuss only relevant issues. Consider announcing a time limit for a particular discussion if you fear that it may continue too long.

- **Handle heated discussions** — Changing focus may be especially important if a discussion becomes too heated or if animosity develops among participants.

- **Distribute minutes** — Meeting notes, or minutes, help all parties see progress result from meetings. Minutes also help everyone identify unfinished business, as well as determine any particular topics that were omitted.

## Considering technical and non-technical concerns

**OBJECTIVE**
2.15.4: Technical concept clarification

In your meetings, you are likely to find that although everyone may share the same goal, they may not be able to communicate specific needs to each other. A common problem is that some team members do not have much technical knowledge, but nevertheless have ideas that are essential for the success of the site. Often, the non-technical employees in your meetings can ensure funding for your project.

It is the project leader's responsibility to ensure that input and requests from team members with little or no technical knowledge are heard and seriously considered. Similarly, you must ensure that project members with technical experience clearly convey their capabilities, limits and needs to non-technical team members. Otherwise, team members will constantly speak past each other, and confusion will result. Confusion can increase especially if project members work remotely. Ways to ensure clarity both in meetings and in communication include:

- **Regularly asking if anyone has questions** — This strategy helps some team members speak up. However, less outgoing individuals who have questions may still hold back.

- **Asking team members to summarize their understanding of decisions** — Although this strategy puts some people on the spot, this is preferable to having team members remain confused about the project's direction.

- **Asking a third party to deliver a summary of progress** — This third party can attend your meeting and ask questions of team members. By listening to responses, you can gauge overall team participation and understanding.

- **Writing regular updates about the project** — Make sure that in your updates you translate technical requirements into non-technical language, and vice versa.

## Developing the site

Once you have obtained enough information and created a definitive plan, you can begin developing the site. As your team develops the site, you will be engaged in various activities, including:

- **Creating markup code** — You will develop pages that fulfill all design standards.

- **Testing functionality** — Make sure that the site performs well technically before it is published to the Web. This involves testing the site in multiple browsers, for example.

- **Approving the site** — All stakeholders will need to approve your team's work. Make sure that all parties have seen the site before publication, and make sure that you have documented this fact.

- **Publishing the site** — The site must be properly placed on a Web server. You may also participate in decisions such as whether you will configure your own Web server or use a Web server configured by another provider.

### Testing pages in multiple Web browsers

**OBJECTIVE**
2.14.3: Pre-launch functionality testing

2.12.3: Testing pages in browsers

As you develop Web pages, make sure that you test your Web pages using multiple Web browsers. A different generation of the same browser may interpret HTML somewhat differently. For example, Internet Explorer 6.x and higher uses an HTML-rendering engine that has been significantly revised from version 4.x. Similarly, current versions of Firefox have a significantly revised rendering engine. You should always consider how each vendor and each version implements HTML standards differently.

If you are preparing a site for public use, it is advisable to write your HTML code using the most widely supported standards.

 *The HTML code used in this course will function in all browsers. However, there will always be subtle differences from browser to browser.*

**OBJECTIVE**
2.7.5: Usability and browser compatibility

In some situations, you may feel it is unnecessary to test your pages on a wide variety of browsers. For example, you may not need to perform as many tests for the company intranet if the company has standardized to one browser, such as Microsoft Internet Explorer. Nevertheless, it is always good practice to ensure that your code is compatible with all browsers so that your browser options are flexible.

## Browser types and versions

Table 2-1 discusses browsers to consider for your Web site testing process.

*Table 2-1: Commonly used Web browsers*

| Browser | Description | Download Location |
|---------|-------------|-------------------|
| **Microsoft Internet Explorer** | The most commonly used browser on the Web today. Included with various versions of Windows operating systems. | *www.microsoft.com* |
| **Mozilla Firefox** | An open-source browser. Firefox versions are available for various operating systems, from Windows to Linux. | *www.mozilla.org* |
| **Google Chrome** | An open-source browser from Google. Chrome has many new features, such as a clean interface, automatic crash recovery, multi-threading capability, improved sandboxing, isolated tabs and privacy mode. | *www.google.com/chrome* |
| **Opera** | An alternative Web browser with extended language support. | *www.opera.com* |
| **Lynx** | A command-line text-only Web browser. Often used by those with shell accounts and those who are visually impaired because it can be used with software that renders text into voice. A binary version is included with most versions of UNIX/Linux. | The source code is available at *http://lynx.isc.org*. A Windows binary is available at *www.fdisk.com/doslynx/lynxport.htm* |

Remember that Web browsers are not the only user agents that render HTML pages. Additional user agents include:

- PDAs.

- Mobile phones.

- Other devices that read markup language.

When testing your Web pages for browser compatibility issues, check the following:

- **Rendering of tables** — If you use HTML tables to format content, some browsers may not render the information proportionally, which can distort the way information appears on the page. Some browsers also do not support table options.

- **Strictness levels** — Older browsers may not be able to render the newer versions of HTML or XHTML well.

- **Color support** — If you use background colors or colors within tables, your customers' browsers may not render them exactly as you have intended.

- **Images** — As you already know, some Web browsers do not support images at all. Some browsers do not render background images, whereas others do. Always provide alternative text descriptions for images, and use background images sparingly.

- **Scripting languages** — Make sure that any scripting language you use is supported by the majority of Web browsers.

- **XHTML/HTML version** — Choose a version of XHTML/HTML that you know most browsers will support. The XHTML 1.0 Transitional standard is a solid choice because it has been adopted by the most browsers.

As a general rule, the closer you adhere to W3C standards, the more consistently your Web pages will render in various browsers. Also, be conservative when using elaborate features that may not render well in certain browsers. Finally, as you develop your Web pages, use features that are supported by the most commonly used browsers.

## Publishing the site

As you and your team prepare to publish your site to the Web, you must determine the following:

- **The IP address and/or DNS name of the site** — Without this information, you will not be able to access the remote server.

- **User name and authentication information** — You must provide this information or else you cannot authenticate with the server to upload files. You will probably be given a user name based on your first and last name. Common administrative user names include:

  — *root* (for UNIX systems, including Linux). This user name is usually all lowercase letters; passwords can be in uppercase and lowercase.

  — *administrator* (for Windows-based systems). User names are not case-specific, but passwords are.

- **The destination directory (i.e., folder) on the Web server** — Even if you are placing the site on a local system, you still must know the exact directory where you will place all of your markup pages, images and other files.

- **Space requirements** — You must know the amount of memory that the site will require on the Web server.

- **The protocol you will use to upload the site** — FTP is a common protocol for uploading files to Web servers.

### Working with service providers

Service providers are organizations that can host and maintain your Web site files and provide other services for a fee. There are two types of service providers:

- **Internet Service Provider (ISP)** — responsible for providing access to the Internet. Most ISPs also provide access to their Web and database servers for an additional fee. Larger ISPs may offer a choice of operating systems and Web servers. Such ISPs also offer CGI scripts that you can modify for your own purposes.

- **Application Service Provider (ASP)** — similar to an ISP, but dedicated to providing database, e-mail and information management services. Many provide access to telephony and voicemail services, as well. All of these applications are centralized, and can be purchased or leased on a periodic basis (e.g., monthly, quarterly, annually or per-use). ASPs help companies save time and money because the ASP usually has all applications configured and ready for use. An ASP can also track IT and Web developer expenditures, and provide Help Desk services. ASPs do more than provide some CGI and database access; they provide access to any Internet-based service you want. Many companies obtain Internet access from an ISP, then use an ASP for e-mail and Web services.

As you work with service providers, you should consider the many features that they provide. Table 2-2 describes typical service provider offerings.

Table 2-2: Typical service provider offerings

| Service | Description |
|---|---|
| **Additional bandwidth** | Companies with particularly busy sites can buy additional bandwidth to improve client response times. |
| **CGI scripts** | ISPs generally offer some form of CGI. Large ISPs may offer choices (e.g., .NET, PHP or JSP). You must ask the ISP to give you execute permissions on your CGI directory. This directory is called a CGI bin and is usually named cgi-bin (e.g., /var/www/cgi-bin in Linux). |
| **Database access** | You can choose which database your site will use (e.g., Oracle, DB2, MySQL). |
| **Backup services** | Some ISPs offer the ability to back up your important files onto tape or other media (e.g., CD-Rs). ISPs and ASPs charge a fee for such services. |
| **Technical support** | ISPs and ASPs can provide expert services. Basic technical support is complimentary. Extensive technical support services are usually fee-based or require an additional contract. |

You will learn more about service providers later in this course.

## Managing the site

You are unlikely to develop and post a site that never needs modification. In fact, managing a site usually requires more time and work than initially developing it. As part of a team that manages a site, you must:

- **Create new content** — The perception that a site has failed to remain current can be damaging. Innovation and fresh content are both essential to managing a site that stays popular.

- **Update dead links** — For various reasons, links that once functioned may fail over time. A link can become invalid because a page's location was changed on the hard drive, or because the link pointed to an external Web site that no longer exists or has changed its structure. You can use automated applications to check your site for dead links. However, someone must still manually alter any invalid links to make them valid again.

- **Remove old sites** — Sometimes an entire site becomes invalid. It is your duty to remove such sites from the Internet.

- **Remove unused pages** — Pages on Web sites sometimes become stale, especially if they are tied to a marketing campaign. If they cannot be updated, they must be removed.

2-23

**trouble ticket**
A record of a problem related to a service provided by an ISP or ASP. Used to record receipt of a complaint and track resolution of the problem.

**OBJECTIVE**
2.13.6: Site feedback and improvement

**troll**
A Web user who publishes negative comments or submits feedback simply to annoy or anger.

**OBJECTIVE**
2.15.1: Management and customer feedback

- **Ensure connectivity** — You or a member of the IT department may be assigned to ensure that the site is active and that enough bandwidth is available. You may have to upgrade or downgrade bandwidth, depending upon customer volume. You do not want customers to be frustrated by slow site access, but you also do not want to pay for unused bandwidth.

- **Report access troubles** — Sometimes you need to contact your ISP and begin a **trouble ticket** to begin resolving a problem. It may also be your responsibility to follow up with problems to ensure they are properly resolved.

- **Process feedback from customers and stakeholders** — Your team will be asked to make changes to the site periodically. Some changes may be subtle; others may require considerable effort on your part to make the site fulfill its potential and truly benefit your organization.

## Obtaining feedback

Your Web team must process various types of feedback. Feedback can include:

- **Direct contact with customers** — People who frequent the site may contact you directly through feedback forms to inform you about desired changes.

- **Feedback from upper management** — Executive officers may request changes to the site in order to improve the company's image.

- **Feedback from sales and marketing** — Sales representatives often receive comments from their customers about desired changes. Addressing such reports of customer requests is essential to the site's success.

As you receive feedback, you must be able to distinguish between serious feedback and nuisance input. Some individuals scour Internet sites and pretend to provide serious feedback, when in fact they are just trying to cause problems. Such users are often called **trolls**. Trolls can employ various tactics, including sending annoying e-mail messages, submitting Web forms full of negative comments, or writing blogs or articles that disparage your site.

You and your team must also be aware that some people who are sincere about their feedback may have idiosyncratic perspectives. In any case, you should always work to obtain a consensus of opinion that includes reliable sources, then obtain appropriate stakeholder approval before making any changes.

## Ways to obtain quality feedback

Your team can ensure that you obtain quality feedback by:

- **Providing Web forms on the site that ask for customer input** — Such forms should be available only to serious customers and/or members of the organization. For example, make the form available only to users who have paid for a service or provided verifiable identity. Otherwise, you increase your chances of receiving prank information from trolls.

- **Conducting surveys in person** — You or other team members can contact customers at the direction of your team leader. Such surveys should be directed to your top customers. Make sure that surveys are quick and to the point. You may also want to offer your customers a valuable product, service or discount in exchange for responding to the survey.

- **Conducting surveys via e-mail** — If you want to contact more people, an e-mail survey may be appropriate. However, be sure to send surveys only to established customers. Otherwise, your organization may receive a bad reputation as a "spammer."

OBJECTIVE
2.15.5: Feedback
interpretation

As you process and interpret feedback, you should ask the following questions:

- Which suggestions should be taken seriously?

- Does this feedback apply directly to the Web site, or could this problem be solved by requesting that sales and/or marketing personnel work directly with complaining customers?

- What changes will please the majority of customers?

- How much will proposed changes cost? You must consider whether requested changes are economically feasible and worth the extra investment.

- How long will it take to make the proposed changes?

- Who must you contact in order to obtain approval and/or funding for the proposed changes?

## Intellectual property

OBJECTIVE
2.14.1: Web site
legal issues

Intellectual property is a unique product or idea created by an individual or organization, and that generally has commercial value. When creating a Web site, you must consider legal issues related to ideas, products and images that are widely available. You cannot "borrow" information from other Web sites. Table 2-3 describes common intellectual property issues and terminology.

*Table 2-3: Intellectual property issues and terms*

| Intellectual Property Term | Description |
|---|---|
| Trade secret | Intellectual property that must remain private for a company to retain viability. Examples include proprietary code, business plans and sales contacts. |
| Copyright | The legal ownership of expression by an author. According to most developed countries, copyrighted intellectual property becomes the property of the author for a certain number of years. Copyright protection ensures that the person or group who owns the copyright has the right to publish or otherwise distribute material, and control how it is redistributed. In most countries, a copyright can be sold by its owner. |
| Trademark | A unique word, phrase or symbol that is claimed or officially registered by an organization with the government. Trademarks can include logos, phrases, company names and so forth. If a logo, word or phrase is trademarked, then only the organization that registered it can use it. |
| Licensing | The legally authorized use of another person's or entity's copyrighted intellectual property. The terms of the license are generally dictated by the copyright holder. Licenses require contracts and usually an exchange of money, services or both. |
| Infringement | Any violation of a copyright or trademark. Copyright and trademark infringement are punishable crimes. |
| Plagiarism | A specific instance of infringement in which an individual or entity claims to have created content (e.g., images, writing or other exact expressions) that was in fact created by other developers. Proven plagiarism can result in severe reprimands, loss of employment, corporate lawsuits and financial penalties. |

## Copyright scope, reach and time limits

No copyright or trademark is permanent. Legal registrations must be renewed, so if you have trademarked or copyrighted a particular portion of your Web site, then you must manage this intellectual property. Research the laws for your own country to avoid surprises.

The legal issues described here apply to all phases of Web development. Do not ignore these concepts; doing so could lead to your dismissal and to legal action against your company. Precedent court rulings have held violators liable even when they claimed ignorance of the law.

 *You may be tempted to use other people's words and ideas when optimizing pages. Avoid that temptation. One way to create original yet relevant content is to work with another individual. Talk out your ideas. You will be surprised at how you can create an optimal page that is both original and relevant.*

## Ethical issues regarding copyright, trademark and plagiarism

**OBJECTIVE**
2.20.4: Web site
ethics

Ethics is the study of making proper choices to ensure that other people's rights are not violated. Consider the following ethical points as you create markup code and design Web pages:

- You cannot copy a site's code or look without the owner's explicit permission. You can create entirely new code that provides a similar look and feel, but consider the perception you present if your site looks just like another.

- Borrowing a lot of code from a site infringes upon the author's copyright.

- The owner of a copyright may allow copyrighted material to be used by others. This permission may be exchanged by contract, for a fee or simply for proper attribution. Most major Web sites post their copyright and licensing contact information.

- All aspects of a Web site are copyrighted. Do not "borrow" images, text, logos, music, scripts, applications or code. Seek proper permission if you find an element on a site that you want to use.

- You cannot provide a link from your Web site to another site without permission because such a link generally implies that the two sites have a business relationship.

- You cannot copy or translate the content of another Web site without explicit permission.

Copyright and trademark laws are country-specific. The World Wide Web allows a person from one country to view information from all over the world. Suppose your employer asks you to research national and international copyright laws. What steps will you take?

## Avoiding copyright infringement, trademark infringement and plagiarism

**OBJECTIVE**
2.20.1: Content
developer
permissions

Stealing the intellectual property of others is a serious matter. You must avoid even appearing as if you have stolen information. Ways to avoid problems include:

- **Reviewing all Web site content for originality** — This includes code, images and text. The review must be independent. In other words, choose someone who is not on your team but who will work diligently to highlight any potential infringement issues.

- **Conducting regular content reviews** — A single content review at the end of the project may not solve infringement problems. Regular reviews are likely to encourage development team members to change their practices so that you do not have a large problem to resolve near a deadline.

- **Obtaining express, written consent for any material you use** — Make sure that written consent is properly stored for later retrieval, and that developers do not take advantage of this consent. Even specific design concepts are copyrighted, so if you "borrow" someone else's unique expression for your own site, you may incur legal action. Of course, images and code are all protected by copyright.

- **Creating reasonable deadlines** — Busy developers often take shortcuts to meet deadlines. Work with your project manager to ensure that deadline pressure does not contribute to a team's tendency to copy content.

 *Plagiarism is never justified. When in doubt, simply consider another approach to expressing an idea. Never steal ideas or expressions of ideas from others and claim them as your own.*

Avoiding copyright and trademark infringement is essential. So is avoiding plagiarism. Suppose your program manager asks you to find authoritative evidence of intellectual property laws. Where could you find this information?

## Outsourcing

Increasingly, Web development work (including site design) is being outsourced to workers in remote locations. When outsourcing occurs, a local team of workers often remains to perform some tasks (sometimes permanently, sometimes only for a short time). This local team is usually charged with managing the project. The outsourced team will probably perform the Web page coding and other tasks that the local team cannot complete.

When working with remote teams and even other companies, you must consider the following:

- **Non-Disclosure Agreement (NDA)** — An NDA is a legally binding contract signed by both parties stating that they will not reveal any trade secrets or intellectual property owned by the other.

- **Legal consultation** — When signing NDAs and other documents is necessary, you should first retain legal counsel. Otherwise, you may make commitments that you cannot fulfill. Any contract breach can make your company liable for a lawsuit.

### Non-Disclosure Agreement (NDA)

**OBJECTIVE**
2.2.20.2: Non-Disclosure Agreement (NDA)

An NDA protects the following intellectual property from unauthorized use by contractors, partners or others who are allowed access to it:

- Ideas and concepts

- Specific plans

- Code

- Written documents

Most NDAs specify penalties if stipulated violations occur. One problem with an NDA is that it takes time to agree about its content. If you involve several individuals on an NDA, then the timeline on a project might increase.

### Consulting with legal teams

**OBJECTIVE**
2.20.3: Legal team consultation

You may have to consult with legal teams in the following situations:

- As you create NDAs

- If you decide to use a marketing campaign, trademark or copyrighted idea similar to another company's

- If you must investigate infringement by other companies against your intellectual property

In the following lab, you will investigate intellectual property concepts and laws. Suppose your project manager assigned you to work closely with a legal team. Before meeting with this team, you want to obtain some preliminary information about intellectual property concepts and laws. The sites you review in this lab provide this type of information.

 **Lab 2-3: Investigating intellectual property concepts and laws**

In this lab, you will learn more about intellectual property concepts and laws.

1. One of the missions of the United Nations Educational, Scientific and Cultural Organization (UNESCO) is to ensure cooperation among nations regarding copyright laws. The UNESCO Universal Copyright Convention enables various countries to cooperate so that copyright is protected across the world. Open your browser, and visit the following site to learn more about the UNESCO Universal Copyright Convention:

   *http://portal.unesco.org/en/ev.php-URL_ID=15241&URL_DO=DO_TOPIC&URL_SECTION=201.html*

2. The Berne Convention is another international effort to protect copyright. Visit the following page of the World Intellectual Property Organization (WIPO) site to read more about it:

   *www.wipo.int/treaties/en/ip/berne/trtdocs_wo001.html*

3. Copyright law has many facets and differs among countries. Visit the following sites to review copyright laws specific to the United States:

   *www.copyright.gov/circs/circ15a.html*

   *www.copyright.gov/title17/*

4. Visit the following site to learn more about general copyright issues:

   *http://whatiscopyright.org*

5. Using Google, AltaVista or another search engine, research the meaning of the word *plagiarism*.

6. As a class, answer the following questions:

   - Which parties are responsible for protecting copyright?

   _____

   - What is plagiarism?

   _____

- What can you do as a developer to ensure that you do not engage in activities such as copyright infringement and plagiarism?

_____

_____

In this lab, you investigated aspects of copyright and trademark law. You also researched the meaning of the word plagiarism.

## Case Study

# Plan It Out

Seamus was assigned to create a Web site plan for a charity organization. He must ensure that the site includes the following features:

- A message stating the purpose of the charity

- An online form that will receive personal information from potential volunteers and place it into a database

Seamus' first step was to discuss the plan with stakeholders. He did not have a stakeholder group, so he obtained representatives from the following departments:

- Marketing

- IT

- Web development

Eventually, all parties were able to agree on a site plan. After creating the site plan, Seamus' project manager asked him to help present this plan to upper management. Seamus decided to use the following:

- Web page examples provided via an overhead projector

- A handout listing the names of the stakeholders, as well as projected costs and timelines

Upper management was very pleased, although they did have a few specific feedback points that they asked Seamus to consider. The project was approved, and Seamus was able to work closely with the project manager to create the site.

*          *          *

As a class, consider this scenario and answer the following questions:

- What other features might benefit this site?

- What other stakeholders could have been consulted?

- What additional presentation aids could have helped Seamus make a positive impression?

## *Lesson Summary*

### Application project

The ability to write markup code manually is important because many GUI editors do not use the latest markup language standards and are not proficient at connecting to databases. XHTML is still an evolving language, so you should be ready to modify existing code at any time.

To research the most current Web standards and recommendations, use your browser to access the W3C site (*www.w3.org*). Locate the following information:

- What is the most recent version of XHTML?

- What new developments have occurred?

- What additional technologies does the W3C discuss in relation to XHTML?

- What is the future of XHTML in general? Why was XHTML deemed necessary?

When you are finished with your research, visit the Habitat For Humanity site (*www.habitat.org*). Then answer the following questions:

- What is the message of this site?

- What technical people would you need to help develop this site? For example, consider the site's search engine.

- What input from non-technical people was necessary to develop this site?

### Skills review

In this lesson, you learned about the origins of HTML and the purpose for its creation. You learned that the W3C is the standards organization governing the evolution of HTML and XHTML. You also learned that HTML editors may provide a simple interface to help you create HTML pages, but without the core knowledge to write HTML code manually, you are limited in your Web page development. After you learn how to write HTML code, the possibilities are limitless. Finally, you studied principles of Web site planning, development and management.

Now that you have completed this lesson, you should be able to:

- ✓ 2.1.1: Relate the history of markup languages to current techniques and technologies, including Standard Generalized Markup Language (SGML), previous versions of Hypertext Markup Language (HTML).

- ✓ 2.1.2: Identify the format and various versions of HTML, including HTML 4.01, Extensible HTML (XHTML).

- ✓ 2.1.8: Explain the importance of consistently developing to a single W3C standard (e.g., XHTML 1.0 Transitional).

- ✓ 2.6.1: Describe the functionality of XML.

- ✓ 2.7.1: Obtain input from stakeholders about acceptable technologies and color combinations.

- ✓ 2.7.2: Create an initial Web site diagram (i.e., a story board or prototype), and translate it into a site map.

- ✓ 2.7.4: Validate Web page design according to technical and audience standards adopted by employers.

✓   2.7.5: Verify Web site usability, viewability and browser compatibility.

✓   2.12.3: Test Web pages in multiple browsers.

✓   2.13.1: Work as a team member to develop pages and sites.

✓   2.13.2: Collaborate with technical (e.g., IT) and non-technical (e.g., marketing) members of the organization to ensure sites meet requirements.

✓   2.13.3: Determine information and audience requirements for a site, including stakeholders such as customers, employees, shareholders, suppliers.

✓   2.13.4: Document a Web site plan.

✓   2.13.5: Communicate the Web site plan effectively, both orally and in writing.

✓   2.13.6: Obtain and document feedback, then improve the site, including working closely with sales and marketing to evaluate site effectiveness.

✓   2.14.1: Define legal issues related to a Web site, including trademarking, licensing, copyrighting, licensing copyrighted materials, scope of copyright, reach of copyright, copyrighting process, copyright infringement and consequences.

✓   2.14.2: Identify fundamentals of project management, including major stages of a Web design/development project cycle.

✓   2.14.3: Identify processes of pre-launch site/application functionality testing, including checking links, testing with various browsers, testing against corruption of your e-commerce site, load testing, access to the site, testing with various speed connections.

✓   2.14.4: Manage existing sites (e.g., remove dead links and/or upgrade connectivity when necessary).

✓   2.14.5: Remove old sites and pages.

✓   2.15.1: Identify ways to elicit useful feedback from management and customers.

✓   2.15.2: Use presentation aids and support material, including charts, tables, figures, written content, overhead projection.

✓   2.15.3: Use presentation software (e.g., slide-based software).

✓   2.15.4: Clarify technical concepts for a non-technical audience, and use strategies to retain listener interest.

✓   2.15.5: Interpret verbal, non-verbal and written feedback.

✓   2.15.6: Address diversity and corporate/organizational culture when communicating your message by customizing meeting and message delivery, and listening for responses.

✓   2.15.7: Identify ways to lead meetings (e.g., make introductions, invite questions, set time frames, set action times, monitor time, ensure proper discussion focus, publish minutes).

✓   2.19.3: Consider corporate/organizational culture when designing page layout.

✓   2.19.4: Demonstrate sensitivity to ethnic and cultural issues in page layout and design.

✓   2.20.1: Obtain proper permissions from developers when repurposing content (e.g., other developers' code, images, concepts).

✓   2.20.2: Create and sign a Non-Disclosure Agreement (NDA) when necessary.

✓   2.20.3: Identify situations in which it is necessary to consult with a legal team.

✓   2.20.4: Identify ethical concerns when developing a Web site.

# Lesson 2 Review

1. What is the primary difference between SGML and XHTML? What do they have in common?

   _____

   _____

   _____

2. List three operating systems and three browsers on which XHTML will function.

   _____

   _____

3. What is the purpose of a tag in markup languages?

   _____

   _____

4. Why is it important to relate technical concepts to non-technical people during planning meetings?

   _____

   _____

5. When working with a service provider to upload a Web site, what is some of the essential information you will need?

   _____

   _____

   _____

   _____

# Lesson 3:
# XHTML Coding

## Objectives

By the end of this lesson, you will be able to:

⇗ 2.1.3: Use HTML tags to format paragraphs and text.

⇗ 2.1.7: Add comments to HTML code and document page/site creation.

⇗ 2.1.8: Explain the importance of consistently developing to a single W3C standard (e.g., XHTML 1.0 Transitional).

⇗ 2.7.4: Validate Web page design according to technical and audience standards adopted by employers.

⇗ 2.8.2: Identify ways to apply styles with CSS.

⇗ 2.9.1: Define the three flavors of the XHTML standard (Strict, Transitional, Frameset).

⇗ 2.9.2: Create a Web page using the XHTML 1.0 standards.

⇗ 2.12.1: Test and validate Web documents.

## Pre-Assessment Questions

1.  Which choice represents valid XHTML tag use?

    a.  Both <p>Web page text</p> and <p/>Web page text
    b.  Only <p>Web page text</p>
    c.  Both </p>Web page text</p> and <p>Web page text<p>
    d.  Only <p/>Web page text</p>

2.  What two XHTML Transitional elements are used to create boldface text?

    a.  <bold> and <s>
    b.  <em> and <big>
    c.  <b> and <strong>
    d.  <dfn> and <sup>

3.  How many heading styles (such as H1, H2, etc.) are available when using XHTML?

    _____

# Introduction to Using XHTML

**OBJECTIVE**
2.1.8: Using a single
W3C standard

In this lesson, you will learn how to use standard XHTML tags to create functional documents. These documents are commonly referred to as pages when written for the Web or for any other application. The default or starting page of a Web site is called the home page for that site.

This course demonstrates the XHTML 1.0 standard. Remember that when you begin creating a Web page or site, you should first choose the W3C standard HTML or XHTML version that you will use. Then stick to your chosen standard, applying it consistently throughout your document, pages and site. This practice ensures that your markup is universal and your pages will render properly in any user agent that your site visitors use. Keep in mind that it is less important which X/HTML standard you choose for your Web pages than it is that you consistently apply the one standard you choose.

# Markup Tags

Markup tags are element names enclosed in angle brackets, or wickets. Tags are the essential building blocks of markup files. Tags embed the markup element information in the document so that a user agent will render text as instructed by the associated element. For example, applying the boldface tags to text would cause the browser to display text contained by such tags in bold font. Text surrounded by tags becomes an element. Text between an opening heading tag and a closing heading tag, for example, would be considered a heading element.

The combination of markup tags and standard text is loosely referred to as either code or markup. Although markup languages are not programming languages, the tags instruct the browser to perform certain actions, and so the use of the term code is appropriate in this context.

## Container tags and empty tags

There are two types of HTML tags:

- **Container tags** — tags that come in pairs. Container tags use opening and closing tags. For example, when you want italic text, you will contain the text between opening and closing <i> </i> tags.

- **Empty tags** — tags that stand alone. Empty tags are those that do not directly format a specified block of text, and therefore one tag can execute the instruction. For example, if you want to create a line break, you insert the <br> tag at the point you want the break to occur.

HTML allows you to use some empty tags, but good coding practice requires you to use container tags. XHTML requires you to use only container tags or alternative "non-empty" tags that can stand alone.

Figure 3-1 demonstrates the proper, traditional use of a container tag. The <title> tag contains text between an opening and a closing tag. Note that the closing tag includes the slash (/) character.

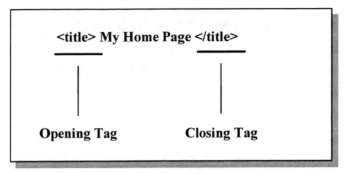

Figure 3-1: <title> tag pair as container for page title text

Container tags are also known as non-empty tags. All versions of XHTML 1.0 allow you to use an alternative method for closing tags, as shown in Figure 3-2.

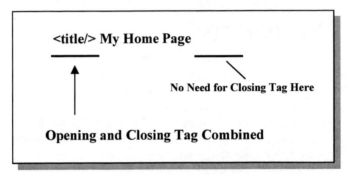

Figure 3-2: Alternative non-empty tag in XHTML

Note that the alternative notation for stand-alone non-empty tags places the slash ( / ) character after the element name (before the closing wicket), rather than before the element name like in a standard closing tag. All XHTML tags must be closed (using either a pair of container tags or the stand-alone non-empty tag), even when you insert images, hyperlinks, tables and lists. You will learn more about creating the appropriate tags throughout the rest of this course.

### Empty tags

An empty HTML tag stands alone and is not closed with the slash character. XHTML does not use empty tags; an empty tag in an XHTML document will prevent the document from validating. However, HTML 4.01 and earlier versions allow empty tags. For example, tags used to insert images, hyperlinks and list items are empty tags in HTML. Figure 3-3 shows an example of an empty tag, although remember that you should not use empty tags if you want to create markup to current standards.

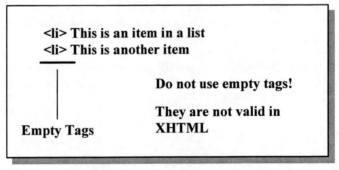

Figure 3-3: List item <li> as empty tag in HTML

**OBJECTIVE**
2.12.1: Validating
Web documents

 *Again, it is important to understand that empty tags are not acceptable in XHTML. However, HTML 4.01 transitional code allows this use of tags.*

## What constitutes a tag?

A tag can consist of the following three items inside the angle brackets:

- **An element** — provides the main instruction of the tag. An element is required in every tag. Elements include <title>, <font>, <table> and many others.

- **An attribute** — specifies a quality or describes a certain aspect of the element. For example, <div> has several attributes, including *align*. Many elements require specified attributes, but some do not. An attribute is required in a tag only if the element requires it.

- **A value** — gives value to the element and its attribute. For example, <div align="center"> has a value that instructs the text to be centered. Like attributes, values are optional in a tag unless required by a specified attribute to the element. Values are used only with attributes; elements do not take values directly. All values must be surrounded by quotation marks in XHTML. If you use HTML 4.01 and earlier, quotes are not necessary, but placing values in quotation marks is considered good coding practice.

 *Be sure to close any quotation marks that you open. If you do not close them, the page content up to the next occurrence of the quotation mark character may disappear.*

Some markup tags use only an element and do not support attributes and values. Others, such as the <div> tag, support attributes and values. It is important that you understand this terminology as you continue throughout the course.

## Document Structure Tags

Every XHTML document must have the following document structure components:

- **A <!DOCTYPE> tag** — The DOCTYPE declaration determines how the interpreter will render all markup in the document. It is an SGML statement. If you declare an XHTML DTD (e.g., XHTML Transitional), then the interpreter will read the document as an XHTML document. If you were to change the declaration to the HTML 4.01 DTD, for example, then the document would be read according to HTML rules for syntax.

- **An <html> tag** — All code up until the <html> tag is not HTML, but is rather SGML.

**OBJECTIVE**
2.1.3: HTML text
formatting

- **A <head> tag** — The head section allows you to insert <meta> tags (which describe the nature of the document), links to style sheets, and the <title> tag.

- **Any <meta> tags** — The <meta> tag can specify various information about the document, known as metadata, or data about data. This metadata includes a document description and keywords that help search engines index the page. It can also specify the character set used in XHTML documents (which is often set by the Web server for HTML documents, rather than by the document itself). The <meta> tag is placed between the <head> </head> tags.

- **A <link> tag that references a style sheet** — This link is recommended for XHTML 1.0 Transitional and required for XHTML 1.0 Strict. A style sheet usually has a .css file name extension and a file name similar to the page to which it is linked (e.g., syb.css for the XHTML page named syb.html). Style sheets are often placed in a subdirectory for the Web page. This subdirectory contains all images and associated files for the page. The <link> tag is placed between the <head> </head> tags.

- **A <title> tag** — This tag inserts the document title. The <title> tag is placed between the <head> </head> tags.

- **A <body> tag** — This tag begins the body of the document.

**OBJECTIVE**
2.7.4: Technical and
audience standards

If your document fails to include these basic structure elements, it will fail validation. The document may or may not still render in browsers. Many of the structure tags (e.g., <html> and <body>) can have attributes and values. Figure 3-4 shows an example of XHTML Transitional code.

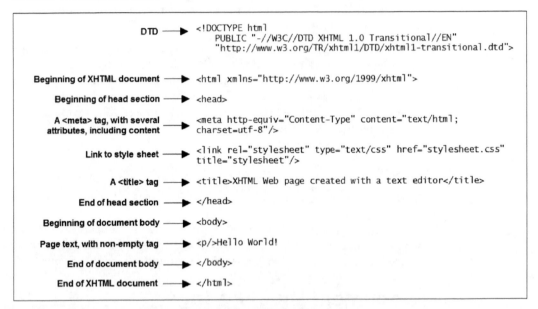

| | |
|---|---|
| DTD ➤ | `<!DOCTYPE html`<br>`        PUBLIC "-//W3C//DTD XHTML 1.0 Transitional//EN"`<br>`        "http://www.w3.org/TR/xhtml1/DTD/xhtml1-transitional.dtd">` |
| Beginning of XHTML document ➤ | `<html xmlns="http://www.w3.org/1999/xhtml">` |
| Beginning of head section ➤ | `<head>` |
| A <meta> tag, with several attributes, including content ➤ | `<meta http-equiv="Content-Type" content="text/html;`<br>`charset=utf-8"/>` |
| Link to style sheet ➤ | `<link rel="stylesheet" type="text/css" href="stylesheet.css"`<br>`title="stylesheet"/>` |
| A <title> tag ➤ | `<title>XHTML Web page created with a text editor</title>` |
| End of head section ➤ | `</head>` |
| Beginning of document body ➤ | `<body>` |
| Page text, with non-empty tag ➤ | `<p/>Hello World!` |
| End of document body ➤ | `</body>` |
| End of XHTML document ➤ | `</html>` |

*Figure 3-4: Sample XHTML code*

An HTML document is almost identical, except that the <!DOCTYPE> declaration would point to a different DTD (one that references an HTML standard version). Following is a discussion of each tag demonstrated in the preceding figure.

 *Notice that all tags in the example are closed.*

## Are XHTML tags case-sensitive?

XHTML tags are case-sensitive and should always be typed in lowercase letters. By contrast, HTML tags are not case-sensitive. Because XML is case-sensitive in that it requires strict conformance to letter case specified in a given DTD, it was decided that all XHTML document elements and attributes should be developed in lowercase letters to ensure consistency, compatibility and conformance. The following code is valid as HTML but invalid as XHTML:

```
<HTML>
<Head>
<Meta http-equiv="Content-Type" content="text/html; charset=utf-8">
```

```
<LINK rel="stylesheet" type="text/css" href="stylesheet.css"
title="stylesheet">
<title> This is an HTML document </Title>
</head>
<Body>
This code will validate as HTML but not as XHTML 1.0 Transitional.
<LIST>
<lI> Make it well-formed
<li> Use existing HTML elements
</list>
</BODY>
</html>
```

Because XHTML requires lowercase tags but HTML has no case requirements, you should always create your markup tags using lowercase letters. Notice that the <!DOCTYPE> tag uses all uppercase letters. This is because <!DOCTYPE> is not an XHTML tag, but an SGML tag that defines the XHTML used in the page. You will learn more about <!DOCTYPE> shortly. The following code is valid as both XHTML and HTML:

```
<!DOCTYPE html PUBLIC "-//W3C//DTD XHTML 1.0 Transitional//EN"
        "http://www.w3.org/TR/xhtml1/DTD/xhtml1-transitional.dtd">
<html>
<head>
<meta http-equiv="Content-Type" content="text/html; charset=utf-8"/>
<link rel="stylesheet" type="text/css" href="stylesheet.css"
title="stylesheet"/>
<title> This is an HTML document </title>
</head>
<body>
This code will validate as XHTML 1.0 Transitional.
</body>
</html>
```

When examining this example code, notice that the only major changes are the addition of closing tags and the use of lowercase type for all the element names. The benefit to these modifications is that the code is now compliant with both HTML and XHTML, and will render in all user agents that follow W3C standards.

*It is important to understand that XML does not require element names and attributes to be written in lowercase. For example, <FirstName> is a valid element name if it is defined in the DTD as such.*

## Document type declaration (DOCTYPE)

The **document type declaration**, or <!DOCTYPE> tag, describes the nature of your code. It is placed at the very top of your document.

The <!DOCTYPE> declaration is technically not XHTML or HTML; it is actually SGML. The DOCTYPE statement specifies the markup version used by the page, as well as the document's primary language. It also includes an optional Web address that contains the proper Document Type Definition (DTD) for the markup version used. For instance, the XHTML 1.0 Transitional DOCTYPE declaration contains the Web site address *www.w3.org/TR/xhtml1/DTD/xhtml1-transitional.dtd*. If you follow this link, you can read the XHTML 1.0 DTD.

*Be careful not to confuse the document type declaration (<!DOCTYPE> tag) with the Document Type Definition (DTD). The <!DOCTYPE> tag is a statement that identifies code versions in a document. The DTD is a separate document containing a set of rules for structure, syntax and vocabulary, used commonly with XHTML and XML. A <!DOCTYPE> tag may contain a URL referencing a DTD document that applies the rules of the specified language version.*

If you do not specify a DOCTYPE, then two problems may arise:

- You will not be able to control how your code renders in the future.

- You will not be able to use a markup validator, because the validator cannot determine the type of markup you are using (e.g., XHTML Transitional or HTML 4.01).

Some examples of DOCTYPE statements follow.

### HTML 2.0
The following DOCTYPE statement is used for HTML 2.0 files:

```
<!DOCTYPE HTML PUBLIC "-//W3C//DTD HTML 2.0//EN">
```

### HTML 3.2
The following DOCTYPE statement is used for HTML 3.2 files:

```
<!DOCTYPE HTML PUBLIC "-//W3C//DTD HTML 3.2 Final//EN">
```

### HTML 4.01
The following DOCTYPE statements are used for files written in the specified flavors of HTML 4.01 (the Web addresses are optional):

- **HTML 4.01 Transitional**

```
<!DOCTYPE HTML PUBLIC "-//W3C//DTD HTML 4.01 Transitional//EN"
"http://www.w3.org/TR/html4/loose.dtd">
```

- **HTML 4.01 Strict**

```
<!DOCTYPE HTML PUBLIC "-//W3C//DTD HTML 4.01//EN"
"http://www.w3.org/TR/html4/strict.dtd">
```

- **HTML 4.01 Frameset**

```
<!DOCTYPE HTML PUBLIC "-//W3C//DTD HTML 4.01 Frameset//EN"
"http://www.w3.org/TR/html4/frameset.dtd">
```

### XHTML
XHTML approximates the HTML 4.01 <!DOCTYPE> tags. If you are using the XHTML Transitional flavor and you are not including XML in your document, there will be little difference between an HTML 4.01 and an XHTML document. The following DOCTYPE statements are used for the specified flavors of XHTML (the Web addresses are optional).

**OBJECTIVE**
2.9.1: XHTML flavors

- **XHTML Transitional**

```
<!DOCTYPE html PUBLIC "-//W3C//DTD XHTML 1.0 Transitional//EN"
"http://www.w3.org/TR/xhtml1/DTD/xhtml1-transitional.dtd">
```

- **XHTML Strict**

```
<!DOCTYPE html PUBLIC "-//W3C//DTD XHTML 1.0 Strict//EN"
"http://www.w3.org/TR/xhtml1/DTD/xhtml1-strict.dtd">
```

- **XHTML Frameset**

```
<!DOCTYPE html PUBLIC "-//W3C//DTD XHTML 1.0 Frameset//EN"
"http://www.w3.org/TR/xhtml1/DTD/xhtml1-frameset.dtd">
```

By using the <!DOCTYPE> tag, you will improve your page's ability to work with browsers. The DOCTYPE statement can help you create a more efficient interface. However, most of its functionality occurs within process.

## The <html> tag

The opening <html> and closing </html> tags must encompass all markup for the entire page. The <html> tag can take several attributes, including:

- **xmlns** — abbreviation for XML namespace, which is called the XPointer scheme because it allows you to create your own XML namespace so that documents can be properly database-enabled, indexed and searched. The default entry is *xmlns="http://www.w3.org/1999/xhtml"*. This attribute is required in the <html> tag, although if you omit it, most browsers will automatically add it.

- **lang** — configures the page to use a particular language. For instance, a Web document written in English would use <html lang="en"> and a document written in French would use <html lang="fr">. This attribute is helpful for search engines and speech synthesizers. You can also use the XML version of the lang attribute. Following are examples of both uses:
  ```
  <html xmlns="http://www.w3.org/1999/xhtml" lang="en">
  <html xmlns="http://www.w3.org/1999/xhtml" xml:lang="en">
  ```

For a list of additional attributes, visit *www.w3schools.com* or *www.w3.org*.

## The <head> tag

The <head> and </head> tags encompass several page elements, including:

- The <meta> tag.
- The <link> tag that references a CSS file, if present.
- The <title> tag.

### The <meta> tag

**character set**
The group of symbols used to render text on a page.

**Unicode**
A universal character set designed to support all written languages, as well as scholarly disciplines (e.g., mathematics).

The <meta> tag can specify various information, or metadata, about the document. For example, it can specify the **character set** used in XHTML documents (which is often set by the Web server for HTML documents, rather than by the document itself). The following example <meta> tag specifies the **Unicode** character set, which is standard in today's Web pages:

```
<meta http-equiv="Content-Type" content="text/html; charset=utf-8"/>
```

The <meta> tag has several attributes, which contain values that generally require a corresponding *content* attribute and value. Attributes include:

- **content-type** — associates the page to HTTP, and includes *http-equiv*.

- **http-equiv** — contains values that allow you to automatically refresh a page or forward a page to another URL, for example.

- **name** — values include "keywords" and "description," and must be accompanied by the *content* attribute. The "keywords" value of the *name* attribute allows you to specify individual words as the value in the accompanying *content* attribute; these words are used by search engines to match pages to searched keywords, and to describe the meaning of the document. The "description" value of the *name* attribute allows you to specify entire sentences as the value in the accompanying *content* attribute; these sentences display in search engines to describe the purpose of the document.

- **content** — used to specify character sets (e.g., the *charset* character coding statement [e.g., charset="utf-8"] attribute, and the "text/html" value) or refresh time periods when paired with the *http-equiv* attribute. When paired with the *name* attribute, the *content* attribute values can supply keywords, author name, page descriptions and so forth, as previously described. Following are some examples.

To provide keywords for search engines, you can use the <meta> tag as follows:

```
<meta name="keywords" content="TCP/IP, networking, Java, CIW, certification">
```

If you want to use the <meta> tag to provide a detailed description of your page, use syntax similar to the following:

```
<meta name="description" content="You can enter a useful description of the
page here. You can use sentences, as you would in an e-mail or letter, but
keep it concise.">
```

To specify the author of the Web page, use the <meta> tag's *name* attribute with the "author" value:

```
<meta name="author" content="Rosa Estelle Rodriguez">
```

Use the <meta > tag to make your page refresh automatically after a specified number of seconds as follows:

```
<meta http-equiv="refresh" content="5; URL=http://www.CIW-certified.com">
```

An extended discussion of the <meta> tag is beyond the scope of this course. However, the <meta> tag is a very effective back-end tool for ensuring that your pages work well across networks. The <meta> tag was discussed in this section because it is placed within the document structure tags.

## The <link> tag

Style sheet references are specified with the <link> tag in the <head> section, usually before the <title> tag. They are recommended for XHTML 1.0 Transitional and required for XHTML 1.0 Strict. The link must point to a standard ASCII text file. Although you can also import style sheets using the <style> tag and the *@import* statement, it is recommended to use the <link> tag to link styles instead.

## The <title> tag

The <title> tag is the first tag that allows you to specify content that will appear on the page. Any text you enclose with this tag appears in the page title box at the top of a browser. This text also appears in the history list and on the page when printed. Title text becomes the Bookmark name if the page is bookmarked or added to a browser Favorites folder.

## The <body> tag

All text to be displayed on the page through the user agent needs to appear between the <body> and </body> tags. The <body> tag takes several attributes. Some of the attributes include:

- **bgcolor** — specifies a background color for the entire page. This attribute cannot be used in XHTML Strict; you must use style sheets instead.

- **background** — inserts an image as a background for the page. This attribute cannot be used in XHTML Strict; you must use style sheets instead.

- **link** — specifies the color of hypertext links for the page. This attribute cannot be used in XHTML Strict; you must use style sheets instead.

The <body> tag takes other attributes as well. Visit *www.w3.org* or *www.w3schools.com* for more information.

### Values in XHTML

In XHTML, attribute values must be placed within quotation marks ( " " ). This means that if you want to specify a page's background color as gray, for example, you would use the following tag:

```
<body bgcolor="gray">
```

In HTML, you do not necessarily need to supply quotation marks, but omitting them is considered poor coding practice.

# Web Site File Structure

When creating a Web page, you must consider the site's structure. Your HTML and images will be uploaded to a server eventually, so it is always good practice to organize your files as you create them. Figure 3-5 illustrates a typical Web site file structure.

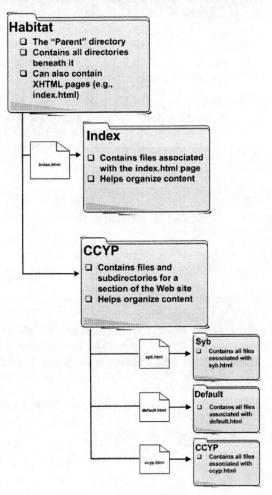

*Figure 3-5: Typical Web site file structure*

As shown in this figure, the XHTML pages are usually placed in a directory, and all images and files used in that page are stored in subfolders with the same name.

In this course, you will work on selected pages from a previously live version of the Habitat For Humanity Web site. All necessary files are provided. Specifically, you will work on a Summer Youth Blitz page, which resides in the Habitat\CCYP\ directory.

# Preparing Your Development Environment

Before you begin creating Web page code, you should:

- **Obtain a text editor** — Most operating systems have their own editors, so you do not need to download and install one. However, you may prefer to obtain a text editor that automatically numbers lines so you can easily reference your code. It is best to use a text editor that automatically saves standard ASCII text. Applications such as Microsoft Word can save to standard ASCII text only if you explicitly command them to do so. Common editors include Notepad, WordPad, Vi, Pico and Emacs.

- **Install multiple browsers** — You will need to test your code in multiple environments.

- **Set file preferences** — The Windows operating systems do not show file name extensions by default. You will be working with files with various extensions (e.g., .html, .css, .txt) so you will need to be able to see them. You can set preferences in Windows Vista by selecting Start | Control Panel | Folder Options, then selecting the View tab. Deselect the Hide Extensions For Known File Types check box so that you can view all file name extensions.

**OBJECTIVE**
2.1.3: HTML text formatting

In the following lab, you will create a simple XHTML page. Suppose you have been assigned to create a basic markup page as a placeholder for a page that will describe a summer youth program for Habitat For Humanity volunteers. This simple file should be named syb.html and should validate as XHTML 1.0 Transitional. What steps would you take to create this simple page?

 **Lab 3-1: Creating a simple XHTML page**

**OBJECTIVE**
2.9.2: Creating pages with XHTML

In this lab, you will create a basic file directory structure, and you will create an XHTML page then validate it as XHTML Transitional.

1.  If necessary, configure your operating system so that you can read the full extensions of all file names. This will allow you to find your XHTML files more easily. In Windows Vista, select **Start | Control Panel | Folder Options**, then select the **View** tab. Deselect the **Hide Extensions For Known File Types** check box. Select the **Show Hidden Files And Folders** radio button. Click **OK** to close the Folder Options dialog box.

2.  Right-click the **Desktop** and select **New | Folder**.

3.  Name the new folder *Habitat*.

4.  Double-click the **Habitat** folder to open it. Inside, create a subfolder and name it **CCYP**.

5.  Double-click the **CCYP** folder to open it.

6.  When you are finished, review the directory structure you have created. In Windows Explorer, it should appear off of your Desktop as Habitat\CCYP\.

7. The Habitat\CCYP\ folder will eventually contain the syb.html file, among others. You have now created a standard directory structure for a Web site in which you can organize your images and CSS pages.

8. Right-click inside the **Habitat\CCYP\** folder, and select **New | Text Document**. Name the new text document *syb.html*.

9. Right-click the **syb.html** file and open it in Notepad. You will see that the syb.html file is currently empty.

10. In the blank syb.html file, enter the following code exactly as written:

```
<!DOCTYPE html
    PUBLIC "-//W3C//DTD XHTML 1.0 Transitional//EN"
    "http://www.w3.org/TR/xhtml1/DTD/xhtml1-transitional.dtd">

<html xmlns="http://www.w3.org/1999/xhtml" xml:lang="en">

<head>
<meta http-equiv="Content-Type" content="text/html; charset=utf-8"/>
<meta name="keywords" content="CIW, XHTML 1.0, Habitat for Humanity"/>
<meta name="Description" content="Simple XHTML page for Habitat site"/>

<title>Habitat for Humanity International Summer Youth Blitz Program</title>
</head>

<body bgcolor="white">

Join a Summer Build for Teen-agers.
The Summer Youth Blitz is a unique service experience for a diverse group of
youth, ages 16 to 18, from high schools and youth organizations around the
United States. This page will validate as XHTML 1.0 Transitional.
</body>
</html>
```

11. Once you have inserted this code, save your changes. Make sure that your file is named syb.html, not syb.txt or anything else. You may have to close Notepad to rename the file.

12. Now, open **syb.html** in a Web browser. It should resemble Figure 3-6.

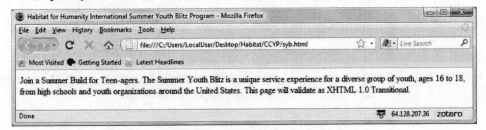

*Figure 3-6: File syb.html in Firefox*

*Note: You can use any Web browser. In fact, you are encouraged to view code in multiple browsers to ensure that you are creating pages that render well in various environments.*

13. As you can see, you have created a rudimentary Web page that will validate as XHTML Transitional, as long as you have entered the code correctly. To verify this, visit ***http://validator.w3.org***. You will see the W3C Markup Validation Service Web page, as shown in Figure 3-7.

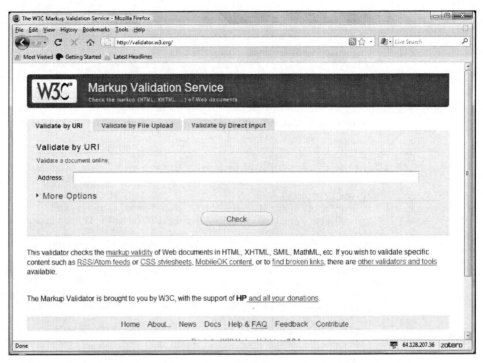

Figure 3-7: W3C Markup Validation Service Web page

**14.** Click the **Validate By File Upload** link. To the right of the File text box, click the **Browse** button. Navigate to the **syb.html** file you have created and select it by double-clicking.

**15.** Click the **Check** button.

**16.** If your code does not validate, make appropriate changes.

**17.** Once your code validates, change the background color of your page to teal, which is a bluish-green color. To do this, find the <body bgcolor="white"> tag, then change the *bgcolor* attribute value to read as follows:

<body bgcolor="**teal**">

**18.** Save **syb.html**, then open it in your Web browser again.

**19.** Notice the change in color. Experiment with changing other values to the *bgcolor* attribute. Then validate your code again.

**20.** Return your Web page to its original state. Change the *bgcolor* attribute back to the value "white" then validate your XHTML again.

**21.** Close your Web browser.

In this lab, you created and validated an XHTML Transitional document.

# Style Sheets

You have already learned that a **Cascading Style Sheets (CSS)** document is an ASCII text file that determines the look and feel for a Web page or site. It contains formatting instructions that can define the font, color and phrase elements used on a particular markup page.

If all pages on your site are linked to the same style sheet, then one simple change to the style sheet will change all elements across the site. If you then want to change those instructions (for example, the style of <h1> headings), you need not change every page manually. You need only change a line in the style sheet file, then all your <h1> headings will change their appearance to conform to the style sheet. This technology can save a great deal of development and maintenance time, as well as make a more consistent, accessible interface.

The Strict flavors of HTML 4.01 and XHTML 1.0 demand that you use only CSS to impose layout and formatting for your pages. You can use style sheets to override some or all of the default properties presented in the body of your pages. The new properties you define will remain in force throughout the document.

Currently, three standards exist for style sheets:

- **Cascading Style Sheets (CSS1)** — governs the basic structure of style sheets.

- **Cascading Style Sheets 2 (CSS2)** — adds more capabilities to the CSS1 specification, including the ability to support media types (such as specific printers) and work with tables.

- **Cascading Style Sheets 3 (CSS3)** — will be modularized so that when changes need to be made to a specification, only a particular module within CSS3 will need to be updated, rather than the entire standard. This will allow for a more flexible and timely upgrade of the standard as a whole. New functions are being added to CSS3 to enhance its support of borders, backgrounds, colors, text effects and so forth.

HTML 4.01 and XHTML both adopt CSS1 and CSS2 as the preferred ways to format a page. Because CSS1 contains the instructions you will use most often, this lesson will focus on the CSS1 standard.

**Tech Tip**  *Proper use of style sheets is foundational for creating pages that rank highly in search engines.*

## CSS terminology

Before you deploy CSS, you should learn its terminology. The most important terms to understand are selector, property, value, declaration and rule. Figure 3-8 illustrates the anatomy of these style sheet elements as they are found in linked, imported and embedded style sheets. Inline styles are declared differently. You will learn more about different ways to define styles shortly.

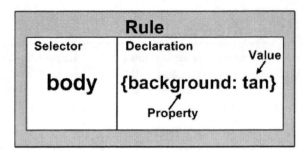

*Figure 3-8: Anatomy of CSS rule*

**selector**
In a style sheet, any element to which designated styles are applied.

Most developers use CSS to override some or all of the properties found in existing tags. As shown in the preceding figure, you could decide to give all pages a background color of tan. To make such a change, you must identify the markup element you want to change, then refer to it in a style sheet. In a style sheet, any element you want to affect is called a **selector**.

After you have chosen a selector, you can customize it by selecting a property and setting a value. By selecting a property, you will change the way the selector renders in the browser. For example, you could alter the selector's color, size, background, font family, font size and so forth. These changes will apply to all subsequent instances of the element you define as a selector.

A property must then have a value. For example, if you want to change a selector's size property, you must set a value to specify that size. Or you could decide to change the color of your pages to blue, and so forth.

In the following example, you will see a CSS declaration, which consists of a property and a value contained within curly brackets:

    body {background-color: teal}

The name for a selector, property and value all grouped together is a **rule**. The following rule will change the color of the body background to teal, then set the font color to white:

    body {background-color: teal; color: whiteitalic}

**rule**
In a style sheet, a format instruction that consists of a specified selector and the properties and values applied to it. Also a line or lines; the word is related to "ruler," a tool of measurement that can be used to draw straight lines.

To define multiple declarations for one selector within a rule, as in the previous example, you must separate each declaration with a semicolon. You can also place a semicolon between a value and the end bracket.

Notice from these examples that the properties and the values must be placed within curly brackets. This practice is standard for all style sheet rules, except when declaring inline styles. You will learn more about different ways to define styles shortly.

*CSS declarations are not case-specific. However, you should use letter case consistently when declaring styles.*

## Proper CSS structure

Following is the accepted structure of rules within an external style sheet:

```
body {
            font-family: arial, verdana, helvetica; color: gray; font-size:
10pt;
       }
h1    {
            font-family: arial, sans-serif; color: black; font-size: 24pt;
       }
```

Notice that the opening and closing curly brackets are indented and placed on separate lines. This indentation and spacing is considered good coding practice.

If you want a particular rule in a style sheet to be ignored, you can "comment out" the entry by placing it in between the /* and */ characters. In the following example, the words "STYLE SHEET FOR SYB.HTML" will not be read:

```
/* STYLE SHEET FOR SYB.HTML */
```

## Inheritance

The concept of inheritance is essential to Cascading Style Sheets. In fact, the word "cascading" refers to inheritance. The style you define will flow, or cascade, throughout the document, unless another style defined inside of a page specifically overrides it. Many styles can be used together to create a completely formatted document. For example, a style sheet rule will override the *bgcolor* attribute, as well as the default *body* font color, which is black. However, certain properties (such as text size) remain in force. All these characteristics, whether they are defined in a style sheet or exist by default, are inherited throughout the rest of the document.

*Formats specified using the <style> tag within a page will override linked CSS entries.*

## CSS and XHTML

Now that you understand CSS terminology and syntax, you need to know how to implement it in a markup page. You can apply CSS styles to X/HTML pages in four ways. You can:

• Declare an inline style.

• Create an embedded style sheet.

• Link to an external style sheet.

• Use an imported style sheet.

## Benefits of using CSS

CSS benefits include:

• **Consistency** — CSS easily makes an entire site retain a consistent look and feel.

• **Easy change management** — You have the ability to change the look and feel of an entire site simply by changing only part of a single line of code, rather than having to change thousands of lines.

## Style sheets and compatibility

Imported style sheets have been known to cause some problems. Certain older browsers may crash when rendering pages with the import statement. If you want to use an external style sheet, use a linked style sheet rather than an imported style sheet.

In the following lab, you will use a style sheet. Suppose your project manager reviews some of your pages and requests that you eliminate the background color from all pages. You could perform this task quickly and simply by editing the style sheet.

**Lab 3-2: Using a style sheet with XHTML**

In this lab, you will attach a style sheet to a document, then edit the style sheet to override the XHTML *bgcolor* attribute.

1. **Windows Explorer:** Navigate to the **Habitat\CCYP\** folder, and create a subfolder named *syb*. This new folder (Habitat\CCYP\syb\) will contain the style sheet as well as all images and other files for the syb.html page.

2. **Windows Explorer:** Navigate to **C:\CIW\Site_Dev\Lab Files\Lesson03\Lab_3-2\**. Copy the file **syb.css** to the Habitat\CCYP\syb\ folder on your system.

   *Note: Remember that you are going to place all files associated with a page in a specific subfolder. In this case, files will be in the syb subfolder.*

3. **Editor:** Open the **syb.html** file, and enter the code shown in bold:

```
<!DOCTYPE html
    PUBLIC "-//W3C//DTD XHTML 1.0 Transitional//EN"
    "http://www.w3.org/TR/xhtml1/DTD/xhtml1-transitional.dtd">

<html xmlns="http://www.w3.org/1999/xhtml" xml:lang="en">

<head>
<meta http-equiv="Content-Type" content="text/html; charset=utf-8"/>
<meta name="keywords" content="CIW, XHTML 1.0, Habitat for Humanity"/>
<meta name="Description" content="Simple XHTML page for Habitat site"/>
<link rel="stylesheet" type="text/css" href="syb/syb.css" title="stylesheet"/>

<title>Habitat for Humanity International Summer Youth Blitz Program</title>
</head>

<body bgcolor="white">

Join a Summer Build for Teen-agers.
The Summer Youth Blitz is a unique service experience for a diverse group of
youth, ages 16 to 18, from high schools and youth organizations around the
United States. This page will validate as XHTML 1.0 Transitional.
</body>
</html>
```

4. **Editor:** Save your changes.

5. Open **syb.html** in your Web browser. You will not notice any changes because the style entries in the CSS file are currently commented out using the syntax /*  */.

6. Open the file **syb.css** in Notepad. Remove the comments from the line that begins with *body*. Make sure to remove both the beginning /* and ending */ characters of the comment. When you are finished, save your changes.

7. Before you close syb.css, review the entry. Note especially the *background: tan* entry.

8. After you have removed the comment from the body entry and reviewed all entries, close **syb.css**, making sure that you have saved your changes.

**serif**
A font style that uses characters with small decorative additions at the outermost points of the characters, called strokes. Includes the Times and Times New Roman fonts.

9. Refresh your browser's display. Notice that the page's background color has changed to tan. In this case, the style sheet has overridden the *bgcolor* attribute found in the XHTML <body> tag. Also, notice that the font type (i.e., the font face) has changed. Instead of the standard **serif** font most Web browsers use, you now see the **sans-serif** Arial font.

10. In syb.html, delete the **bgcolor** attribute from the <body> tag, then save and close the file.

**sans-serif**
A font style that does not use decorative strokes at the tips of characters. Includes the Arial font family.

11. Open **syb.css** again and change the *body* entry so that it reads *background: white*, then save and close the file.

12. Refresh your browser's display. What color is the background?

13. Close any **Notepad** windows.

# Paragraph Formatting and Block-Level Elements

**block-level element**
A markup element that affects at least an entire paragraph.

Markup elements that affect an entire paragraph or multiple paragraphs are referred to as **block-level elements**. Elements that can affect something as small as a character or a word are referred to as **text-level elements**. Block-level elements are automatically preceded and followed by paragraph breaks. Text-level elements are not followed by breaks unless the breaks are manually added.

**text-level element**
A markup element that affects single characters or words.

## Paragraph breaks and line breaks

The most basic block-level element is the paragraph element. The line break element is technically a text-level element, but it is included here in the context of formatting paragraphs. The <p> tag defines the start of a new paragraph, and a closing </p> tag specifies the end of the paragraph.

The <br> tag inserts a simple line break into the document. Because the <br> tag usually breaks a line of text, it never spans words or multiple lines of text, as does the <p> tag. The <br> tag does not use a separate closing tag, so it is best to include a closing slash in every line break tag to make it a stand-alone non-empty tag, as follows: <br/>

In the following lab, you will use XHTML tags to insert paragraph and line breaks. Suppose the marketing and legal departments have created several paragraphs of text for the syb.html page, and you are assigned to insert this text. You can use the <p> and <br> tags to format information on the page and make it easy to read.

 **Lab 3-3: Creating paragraph breaks and line breaks with XHTML**

In this lab, you will use the <p> and <br> tags to add paragraph breaks and line breaks to a Web page.

1. **Editor:** Open the file **syb.html**, which you edited in the previous lab.

2. **Editor:** Delete all text located between the <body></body> tags except for the "Join a Summer Build for Teen-agers" line. Place your cursor on a new line just below "Join a Summer Build for Teen-agers."

3. **Editor:** Minimize **syb.html**.

4. Navigate to the **C:\CIW\Site_Dev\Lab Files\Lesson03\Lab_3-3\** directory. Copy the file **syb.txt** to your Desktop, then open it in the text editor. Notice that the text is organized into five separate paragraphs.

5. Copy the contents of the syb.txt file into **syb.html**, then save **syb.html**.

6. Load **syb.html** into a browser. You will now see more text on the Web page, but it is not organized into paragraphs when you view it in a browser.

7. Edit the text in syb.html to add paragraphs breaks that will be recognized by a browser. Add the following code shown in bold:

```
Join a Summer Build for Teen-agers.
<p>
The Summer Youth Blitz is a unique service experience for a diverse group of
youth, ages 16 to 18, from high schools and youth organizations around the
United States. During this program, 15 to 20 youth participants and adult
leaders "blitz build" an entire Habitat house in two weeks.
</p>
<p>
The house build, an unfamiliar activity for most, provides a common,
nonthreatening ground for building relationships and teams.
</p>
<p>
In the evenings, the youth participate in activities like team-building games,
leadership development, local cultural events or community dinners.
</p>
<p>
This program is sponsored by national grant donations and coordinated by the
Campus Chapters and Youth Programs department of Habitat for Humanity
International. For the past several years, funding has allowed for three blitz
builds per summer--two in the United States and one outside the country. The
builds take place during the months of June, July and August.
</p>
<p>
If you're interested in participating, and are between the ages of 16 and 18
years old, you must submit an application, which is available during January
and February.
</p>
</body>
</html>
```

8. Load **syb.html** into your browser. You will see that the text is now separated into paragraphs, as shown in Figure 3-9.

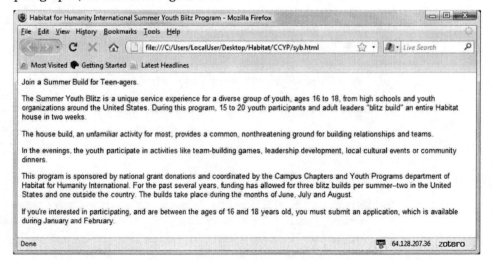

*Figure 3-9: File syb.html after adding <p> tags*

9. Notice that using the <p> tags has created paragraphs. Now, add some <br/> tags to see the difference between a line break and a paragraph break in HTML. Open the **syb.html** file again and enter the following <br/> tags as indicated in bold:

```
<p>
The Summer Youth Blitz is a unique service experience for a diverse group of
youth,<br/>ages 16 to 18,
from high schools and youth organizations around the United States.
<br/>During this program, 15 to 20
youth participants and adult leaders <br/>"blitz build" an entire Habitat
house in two weeks.
</p>
<p>
The house build, an unfamiliar activity for most, provides a common,
<br/>nonthreatening ground for building
relationships and teams.
</p>
<p>
In the evenings, the youth participate in activities like team-building games,
<br/>leadership development,
local cultural events or community dinners.
</p>
<p>
This program is sponsored by national grant donations and coordinated by the
Campus Chapters<br/> and Youth
Programs department of Habitat for Humanity International. For the past
several years, <br/>funding has allowed
for three blitz builds per summer--two in the United States and one outside
<br/>the country. The builds take
place during the months of June, July and August.
</p>
<p>
If you're interested in participating, and are between the ages of 16 and 18
years old, <br/>you must submit
an application, which is available during January and February.
</p>
```

10. Notice that you entered the stand-alone non-empty <br/> tag, rather than encompassing text between <br> and </br>.

11. Reload your file in the browser. You should now see the lines break across the page, as shown in Figure 3-10. Notice that although the lines break, no extra returns are added after the line breaks, as they are with the paragraph breaks.

      

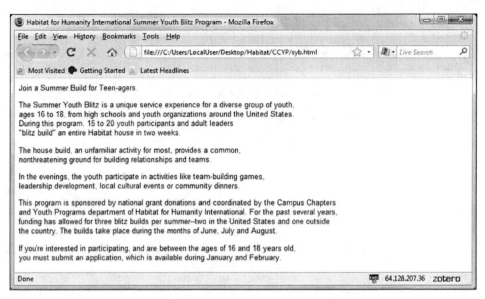

Figure 3-10 browser window content:

Join a Summer Build for Teen-agers.

The Summer Youth Blitz is a unique service experience for a diverse group of youth,
ages 16 to 18, from high schools and youth organizations around the United States.
During this program, 15 to 20 youth participants and adult leaders
"blitz build" an entire Habitat house in two weeks.

The house build, an unfamiliar activity for most, provides a common,
nonthreatening ground for building relationships and teams.

In the evenings, the youth participate in activities like team-building games,
leadership development, local cultural events or community dinners.

This program is sponsored by national grant donations and coordinated by the Campus Chapters
and Youth Programs department of Habitat for Humanity International. For the past several years,
funding has allowed for three blitz builds per summer--two in the United States and one outside
the country. The builds take place during the months of June, July and August.

If you're interested in participating, and are between the ages of 16 and 18 years old,
you must submit an application, which is available during January and February.

*Figure 3-10: After adding <br> tags to create line breaks*

**12.** Close all browser and editor windows.

The preceding lab demonstrates that the appearance of text in the editor will not
necessarily match the appearance of text in the browser. Do not become frustrated when
the text in your browser does not appear as you intended. Determine what needs to be
done to achieve the desired appearance, and add the appropriate code to your file.

## Heading levels

OBJECTIVE
2.9.2: Creating
pages with XHTML

Even the most basic documents will usually include at least one heading, and more likely
several. Denoting text as heading elements emphasizes the start of different sections on
your page and draws attention to that text. Heading tags have built-in styles associated
with them. For example, text formatted as a heading level 1 element is rendered by
default in a large, bold, serif font.

HTML and XHTML Transitional 1.0 use six heading styles. Heading tags are container
tags that encompass the affected text. The <h1> and </h1> tags cause enclosed text to be
rendered in the heading level 1 style; the <h4> and </h4> tags cause enclosed text to be
rendered in the heading level 4 style, and so forth. The largest heading is level 1. Heading
level 4 text is rendered the same size as normal text. Heading levels 5 and 6 are smaller
than normal text and should be used sparingly, if at all. Figure 3-11 shows heading
appearances relative to normal text.

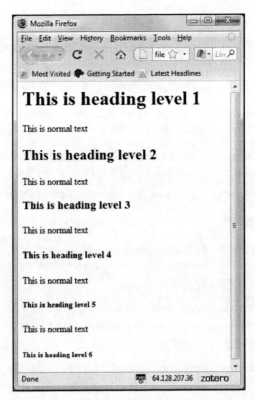

Figure 3-11: Heading-level text and normal text

Because headings are block-level elements, they are automatically preceded and followed by paragraph breaks, regardless of the relative position of the element to other text in the source code. It is important to note that you cannot place any header elements within a set of <p> </p> tags. If you do, your code will not validate as XHTML 1.0 and it may not render properly.

## Tag nesting in markup

You will often use multiple sets of tags to format some text. Placing a pair of tags within another pair of tags is called tag nesting. You must ensure that your code is properly nested. Proper nesting means that you must open and close a pair of tags within another pair. The following two examples show both proper and improper tag nesting techniques.

**Proper**: <h1> <i> ... </i> </h1>

**Improper**: <h1> <i> ... </h1> </i>

Notice that in the improper example, the <i> tag is opened within the <h1> tag, but then closed outside the </h1> tag. If you fail to properly nest code, your pages may still render in some user agents, but they will not validate and may fail to render in the future.

Similarly, heading tags (e.g., <h1>, <h2>) should not be used within formatting tags (e.g., <i>, <p>). This tag combination constitutes improper nesting because the elements are incompatible, and will therefore prevent your code from validating.

In the following lab, you will use XHTML to create headings. Suppose your project manager has assigned you to add headings to a Web page so that readers immediately understand the page's topics. The headings must help organize the content. The page content includes an introduction, the program's sponsors and an application section.

OBJECTIVE
2.1.3: HTML text
formatting

## Lab 3-4: Using headings in XHTML

In this lab, you will add heading tags to Web page code to help organize the content.

1. **Editor:** Open **syb.html**. Remove the style sheet entry from the document so that you can see standard heading fonts.

2. Add and edit the code as shown in bold so that it has <h1> tags but no period at the end:

   `<h1>Join a Summer Build for Teen-agers</h1>`

   *Note: Make sure that the <h1> line is not placed between a set of <p>...</p> tags.*

3. **Editor:** Add a line that says ***Sponsors*** just above the fourth paragraph, and make it an h2 heading. Again, make sure that your heading is not between a set of <p>...</p> tags.

4. **Editor:** Add a line that says ***Apply now!*** just above the last (fifth) paragraph, and make it an h3 heading. Again, make sure that your heading is not between a set of <p>...</p> tags.

5. **Editor:** Save your changes and load the file into a browser. Your screen should resemble Figure 3-12. When you are finished, validate your code.

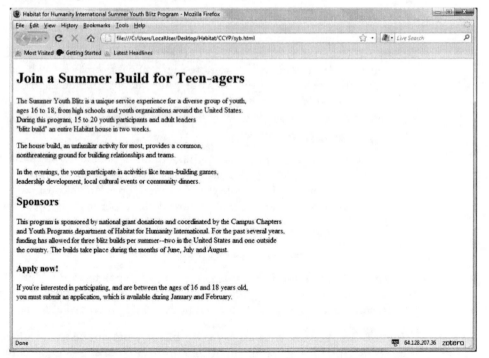

*Figure 3-12: After adding heading, paragraph and line break tags*

6. Close all browser and editor windows.

In this lab, you used markup headings.

## Primitive formatting with the <pre> tag

**OBJECTIVE**
2.9.2: Creating
pages with XHTML

Sometimes, you may want to use text that has already been formatted in a table or with a **fixed-width font**, such as Courier or Lucida Sans Typewriter. With the preformatted text tag (<pre>), all line breaks and spacing will be displayed in the browser exactly as they appear in the original text. The text will display in a fixed-width font, usually Courier.

**fixed-width font**
A font in which every character, including the space character, has equal width. In proportional-width fonts, letters such as I and J have less width than M or B.

The <pre> tag allows you to display plain text files in their original format. It is commonly used to display tabular data. The <pre> tag is a container tag, requiring a closing </pre> tag. The code shown in Figure 3-13 will render as shown in Figure 3-14.

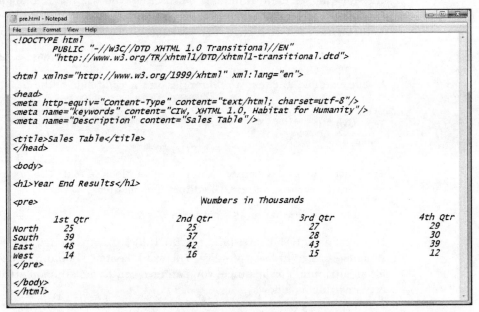

*Figure 3-13: Table created using <pre> tag*

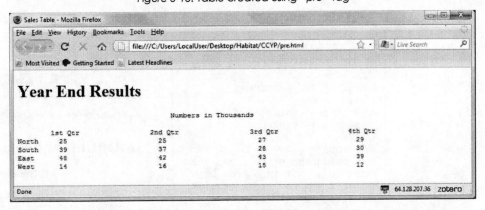

*Figure 3-14: Preformatted tabular data rendered in browser*

As you will learn in a later lesson, HTML tables are more attractive and functional for presenting tabular data. However, if you have preformatted data and little time, the <pre> tag is quick and simple to use.

## Indenting and centering text

When you want to center a paragraph of text, you have several options. First, you can use the division (<div>) tag. The syntax is as follows:

```
<div align="center"> This text is centered. </div>
```

This code shows the standard way to create centered text using XHTML or HTML 4.01. In this example, the div tags encompass the text you want to format. The *align* attribute tells the browser that the text should be aligned to the specified value, "center". You can use the <div> tag for many functions. Most often, you will use it to align content. For example, you can center text, tables and images. You can also use <div> to justify items to the right or left on a page. For example, consider the following code:

```
<div align="right"> This text is aligned to the right. </div>
```

In this example, the text would render on the right side of the page.

 *You will use the <div> tag to divide a document into discrete sections in a later lesson.*

The <blockquote> tag centers and indents a block of text. The <center> tag also centers text. Many developers and GUI editors use <center>:

```
<center> This text is centered.</center>
```

However, as of HTML 4.01 (and also XHTML 1.0 Transitional) the <center> element has been deprecated in favor of <div>. The word "center" should now be used only as a value for an attribute. For instance, you can use "center" as an *align* attribute value in the <p> container tag as follows:

```
<p align="center"> Your text here. </p>
```

In Figure 3-15, the source code on the left displays in the browser as shown on the right. This example demonstrates the effects of the <blockquote> and <div> tags.

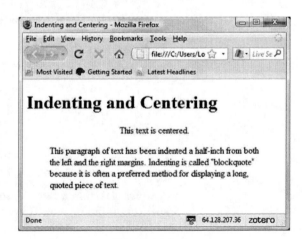

*Figure 3-15: <blockquote> and <div> tags rendered in browser*

Do not use <blockquote> tags within <p> tags, and do not use <h1> tags within <blockquote> tags. Doing so will prevent your code from validating.

In the following lab, you will use XHTML to center and indent text on a Web page. Suppose your project manager has seen your XHTML work thus far and asked you to continue formatting the document. She has suggested indenting and centering some text to enhance the page's appearance. She has also asked you to add some contact information at the bottom of the page.

## Lab 3-5: Indenting and centering text with XHTML

**OBJECTIVE**
2.1.3: HTML text formatting

In this lab, you will use XHTML to indent and center text in the file you created in previous labs.

1.  **Editor:** Open **syb.html** and scroll to the bottom of the file.

2.  **Editor:** Add the following line just above the </body> tag:

    ```
    <center>For more information, contact us at (800) 422-4828, ext.
    2220.</center>
    ```

3.  **Browser:** Load the **syb.html** file. You will see that your new line is centered. Validate your code at ***http://validator.w3.org***.

    *Note: Properly nest code, or else it may fail validation, render incorrectly, or both.*

4.  **Editor:** Replace the <center> and </center> tags with **<div align="center">** and **</div>,** respectively, then check your work by both reviewing the code and validating it automatically.

5.  Notice that the centering looks awkward. Use the **<blockquote>** tag to indent all of the text beneath each header, as follows:

    ```
    <h1>Join a Summer Build for Teen-agers</h1>
    <blockquote>
    <p>
    The Summer Youth Blitz is a unique service experience for a diverse group of
    youth, <br/>ages 16 to 18,
    from high schools and youth organizations around the United States.
    <br/>During this program, 15 to 20
    youth participants and adult leaders <br/>"blitz build" an entire Habitat
    house in two weeks.
    </p>
    </blockquote>
    ```

6.  Repeat this formatting for the entire page by enclosing each text paragraph in <blockquote> tags. Do not format headings as blockquotes. Notice that the tags are properly nested: The <blockquote> tags are not placed inside of the <p> tags, nor are the <h1> tags inside of a <blockquote> tag. When you are finished, resize your browser window so your page resembles Figure 3-16.

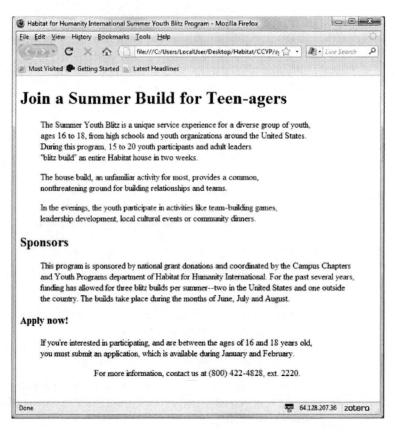

Figure 3-16: After indenting with <blockquote> and centering with <div>

**7.** Close all browser and editor windows.

In this lab, you used XHTML to center and indent text in a Web page.

## Additional block-level elements

You can incorporate additional block-level elements into your pages. These include forms, horizontal ruling lines, and lists.

By this point, you should understand how to use the most common block-level tags:

- <p>
- <h1> through <h6>
- <blockquote>
- <div>

Other elements are discussed later in this lesson and in the lessons that follow. The key point to remember is that all block-level elements are automatically preceded and followed by paragraph breaks.

*Additional paragraph tags are not added to your code when you use block-level elements. The block-level elements are interpreted by the client browser, which automatically includes the additional spacing.*

# Text-Level Elements

Text-level elements can affect a section of text as small as a single character or as large as an entire page. In the discussion that follows, you will learn how to use several text-formatting elements to emphasize text and embellish your pages.

## Bold, italic and underlined text

**OBJECTIVE**
2.1.3: HTML text formatting

Simple text-level elements include the following:

- <b> and <strong> for **bold** text

- <i> and <em> for *italic* text

- <u> for <u>underlined</u> text

The <strong> and <em> elements are standard; it is recommended that you use them instead of <b> and <i>.

*As a general rule, you should limit the use of underline because this convention predominantly designates hyperlinks in Web page text.*

The code in Figure 3-17 shows text that will appear underlined, as well as in bold and italic type. This example also shows how you can combine elements. Note especially the sequence of tags used around the text that is both bold and italic. Again notice the nesting: The tag that opens first closes last, and the tag that opens last closes first.

```
text-level_elements.html - Notepad
File  Edit  Format  View  Help
<!DOCTYPE html
          PUBLIC "-//W3C//DTD XHTML 1.0 Transitional//EN"
          "http://www.w3.org/TR/xhtml1/DTD/xhtml1-transitional.dtd">

<html xmlns="http://www.w3.org/1999/xhtml" xml:lang="en">

<head>
<meta http-equiv="Content-Type" content="text/html; charset=utf-8"/>
<meta name="keywords" content="CIW, XHTML 1.0, Habitat for Humanity"/>
<meta name="Description" content="Text-level Elements"/>

<title>Text-level Elements</title>
</head>

<body>

<h1>Text Formatting</h1>
<u>This line will appear as underlined text (using the u tag).</u>
<br/>
<b>This line will appear in boldface (using the b tag).</b>
<br/>
<strong>This line will also appear in boldface (using the strong tag).</strong>
<br/>
<i>This line will appear in italic (using the i tag).</i>
<br/>
<em>This line will also appear in italic (using the em tag).</em>
<br/>
<b><i>This line will appear in both boldface and italic (using the i and b tags).</i></b>
<br/>
<strong><em><u>This line will be underlined, as well as appear in boldface and italic
(using the strong, em and u tags).</u></em></strong>

</body>
</html>
```

*Figure 3-17: Text formatted using <strong>, <b> and <i> tags, among others*

Figure 3-18 shows the effects of such formatting.

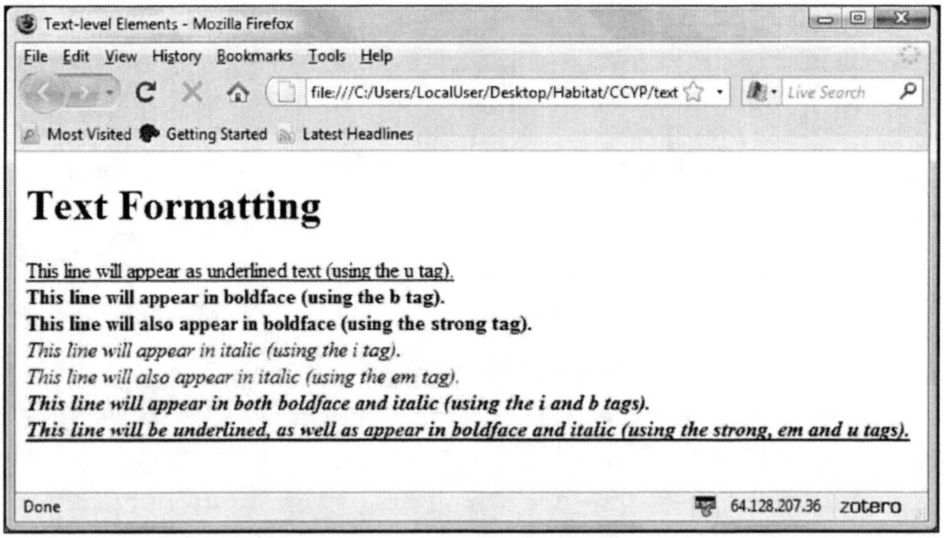

*Figure 3-18: Effects of adding formatting elements to text*

Text-formatting tags are simple to use. Open the tag before the text to be affected, and close the tag where you want that effect to end.

## Font style elements vs. phrase elements

**OBJECTIVE**
2.1.3: HTML text
formatting

The <b> and <strong> elements both create bold text. However, each element accomplishes this effect differently. The difference is that <b> specifically means apply the bold font style, whereas <strong> indicates that the text is to be given a strong appearance. In short, <b> represents a font appearance instruction, whereas <strong> represents the weighting of the phrase relative to surrounding text. The <b> element is called a font style element; <strong> is called a phrase element. The same is true of <i> and <em>, respectively, which both create italic or emphasized text.

HTML was originally created to describe the *function*, not *appearance*, of text. However, it has evolved into use as primarily an appearance-formatting language. XHTML was designed to improve upon this. Markup was and is viewed as a language that can describe more than text. Markup can also be used by speech-output systems. Outside of ancient rhetoric, there is no such thing as "bold" speech, but the term "strong" can be used both to denote bold text when printed and strongly spoken text when output through an audio device.

For printed output, you can use phrase and font elements interchangeably. However, if you are coding for the future (as you should be), you should consider how the markup might be used in a different context, then apply the most appropriate tag.

Table 3-1 lists text-level elements, their usage and their appearances.

Table 3-1: Text-level XHTML elements

| Element | Usage | Appearance |
|---|---|---|
| <b> | Font style element | **bold text** |
| <big> | Font style element | larger text |
| <cite> | Phrase element (for program sample output) | *italic text* |
| <code> | Phrase element (for program code examples) | `fixed-space font` |
| <dfn> | Phrase element (for word definitions) | normal text (or *italic* text in Internet Explorer) |
| <em> | Phrase element (for emphasis) | *italic text* |
| <i> | Font style element | *italic text* |
| <kbd> | Phrase element (for user text to be typed) | `fixed-space font` |
| <samp> | Phrase element (for program sample output) | `fixed-space font` |
| <small> | Font style element | smaller text |
| <strong> | Phrase element | **bold text** |
| <sub> | Font style element (for subscript) | smaller text lowered below the baseline, as in $H_2O$ |
| <sup> | Font style element (for superscript) | smaller text raised above the baseline, as in $E=MC^2$ |
| <strike> | Font style element | ~~strikethrough text~~ |
| <tt> | Font style element | `fixed-space font` |
| <u> | Font style element | underline |
| <var> | Phrase element (for variable text in program code) | *italic text* |

## The <code>, <kbd> and <samp> tags

Take special note of the <code>, <kbd> and <samp> tags. All of these tags can make text appear in a fixed-space font in an HTML 4.0-compliant browser window. They are available to both HTML 4.0 and XHTML.

In the following lab, you will use text-level XHTML tags to format text on a Web page. Suppose your project manager has asked you to add emphasis to certain phrases with formatting such as italic, bold and underlined type. You could perform these steps to add font-level elements to your Web page code.

## Lab 3-6: Using text-level formatting tags in XHTML

**OBJECTIVE**
2.1.3: HTML text formatting

In this lab, you will add text-level formatting tags to the file you worked with in previous labs.

1. **Editor:** Open **syb.html**.

2. **Editor:** In the first full paragraph, find the phrase "*Summer Youth Blitz*" and add the <em> tag as shown:

   **<em>**Summer Youth Blitz**</em>**

3. **Editor:** Save the file.

4. Review your work in a browser, and then validate it.

5. **Editor:** Find the phrase "*Campus Chapters and Youth Programs*" and surround it with the <u> tags as shown:

   **<u>**Campus Chapters and Youth Programs**</u>**

6. Find the phrase "*and are between the ages of 16 and 18 years old*," and add the <strong> tags as shown:

   **<strong>**and are between the ages of 16 and 18 years old**</strong>**,

7. Save your code and load it into a browser. Your page should resemble Figure 3-19.

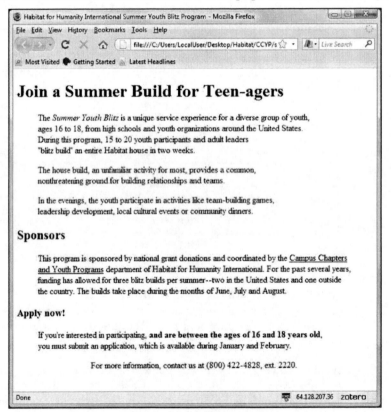

*Figure 3-19: After adding text-level formatting tags*

8. **When time permits:** Experiment with using the <code>, <kbd> and <samp> tags. Be sure to delete these tags when you are finished experimenting.

9. Close all browser and editor windows.

Now that you know how to use the text-level formatting tags, you will work with lists.

# Lists

A common markup function is to create bulleted and numbered lists. Lists are compound, block-level elements. Encompassed within list definition tags are individual list item tags. A paragraph break automatically precedes and follows the entire list. Individual list items are separated automatically by single line breaks.

There are two types of lists:

- **Ordered list** — a numbered list. Uses the <ol> element and requires a closing tag.

- **Unordered list** — a bulleted list. Uses the <ul> element and also requires a closing tag.

Both list types use identical syntax. Each list item is specified using the list item element:

- **List item** — specifies list items in an ordered or unordered list. Uses the <li> element; the closing </li> tag is optional in HTML. Remember that in XHTML you must close all tags.

Contrast the code in the left column of Table 3-2 and its resulting display in Figure 3-20, with the code in the right column of Table 3-2 and its resulting display in Figure 3-21.

Table 3-2: Ordered and unordered list syntax and display

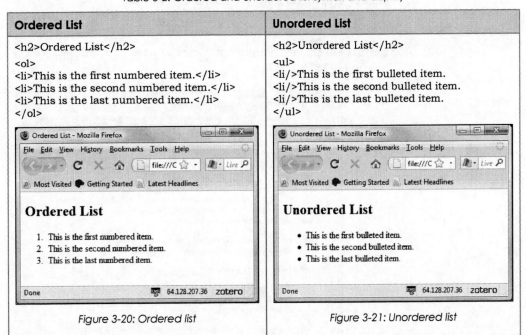

| Ordered List | Unordered List |
| --- | --- |
| <h2>Ordered List</h2><br><br><ol><br><li>This is the first numbered item.</li><br><li>This is the second numbered item.</li><br><li>This is the last numbered item.</li><br></ol> | <h2>Unordered List</h2><br><br><ul><br><li/>This is the first bulleted item.<br><li/>This is the second bulleted item.<br><li/>This is the last bulleted item.<br></ul> |
| *Figure 3-20: Ordered list* | *Figure 3-21: Unordered list* |

In the following lab, you will use XHTML to create bulleted and numbered lists. Suppose your supervisor has given you the following text to add to the Web page:

> "During the house build, you will: help lay the foundation, assist in framing the home, and do simple carpentry under supervision."

You can see that a list format would work well for this multi-point information. You can experiment with both an ordered and an unordered list. Which is most appropriate for the information?

## Lab 3-7: Creating lists with XHTML

**OBJECTIVE**
2.1.3: HTML text formatting

In this lab, you will create a bulleted list and a numbered list on a Web page.

1. **Editor:** Open **syb.html**.

2. Create empty space by adding a return immediately beneath the </p> tag located after the text that reads "*for building relationships and teams.*"

3. Add the text shown and format it as an unordered (bulleted) list. Make sure that the list (beginning with the <ul> tag) is not placed within a set of <p> tags:

```
<blockquote>
<p>
The house build, an unfamiliar activity for most, provides a common,
<br/>nonthreatening ground for building relationships and teams.
</p>
<p>During the house build, you will:</p>
<ul>
<li>Help lay the foundation. </li>
<li>Assist in framing the home. </li>
<li>Do simple carpentry, under supervision. </li>
</ul>
</blockquote>
```

4. **Editor:** Save your changes and view the page in a browser. Your page should resemble Figure 3-22.

*Figure 3-22: Adding bulleted list*

5. Validate your code at ***http://validator.w3.org***.

6.  Change your unordered list to an ordered list, then validate your code again. View the page with the ordered list in the browser. Do you think a numbered list format is more appropriate for this information than a bulleted list?

7.  Change your code back to an unordered list, then close all editors and browsers.

In this lab, you created ordered and unordered lists.

# Good Coding Practice

Now that you have learned the basics of working with HTML and XHTML tags, you should consider not simply which tags to use, but how to best use them in conjunction with your text.

## Forward compatibility

Remember that good coding practice involves writing code for forward-compatibility. That means that even if you are following an HTML standard for your code, for example, you can still apply some XHTML practices to make your code cleaner and allow an easier transition to updated standards in the future. Such practices include:

*   Closing all tags.

*   Using lowercase letters for tags.

*   Surrounding attribute values with quotation marks.

## Universal markup and consistency

OBJECTIVE
2.1.8: Using a single
W3C standard

As previously discussed, another facet of good coding practice is creating universal markup that applies W3C standards consistently and thus renders consistently across most or all browsers. Remember to choose one X/HTML standard for your Web document, pages or site, then apply that standard carefully and consistently throughout. Applying the syntax rules of multiple standards in the same document or site not only prevents your code from validating but also produces unexpected rendering results in your users' browsers.

Note that this point does not contradict the previous point about applying the stricter syntax rules of XHTML in your HTML documents for the purpose of forward-compatibility. Using stricter syntax than required will rarely produce output problems. Inconsistency is mostly an issue with the older HTML standards because their looser rules allowed some sloppier coding practices to render without penalty. Keep in mind that you should understand the requirements of whichever standard you are using, and be particularly aware of syntax and tag usage when using the strictest standards, such as HTML or XHTML Strict or Frameset flavors.

## Readability

If you are coding an HTML page and you are the only one who will ever look at the code, you may think the appearance of your code does not matter. This statement is basically true. But suppose you must share your work with others. Some coding techniques provide better readability, and make finding and changing code a simple operation. Other coding techniques produce a busy, confusing format that makes it difficult to decipher and edit the code.

Examine the two boxes of HTML code in Figure 3-23. Both sets of code will render the same in a browser, but clearly one set of markup is easier to read than the other. Suppose you were hiring someone to write HTML code for you. Would you be more inclined to hire the developer of the code on the left, or the developer of the code on the right? The code on the right is much more readable.

```
<html><head><title>Overview
</title></head><body><h1>
Looking Back</h1></body>
</html>
```

```
<html>
<head>
<title>Overview</title>
</head>
<body>
<h1>Looking Back</h1>
</body>
</html>
```

*Figure 3-23: Same HTML code with different line breaks*

## Exceptions

In some cases, you may find it impossible to make the code more readable without affecting the way it renders in the browser. With XHTML code involving images or the <div> tag, you may find that entering random white space can affect rendering in certain browsers. Always try to make your code readable, but verify that it renders properly.

## Adding hidden comments

OBJECTIVE
2.1.7: HTML code
comments

You can hide comments within your HTML source code that will not appear on the page. The syntax for including a comment within your HTML document is as follows:

```
<!-- comment text here -->
```

As you read earlier, you can comment out style sheet entries by placing any entry in between the /* and */ characters.

## When to use comments

When creating markup pages, you can use comments to:

- "Comment out" code to see how a page will appear without a particular markup element.

- Inform others about important elements in the code you are creating.

- Remind yourself why you inserted a particular piece of code.

- Insert programming code, such as JavaScript.

In the following lab, you will insert hidden comments into your XHTML code. Suppose your project has incurred a change and you have been asked to temporarily remove the bulleted list. You can use hidden comments to add notes to the file that document this change, and also make it easy to reverse it if necessary.

**Lab 3-8: Documenting and commenting XHTML code**

In this lab, you will document your XHTML code and "comment out" certain portions.

1. **Editor:** Open the **syb.html** file.

2. **Editor:** Comment out your bulleted list and the introduction to it using the <!-- and --> tags.

```
</p>
<!-- <p>During the house build, you will:</p>
<ul>
<li>Help lay the foundation. </li>
<li>Assist in framing the home.</li>
<li>Do simple carpentry, under supervision. </li>
</ul>

-->

</blockquote>
```

3. Save your changes and view your edited file in a browser. You will no longer see the bulleted list and its introduction.

4. Validate your code to ensure that you have used the comments properly. Sometimes adding comments can cause you to mistakenly omit closing tags and/or interrupt a nesting sequence.

5. Document the reason that you removed the bulleted list by creating another comment immediately after the bulleted list you just commented out:

```
<!-- Bulleted list removed at the request of supervisor, Jane Doe.-->
```

6. Near the bottom of the file, just above the </body> tag, document your code so that another developer can identify who wrote it. Insert your name, the date, and a statement that this code validates to XHTML 1.0 Transitional:

```
<!-- Your Name, Today's Date. This code validates to XHTML 1.0 Transitional -->
```

7. Validate your code again.

8. Review your code in the text editor. Make sure that it is easy to read in terms of good coding practice.

9. **If time permits:** Create additional comments explaining the code.

10. Close all editors and browsers.

In this lab, you documented and commented out portions of your markup.

## Case Study

# XHTML Convert

Vlad works as a developer on his company's Web team. He has been assigned to convert the Web site's code from HTML 4.0 to XHTML 1.0. He developed a conversion plan that included the following steps:

- Use a valid DTD for all pages.

- Ideally, use style sheets. If developers decide to use XHTML 1.0 Transitional, they do not necessarily need to use CSS, but it is recommended.

- Identify deprecated and forbidden tags already in use. Determine replacement tags and/or other methods of achieving the same effects using proper XHTML markup.

- Estimate the necessary time and resources to make these changes.

Vlad presented to his project manager an example of a converted page, a new style sheet, and an estimate for the time it would take to complete the conversion process. His project manager was able to obtain funding for the conversion.

\*     \*     \*

As a class, discuss the following questions.

- Suppose Vlad uses a GUI HTML editor. What changes and/or updates must he make?

- What DTD should Vlad choose if he wants the site to be XHTML-compliant as quickly as possible?

- Considering that Vlad must identify and change deprecated tags, should he add time to the project?

## Lesson Summary

### Application project

You have already learned many of the basic tags that XHTML provides for formatting text and paragraphs. In the lessons that follow, you will learn how to incorporate graphics, create links, work with tables and create XHTML forms. Now, consider the following:

- What is the difference between a container element and an empty element? Consider that a container element must contain the text that it formats between opening and closing tags.

- Review all the HTML code you have created. Verify that it adheres to the good coding practices discussed in this lesson. If not, modify your code as necessary and save the files. As your Web site becomes more complicated throughout this course, you will be able to quickly locate code for modification within your files.

### Skills review

In this lesson, you learned to use container and stand-alone HTML and XHTML tags. You learned the basic structure tags that must be present in any XHTML document. You learned how to format both text and paragraphs, and you learned how to use the <pre> tag. You also created a bulleted list and a numbered list. Finally, you were introduced to the concept of good coding practice, and the importance of correct application and sequence of your code.

Now that you have completed this lesson, you should be able to:

✓  2.1.3: Use HTML tags to format paragraphs and text.

✓  2.1.7: Add comments to HTML code and document page/site creation.

✓  2.1.8: Explain the importance of consistently developing to a single W3C standard (e.g., XHTML 1.0 Transitional).

✓  2.7.4: Validate Web page design according to technical and audience standards adopted by employers.

✓  2.8.2: Identify ways to apply styles with CSS.

✓  2.9.1: Define the three flavors of the XHTML standard (Strict, Transitional, Frameset).

✓  2.9.2: Create a Web page using the XHTML 1.0 standards.

✓  2.12.1: Test and validate Web documents.

# Lesson 3 Review

1.  Markup tags include container, empty and stand-alone non-empty tags. Which tag types are valid in XHTML?

    _____

    _____

2.  Are HTML and XHTML tags case-sensitive?

    _____

    _____

3.  What three items can be contained inside the angle brackets (wickets) of an HTML tag?

    _____

    _____

4.  What is the function of the document type declaration or <!DOCTYPE> tag?

    _____

    _____

5.  Define text-level element.

    _____

    _____

6.  What notation can you use to write a note to yourself or others in the HTML code that will not appear in the page when rendered in a browser?

    _____

    _____

7.  Should all values be placed in quotation marks for XHTML? For HTML?

    _____

    _____

# Lesson 4:
# Horizontal Rules and Graphical Elements

## Objectives

By the end of this lesson, you will be able to:

- 2.2.1: Incorporate graphical images into HTML pages.

- 2.2.2: Distinguish among and identify the uses and benefits of various graphic file formats, including GIF, GIF89a, JPEG, PNG, TIFF, BMP.

- 2.2.3: Add lines, colors and tiled background images to HTML pages.

- 2.2.6: Insert horizontal rules into Web pages.

- 2.3.1: Define the browser-safe color palette.

- 2.3.2: Identify ways that color affects the principles of line, value, shape and form in Web pages.

- 2.3.3: Identify and demonstrate the impact of color combinations to various audiences and cultures.

- 2.3.4: Evaluate Web page design and layout.

- 2.8.1: Explain how to structure Web documents with CSS.

- 2.21.1: Use CSS and the <div> tag to create layers.

- 2.21.2: Distinguish between fixed-width and liquid design layouts.

# Pre-Assessment Questions

1. Name the three standard image file formats supported across the Web.

   _____

   _____

2. Define hexadecimal color values. Why would you use a hexadecimal value instead of the name of a color?

   _____

   _____

   _____

   _____

3. Which attribute determines the image that will be tiled behind the contents of a page?

   a.  The bgcolor attribute of the <html> tag
   b.  The text attribute of the <img> tag
   c.  The background attribute of the <body> tag
   d.  The img attribute of the <background> tag

# Horizontal Rules in XHTML

Several simple graphical elements can be added to a Web page to provide structure and visual interest. One such element is the horizontal rule, which is easy to add in HTML or XHTML. To add a horizontal rule to your page, insert the <hr> tag at the position where you want the line to appear. In HTML, <hr> is an empty tag, requiring no closing tag. XHTML requires you to close the tag, either using the container tag syntax <hr> </hr> or the alternative stand-alone non-empty tag <hr/>.

Horizontal rules do not appear as distinctly on a white background as they do on a colored or textured background. You will learn how to change the page background later in this lesson.

**OBJECTIVE**
2.2.3: Lines, colors and backgrounds

2.2.6: Horizontal rules

Consider the following code:

```
<h1>Horizontal Rules</h1>
<hr/>
Horizontal rules: Lines used to make visual divisions in your document.
```

This code will render in a browser as shown in Figure 4-1.

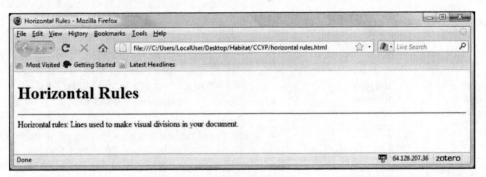

*Figure 4-1: Page displaying horizontal rule*

By default, these lines include a 3-D shading effect, which can be removed. In addition, the lines can be set to various sizes, widths and alignments. Because the line is added by a single tag, <hr>, how is this other information passed to the browser?

## Horizontal rule attributes

In the previous lesson, you learned about the three components of a tag: an element, attributes and values. You also learned about the <div> element's associated attributes and values. The <hr> element has a *width* attribute that controls how far the line extends across the screen. By default, the value of the *width* attribute is 100 percent. Thus the line in the preceding figure extends from the left margin across to the right margin in the browser window, or the entire width of the window. If you want the line to extend across only 50 percent of the window, you would write the tag as follows:

```
<hr width="50%"/>
```

Note that the attribute name (in this case, *width*) precedes an equal sign (=). Following the equal sign is the desired value for this attribute, in this case "50%". The value must always be enclosed in quotation marks.

You are already familiar with the *align* attribute from your work with the <div> element. You can use the *align* attribute with the <hr> element as well. For example, to create a line starting at the left margin that extends halfway across the page, you could use either of the following two tags:

```
<hr width="50%" align="left"/>
<hr align="left" width="50%"/>
```

The element name must always be the first text in the tag. The order in which the attributes appear is not dictated. However, you cannot reverse the attribute and value; the attribute must always precede the equal sign and value, and the value must always appear in quotes.

Table 4-1 lists the attributes and accepted values for the <hr> element.

*Table 4-1: Horizontal rule (<hr>) attributes*

| Attribute Name | Accepted Values |
|---|---|
| **align** | The *align* attribute takes three values:<br>• - "left"<br>• - "right"<br>• - "center"<br>If no alignment is specified, the default value for this attribute is center. |
| **size** | The *size* attribute can be specified in terms of pixels, which are very small units of the screen. Pixels are not an absolute measurement, but are relative to the display resolution. When specifying pixels, you need only specify a numeral value. |
| **width** | The *width* attribute can be specified in terms of:<br>• - Percentage of the window width.<br>• - Pixels.<br>• When specifying a percentage, you must include the percent ( % ) symbol after the numeral value.<br>• When specifying pixels, you need only specify a numeral value. |
| **noshade** | The *noshade* attribute takes two values:<br>- "true" (the rule renders as a solid color)<br>- "false" (the rule renders in two colors)<br>This attribute has been deprecated and will not validate in XHTML. Use style sheets instead. |

In the following lab, you will add horizontal rules to a Web page. Suppose your project manager suggests that the syb.html page could use a visual separation or graphic of some sort between the page content and the contact information at the bottom. You can add a horizontal rule to serve this purpose.

 **Lab 4-1: Assigning attribute values to the <hr> tag in XHTML**

In this lab, you will learn how to assign and change the values of attributes in the <hr> tag.

1. **Editor:** Open the version of **syb.html** you edited in the previous lesson's labs.

   *Note: If necessary, go to the **C:\CIW\Site_Dev\Lab Files\Lesson03\Finished** folder and use the **lab_3-8_syb.html** file.*

2. **Editor:** Enter the following code, just above the "*For more information . . .*" line near the bottom of the page:

   `<hr/>`

3. **Editor:** Save your changes.

4. **Browser:** Load **syb.html**. You will see a horizontal line appear in the document.

5. Edit the <hr> tag you have inserted so that the line is 5 pixels in size, 800 pixels wide, and centered. When you are finished, a horizontal line will appear, as shown in Figure 4-2.

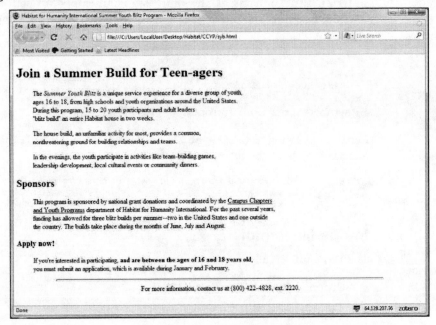

*Figure 4-2: Customizing the <hr/> tag*

6. Visit the W3C MarkUp Validation Service at ***http://validator.w3.org*** and validate your code.

In this lab, you inserted and customized a horizontal line in your XHTML page.

Many Web authors choose to insert images and bars instead of using HTML horizontal lines. Remember that XHTML and HTML can define function as well as appearance. You may have a reason to choose the <hr> element in the future because it may designate some contextual meaning.

# Images in Web Pages

**OBJECTIVE**
2.2.1: Images

2.2.3: Lines, colors and backgrounds

You may have heard the saying that a picture is worth a thousand words. Most Web pages incorporate graphical images in their designs. Images add interest to a page, but they provide more than just aesthetics. Images are memorable and can be used to create a mood, emphasize a point or sell a product.

Images can be big or small; they can function as links; they can be used to launch script actions; and they can be used as image maps. Although scripting is not discussed in this course, you will be introduced to clickable image maps in a later lesson. In this lesson, you will focus on using images purely as graphical enhancements.

*When chosen carefully, images can greatly enhance your pages. However, too many images can slow page loading, waste costly online time, and even displease users by making the page look too cluttered. Be creative but sparing in your use of images.*

The <img> tag displays a graphical image on your page. The key attribute that is required in this tag is *src* (abbreviation for source). You use the *src* attribute to specify the name and, if necessary, the location of your image file.

In HTML 4.01 Transitional, the <img> tag is an empty tag, so it requires no closing tag. In XHTML, however, you must close the tag. You can close the <img> tag in either of two ways in XHTML:

```
<img src="imagefile.gif"> </img>

<img src="imagefile.gif"/>
```

Either syntax will render properly in a browser.

For the <img> tag to validate as XHTML, it must also include the *alt* attribute. You will learn more about the *alt* attribute shortly.

*If you upload your Web pages to a Web server and the images do not appear, check the <img src=" "> value of each image. If you created all of your images in a separate directory, make sure you uploaded that directory as well.*

## Image file formats

OBJECTIVE
2.2.2: Graphic file formats

The three universally supported Web image formats are:

• Graphics Interchange Format (GIF).

• Joint Photographic Experts Group (JPEG).

• Portable Network Graphics (PNG).

Microsoft Internet Explorer and Mozilla Firefox also support the display of Windows Bitmap (BMP) images when used in HTML documents.

### JPEG

The Joint Photographic Experts Group (JPEG) format supports literally millions of colors, and is typically used for photographs and complex images. If you want the highest image quality, generally you would use a JPEG file.

This format also supports compression, meaning that you can reduce the image's file size. However, the more an image is compressed, the more its quality is reduced. For this reason, standard JPEG image compression is called "lossy" compression. JPEG compression is copyrighted in many countries. As a result, applications that use JPEG and other copyrighted materials may cost more or have limitations placed on them.

A newer JPEG format, called JPEG 2000, supports lossless compression. To learn more about the JPEG format, visit The JPEG Committee home page (*www.jpeg.org*) and the Independent JPEG Group home page (*www.ijg.org*).

### GIF

Graphics Interchange Format (GIF) files support 256 colors, rather than the millions of colors available to JPEG images. GIFs are best suited for line art, custom drawings and navigational images. GIF has two versions:

- GIF 87a

- GIF 89a

GIF 89a is more popular because it supports the following techniques:

- **Transparency** — the ability to make any part of the image invisible so the page background shows through. The image thus appears to blend into the background.

- **Interlacing** — the ability for an image to render gradually as it downloads.

- **Animation** — a series of images appearing in sequence to create the effect of motion.

GIF and its compression format are also copyrighted in many countries, making it somewhat controversial. You will learn more about animation, transparency and interlacing later in the course.

### PNG

Portable Network Graphics (PNG) has emerged as a standard format and is now widely implemented. The PNG format was developed using open standards, which means that it does not have the same legal liabilities as other formats (e.g., GIF). However, older browsers do not render the PNG format. PNG images provide the following features:

- **Transparency** — similar to GIF 89a.

- **Interlacing** — similar to GIF 89a.

- **Compression** — lossless, unlike standard JPEG compression. Also, the compression used in the PNG format is not copyrighted, which has helped ensure developer and user agent vendor support.

- **Animation** —less popular than animated GIF, but gaining attention.

You can learn more about the PNG format at LibPNG.org (*www.libpng.org*), the free reference library for PNG images. Table 4-2 provides a summary of the features provided by the three common image formats.

*Table 4-2: Features common to major image file formats*

| Format | Transparency | Interlacing | Compression | Animation |
|---|---|---|---|---|
| GIF 89a | Yes | Yes | Yes | Yes |
| JPEG (standard) | No | No | Yes | No |
| PNG | Yes | Yes | Yes | Yes |

 If you spend time browsing images on the Internet, you may be tempted to use graphics created by others in your Web pages. Be aware that any content — text, sound files or images — is the sole property of the original owner. You may be subject to penalties under copyright laws if you use someone else's creation without express, written permission.

## Using the *alt* attribute with images

Every image used in XHTML must follow good coding practice by containing the *alt* attribute with a corresponding value. The *alt* attribute specifies alternative text to appear while the graphic is loading, or in place of the graphic in non-graphical browsers such as Lynx. This alternative text will also display if the image fails to load or if the user has configured his or her browser not to display images. HTML 4.01 code does not require the *alt* attribute, but it is good coding practice to include it so that your code is forward-compatible.

The syntax for using the *alt* attribute is as follows:

```
<img src="image.gif" alt="This text should describe the image."/>
```

Notice that this tag is closed using the XHTML non-empty tag format. Any other use of the <img> tag will not validate as XHTML.

**Tech Tip**  *Search engines will rank a page higher in a search engine results page if it consistently uses the alt attribute effectively. Remember to include a short but useful description of every image.*

## Combining background images and background colors

You can specify both an image and a color for the background in a Web page. In fact, it can be advantageous to specify both, in case a background image becomes unavailable for some reason.

If you use the *bgcolor* and *background* attributes in the same <body> tag, then only the attribute given last in the tag will be rendered. If you use a style sheet and specify both image and color as a background, then the background image will always render first. If the image cannot be found, a background color will then appear. All values specified in style sheets will override anything specified in the HTML or XHTML itself.

In the following lab, you will incorporate images in a Web page. Suppose the marketing team and another member of your Web development team have collaborated to create an image for your Web site. You have been asked to insert the image into a page you have developed, and you have been given the same image in the three standard file formats. You must choose an image format and insert it in the appropriate location on the page.

**Lab 4-2: Incorporating images in an XHTML page**

In this lab, you will learn how to place and align an image relative to text in a Web page.

1.  Navigate to the **C:\CIW\Site_Dev\Lab Files\Lesson04\Lab_4-2\** directory, and copy the following files to the **Habitat\CCYP\Syb\** directory:

    **SYBcollage2.gif**
    **SYBcollage2.jpg**
    **SYBcollage2.png**

2.  Open the **Habitat\CCYP\Syb\** directory, and view each image by double-clicking on it. See if you notice any difference among the three image formats.

3.  Right-click each image and select **Properties**. What is the file size of each image type (GIF, JPEG and PNG)?

4.  As a class, discuss the following points about these image formats:

    •   The larger the image file size, the longer it takes users to download.

    •   Older browsers may not be able to render PNG images.

    •   GIF and PNG images can be interlaced, animated or made transparent. Standard JPEG images do not support these features.

    •   JPEG images offer the highest image quality.

    •   PNG and standard JPEG images can be compressed; however, the higher the compression, the lower the image quality.

5.  Now you will insert an image into your Web page. Open **syb.html** in a text editor.

6.  Insert the SYBcollage2.png image by entering the code indicated in bold:

```
<blockquote>
<img src="syb/SYBcollage2.png" alt="Join a summer build!"/>
</blockquote>
<h1>Join a Summer Build for Teen-agers</h1>
```

*Note: The code you typed inserted a file from the Syb\ subfolder. You will learn more about how to specify files in other directories later in this lesson.*

7.  Load your edited page into a browser. You should see the image shown in Figure 4-3.

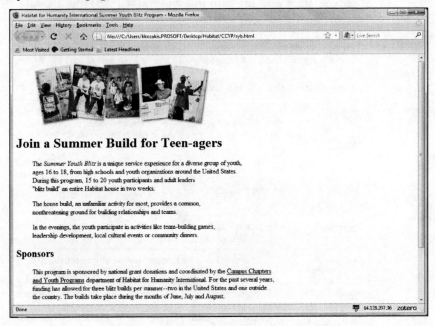

*Figure 4-3: Page syb.html after adding image*

8.  Validate your code.

9.  Delete the code *alt="Join a summer build!"*. Now revalidate your code. What were the results, and why? How does validated XHTML help users with disabilities?

_____

_____

10. Reinsert the code **alt="*Join a summer build!*"** where it was.

11. Comment out the **<blockquote>** tags that encompass the <img> tag using the **<!-- ... -->** comment tags.

12. Create a new line that inserts and centers the JPEG image using the <div> tags as follows:

```
<div align="center">
<img src="syb/SYBcollage2.jpg" alt="Join a summer build!"/>
</div>
```

13. Experiment by aligning the image to the right, then to the left. Be sure to view it in the browser each time to see the differences.

14. When you are finished experimenting, comment out the **<div>** tags, and remove the comment notation from the **<blockquote>** tags around <img>. You code should now render as shown in the previous figure.

In this lab, you added image files to a Web page. You used the required *alt* attribute, and you experimented with image placement using the <blockquote> and <div> tags.

OBJECTIVE
2.2.1: Images

2.2.3: Lines, colors and backgrounds

## Aligning images relative to text

After you start working with images, you will see that placing an image on your page is only the first step. You must know how to position images relative to text on a page. The syntax for the *align* attribute is as follows:

```
<img src="imagefile.gif" align="alignment value"/>
```

Table 4-3 lists the values that you can use with the *align* attribute in the <img> tag.

 The align attribute to <img> has been deprecated for XHTML. It is recommended that you use style sheets instead. The CIW Site Designer course teaches you to do this, as well as to create advanced style sheets.

Table 4-3: Values for align attribute in <img> tag

| Attribute Value for *align* | Description |
|---|---|
| "bottom" | The default alignment. The bottom of the image is aligned with the baseline of adjoining text. |
| "middle" | A vertical — not horizontal — alignment option. This value aligns the middle of the image to the baseline of adjoining text. |
| "top" | Aligns the top of the image with the top of adjoining text. |
| "left" | Floats the image to the left of the text paragraph into which the <img> tag is inserted. The top of the image will align with the left and top of the adjoining text. |
| "right" | Floats the image to the right of the text paragraph into which the <img> tag is inserted. The top of the image will align with the right and top of the adjoining text. |

Additional <img> attributes include:

- *hspace* — aligns the image horizontally, moving it to the right

- *vspace* — aligns the image vertically, moving it down from the top

- *height* — resizes the image's original height dimension

- *width* — resizes the image's original width dimension

In the following lab, you will use <img> tag attributes to align images relative to text on your Web page. Suppose your project manager has notified you that several images will be incorporated into a Web page you are developing. You will need to experiment with aligning the images and text. Proper alignment of page components in relation to each other are an important part of Web design that can greatly improve — or degrade — a page's appearance and effectiveness.

 **Lab 4-3: Aligning images relative to text with XHTML**

In this lab, you will learn additional <img> tag attributes that will help you align your images relative to nearby text.

1. **Editor:** Open **syb.html**.

2. Find the <img> tag and edit it as follows so that it aligns to the right of the text:

```
<blockquote>
<img src="syb/SYBcollage2.png" alt="Join a summer build!" align="right"/>
</blockquote>
```

3. View your page in a browser. It should resemble Figure 4-4.

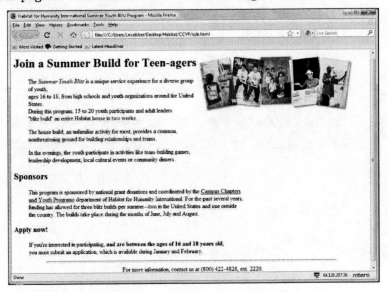

*Figure 4-4: Aligning image to right of text*

4. Change your code so that the image aligns to the left and the text wraps to its right. Then change it so the text wraps to the top of the image, then again so text wraps to the middle of the image. Be sure to view the page each time in your browser, and note the differences.

5.  Use both the "middle" value and the "top" value with the *align* attribute. Notice that the *align* attribute values "top" and "middle" produce the same effect.

6.  Now, use the *hspace* attribute as shown:

```
<blockquote>
<img src="syb/SYBcollage2.png" alt="Join a summer build!" align="middle"
hspace="20"/>
</blockquote>
```

7.  Refresh your browser. Notice that the image moves to the right. Experiment with a larger value, such as **"60"**, **"100"** or **"200"**.

    *Note: These values may seem large, and will probably make the image seem out of place. Simply experiment with these values. Remember that a pixel is a very small unit of measurement. The number of pixels per inch is determined by the monitor's screen resolution.*

8.  When you are finished experimenting, change the *hspace* value back to **"20"**.

9.  Add the **vspace** attribute, and assign it a value of **"20"**. Notice that the image appears 20 pixels lower on the screen.

10. Validate your code.

    This lab provides a good introduction to various issues of alignment. The <br> element provides a special attribute called *clear* that you can use to force text to clear an image, so that a line of text starts below the image. The syntax is as follows, where the value is either "left", "right" or "all":

    ```
    <br clear="right"/>
    ```

    This code causes the text following the break to clear the image at the right margin. To clear an image at the left margin, use the "left" value. To clear images at both margins and to force text to the next line below the image, use the "all" value.

11. **Editor:** Finish this lab by adding a break in the text below the image as follows:

    ```
    <br clear="all"/>
    ```

12. View your page in at least one browser, then validate your code.

In this lab, you learned to position images in relation to text with XHTML.

### Resizing images

At times, you will want to use an image in a size other than its natural size. If you need to resize an image, you must maintain its relative measurements. For example, if you have an image that is 200 pixels wide by 300 pixels tall, you probably would not want to change the size to be 100 pixels wide by 300 pixels tall because this would distort the image, making it appear taller and narrower than it was originally. If you were trying to shrink this image to one-half its size, you would instead change the width to 100 and the height to 150. By shrinking both dimensions by an equal percentage (in this case, by 50 percent), you maintain the original ratio of the image.

The syntax for specifying image height and width information is as follows:

```
<img src="imagename.gif" height="HeightInPixels" width="WidthInPixels"/>
```

If you are not certain of the original dimensions of your image, you can ensure that the size will be changed proportionately by specifying either the height or the width; the other measurement will then be calculated proportionately for you based on the original image size.

## Special Characters

Occasionally, you will need to include a non-keyboard character in your Web page. For example, mathematics professors who use XHTML pages to show math problems may want to use the "less than" (<) and "greater than" signs (>). And most companies use the © and ® symbols to indicate their copyrights and trademarks on their Web sites.

You can include non-keyboard characters in Web pages by using either the ANSI character value or the special HTML code for the character. These special character values can be read by HTML interpreters, which cannot otherwise recognize non-keyboard characters. The HTML code combination, called the escape sequence, consists of the ampersand ( & ), followed by a code for the specific character you want to generate on the page, followed by a semicolon ( ; ). For example, to generate the "less than" symbol on a Web page, you would use the following special character code as text on your HTML page:

```
&lt;
```

Using the escape sequence is also called "escaping" because it does not allow the browser's HTML interpreter to read the characters as literal text or HTML commands. In the Resources directory of your supplemental CD-ROM, the file named charcodes.html provides a list of codes for special characters. Table 4-4 defines some of the most commonly used special characters. As you can see, each special character code begins with the ampersand and ends with the semicolon character.

Table 4-4: HTML/XHTML special character codes

| Character | Description | Code |
|---|---|---|
| © | Copyright symbol | `&copy;`<br>or<br>`&#169;` |
| ® | Registered trademark symbol | `&reg;`<br>or<br>`&#174;` |
| é | Acute accent (over letter e) | `&eacute;`<br><br>To create an acute accent over another character, such as o, enter:<br>`&oacute;` |
| < | Less-than symbol | `&lt;` |
| > | Greater-than symbol | `&gt;` |
| & | Ampersand ("and") | `&amp;`<br>or<br>`&#38;` |
| £ | Pound sterling sign | `&#163;` |
| ü | Umlaut (over letter u) | `&uuml;`<br><br>To create an umlaut over another character, such as i, enter:<br>`&iuml;` |
| ñ | Tilde (over letter n) | `&ntilde;`<br><br>To create a tilde over another character, such as o, enter:<br>`&otilde;` |
| " | Quotation marks | `&quot;` |
| @ | At symbol | `&#64;` |
| Non-breaking space | Inserts an extra space. Often used to create indentations in a paragraph, or create additional spaces between words. | ` ` |

Visit *www.w3.org/TR/REC-html40/charset.html#h-5.3.2* to learn more about special character references. For a list of additional special characters, visit *www.w3.org/MarkUp/html-spec/html-spec_13.html*.

## Non-breaking spaces

You will often see * * in HTML and XHTML code, especially in code created by GUI-based Web authoring applications. The HTML special character code for a non-breaking space can be used to insert more than one space in succession when needed. You will find this character to be useful because more than one successive space is ignored in HTML. However, a non-breaking space is never ignored. The following code ensures an indentation before the line "This begins an indented paragraph":

```
<p>
      This begins an indented paragraph.
</p>
```

Use non-breaking spaces sparingly. For more information about all special characters, visit *www.w3.org/TR/REC-html40/sgml/entities.html*.

In the following lab, you will create a symbol on a Web page using HTML special character code. Suppose your project manager mentions that the Web page you will post to the public contains original text and images that could be subject to copyright infringement. You can use HTML special character code to add a copyright statement to your page.

## Lab 4-4: Adding a copyright statement with HTML special characters

In this lab, you will add a copyright statement to your page using the HTML special character code to create the copyright symbol.

1. **Editor:** Open **syb.html**.

2. Insert the following statement at the bottom of the page, just above the </body> tag:

```
<p/>
<div align="center">&copy; 2009 Habitat for Humanity International</div>
```

3. Save your changes, then view your page in a browser. You will see the copyright symbol at the bottom of the page, as shown in Figure 4-5.

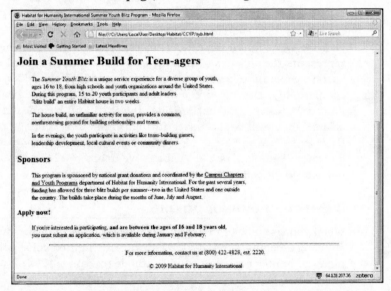

*Figure 4-5: Adding copyright symbol to a Web page*

4. Validate your code, and test it in multiple browsers.

In this lab, you added a copyright statement using HTML special character code.

# Specifying Colors

**OBJECTIVE**
2.2.3: Lines, colors
and backgrounds

**hexadecimal**
A base-16 number
system that allows
large numbers to be
displayed by fewer
characters than if
the number were
displayed in the
regular base-10
system. In
hexadecimal, the
number 10 is
represented as the
letter A, 15 is
represented as F,
and 16 is
represented as 10..

You have learned that you can specify colors for the page background in HTML, XHTML and CSS documents. In the previous examples, you used words for values, such as "teal" and "tan". Alternatively, you can also use a **hexadecimal** code to specify color values.

Colors are often specified in terms of their RGB values. RGB stands for Red Green Blue. You may know that if you were mixing paint, the mixture of red, green and blue together creates a rather muddy color. But on a monitor screen, you are mixing light, and the mixture of red, green and blue light produces white, which is the presence of all colors. Black is the absence of all colors. In RGB code, the higher the numeric value representing a color, the lighter that color will be. The lower the value, the darker the color. Figure 4-6 demonstrates the composition of a hexadecimal color code.

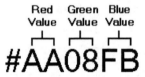

Red     Green   Blue
Value   Value   Value

**#AA08FB**

*Figure 4-6: Red hex value + green hex value + blue hex value = hexadecimal color code*

Colors are specified in RGB values ranging from 0 to 255. The hexadecimal value FF represents 255. Therefore, the hexadecimal value #FFFFFF represents the highest possible value for all three RGB colors, producing white. The hexadecimal value #000000 represents the absence of all colors, or black. The number symbol ( # ) is not required by current generation browsers, but you should include this symbol for full backward-compatibility. The Resources directory from your supplemental CD-ROM contains a file named 216color.html that provides the RGB and hexadecimal codes for browser-safe colors, which will be discussed further in the next section. You can also visit the Browser-Safe Web Palette page at *www.lynda.com/resources/webpalette.aspx* (provided by Lynda Weinman) or the Visibone Webmaster's Color Laboratory at *www.visibone.com/colorlab* (provided by Bob Stein).

## Browser-safe color palette

**OBJECTIVE**
2.3.1: Browser-safe
color palette

**dithering**
The ability for a
computer to
approximate a
color by combining
the RGB values.

**inline images**
Images rendered in
a Web page.

When you use a color in a Web page (whether for a background, font or image), you are enabling a combination of RGB values. This limited color palette is necessary because many computer screens are still cathode ray tubes (CRTs), which have certain limitations. Liquid crystal display (LCD) screens also have similar limitations.

You will want your pages to render consistently no matter which browser or operating system is used to view them. In other words, if you define a blue background color, you will want it to appear the same in a Macintosh system using a version of Mozilla Firefox as it would in a Windows system using a version of Microsoft Internet Explorer. You also want your image colors to appear consistently. If your HTML code asks for a color that the browser or operating system cannot support, the computer will compensate through **dithering**. The results of dithering are unpredictable and often unattractive.

When Netscape Corporation marketed the first browser that supported **inline images**, it created a standard of 216 colors that would render consistently, known as the browser-safe color palette. Microsoft Internet Explorer, NCSA Mosaic and other browsers conform to this list of colors.

*Sometimes the browser-safe color palette is called the Web-safe color palette.*

As mentioned earlier, the file in your Resources directory named 216color.html contains a list of the 216 colors in the browser-safe palette. To further ensure cross-browser capability, you can specify colors in hexadecimal format, rather than by name.

# Page Colors and Backgrounds

**OBJECTIVE**
2.2.3: Lines, colors and backgrounds

2.3.2: Color vs. line, value, shape and form

As you already learned briefly, you can add color information to the <body> tag in an HTML page to control the colors of the page background, as well as the colors of the text and links on the page. In addition, you can tile an image across the page for a background.

To specify a color for a page background, add the *bgcolor* attribute to the <body> element using the following syntax:

```
<body bgcolor="colorNameOrCode">
```

If you set the *bgcolor* attribute to the hexadecimal value given in an earlier example (#AA08FB), the background color of the page will be bright purple.

To designate the color of text on a page, use the *text* attribute of the <body> element. In the next lesson, you will learn how to create hyperlinks. If you are using links, you can control the colors of links from the <body> tag as well. Table 4-5 describes the <body> tag color attributes.

Table 4-5: Color attributes to <body> tag

| Attribute | Sample Values | Description |
|---|---|---|
| *bgcolor* | "#FF0000"<br>"FF0000"<br>"red" | Determines the background color of the page |
| *text* | "#00FF00"<br>"00FF00"<br>"green" | Determines the color of non-link text on the page |
| *alink* | "#0000FF"<br>"0000FF"<br>"blue" | Determines the color of the link when the mouse is pressed but not released over the link |
| *link* | "#FFFFFF"<br>"FFFFFF"<br>"white" | Determines the color of unvisited links |
| *vlink* | "#000000"<br>"000000"<br>"black" | Determines the color of visited links |
| *background* | "backgrnd.png"<br>"tiledimage.jpg" | Determines the image that will be tiled behind the page content as a background for the page |

*If the background and bgcolor attributes are both used, the background attribute will take precedence and the bgcolor attribute will be ignored.*

In the following lab, you will change Web page colors and backgrounds. Suppose your project manager has asked you to experiment with color combinations for your Web site's pages, text and links. She has also given you an image to use as a page background. Which background will work better for the Web page? And should you specify colors using color names or hexadecimal codes?

# Lab 4-5: Changing page colors and backgrounds with XHTML

In this lab, you will use hexadecimal code to specify Web page colors. You will also use an image for a page background.

1. **Editor:** Open **syb.html**.

2. **Editor:** Add the following attribute and value to the <body> tag:

   **bgcolor="#CCCCCC"**

3. View the page in a browser. You will see that the background is gray.

4. Edit the <body> tag to add the *text* attribute as shown:

   bgcolor="#CCCCCC" **text="#0099FF"**

5. Load your page into the browser again. Notice that the text color has changed.

   *Note: Remember that it is considered best practice to use style sheets for this purpose instead of the bgcolor attribute.*

6. Delete the ***bgcolor*** and ***text*** attributes from the **<body>** tag.

7. In the Syb\ subfolder, open **syb.css**, then save it into the **Syb\** subfolder as **Lab_4-5_stylesheet.css**.

8. In the file **Lab_4-5_stylesheet.css**, make the following changes to the body line of the code:

   font-family: arial, verdana, helvetica; color: #0099FF; font-size: 10pt; background: #CCCCCC;

9. Save and close **Lab_4-5_stylesheet.css**.

10. **Editor:** Open **syb.html**. Enter the following style sheet reference to include a link to the style sheet Syb\Lab_4-5_stylesheet.css:

    <link rel="stylesheet" type="text/css" href="Syb/Lab_4-5_stylesheet.css" title="stylesheet"/>

11. Refresh your browser. The page should appear the same (a gray background with light blue text). Validate this code.

12. Now, comment out this linked style sheet so that the document uses the default white background and black Times fonts.

13. Go to **C:\CIW\Site_Dev\Lab Files\Lesson04\Lab_4-5\** directory, and copy the file **background.jpg** to the **Syb** subfolder you have been using.

14. Now add this image as a background image by editing the <body> tag as follows:

    <body background="syb/background.jpg">

15. Refresh your browser. Your page will now have a purple background, due to the JPEG image you just inserted.

16. Remove the purple background image (background.jpg) so that your document's background is white.

17. When your page renders as expected, validate it at ***http://validator.w3.org***.

In this lab, you used hexadecimal color values and inserted a background image using XHTML.

# Specifying Font Information

The <font> tag is a container tag that allows you to change the size, color and typeface of the enclosed text. The <font> tag supports three attributes:

- *size* — takes values "1" through "7", with 7 being largest, 3 being the normal size of default text, and 1 being two sizes smaller than normal. In addition, you can set the value of the <font> tag's *size* attribute to "+1", "-2" and so forth to make changes relative to the font's default size.

- *color* — uses the same values that you learned for specifying a page background color.

- *face* — specifies the typeface (i.e., font name) to be used.

Remember to always close your <font> tag with </font> at the end of the text to be affected.

 *If you specify a font that is not available on all systems, some users will not see the font face you chose. Instead, the font will display as a default font face. Be aware of this when planning your pages.*

Both XHTML 1.0 and HTML 4.01 have deprecated the <font> tag in favor of using CSS to format fonts. This means that future versions of XHTML — and Web browsers — may not support <font>. However, this tag is still quite popular.

Many professionals prefer not to use the <font> tag because it has been deprecated. Also, it sometimes renders in unexpected ways in the browser. Nevertheless, you should know how to use the <font> tag. Many GUI editors still use this tag as well.

In the following lab, you will format text on a Web page. Suppose your Web team agrees that you should experiment with one of the site pages to see if a different font style would work well. You can use the <font> tag to try some different font formatting styles.

 **Lab 4-6: Formatting text with the <font> tag**

In this lab, you will learn how to change the font style of text using the HTML <font> tag.

1. **Editor:** Open **syb.html**.

2. Comment out the <h1> tag, and replace it with a <font> tag entry as shown:

   ```
   <!-- <h1>Join a Summer Build for Teen-agers</h1> -->
   <font size="7">Join a Summer Build for Teen-agers</font>
   ```

3. Comment out the <h2> tag and replace it with a **<font>** tag that has a ***size*** attribute value of **"6"**.

4. Replace the <h3> tag with a **<font>** tag that has a ***size*** attribute value of "5". When you are finished, your page should resemble Figure 4-7.

*Note: When you tagged text to appear as a heading level 1 element, the text became larger and bold. The same is not true when you increase size using the <font> tag.*

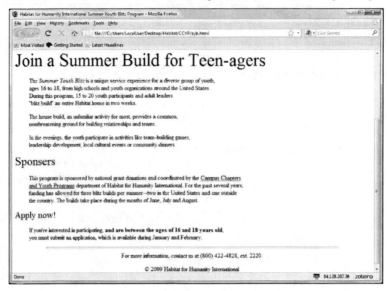

*Figure 4-7: Replacing heading tags with <font> tags*

**5.** Edit the first <font> tag, adding the *color* attribute to make the font purple, and adding the *face* attribute to use the Arial font face, as follows:

```
<font size="7" color="#993399" face="arial">
```

*Note: You can use the word "purple" instead of the hexadecimal value for the font color.*

**6.** When your page renders as expected, validate your code at ***http://validator.w3.org***.

In this lab, you used the <font> tag to format Web page text.

As you have learned, you can specify certain font information for a Web page by using the <font> tag. However, some formats such as boldface and italic type cannot be specified using the <font> tag.

With practice, you can embellish your HTML pages quickly and easily by using simple graphical elements and by adding attributes to the basic elements of the page.

# Web Design Issues

Thus far, you have created a Web page that validates to XHTML 1.0 Transitional. You have also learned many page elements. Before continuing, it is important to consider some Web design issues, including color combinations and ways to structure documents.

**OBJECTIVE**
2.2.3: Lines, colors and backgrounds

2.3.3: Impact of color choices

## Color combinations

Color combinations are important to a Web site's look and feel because they can impose tone and mood. Color choices can convey the personality of a site, and thus its sponsoring organization, as serious, playful, trendy, conservative, creative, studious or authoritative, for example. Certain color combinations can also make a site easier — or more difficult — to read and view. Following are some examples of popular color combinations for Web sites:

- Gray and white (e.g., *www.w3schools.com*)

- Blue and white (e.g., current live Habitat For Humanity site, *www.habitat.org*)

- Red and white (e.g., *www.linux.org*)

- Red, white and gray (e.g., *www.cnn.com*)

- Red and gray (e.g., *http://espn.go.com*)

Once a color scheme is chosen, most sites use lighter shades of chosen colors for background. A lighter background acts as a foil (i.e., contrast) to the foreground text and images, making the site appear more polished and professional.

## Culture and audience issues

Remember that the Web pages and sites you help develop may be available to anyone in the world with a browser and an Internet connection. Consider the following issues:

- From what culture(s) are the people who will primarily view this site?

- Is your chosen color combination effective in the cultures this site targets or in most cultures?

- What is considered "professional" for the audience that will most likely view this site?

In the following lab, you will consider some color combinations that could be used for a Web site. Suppose the marketing department is in charge of branding for your organization. That team will determine the best color combinations for all company materials, sites and advertising. Although you are not responsible for choosing the color scheme, your project manager has asked you to research and compare some color combinations so that you can present information to the marketing team about the way that colors in the company Web pages will render in browsers.

 **Lab 4-7: Comparing Web site color combinations**

In this lab, you will compare color schemes used in organization and corporate Web sites.

1.  Open your browser and visit ***www.w3schools.com***.

2.  What color scheme is used for this Web site? Is it easy to read, distracting or unnoticeable? What type of mood or personality does this site's color scheme convey? And what does the look and feel of the home page make you think about its sponsoring organization?

3.  Visit the following sites and consider the same questions for each:

    ***www.habitat.org***
    ***www.microsoft.com***
    ***www.CIW-certified.com***

In this lab, you compared common color combinations used in Web sites, and you considered their effects on users.

## Page layout

OBJECTIVE
2.3.4: Page design
and layout

Web page layout is the placement of all page elements — including text, images, headings, navigation menus and so forth — relative to each other. A good page layout makes the page aesthetically pleasing, and easy to scan, read and navigate. Following are some layout guidelines to consider when designing your Web pages:

- **Be succinct** — Limit words to clear, necessary verbiage, especially on the home page. Most users simply scan pages quickly looking for specific information or links to it. Let users navigate to additional pages if they want more information.

- **Make sure that each page focuses on one topic** — No tangent message, regardless of its importance, should be added to a page. Use links to point users to appropriate related topics on separate pages.

- **Divide the page into three sections** — Use the left side of the page for navigation, the upper section of the page for a topic title (as well as navigation), and the middle section of the page for the information.

- **Include navigation aids** — A common way to enable navigation is to place links at the top and bottom of the page, and within the body of the page, to reduce the need for users to scroll.

- **Place comments in each section of code** — Comments help explain changes you have made to the code or page. You can indicate the nature of the change, including the date you made the change and your name or initials, or you can explain the nature of the markup. For example, the syb.html page has three headings (h1, h2 and h3). You could comment each of these sections of the narrative.

 Tech Tip    *Effective page layout is essential for effective search engine optimization.*

### *Document structure, the <div> tag and style sheets*

OBJECTIVE
2.8.1: Structuring
documents with CSS

2.21.1: Layers with
CSS and <div>

When Web pages were first being developed, early designers would use the <table> tag to format pages. Tables were necessary to divide the pages into sections because the Cascading Style Sheets (CSS) standard had not yet been developed. By using tables, designers could ensure that all page elements aligned and rendered consistently.

Today, the use of the <table> tag to format pages is considered improper practice by the W3C. Pages formatted with the <table> tag will not pass W3C validation tests, no matter what standard you use. Instead of using tables, you should use CSS and the <div> tag.

You have already learned that the <div> tag can be used to align text and images. You can also use it to add structure to an entire page by using the <div> tag's *id* attribute. Once you specify a name for a document section using the *id* attribute, you can define this section's place in the document (as well as its contents) in a linked style sheet. This strategy gives you granular control over your document, and ensures that the style sheet — rather than the HTML tags — governs the document's structure. Previous versions of HTML required you to use tables for this type of document structure control.

You can also add background images using the <div> tag. In HTML 4.01 and earlier, you could create a table and specify a background image for it; however, you should now use CSS instead. The following XHTML sample demonstrates a way to define part of a document's overall structure and add images using the <div> tag:

```
<!-- SIDEBAR HERE -->
<div id="sidebar">
<img height="129" src="syb/SYBSumReptCV.jpg" width="100" border="0"
hspace="10" alt="Link to a PDF file. Go to www.adobe.com to download Acrobat
Reader"/>
<br/>
<br/>SYB
<br/>Summary Report
</div>
```

This XHTML code can now be controlled through an external style sheet. The following style sheet entry defines formatting for the section of code created by the <div id="sidebar"> tag in the preceding XHTML sample:

```
#sidebar {
            float: left;
            width: 165px;
            background: #fc3 url(navbg_04.gif) repeat-y top right;
            height: 662px;
        }s
```

In this CSS code, the sidebar is made to appear (i.e., float) on the left side of the document. A background image (navbg_04.gif) is specified and will appear at the top right of the page. The *repeat-y* entry ensures that the image is tiled vertically in the background. The document will always appear 165 pixels wide and 662 pixels high. You could repeat this type of <div> tag for each section of the XHTML document, then use CSS to control the rendering of each section in the document.

If necessary, you can adjust the formatting any time by modifying the CSS entries. For example, suppose you were to add more text to a page, which makes the page longer. If you were using a sidebar image, this image may then be too short, making the page look awkward. To solve this problem, you could increase the sidebar image's height to accommodate the change by adjusting the *height* attribute's pixel value in the style sheet. You can also use CSS to move images to specific locations on your pages.

Alternatively, the following example shows a style declared inside an XHTML <p> tag:

```
<p style="text-align:center; margin-right:12px;"/>
```

This tag uses an inline style to align text to the center of a right margin that begins 12 pixels into the document. This style will apply only to this <p> tag, and not to any others.

For more information about using proper CSS layout, visit the following sites:

- W3C — Home Page Table-less Layout (*www.w3.org/2002/11/homepage*)

- Greytower Technologies — Layering the CSS Way (*www.greytower.net/archive/articles/layers.html*)

- HTMLSource — CSS Layout page (*www.yourhtmlsource.com/stylesheets/csslayout.html*)

- DeveloperTutorials — How to Position Text and Images Exactly (*www.developertutorials.com/tutorials/css/css-position-text-images-050629/page1.html*)

- EchoEcho.Com — CSS Layers (*www.echoecho.com/csslayers.htm*)

You will learn more about applying styles with CSS later in this course.

## Fixed-width vs. liquid design layouts

**OBJECTIVE**
2.21.2: Fixed-width
vs. liquid design

Web designers have no control over their site visitors' browser window sizes, the Web browsers used or the fonts installed on visitors' computers. Yet despite this, many designers try to control the way that Web page elements will render on the screen.

There are two page-layout methods that designers use to control the placement of Web page elements when rendered in the browser:

- **Fixed-width layout** — also known as absolute positioning. Achieved by assigning specific pixel widths to elements using the <div> tag. This layout ensures that the text, images and layout will not vary from browser to browser. The problem with using a fixed-width layout is that the elements may not render as expected when users change the size of their browser windows.

- **Liquid layout** — also known as relative positioning. Achieved by assigning percentage values to elements. With this layout, the size of an element is flexible and will change dynamically depending on the size of the browser window. For example, you can specify in the <div> tag that Element A will occupy 35 percent of the screen and Element B will occupy the remaining 65 percent. If the user resizes the browser window, the elements will resize correspondingly.

There is great debate concerning the use of fixed-width versus liquid design layouts in Web pages. General industry consensus indicates that implementing a liquid design layout using CSS is the preferred method of designing Web pages.

For more information about this long-running debate, visit the following Web sites:

- Molly.com — "Fixed Versus Liquid: The Beat(ing) Goes On" by Molly Herschlag *(www.molly.com/2005/04/16/fixed-versus-liquid-the-beating-goes-on)*

- 456 Berea Street — "About fluid and fixed width layouts" by Roger Johansson *(www.456bereastreet.com/archive/200504/about_fluid_and_fixed_width_layouts)*

- 456 Berea Street — "Fixed or fluid width? Elastic!" by Roger Johansson *(www.456bereastreet.com/archive/200504/fixed_or_fluid_width_elastic)*

- MaxDesign — "Liquid layouts the easy way" by Russ Weakley *(www.maxdesign.com.au/presentation/liquid)*

- Amazines — "Most crucial factors in determining the success of a website" *(https://www.amazines.com/Business_News/article_detail.cfm/784012?articleid=78 4012)*

- CSSTricks — "The Perfect Fluid Width Layout" by Chris Coyier *(http://css-tricks.com/the-perfect-fluid-width-layout)*

## Relative path names

Most Web developers use subfolders to organize images, style sheets and Web pages. Currently, your XHTML pages are configured to refer to all images and style sheets in the same directory (e.g., a folder on your Desktop). As the site grows, your XHTML pages will refer to subdirectories. A reference to a file within a directory or subdirectory is called a relative path.

A relative path statement allows you to specify subdirectories (i.e., subfolders), as well as directories above the one where your page currently resides. A relative path assumes that the directory in which the XHTML file resides is the current (i.e., "home") directory. All other directories exist either beneath the current directory (i.e., subdirectories) or above the current directory (i.e., parent directories) in a hierarchical structure.

For example, if you place the SYBcollage2.png file into the Syb\ directory, and your Web page's <img> tag needs to reference this image file, then you must change your *src* attribute value to include the new subdirectory location, as follows:

```
<img src="Syb/SYBcollage2.png" alt="PNG image"/>
```

If you omit the subdirectory reference to Syb/ before the image file name, then your XHTML page will look for the SYBcollage2.png image file in its existing directory, and not in a subdirectory named Syb. Thus the page will render without the image file, and a small box with an X will appear in its place.

### *White space, the <img> tag and XHTML*

With HTML, if you add a space or use the ENTER key to create a return within the <img> tag, the additional space will not be rendered in a browser. In XHTML, however, sometimes adding spaces or hard returns within or even between <img> tags will cause white space to appear on the page. Therefore, be careful when working with <img> tags so that you do not add unintentional white space. Avoid adding returns within an <img> tag or between multiple <img> tags, even though this practice generally makes code easier to read. It is more important that your images render as expected in a browser.

In the following lab, you will see how the <div> tag and CSS can be used to create document sections. Suppose members of your Web team have added images and page structure to an XHTML page. The new document structure includes four sections:

- **A navigation bar at the top of the page** — with links to the rest of the site. This section will contain several images.

- **A navigation bar on the left side of the page** — with links that explain additional Habitat youth programs. This section will contain a background image, an image that will eventually link to a PDF file, and several button-style images, the first of which will eventually link to another page.

- **A body content section** — with the narrative (which you have already marked up) about the Summer Youth Blitz program.

- **A footer section** — with text-based navigation to help ensure accessibility.

The page and a style sheet have been developed already. You have been assigned to review the page and add comments to make sure that the document is properly structured. You have also been asked to verify that the document refers to the correct style sheet.

 **Lab 4-8: Using CSS and <div> to structure a page and add images**

In this lab, you will review the structure of a Web page. Specifically, you will see the way that the <div> tag and CSS can be used to create document sections.

1. **Editor:** Close **syb.html**.

2. **Windows Explorer:** Create a subdirectory off of **Habitat\CCYP\Syb\** named *Old*.

3. **Windows Explorer:** Move the contents of the Habitat\CCYP\Syb\ folder to the **Habitat\CCYP\Syb\Old\** folder.

   *Note: These actions will not delete or move your existing syb.html page, because it is not in the Habitat\CCYP\Syb\ folder.*

---

**4.** Move the existing **syb.html** file into the **Habitat\CCYP\Syb\Old\** folder.

**5.** **Windows Explorer:** Go to the **C:\CIW\Site_Dev\Lab Files\Lesson04\Lab_4-8\** directory, and copy the contents of the Syb\ folder into the **Habitat\CCYP\Syb\** folder.

*Note: Copy the contents of the Syb\ folder, but not the folder itself.*

**6.** Go to the **C:\CIW\Site_Dev\Lab Files\Lesson04\Lab_4-8\** folder, and copy the **syb.txt** file from this folder to your **Habitat\CCYP\** directory.

**7.** Open **syb.txt**. Verify that the style sheet links to the **\Syb\syb.css** file.

**8.** In **syb.txt**, scroll down to the following code block:

```
<div id="container">
<div id="banner">
<div id="head"></div>
<div id="navbar">
```

**9.** Add the following comment immediately above the code block:

```
<!-- TOP NAVIGATION BAR-->
```

**10.** You have identified the top section of the page. Now, find the following text:

```
<div id="sidebar">
```

**11.** Immediately above this text, enter the following comment:

```
<!-- SIDEBAR HERE -->
```

**12.** You have just marked the sidebar section of this page. Next, find the following text:

```
<div id="content">
```

**13.** Immediately above the text you just found, enter the following comment:

```
<!-- CONTENT BODY -->
```

**14.** Find the following text:

```
<div id="footer">
```

**15.** Immediately above the text you just found, enter the following comment:

```
<!-- FOOTER -->
```

**16.** You have now commented each of the sections of your page. Review each section carefully. Notice that the <div> tag is used to create each section.

**17.** Save syb.txt as **syb.html** in the Habitat\CCYP directory, and view it in a browser. Your page should resemble Figure 4-8.

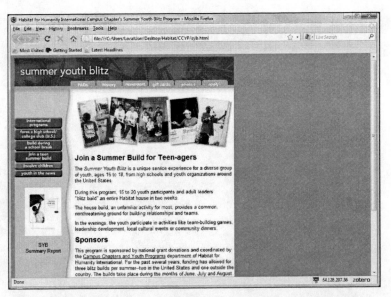

*Figure 4-8: Page syb.html using additional images, <div> tags and style sheet*

18. **Editor:** Open **syb.html** in your editor. Find the section marked with the comment `<!-- TOP NAVIGATION BAR-->`. Notice the `<div>` tags immediately beneath the comment. Each of these tags has a counterpart in the Syb\syb.css file because each `<div>` tag, in conjunction with your linked style sheet, helps define the structure of this XHTML page.

19. **Editor:** Open the **Syb\syb.css** file. Compare the `<div>` tags with the corresponding entries in the style sheet. For example, notice that the *#head* entry in syb.css inserts an image named sybheaders_01.jpg into the file. No reference to this image exists in syb.html. Therefore, you can use style sheets to add images.

20. Review the other sections of your page, and compare them to the style sheet.

21. Cut one of the **<div>** tags, then load the page in a browser to see the impact. Return to the editor, and Undo your changes to restore the document.

    *Note: You can restore the document by using the Undo feature in WordPad or Notepad. If necessary, you can also copy the complete file from the Finished folder for this lab.*

22. From **syb.html**, comment the reference to the style sheet, then reload the page in the browser. Notice that the document's structure is no longer intact because the style sheet, in conjunction with the `<div>` tags, now defines the structure of this XHTML page. Remove the comment notation.

23. Validate your code. Correct all problems so that the code validates as XHTML 1.0 Transitional.

24. If you like, remove the background image (background.jpg) from the page. What background color would you recommend for this page? Add it now.

In this lab, you added structure to your page using images and CSS.

## Case Study

# A Sharper Image

Iain works on the Web development team for a prominent community college system in the Southwest part of the United States. He was assigned to create several new Web pages, most of which would include detailed images. These images would aid navigation and provide vital registration instructions for the college students.

Iain was experienced with XHTML and did not feel it was important to spend time validating all code because he was very busy. After creating and posting the new pages, however, Iain began receiving complaints from students who used text-based browsers. These students complained that they could not see (or hear) the registration instructions.

To solve this problem, Iain added the *alt* attribute to each <img> tag to describe each image with text. Although it would have taken him more time to include the *alt* attribute in his initial page development, Iain found that the *alt* attribute resolved the complaints.

\*　　　\*　　　\*

As a class, discuss the following issues that might arise when incorporating images in Web pages:

*   Most people use browsers that support images. Why is it important to support all browser types in this situation?

*   How could validation have saved Iain development time? What other advantages would have come from initial validation?

## Lesson Summary

### Application project

When you incorporate an image into your Web page, you should consider the image's usefulness to the rest of the page. Images are generally effective only if they complement the text or overall message of the page.

Many Web sites offer copyright-free graphic files for site designers to use. These sites provide coordinated graphics such as buttons, bullets, rules and backgrounds that can help create a theme for your site. Use a search engine to locate free Web graphics, or visit the Yahoo! Directory at *http://dir.yahoo.com/*, and navigate to Arts & Humanities | Design Arts | Graphic Design | Web Page Design And Layout | Graphics. Add a new, free, non-copyrighted image to your Web page. After you finish, revert your file to its original state for the remaining lessons.

### Skills review

In this lesson, you were introduced to graphical Web page elements such as horizontal rules, images and colors. You learned how to position graphics relative to text on a page, and how to resize images for display. In addition, you were introduced to the <font> tag, which specifies font face, size and color information. You also learned about special characters, and about using the <div> tag and CSS to add structure to a Web document.

Now that you have completed this lesson, you should be able to:

✓ 2.2.1: Incorporate graphical images into HTML pages.

✓ 2.2.2: Distinguish among and identify the uses and benefits of various graphic file formats, including GIF, GIF89a, JPEG, PNG TIFF, BMP.

✓ 2.2.3: Add lines, colors and tiled background images to HTML pages.

✓ 2.2.6: Insert horizontal rules into Web pages.

✓ 2.3.1: Define the browser-safe color palette.

✓ 2.3.2: Identify ways that color affects the principles of line, value, shape and form in Web pages.

✓ 2.3.3: Identify and demonstrate the impact of color combinations to various audiences and cultures.

✓ 2.3.4: Evaluate Web page design and layout.

✓ 2.8.1: Explain how to structure Web documents with CSS.

✓ 2.21.1: Use CSS and the <div> tag to create layers.

✓ 2.21.2: Distinguish between fixed-width and liquid design layouts.

# Lesson 4 Review

1. What is another term for a horizontal line on a Web page?

   _____

2. What is the default alignment attribute value for horizontal lines?

   _____

3. Name the alignment options available for aligning images relative to text.

   _____

4. What is the function of the *alt* attribute?

   _____

   _____

5. What standard of 216 colors was introduced to render Web page colors consistently across different browsers?

   _____

   _____

# Lesson 5: Hyperlinks

## Objectives

By the end of this lesson, you will be able to:

🖘 2.1.4: Create HTML hyperlinks for text, images, local files and remote sites (internal and external links).

🖘 2.14.4: Manage existing sites (e.g., remove dead links and/or upgrade connectivity when necessary).

🖘 2.16.6: Identify the importance of online indexing and cataloging.

# Pre-Assessment Questions

1.  Which term describes the underlined, colored text on a Web page that a user can click to access another Web page?

    a.  Fully qualified URL
    b.  Anchor
    c.  Hyperlink
    d.  Partial URL

2.  When are partial URLs used with hyperlinks?

    a.  When using an external image as a link
    b.  When linking to another location on the same site
    c.  When linking to an external Web site
    d.  When accessing a system file on the Web server

3.  What is the term recommended by the W3C for a link to a resource? What is the other common term for such a link?

_____

# Introduction to Hyperlinks

The characteristic that makes the World Wide Web a "web" is the linking capability that connects Web pages to other files across the Internet. Hyperlinks are in fact more fundamental than the ability to include multimedia objects in your HTML documents. Even users with non-graphical browsers, such as Lynx, can select hyperlinks in Web pages to navigate and explore the Web. The critical element is the ability to move from page to page by clicking linked text or images.

A hypertext link is a word or phrase in an HTML document that is specially tagged as a link using the anchor tag, <a>. By default, hyperlinks appear blue and underlined in the browser. You can use CSS or the *alink* attribute of the <body> tag to make hyperlinks appear in any color you like. An image or icon can also be enclosed in anchor tags and used as a link to another file. In both cases, clicking the link will take the user to the link's specified destination.

You can create links to external files as well as to points within the current file. On a long page, you can use links to jump between sections of the page; such a link is called an internal link.

# The Anchor Tag

**OBJECTIVE**
2.1.4: HTML hyperlinks

Links are created with the anchor tag, <a>. Anchor tags are container tags that encompass the text or image (or both) to be used as the link. The *href* attribute is used to specify the link's hypertext reference, or the target of the link. You can specify a fully qualified URL or a relative URL reference for any file, page or site. The W3C prefers the phrase Uniform Resource Identifier (URI) to URL. However, most professionals still use the term URL, so this course will use URL throughout.

The syntax for using the anchor tag to create a link is as follows:

```
<a href="URL"> linked text or image (or both) </a>
```

Table 5-1 lists examples of values for the URL when referencing external links.

*Table 5-1: URL options for external links*

| Type of Reference | Description | Examples |
|---|---|---|
| **Fully qualified URL (also called absolute URL)** | A URL (i.e., URI) that contains a full path to a resource, including the protocol indicator. Also known as a hard link. | *http://www.someserver.com/somepage.html*<br>or<br>*ftp://ftp.someserver.com/pub/somefile.ext*<br>or<br>*c:\intetpub\wwwroot\ccyp\syb\syb.html* |
| **Partial URL (also called relative URL)** | A URL that assumes the current document's path. All references are made from the document's current directory. | *syb.html*<br>or<br>*../css/stylesheet.css*<br>or<br>*pub/images/mybullet.gif* |

As you read absolute and relative URLs, you must understand how browsers interpret them. Table 5-2 summarizes common URL paths. As you read this table, assume that all references are to the same page, index.html.

*Table 5-2: URL paths*

| URL | Description |
|---|---|
| **/mysite/index.html** | The initial forward slash ( / ) instructs the browser to look for a directory named mysite that is off of the root directory. If you were to insert this reference into a page on your Windows XP system, your browser would interpret the first forward slash as C:\, and would look for the mysite/ directory, which would contain the index.html file. If this page were on a Web server, the link would refer to the Web server's root directory (e.g., /var/www/mysite/ in Linux/UNIX or C:\inetpub\wwwroot\ in Windows). |
| **mysite/index.html** | The absence of any initial characters instructs the browser to look for the mysite subdirectory. This subdirectory begins off of the same level as the current page. The index.html page resides inside of the mysite subdirectory. |
| **../mysite/index.html** | The initial two periods and forward slash ( ../ ) instruct the browser to look for a directory named mysite that begins one level higher than the page you are currently viewing. |

**Tech Tip**

*Windows and UNIX/Linux systems use different naming conventions for their paths. Windows path names use back slashes, whereas UNIX/Linux paths use forward slashes. Also, Windows paths can use drive names (e.g., C:\), whereas Unix/Linux paths do not.*

## Specifying protocols

Hyperlinks do not have to point only to HTTP addresses. You can create hyperlinks for various protocols. Table 5-3 describes several protocols you can specify in a hyperlink URL.

*Table 5-3: Protocols in hyperlink URL references*

| Protocol | Hyperlink HTML Example |
|---|---|
| **HTTP** | Visit the &lt;a href="http://www.CIW-certified.com"&gt;CIW&lt;a/&gt; site. |
| **HTTPS (Secure HTTP)** | Visit our &lt;a href="https://www.CIW-certified.com"&gt;secure CIW&lt;a/&gt; site. |
| **FTP** | Download the file from our &lt;a href="ftp://ftp.server.com"&gt;FTP server.&lt;/a&gt; |
| **E-mail** | You can send e-mail to us at &lt;a href="mailto:info@ciwcertified.com"&gt; info@ciwcertified.com&lt;/a&gt;. |
| **Telnet** | Please visit our &lt;a href="telnet:cals.evergreen.edu"&gt;Telnet server.&lt;/a&gt; |

## Problems when creating hyperlinks

Many Web developers commit the same common errors when writing HTML code to create hyperlinks on their Web pages. As you use the &lt;a&gt; element, make sure that you:

- **Use a closing anchor tag** — You must place the &lt;/a&gt; tag after the page text to be affected.

- **Place quotation marks around the value** — The value of the *href* attribute is the target of your link; for example:
  *"http://www.habitat.org"*

- **Include the closing bracket at the end of the opening &lt;a&gt; tag** — The following example is a common oversight:
  *&lt;a href="http://www.habitat.org" Habitat &lt;/a&gt;*
  The tag should read as follows:
  *&lt;a href="http://www.habitat.org"&gt; Habitat &lt;/a&gt;*

Table 5-4 lists some problems you might experience when creating links in HTML, with troubleshooting techniques that you can use to solve these problems.

Table 5-4: Troubleshooting HTML hyperlink problems

| Problem | Solution |
|---------|----------|
| **Text and images disappear** | The <a> tag is not properly closed with </a>, or you have not placed quotation marks around a value. Review your tags carefully. |
| **All successive Web page text is a hyperlink** | The <a> tag is not properly closed with </a> in the correct location. Review your tags carefully. |
| **Garbled code appears on screen** | One or more <a> tags may be missing an opening or closing angle bracket (i.e., wicket). Review each <a> tag carefully. |
| **Code will not validate due to a problem <a> tag** | A closing tag may be missing or mistyped (such as <a/> instead of </a>). Review your tags carefully. |

# Creating Local Hyperlinks

OBJECTIVE
2.1.4: HTML
hyperlinks

A local hyperlink is a link you create from one file on your local system to another file on your local system. You create these types of links when you are developing your own pages and linking them to form a site. Your files can be uploaded to a Web server in the same directory structure you save on your system, so your file references can remain unchanged as long as your directory structure persists. Creating local hyperlinks involves determining the location of the file to which you want to link, relative to the location of the file from which you are linking.

In the following lab, you will create local hypertext links in a document. Suppose you have been assigned to link your Web page to other pages on the site. You need to determine page text that will clearly identify hyperlinks so your users know where each link will take them. You also need to provide a link to a report in PDF format. You must supply page text for each hyperlink, as well as the HTML code that will create the hyperlink function that links the pages of your site to each other.

 **Lab 5-1: Creating local text hyperlinks in XHTML**

OBJECTIVE
2.1.4: HTML
hyperlinks

In this lab, you will create local hyperlinks from the syb.html page to other pages that are stored on your hard drive.

In the first five steps, you will populate and verify the Habitat folders on your Desktop. In the rest of the lab, you will create links from syb.html to files in these directories.

1. Navigate to the **C:\CIW\Site_Dev\Lab Files\Lesson05\Lab_5-1** folder. Copy the **index.html** file and the **index\** directory to the **Habitat\** folder on your system. This page and its associated directory re-create a prototype version of the Habitat For Humanity home page.

2. From the **Lab Files\Lesson05\Lab_5-1** folder, copy the **default.html** file and the **default\** directory to the **Habitat\CCYP\** subfolder. (Notice that you are copying to a different location than in Step 1.) This file and directory re-create a prototype Campus Chapters And Youth Programs page.

3.  From the **Lab Files\Lesson05\Lab_5-1** folder, copy the **ccypintl.html** file and the **ccypintl\** directory to the **Habitat\CCYP\** subfolder (the same location as in Step 2). This file and directory re-create a prototype International Programs page.

4.  From the **Lab Files\Lesson05\Lab_5-1** folder, copy the file **application.html** and the **application\** directory to the **Habitat\CCYP\** subfolder (the same location as in Steps 2 and 3). This file and directory re-create a prototype Summer Youth Blitz Application Form page.

5.  Verify that your Desktop directories are now populated as follows:
    *   **Habitat\** should contain **index.html** and the **index\** directory.

    *   **Habitat\CCYP\** should contain **application.html**, **ccypintl.html** and **default.html** (and all associated directories for these files), and should also contain **syb.html** and the **Syb\** directory. You should be using the copy of syb.html from the last lab in the preceding lesson (Lab 4-8).

    *Note: The directories you copied and verified in Steps 1 through 5 contain Web pages to which you will link in this lab. You will create links to these directories in the following steps.*

6.  Open **syb.html** in a text editor. Scroll to the bottom of the page, to the footer section.

7.  At the bottom of the page, find the text that reads *International Programs*. Surround this text with the opening and closing anchor tags to create a hyperlink to the ccypintl.html page:

    ```
    <a href="ccypintl.html">International Programs</a>
    ```

    *Note: You do not need to specify a subfolder for this relative URL because ccypintl.html is in the same folder as syb.html.*

8.  Save the page, then open it in a browser. Scroll to the bottom of the page. The phrase International Programs should now be a hyperlink, indicated as blue underlined text, as shown in Figure 5-1.

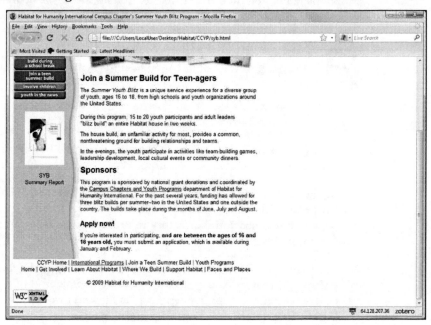

*Figure 5-1: Page syb.html with hyperlink in footer section*

9. Click your new link to verify that it is valid. The International Programs page should appear in your browser.

10. Validate your code at ***http://validator.w3.org***.

11. Open **syb.html** in the text editor and again scroll to the bottom. Find the text that reads *CCYP Home*. Surround this text with the opening and closing anchor tags to create a hyperlink to the **default.html** page that resides in the same folder (i.e., on the same level) as syb.html:

    ```
    <a href="default.html">CCYP Home</a>
    ```

    *Note: Understand that this code refers to a page on the same level (in the same directory) as the page you are currently editing.*

12. Save the file. Test your code in a browser. You should see that the text CCYP Home at the bottom of the page is now a hyperlink.

13. Click the link to verify that it points to the correct page. You should see the Campus Chapters And Youth Programs home page appear in the browser.

14. Open **syb.html** again in the text editor and again scroll to the footer. Find the text that reads *Home*. Create a link for this text pointing visitors to the **index.html** page that resides in the **Habitat\** directory (one directory up from syb.html):

    ```
    <a href="../index.html">Home</a>
    ```

    *Note: This code refers to a page one directory up from the current directory. Remember that in Step 1, you copied this file and a directory to the Habitat\ folder, not to the Habitat\CCYP\ folder.*

15. Save the file. Test your code in a browser, then validate it at ***http://validator.w3.org***. Resolve any code problems before continuing the lab.

16. In **syb.html**, find the text that reads *...You Must Submit An Application* (in the Apply Now! section). Create a hyperlink from the word ***Application*** to the file **application.html**, which resides in the same directory as syb.html.

17. Find the phrase *Join A Teen Summer Build*, and create a hyperlink from this phrase to the current page (syb.html). Save the file.

18. Check your work by viewing it in a browser then validating it. Resolve any problems.

19. Next, you will link to a PDF document. Verify that Adobe Reader is installed on your system by selecting **Start | All Programs** and looking for the Adobe Reader icon. If your system does not have Adobe Reader, go to ***www.adobe.com*** to download and install it. Adobe Reader 9.0 is free software that allows you to view PDF files.

20. Verify that the file **SYBSumRept06.pdf** is in the Habitat\CCYP\Syb\ subfolder. If it is not present, copy the PDF file from **C:\CIW\Site_Dev\Lab Files\Lesson05\Lab_5-1** to the **Habitat\CCYP\Syb\** subfolder.

21. In **syb.html**, find the text that reads *SYB<br/>Summary Report*. Create a link from this text to the PDF file.

22. Save the file, then refresh **syb.html** in the browser. Verify your relative link to the PDF. When you click the **SYB Summary Report** link, Adobe Reader should automatically launch and download the report file.

**23.** Browse all your local links to verify that they work.

**24.** You can change the default appearance of a hyperlink using CSS. In your editor, open the file **Habitat\CCYP\Syb\syb.css** (which is the style sheet for syb.html) and find the following entry:

```
/*
  a {
     color: #093
     }
*/
```

**25.** Notice that this CSS entry for hyperlinks is commented out. The entry instructs all hyperlinks to be displayed in green, rather than the default blue. Delete the comment notation **/* */**, then save and close the **syb.css** file.

**26.** Reload the **syb.html** page in the browser, and notice that the hyperlink is now green instead of blue. All links on this page will now appear green, even if visitors click them.

**27.** Now, change all of your headings (e.g., <h2> and <h3>) to appear purple. Do this by opening the **Habitat\CCYP\Syb\syb.css** style sheet file and adding the following line to the end of the h2 and h3 styles:

**color: purple**

*Note: Be sure to add a semicolon ( ; ) after the preceding style to separate it from the new color style you are adding.*

**28.** Save your changes to **syb.css** and to **syb.html**. Verify and validate your work. Resolve any problems. When you are finished, your page should resemble Figure 5-2.

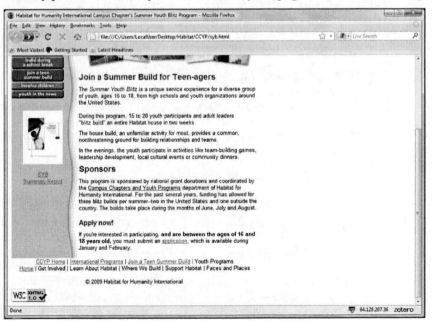

*Figure 5-2: Page syb.html after adding local hyperlinks*

**29. If time permits:** Create additional directories and XHTML files to act as placeholders for more local links.

In this lab, you created hyperlinks in a Web document.

# Creating External Hyperlinks

An external hyperlink is a link you create from a file on your system to a separate file on the Internet. You add these types of links to your own pages to reference other Web sites' pages. Creating external hyperlinks involves determining the full URL, including the protocol indicator, for the Web page to which you want to link. Remember that you should not provide a link from your site to another site without first obtaining permission from that site's owner, because such a link may imply a business relationship or endorsement.

In the following lab, you will create external hyperlinks. Suppose your project manager has assigned you to work on the Summer Youth Blitz page for a sister site to Habitat. You need to link this page to the live *www.habitat.org* site. However, some of the links should remain local.

 **Lab 5-2: Creating external hyperlinks in XHTML**

In this lab, you will use the anchor tag to link text from one file to another file on an external Web site.

**OBJECTIVE**
2.1.4: HTML
hyperlinks

1.  Open **syb.html** in a text editor. Scroll to the bottom of the page, to the footer section.

2.  Your project manager has provided you with the information in the following table. Using this information, add the appropriate links from specified page text in the footer section of syb.html to the specified external pages on your system.

| Page Text to Tag as Hyperlink | URL Value to Reference |
|---|---|
| Youth Programs | *http://www.habitat.org/youthprograms/* |
| Get Involved | *http://www.habitat.org/getinv/* |
| Learn About Habitat | *http://www.habitat.org/how/* |
| Where We Build | *http://www.habitat.org/build/* |
| Support Habitat | *http://www.habitat.org/donation/default.aspx* |
| Faces and Places | *http://www.habitat.org/faces_places/* |

3.  When you are finished adding all XHTML anchor tags to the file, save **syb.html**. Then load the page in a browser. It should resemble Figure 5-3.

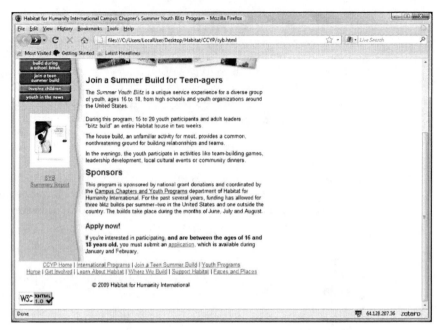

Figure 5-3: Page syb.html after adding remote hyperlinks

4.  Validate your code at **http://validator.w3.org**. Resolve any problems, then save and close **syb.html**.

5.  Consider the names of the images that you inserted. How might you change the image names so that they are more descriptive? Search engines will rank a page higher if they see that images have been given descriptive names.

In this lab, you created absolute links to an external site.

# Using Images as Hyperlinks

You are not limited to using text to provide a link to another file. You can create a hyperlink from a graphical image by surrounding the image tag with opening and closing anchor tags.

In the following lab, you will create hyperlinks from image files. Suppose your project manager has suggested that the images on your Web page serve no purpose other than to be aesthetically appealing. Although this role is acceptable for images, you consider a way to add functionality to the images on your Web page.

**Lab 5-3: Using images as hyperlinks with XHTML**

OBJECTIVE
2.1.4: HTML
hyperlinks

In this lab, you will create hyperlinks from several images on a Web page.

1.  Before beginning this lab, you should have already completed Lab 5-1. Verify that you have copied the following files and folders to your Desktop from the **C:\CIW\Site_Dev\Lab Files\Lesson05\Lab_5-1** folder:

    •   The index.html file and the index\ directory

    •   The default.html file and the default\ directory

- The ccypintl.html file and the ccypintl\ directory

- The application.html file and the application\ directory

2. Open **syb.html** in a text editor.

3. Find the <img> tag for the **sybheaders_03.jpg** image. You can use the search feature in your text editor (e.g., select **Edit | Find** in Notepad).

4. Create a hyperlink from this image as follows:

```
<a href="http://www.habitat.org/how/factsheet.aspx"><img height="22"
src="syb/sybheaders_03.jpg" width="72" border="0" name="FAQs" alt="Click here
to get facts about Habitat."/></a>
```

*Note: Do not introduce any additional spaces or returns in your code. Otherwise, your page may not render as expected because XHTML code sometimes reflects spaces you introduce. Enter this code exactly as it appears.*

5. Your project manager has provided you with the information in the following table. Using this information, create links to the indicated images.

| Image File to Tag as Hyperlink | Image Label | URL Value to Reference |
|---|---|---|
| sybheaders_03.jpg | FAQs | *http://www.habitat.org/how/factsheet.aspx* |
| sybheaders_04.jpg | History | *http://www.habitat.org/how/historytext.aspx* |
| sybheaders_05.jpg | Newsroom | *http://www.habitat.org/newsroom/default.aspx* |
| sybheaders_06.jpg | Gift cards | *http://www.habitat.org/donation/gfth/default.aspx* |
| sybheaders_07.jpg | Photos | *http://www.habitat.org/photogallery/album.aspx* |
| sybheaders_08.jpg | Apply! | *http://www.habitat.org/youthprograms/actspeakbuild/register.aspx* |
| Intlbutton1.gif | International programs | *http://www.habitat.org/youthprograms/int/international.aspx* |

6. When you are finished adding all XHTML anchor tags to the file, save **syb.html**. Then load the page in a browser. Verify that the page renders as expected, and click your new links to test them.

7. Validate your code at ***http://validator.w3.org***. Resolve any problems, then save and close **syb.html**.

In this lab, you created hyperlinks from images to related Web site pages.

So far, you have created external links using full and partial URLs. In the next section, you will learn how to create an internal link to a different area within the same page.

# Creating Internal Links

OBJECTIVE
2.1.4: HTML
hyperlinks

On a long Web page, you may want to include links that target other areas within the same page so that users can easily find the information that interests them. An internal hyperlink provides this link from one point to another in a Web page.

Internal links require internal bookmarks, called anchors, to identify the point that the link will reference within the page. Creating an internal link requires two steps. You must first use the anchor tag, <a>, with the *name* attribute to define an area as a target (the bookmark or anchor). Then, in another portion of the page, you create the link that points to the bookmark using the anchor tag with the hypertext reference (*href*) attribute as you have already learned. The syntax for creating an internal link is as follows:

```
<a name="targetArea1">
target anchor text or image (or both)
</a>

… other page content here …

<a href="#targetArea1"> text/images linking to targetArea1 </a>
```

The *name* attribute of the <a> tag defines an internal bookmark or anchor in the page. Note that for the *href* value, the # symbol is used. This symbol, called a hash, tells the browser to look for an anchor by this name within the current document. Without this hash, the browser will look for an external file by that name.

*In this example, the <a name> tag appears above the <a href> tag in the code. These tags can appear in either order in a document — it simply depends on whether the target <a name> appears above or below the link to it <a href> on the rendered page.*

## Creating a glossary

**OBJECTIVE**
2.16.6: Online indexing and catalogs

A glossary provides a helpful navigation feature, especially if your site introduces concepts and terms to an audience that is unfamiliar with your practices. A glossary is one way to help index and catalog your site.

In the following lab, you will learn how internal hyperlinks are created. Suppose your project manager has asked you to help index and catalog the Web site. You know that a glossary is a useful way to do this. You can create a glossary using internal hyperlinks to index your site and provide helpful information to your site's visitors.

### Lab 5-4: Using internal hyperlinks

In this lab, you will examine and use an XHTML document that includes internal hyperlinks.

1.  **Windows Explorer:** Copy the **internal.txt** file and the **internal** folder to your Desktop from the **C:\CIW\Site_Dev\Lab Files\Lesson05\Lab_5-4** folder.

    *Note: Be sure to copy both the file and folder.*

2.  **Editor:** Open **internal.txt**.

3.  **Editor:** Save this file as **internal.html**. Make sure that both internal.html and the internal\ directory are on your Desktop. The code in internal.html refers to files in the internal\ directory using relative paths.

4.  Examine the following code with your instructor:

```
<!DOCTYPE html
    PUBLIC "-//W3C//DTD XHTML 1.0 Transitional//EN"
    "http://www.w3.org/TR/xhtml1/DTD/xhtml1-transitional.dtd">
<html xmlns="http://www.w3.org/1999/xhtml" xml:lang="en">
<head>
<meta name="Keywords" content="CIW, Foundations, Example"/>
<meta name="Description" content="For the CIW Foundations Course"/>
<meta http-equiv="Content-Type" content="text/html; charset=utf-8"/>
<link rel="stylesheet" type="text/css" href="internal/internal.css"
title="stylesheet"/>
<title>Habitat for Humanity International Glossary </title>
</head>
<body>

<h1>
<a name="TermTop">Glossary of Terms</a>
</h1>

<h3>
<a href="#First">A-D</a> |
<a href="#Second">E-H</a>|
<a href="#Third">I-K</a>|
<a href="#Fourth">L-O</a>|
<a href="#Fifth">P-T</a>|
<a href="#Sixth">U-Z</a>|
</h3>
<blockquote><p>Click the link for the group of letters representing the start
of the term you want to see defined.</p></blockquote>
<p/>

<h3><a name="First">A-D</a></h3>
<p/>
<strong>Term:</strong> Definition of term.<br/>
<strong>Term:</strong> Definition of term.<br/>
<strong>Term:</strong> Definition of term.<br/>
<strong>Term:</strong> Definition of term.<br/>

<br/>
<blockquote><a href="#TermTop"><img src="internal/returnup2.gif" border="0"
alt="Return to the top"></img></a> Click on the image to the left, or <a
href="#TermTop">here</a>, to return to the top.</blockquote>
<p/>

<h3><a name="Second">E-H</a></h3>
<p/>
<strong>Term:</strong> Definition of term.<br/>
<strong>Term:</strong> Definition of term.<br/>
<strong>Term:</strong> Definition of term.<br/>
<strong>Term:</strong> Definition of term.<br/>

<br/>
<blockquote>
<a href="#TermTop">
<img src="internal/returnup2.gif" border="0" alt="Return to the top">
</img></a> Click on the image to the left, or
<a href="#TermTop">here</a>, to return to the top.</blockquote>

<h3><a name="Third">I-K</a></h3>
<p/>
<strong>Term:</strong> Definition of term.<br/>
<strong>Term:</strong> Definition of term.<br/>
<strong>Term:</strong> Definition of term.<br/>
<strong>Term:</strong> Definition of term.<br/>

<br/>
```

```
<blockquote><a href="#TermTop"><img src="internal/returnup2.gif" border="0"
alt="Return to the top" ></img></a> Click on the image to the left, or <a
href="#TermTop">here</a>, to return to the top.</blockquote>

<h3><a name="Fourth">L-O</a></h3>
<p/>
<strong>Term:</strong> Definition of term.<br/>
<strong>Term:</strong> Definition of term.<br/>
<strong>Term:</strong> Definition of term.<br/>
<strong>Term:</strong> Definition of term.<br/>

<br/>
<blockquote><a href="#TermTop"><img src="internal/returnup2.gif" border="0"
alt="Return to the top" ></img></a> Click on the image to the left, or <a
href="#TermTop">here</a>, to return to the top.</blockquote>

<h3><a name="Fifth">P-T</a></h3>
<p/>
<strong>Term:</strong> Definition of term.<br/>
<strong>Term:</strong> Definition of term.<br/>
<strong>Term:</strong> Definition of term.<br/>
<strong>Term:</strong> Definition of term.<br/>

<br/>
<blockquote><a href="#TermTop"><img src="internal/returnup2.gif" border="0"
alt="Return to the top" ></img></a> Click on the image to the left, or <a
href="#TermTop">here</a>, to return to the top.</blockquote>

<h3><a name="Sixth">U-Z</a></h3>
<p/>
<strong>Term:</strong> Definition of term.<br/>
<strong>Term:</strong> Definition of term.<br/>
<strong>Term:</strong> Definition of term.<br/>
<strong>Term:</strong> Definition of term.<br/>

<br/>
<blockquote><a href="#TermTop"><img src="internal/returnup2.gif" border="0"
alt="Return to the top" ></img></a> Click on the image to the left, or <a
href="#TermTop">here</a>, to return to the top.</blockquote>

<hr/>

<p>
    <a href="http://validator.w3.org/check/referer"><img
        src="internal/valid-xhtml10.png" border="no"
        alt="Valid XHTML 1.0!" height="31" width="88"/></a>
  </p>


</body>
</html>
```

5. **Browser:** Load the file **internal.html**. Your page should resemble Figure 5-4.

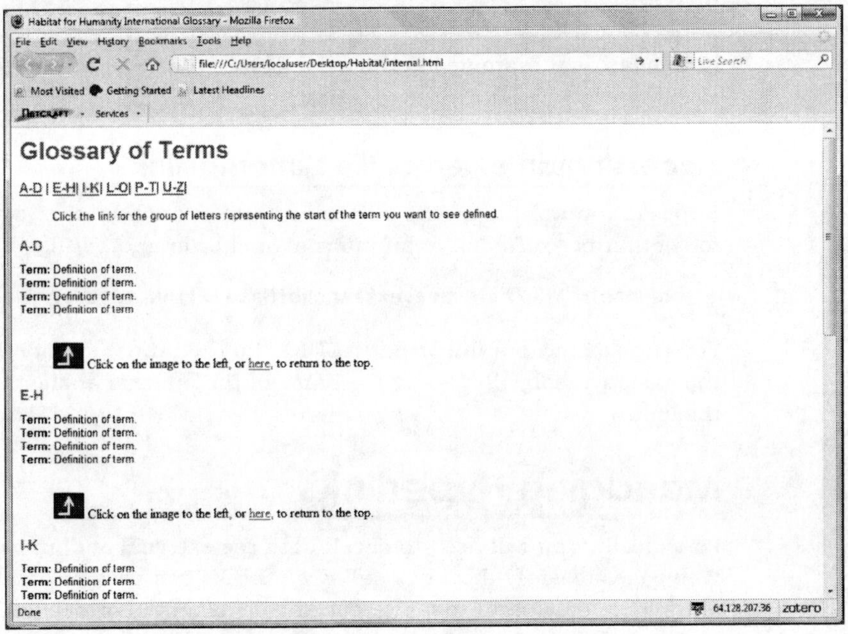

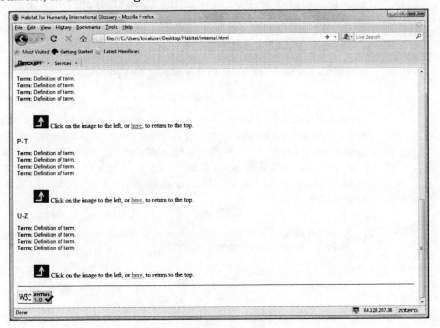

*Figure 5-4: Demonstration glossary file for internal links*

6. **Browser:** Click **U-Z**, the last link at the top of the page. You should see the section heading that matches the link you clicked. This section is near the end of the document, as shown in Figure 5-5.

*Figure 5-5: After accessing internal link*

7. **Browser:** Click any of the arrow images to return to the top of the page.

8. Practice navigating through this page to make sure that all links work correctly.

9. Validate the code at ***http://validator.w3.org***. When you are finished, close your browser.

In this lab, you examined and used a glossary that demonstrates internal hyperlinks.

### Accessing an external file's internal link

Suppose you want to link to a specific point in another page without first accessing the top of that page. To link to an internal anchor in another file, use the following syntax:

```
<a href="URL/filename.ext#AnchorName">link text or image</a>
```

You can start with a full or partial URL, but you must specify the file name, followed by the hash symbol, followed by the name of the internal anchor to which you want to direct the link.

# Managing Hyperlinks

**OBJECTIVE**
2.14.4: Existing site management

**link rot**
The phenomenon in which hyperlinks on a Web site gradually become invalid as referenced Web page content, links and page locations change.

Periodically, you will need to check both the external and internal hyperlinks on your Web pages to verify that they still work. Links can become invalid for a variety of reasons, most commonly because a referenced page is moved or deleted, or because page content is changed and anchors are renamed or lost. This phenomenon is known as **link rot**.

In addition to annoying users, a bad hyperlink will cause a page to be ranked lower by a search engine such as Google, Yahoo! or MSN. To avoid this problem, you can use automated link-checking software to validate the hyperlinks on your pages. This type of software has the ability to report the state of all site links. Following are some common automated link-checking software products:

- **Linklint** (*www.linklint.org*)

- **Link Controller** (*http://freshmeat.net/projects/linkcont*)

- **Checkbot** (*http://degraaff.org/checkbot*)

Consider that automatic link-checking software can identify invalid links for you, but you still must manually update your XHTML code to delete or modify any invalid links. Even if you use automatic link-checking software, it is advisable to check your hyperlinks manually as well. Although a link may still be valid, the content of either the target page or the page with the link can change in ways such that a link is no longer relevant or appropriate.

**Tech Tip**

*Dead hyperlinks are a major factor in having an otherwise good page get ranked lowly by a search engine.*

## Case Study

# The Missing Link

Omar works on a Web development team that just posted a site. This site contains both internal and external hyperlinks. Only three days after the site was posted to the production server, Omar found that four external hyperlinks were already invalid. To solve this problem, he checked each link manually and edited the XHTML code to validate each one.

After this experience, Omar wanted to manage the hyperlinks more closely and be notified of any problem links immediately. He obtained automatic link-checking software, which checks all site links periodically then sends an e-mail message reporting the status of every link. After installing this software, Omar was confident that his site's links would always remain valid.

       *                *                *

As a class, consider this scenario and discuss the following points:

* After Omar installs automatic link-checking software, will his site links always remain valid? Why or why not?

* Why would it be important to occasionally check your hyperlinks manually?

* Why would it be important to use both external and internal links on your Web site?

## *Lesson Summary*

### Application project

This lesson taught you about internal, external and local hyperlinks in Web documents. Take some time to learn more about the attributes available to the <a> tag. Visit the following sites to read about hyperlink options:

- W3C (*www.w3.org*)

- W3Schools (*www.w3schools.com*)

As you visit these sites, research the capabilities and limitations of XHTML 1.0 and HTML 4.0 in relation to the <a> tag.

### Skills review

In this lesson, you learned to create hyperlinks from text and images to other Web files and sites. You learned that you could use full or partial URLs in your links, and you learned to link to an internal anchor point within the current document or even in another document.

Now that you have completed this lesson, you should be able to:

✓ 2.1.4: Create HTML hyperlinks for text, images, local files and remote sites (internal and external links).

✓ 2.14.4: Manage existing sites (e.g., remove dead links and/or upgrade connectivity when necessary).

✓ 2.16.6: Identify the importance of online indexing and cataloging.

# Lesson 5 Review

1. Name the two types of URL you can reference when creating hyperlinks to an external site or to another page on the same site.

   _____

2. Within an anchor tag ( <a> ), the *href* attribute performs what function?

   _____

   _____

3. You are creating an image hyperlink. What HTML code links the image *zoomap.jpg* to the *map.htm* Web page?

   _____

4. You want to create a hyperlink that provides the end user with a pre-addressed blank e-mail message when he or she clicks the link. You want to pre-address the e-mail messages to *info@habitat.org*. The hyperlink text should read "*Please send e-mail to info@habitat.org.*" What HTML code would create this hyperlink?

   _____

5. Describe the syntax used to link to an internal anchor in another file without first accessing the top of that page.

   _____

   _____

   _____

# Lesson 6:
# HTML Tables

## Objectives

By the end of this lesson, you will be able to:

☞ 2.1.5: Design and format HTML tables to present information in an organized way.

# Pre-Assessment Questions

1. Which table tag encloses table cell contents?

   a.  &lt;tr&gt;
   b.  &lt;th&gt;
   c.  &lt;td&gt;
   d.  &lt;table&gt;

2. Which table tag allows you to add a descriptive title that appears above the table by default?

   a.  &lt;border&gt;
   b.  &lt;caption&gt;
   c.  &lt;title&gt;
   d.  &lt;table&gt;

3. What &lt;table&gt; attribute manipulates the amount of space between cells in a table?

   _____

# Introduction to HTML Tables

When you want to display data that is best suited to a tabular format, you can use the set of table tags provided in HTML and XHTML. Tables can provide useful and attractive grids for Web page content. As you learned earlier in this course, you can also use the <pre> tag to structure tabular data. However, the <pre> tag does not allow you to format data exactly as you want it. The <table> tag gives you many formatting options.

Figure 6-1 describes the individual elements that compose a table. Each of these elements will be explored in this lesson.

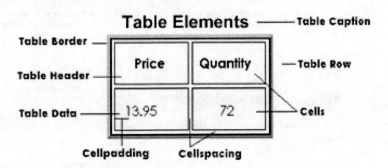

*Figure 6-1: Table elements for HTML and XHTML pages*

The code for the table in the preceding figure could be written as follows:

```
<table border="3" cellpadding="4" cellspacing="2">
<caption>Table Elements</caption>
<tr>
<th>Price</th>
<th>Quantity</th>
</tr>
<tr>
<td>13.95</td>
<td align="center">72</td>
</tr>
</table>
```

Table 6-1 describes the table element tags that correspond to each element in the preceding figure.

*Table 6-1: Table element tags*

| Element | Tag | Required? | Description |
|---------|-----|-----------|-------------|
| **Table** | <table>...</table> | Required | Creates a table. Contains all other table elements. |
| **Table caption** | <caption>...</caption> | Optional | Adds a caption or title, which appears above the table by default. |
| **Table row** | <tr>...</tr> | Required | Contains all data for a table row. |
| **Table header** | <th>...</th> | Optional | Typically designates cells in the top row or left column. By default, text in a header cell will appear bold and centered. |
| **Table data** | <td>...</td> | Required (unless <th> is being used) | Designates table cell contents. |

Tables can be very complex or very simple, as is the one you will create in the next lab. Straightforward tables are easy to create if you understand where to place each element.

## XHTML and tables

HTML tables have often been used to create content structure for entire Web pages. In XHTML, however, you should not use tables to structure a page. Instead, the W3C recommends that you use style sheets and the <div> tag. While useful, <table> tags can make pages harder to update. Most Web developers no longer use tables to structure all the visual elements of their pages, instead using them only where appropriate.

 *A search engine will automatically rank a page lower if the page uses tables for structure. Use CSS instead. Also, if you overuse a table on a page, you may also experience problems. Use tables tastefully and sparingly.*

## Attributes for <table>

The <table> tag defines the overall table structure. Table 6-2 describes attributes of the <table> tag.

*Table 6-2: Attributes of <table> tag*

| Attribute | Description | Values |
|-----------|-------------|--------|
| **align** | Aligns the entire table horizontally on the page. Deprecated for XHTML 1.0, although code will still validate. | - "left"<br>- "center"<br>- "right" |
| **border** | Determines whether a border will appear around the table. By default, borders do not appear on tables. | - "1" (border appears)<br>- "0" (no border appears) |
| **cellpadding** | Determines the amount of space between cell content and the inner cell border. | - Number of pixels<br>- Percentage of the browser window, number followed by percent symbol ( % ) |
| **cellspacing** | Determines the amount of space between table cells. | - Number of pixels<br>- Percentage of the browser window, number followed by percent symbol ( % ) |
| **width** | Determines how far the table will extend horizontally across the page. | - Number of pixels<br>- Percentage of the browser window, number followed by percent symbol ( % ) |
| **summary** | Provides an alternative description of the table for use by applications such as voice-recognition software. | Descriptive text |

## Attributes for <tr>

The <tr> tag defines a single table row. Table 6-3 describes several attributes of the <tr> tag.

*Table 6-3: Attributes of <tr> tag*

| Attribute | Description | Values |
|---|---|---|
| **align** | Aligns content horizontally in all cells in the row. | Same values as for the *align* attribute in the <table> tag:<br>- "left"<br>- "center"<br>- "right" |
| **valign** | Aligns content vertically in all cells in the row. | - "top"<br>- "bottom"<br>- "middle"<br>- "baseline" |
| **bgcolor** | Determines the background color for a row of cells. Deprecated in favor of styles. | - Color name (e.g., "green")<br>- Hexadecimal code (e.g., "#00FF00") |
| **style** | Specifies custom formatting for a row of cells. | A text or numeric definition for an inline style, such as a font, size, color, etc. |

## Attributes for <td>

The <td> tag encompasses the content (text or other data) presented in the table cells, so it has several attributes. Table 6-4 describes the most commonly used attributes of the <td> tag.

*Table 6-4: Attributes of <td> tag*

| Attribute | Description | Values |
|---|---|---|
| **align** | Aligns content horizontally within a single cell. | Same values as for the *align* attribute in the <table> tag:<br>- "left"<br>- "center"<br>- "right" |
| **valign** | Aligns content vertically within a single cell. | - "top"<br>- "middle"<br>- "bottom"<br>- "baseline" |
| **colspan** | Specifies the number of columns that a cell will span across (i.e., occupy). | Number of columns (e.g., "2", "3", "4") |
| **rowspan** | Specifies the number of rows that a cell will span (i.e., occupy). | Number of rows (e.g., "2", "3", "4") |
| **bgcolor** | Determines the background color for a single cell. Deprecated in favor of styles. | - Color name (e.g., "green")<br>- Hexadecimal code (e.g., "#00FF00") |
| **height** | Determines the vertical height of the cell. | Number of pixels |
| **width** | Determines the horizontal width of the cell. Deprecated in favor of styles. | - Number of pixels<br>- Percentage of the browser window, number followed by percent symbol ( % ) |

## Differences between HTML and XHTML

When creating your own tables for a Web page, consider the following differences between HTML and XHTML:

- The HTML 4.01 standard deprecated the use of the *align* attribute with the <table> tag. Although *align* is still allowed in XHTML 1.0 Transitional, it is not supported in XHTML 1.0 Strict. You are encouraged to use style sheets or inline styles to align tables.

- Similarly, the HTML 4.01 standard deprecated the use of the *bgcolor* attribute with the <table> tag. Although this attribute is still allowed in XHTML 1.0 Transitional, it is not supported in XHTML 1.0 Strict. You are encouraged to use style sheets or inline styles to specify background colors for tables.

In the following lab, you will create tables using XHTML. Suppose you notice that the content on the syb_day.html page would work well in a tabular format, which improves readability and adds visual interest. You can organize the existing content into an XHTML table by adding the appropriate tag structure. Then you can supply a couple sentences to introduce the table, as well as a table caption with the title for the table: "A Day in the Life of a Habitat Worker."

### Lab 6-1: Creating XHTML tables to organize content

OBJECTIVE
2.1.5: HTML tables

In this lab, you will convert existing content into tabular format by creating an XHTML table structure.

1. From **C:\CIW\Site_Dev\Lab Files\Lesson06\Lab_6-1\**, copy the file **syb_day.html** and the **syb_day\** folder to the **Habitat\CCYP\** directory. The syb_day.html file should reside on the same level as syb.html, default.html and other Web page files.

2. Load the file **syb_day.html** into your browser. It should resemble Figure 6-2. Notice that the content is not presented in tabular format.

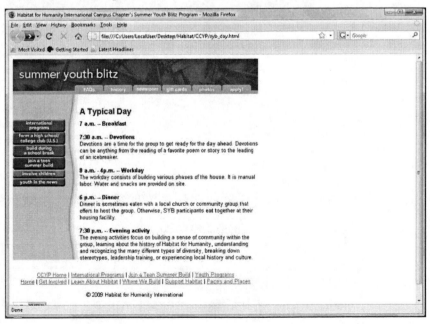

*Figure 6-2: Page syb_day.html presented without table*

3. Open **syb_day.html** in a text editor.

4. Search for the following line of code:

```
<h2>A Typical Day</h2>
```

5. Use the **Edit | Cut** command ( or **CTRL+X**) to cut all content that refers to the "*typical day*," including all text and markup tags. Start by cutting the <p> tag located below the line specified in the previous step, continue through the text that ends with "*experiencing local history and culture*," and also include the **<br/>** tags and the **</p>** tag just above the closing </div> tag. (Do not cut the </div> tag.)

6. Open a second instance of Notepad, and paste the text you just cut into a new file.

7. Save this new file as **old.txt**. In later steps in this lab, you will copy the content (but not the markup) from this text file into the new table you create in syb_day.html. For the purpose of learning tables, it is best to begin by creating the table elements first, then adding content to the table later.

8. Minimize **old.txt**.

9. Maximize **syb_day.html**. Add opening and closing tags to create a table where the text once existed:

```
<table>
</table>
```

10. In **syb_day.html**, create some white space by entering several returns between the opening and closing <table> tags you just entered.

11. By default, tables do not render with a visible border. Give the table a border by adding the **border="1"** attribute and value to the opening **<table>** tag. You now will be able to see your work better.

12. Create a table caption that reads *A Day in the Life of a Habitat Worker*.

13. Consider the content on the original page. As you format the content into a table, you will need to label each column heading with the type of information that column will contain. What categories of information does the existing content provide? Answer the following question in the space provided: How many columns will your table need, and what will each column be titled?

_____

14. You are now ready to create a header row for the table. Between the opening and closing <table> tags, insert a **<tr>** tag. Remember to close the table row with a **</tr>** tag, and use good coding practice by placing each new element on its own line.

15. Now, insert the necessary number of **<th>** tags between the <tr> </tr> tags to create the table header cells. When you are done, you should have three <th> tags, all properly closed with </th>.

16. The table header row will require the most tag information. When you are finished, your code should appear as follows:

```
<table border="1">
<caption>
A Day in the Life of a Habitat Worker
</caption>
```

```
<tr>
<th>Time</th>
<th>Activity</th>
<th>Description</th>
</tr>
</table>
```

17. Add the next row to your table. Use the **<tr> </tr>** tags again, but instead of using three sets of <th> tags within the row, use three sets of **<td>** tags to create the cells in because this row is not a table header.

18. Within the <td> tags, enter the following content from old.txt:

    *7 a.m.*

    *Breakfast*

    *You will cook your own breakfasts and work with others to make sure you are all ready for the day.*

19. Add the **align** attribute with the value **"center"** to center the content that appears in the first two cells you specify with <td> tags. When you are finished, your code should appear as follows:

```
<tr>
<td align="center">7 a.m.</td>
<td align="center">Breakfast</td>
<td>You will cook your own breakfasts and work with others to make sure you
are all ready for the day.</td>
</tr>
```

20. Insert the following text, with <p> </p> tags, just above the table and just below the phrase *A Typical Day*:

```
<p>Why is our program so popular? Because it gives you the opportunity to help
others. Below are some examples of activities.</p>
```

21. Save the file, then view your page in a browser. You should see a table caption introducing a table with three columns, a header row and one row of information, as shown in Figure 6-3.

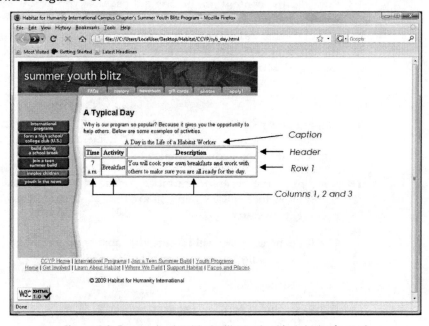

*Figure 6-3: Page syb_day.html with content in tabular format*

22. If your table does not render correctly, review your code and make any necessary changes. When the page renders correctly in the browser, validate your code at *http://validator.w3.org*. The file is short at this point so errors will be easier to locate and correct.

23. Add four more rows to your table, so that you have five rows containing the content you cut from the page. (This content is now in the old.txt file you created, so copy it from there.) Center the content that appears in the first two cells you specify with <td> tags in each row.

24. Notice that the <tr> tags add rows, but that the <td> tags add cells to contain content. The content in each cell is categorized by the column headers, which are defined by the <th> tags.

25. When you are finished, save **syb_day.html** and load it into a browser. If your table does not render as expected, review your code. Edit the code as necessary until it renders as shown in Figure 6-4.

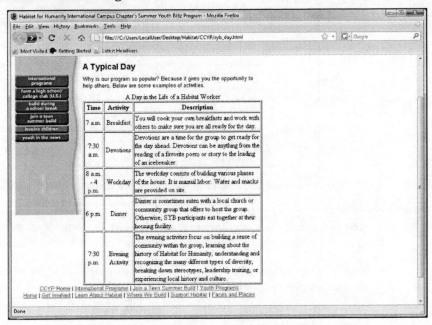

Figure 6-4: Page syb_day.html with table

26. Validate your code and resolve any issues. You will edit this table further in a later lab.

In this lab, you converted existing content into tabular format by creating an XHTML table.

OBJECTIVE
2.1.5: HTML tables

# Table and Data Alignment Options

Frequently you will want to align cell content in a manner that differs from the default alignment. Following are the defaults for table data:

• Content in table header cells is aligned both horizontally and vertically to the center of the cell.

- Content in table data cells is aligned horizontally to the left and vertically to the center.

Table data alignment can drastically affect the look of a table. For instance, if each row uses a different horizontal alignment, the table may not appeal to viewers. For the best visual result, align content consistently within columns.

So far, you have examined only tables with single lines of cell content. Now consider the example in Figure 6-5.

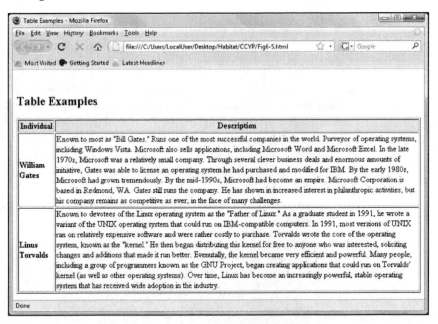

Figure 6-5: Alignment of cell content

You can change the alignment for an individual cell or for an entire row. The attribute you use to specify horizontal alignment is *align*. For vertical alignment, use the *valign* attribute.

Either of the following code samples in Figure 6-6 could be used to produce the alignment shown in Figure 6-7.

```
<tr valign="top">
<td>
William Gates
</td>
```

```
<tr>
<td valign="top">
William Gates
</td>
```

Figure 6-6: Two ways to change vertical alignment

The code example on the left in the preceding figure sets the alignment of the entire row to "top", meaning that all cell content in that row will start at the top of the cell. The code example on the right specifies a vertical alignment only for the cell containing William Gates. The cell to the right of William Gates is already aligned to the top because it is completely full, so the appearance generated by either choice will match that shown in Figure 6-7. (The second row was left unchanged for contrast.)

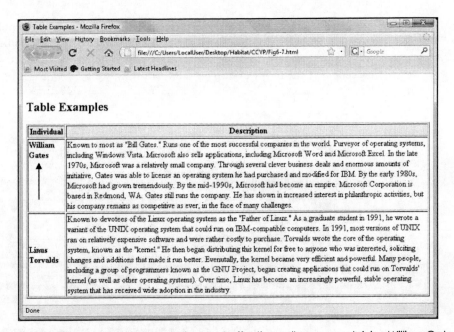

*Figure 6-7: After specifying vertical alignment affecting cell or row containing William Gates*

You can also align the contents of any table cell horizontally to the left, right or center.

# Height and Width of Table Elements

OBJECTIVE
2.1.5: HTML tables

You can change the height or width of the table and individual cells by specifying pixel or percentage values. Examine Figure 6-8.

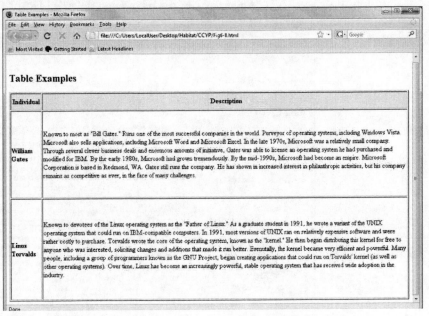

*Figure 6-8: After increasing table height*

In the preceding figure, the table rows increased in size because the *height* attribute of the <table> tag was set to 500 pixels. You could also specify a percentage of the browser window. Note that the additional height was equally distributed among the various rows.

In Figure 6-9, the *height* attribute has been deleted from the <table> tag, and is set only for the cell containing the word *Description*. The cell height has been set to 75 pixels. If you mistakenly set multiple values in multiple cells, the highest value will take precedence; the order of entries does not matter.

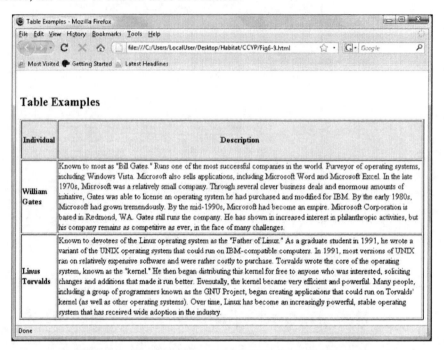

*Figure 6-9: After specifying height="75" (pixels) in table cell*

In Figure 6-10, all *height* attributes have been deleted, except that the width of the first column (with the title *Individual*) has been set to 50 percent of the browser window.

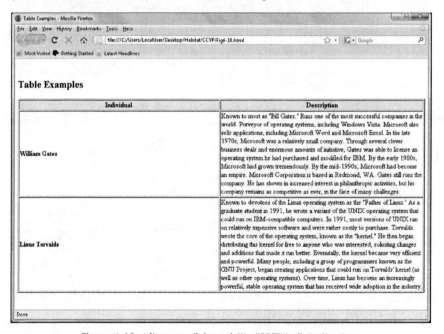

*Figure 6-10: After specifying width="50%" in first <th> tag*

In Figure 6-11, the table width has been changed to 70 percent of the screen and the table has been centered.

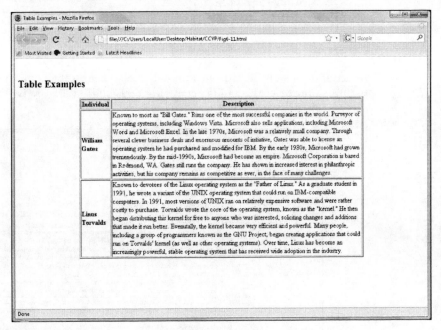

Figure 6-11: After centering table

# Column and Row Spanning

OBJECTIVE
2.1.5: HTML tables

Sometimes you will want a column to span across two or more cells. In other cases, you may need a cell to span more than one row. Figure 6-12 demonstrates a cell that horizontally spans two columns.

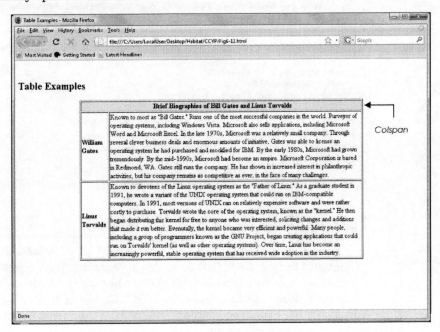

Figure 6-12: Using colspan attribute

The following code created the spanned column in the preceding figure:

```
<tr bgcolor="yellow">
<th colspan="2">
Brief Biographies of Bill Gates and Linus Torvalds
</th>
</tr>
```

Notice that one of the <th> headings has also been removed. This change is logical because now one <th> tag is occupying both spaces. Figure 6-13 shows a cell (i.e., column) that vertically spans two rows.

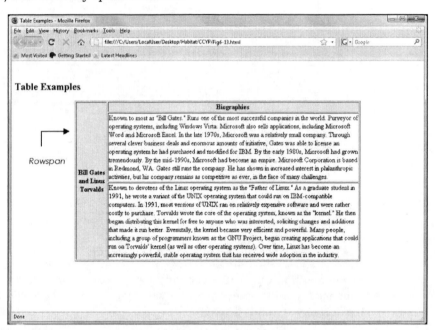

*Figure 6-13: Using rowspan attribute*

The following code created the spanned row in the preceding figure:

```
<tr bgcolor="yellow">
<th rowspan="3">
Bill Gates and Linus Torvalds
</th>
<th>
Biographies
</th>
</tr>
```

Note that the *colspan* and *rowspan* attributes can also be used with the <td> tag.

# Formatting Content in Tables

**OBJECTIVE**
2.1.5: HTML tables

You can format the content that appears within HTML tables. In the past, many developers have used HTML 4.01 tables to organize all content on the Web page. This practice is not recommended by the W3C when writing code in XHTML. You can still insert formatting tags into tables with XHTML. However, the W3C now recommends tables only for organizing content, and not for structuring entire pages. Use the <div> tag for page structuring instead.

Figure 6-14 shows the results of inserting the <strong>, <font> and <center> tags into an XHTML table so that the content "William Gates" and "Linus Torvalds" is emphasized within the table.

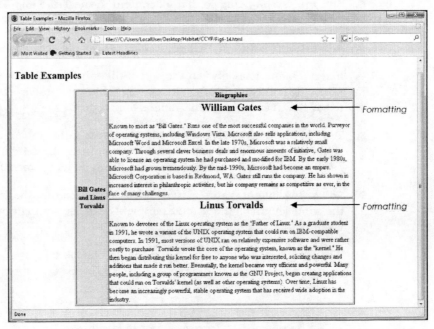

*Figure 6-14: Formatting content within table*

The following code applied this content formatting to the first <td> tag in the document:

```
<td align="left">
<center>
<strong>
<font size="5">William Gates</font>
</strong>
</center>
<br/>
```

In the following lab, you will customize an XHTML table. Suppose you want to add some formatting to your Web page table and the content organized within it. You can use font style, color, alignment and spacing options to modify the table's appearance. Your formatting choices will improve the table's readability, as well as make it more visually exciting.

 ### Lab 6-2: Customizing XHTML tables with formatting

OBJECTIVE
2.1.5: HTML tables

In this lab, you will modify table data with formatting options to make it more aesthetically pleasing.

1.  Open **syb_day.html** in an editor.

2.  Find the table caption, which reads *A Day in the Life of a Habitat Worker*. Notice that it is in a standard font. Add the ***<strong>*** tag to make this caption bold.

3.  Edit the first **<tr>** tag so that its background color is light blue *("#6699FF")*. Load the page in a browser to see how it renders, then validate your code at ***http://validator.w3.org***.

4. Find the first **\<th\>** heading tag. Add the ***width*** attribute to it with a value of ***"93"***. Load the page in a browser to see how it renders, then validate your code.

5. Add the **\<strong\>** tag so that all content in the **Time** and **Activity** columns is bold. (For example, the phrases *7 a.m.* and *Breakfast* should be bold.)

6. Add the ***cellpadding*** attribute to the **\<table\>** tag with a value of ***"5"***.

7. Insert a blank line between the end of the table and the footer section by adding a **\<br/\>** tag immediately after the closing table tag \</table\>. Load the page in a browser to see how it renders, then validate your code.

8. You have now placed all of the page's content into a table. However, the changes you made have caused the yellow sidebar graphic (navbg_04.gif) to be too short for the page. Open the **syb_day/syb_day.css** file in an editor, and find the ***#sidebar*** entry.

9. Adjust the ***height:*** value of the *#sidebar* entry so that the yellow sidebar graphic is the same length as the text. Experiment with the setting until the sidebar looks even when rendered in the browser.

10. When you are finished, your page should resemble Figure 6-15.

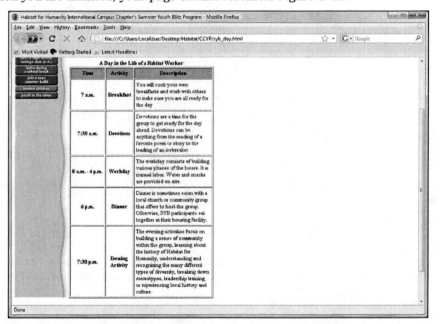

*Figure 6-15: Page syb_day.html with customized formatting*

11. **When time permits:** Remove the border around the table and refresh your browser. Use the ***border="1"*** attribute and value in the **\<table\>** tag to reapply the border.

12. **When time permits:** Experiment with this table by adding formatting to table cells, or by using the \<th\> *colspan* and *rowspan* attributes.

In this lab, you customized the appearance of a table and its content.

## Case Study

# To Use Tables or Not To Use Tables

An-Mei supervised a Web development team responsible for converting the company Web site's HTML 4.0 code into XHTML 1.0. She began the project by reviewing the existing Web pages and code with her team.

An-Mei and her team found that most of the existing pages had used HTML tables to structure all content, rather than only the content that lent itself to a tabular format.

An-Mei chose to limit the use of tables whenever possible, reserving them for content that required a structured layout, such as numbers, dates and other items often viewed within spreadsheets or complex lists.

An-Mei directed the team to remove all HTML tables used for page structuring, and to replace the structure using the <div> tag instead. Although this change required a significant investment of time, the team found that the time was well spent. Without the table structuring, all pages could be quickly updated, and future modifications to the site content were easier. Upper management was pleased that Web site updates were implemented more readily than in the past.

*          *          *

As a class, discuss the ways that HTML tables can improve a Web page.

*   What types of content benefit from a tabular structure? What types of content do not?

*   What advantages do you see in using an invisible HTML table to structure an entire Web page? What disadvantages does the table structure pose?

*   Can you think of examples in which the advantages of using a table page structure would outweigh the disadvantages?

*   Is such a situation likely to occur in the workplace when you are dealing with a business or organization Web site? Why or why not?

## *Lesson Summary*

### Application project

Tables are useful for presenting information that naturally lends itself to tabular format. Both XHTML and HTML allow you to do this. In the past, tables have been used to add structure to a Web page. However, the W3C recommends against this practice for XHTML, so you should use the <div> tag instead.

Visit *www.w3schools.com* and *www.w3.org*, and review attributes to the <table> tag. Then browse some sites, visiting some that include tables. See how other Web developers use tables to organize content. Do you think tables provide an effective presentation? What types of content are best suited for tabular presentation?

### Skills review

In this lesson, you learned to create and manipulate HTML tables. You used the basic structure tags to generate a table, rows and individual cells. You also aligned cell content, spanned cell content across rows and columns, and added background colors to both tables and cells. Finally, you learned that manipulating a border can dramatically affect the appearance of your table.

Now that you have completed this lesson, you should be able to:

✓ 2.1.5: Design and format HTML tables to present information in an organized way.

# Lesson 6 Review

1. The size of an HTML table can be modified by specifying measurements in either of which two units of measure?

   _____

2. What tag can be used instead of the <table> tag to create a simple table by preserving spacing and line breaks in preformatted text?

   _____

3. What components of table appearance can be formatted using the *align* attribute?

   _____

   _____

4. What is the default alignment of the content in table data cells?

   _____

5. What attributes are used to span a single cell across multiple rows or columns, respectively?

   _____

      *Version 2.0*

# Lesson 7:
# Web Forms

## Objectives

By the end of this lesson, you will be able to:

- ✎ 2.4.1: Construct and test HTML forms.

- ✎ 2.4.2: Identify ways that CGI scripts can parse and transmit information from a form, including e-mail, FTP, HTTP, HTTPS.

- ✎ 2.4.3: Diagram a fundamental CGI session.

## Pre-Assessment Questions

1. Which form field offers a round option field in a group of two or more mutually exclusive options?

   a. Submit button
   b. Check box
   c. Scrolling select list
   d. Radio button

2. Which type of button clears all form data and sets all form fields back to the default values?

   a. Default button
   b. Radio button
   c. Reset button
   d. Submit button

3. What tag is used in a select list to identify the text that will appear as list choices?

_____

# Introduction to Web Forms

Web sites use forms to obtain input from users. You can create several types of fields in one form to collect various types of user input. Such input can include the user's name, address and credit card number, for example. The information a user enters into the form is then submitted to a server where it is stored and/or processed.

After a user has entered information into a Web form, he or she clicks the form's Submit button. Submitting the form uploads or e-mails the user's information to the receiving server. Many Web forms also provide a Reset button that clears entered data instead of submitting it, and resets the form fields to the default values.

Forms are of little use without an application on a Web server to process the submitted information. CGI scripts perform this information processing. The following sections discuss the ways that CGI scripts receive and process Web form information. The rest of the lesson will teach you how to develop Web forms using HTML.

# Web Forms and CGI

**Common Gateway Interface (CGI)**
A program that processes data submitted by the user. Allows a Web server to pass control to a software application, based on user request. The application receives and organizes data, then returns it in a consistent format.

To be truly functional, a form requires the use of a **Common Gateway Interface (CGI)** program to process the script. CGI is the de facto standard, but other technologies can be used to process forms, such as Active Server Pages (ASP) and JavaServer Pages (JSP). CGI programs use **server-side script**. By contrast, **client-side script** is executed on the client computer or browser.

A CGI script residing on a server performs two important functions:

**server-side script**
Code that resides on a server to help process Web form input. Server-side CGI scripts are commonly written in Perl.

- It receives data from a Web browser.

- Then it processes and formats the data.

Without some sort of CGI script running on the server, the server cannot receive Web form data. Most CGI scripts do more than just receive data; they also remove extraneous information (such as delimiters) and format the data. Many scripts, servers and utilities are available for UNIX, Macintosh and Windows platforms to simplify this process. Such scripting utilities are available commercially, or as freeware or shareware.

**client-side script**
Code embedded into an HTML page and downloaded by a user; resides on the client and helps process Web form input. Common client-side scripting languages include JavaScript and VBScript.

## Diagramming a CGI session

The following elements are necessary for a CGI session:

- Web browser

- CGI script (a file that contains a programming language such as Perl or PHP)

- Web form

- Web server, with a CGI interpreter

**OBJECTIVE**
2.4.3 Diagramming CGI sessions

A CGI script remains on a Web server. The Web forms you will learn to create in this lesson allow users to upload information to your Web server, where information can be processed and acted upon. Actions taken by the Web server and CGI interpreter can include:

- Storing information in a database (for example, bank account updates).

- Searching a database for a product (for example, a book or DVD at Amazon.com).

- Sending processed information back to the end user (for example, a new bank account balance or a confirmation that a book was shipped).

Figure 7-1 illustrates the Web form data processing performed via CGI.

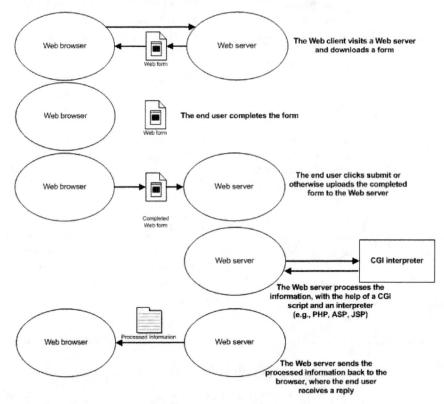

Figure 7-1: CGI session

OBJECTIVE
2.4.2 CGI scripts

## Parsing data: Form handling, name=value pairs and CGI

You now understand that a CGI script residing on a server receives data from a Web browser, then processes the data into human-readable format (or any other format you require). Before a CGI script receives any data, however, a user must enter the data into a Web form and submit it. Figure 7-2 shows a simple Web form.

Figure 7-2: Simple HTML form

In this figure, a form allows the user to provide his name and e-mail address, then indicate whether he wants to be placed on the company's mailing list. When the user clicks the Submit Query button, the browser sends the information entered in this form to the Web server as a raw text string.

The basic element of a raw text string is a name=value pair. The *name* attribute of the <form> element organizes information input by the user into name=value pairs. For example, the Web form in the preceding figure organizes user input according to the following code. Pay special attention to the code shown in bold:

```
Enter Your Name: <input type="text" name="Name" size="40"/>

Enter Your E-mail: <input type="text" name="Email" size="40"/>

Should we add you to our mailing list? <br/>
<input type="radio" name="AddToList" value="yes"/> Yes
<input type="radio" name="AddToList" value="no"/> No
```

*Notice that in XHTML, you must properly close all tags used to create Web forms.*

When the browser sends this data, it will use the *name* attribute values "Name", "Email" and "AddToList" as the basis for creating the raw text string. You can specify any words as *name* values. In this example, the server receives a raw text string that resembles the following:

```
Name=Dimitri+Pappas&Email=student50@class.com&AddToList=yes
```

This raw text string consists of name=value pairs, delimited by ampersands (&). In a name=value pair, entered spaces are replaced with plus signs (+). If a form field is left empty, only the first part of the name=value pair will be returned. For example, if this user left the mailing list option blank, the corresponding name=value pair would return "Email=" without any information after the equal symbol.

After the server receives this information, a CGI script can parse and format the raw text string into a human-readable format similar to the following:

| | |
|---|---|
| **Name:** | Dimitri Pappas |
| **E-Mail:** | student50@class.com |
| **Mailing List:** | Yes |

The Web form you will create in this lesson will use Name and Email, as well as other name values that correspond to their functions. Now that you understand how a basic script processes Web form data, consider a commonly used CGI script: FormMail.

## Applied example: FormMail

One example of a CGI script is the venerable FormMail script, written by Matt Wright. This script has existed in various versions since 1997. It is written in Practical Extraction and Report Language (Perl) and has the file name FormMail.pl.

FormMail is designed to receive information from a Web form via the Perl interpreter. The script then sends the form information to you via e-mail. You simply check your e-mail to receive results from the script. You can learn more about FormMail at Matt's Script Archive (*www.scriptarchive.com/formmail.html*).

FormMail is popular for many reasons, including the following:

- It is available free of charge from Matt's Script Archive (MSA).

- It is written in Perl, which allows developers to use a free CGI interpreter available in many places, including *www.cpan.org*. Most modern operating systems allow the Perl interpreter to be installed, making Perl one of the more ubiquitous languages. The combination of a free, powerful Perl interpreter and a free, well-written FormMail script is widely appealing.

- FormMail is easy to customize. Wright specifically designed FormMail for ease of use: The developer simply modifies a few portions of the script and it is ready to perform whatever tasks a particular Web form requires.

After you download FormMail, you perform the following simple steps:

- Install Perl on your Web server. Many Web servers already have Perl installed.

- Define the FormMail variables so that the script is capable of receiving information and sending it to you.

- Give executable permissions to the FormMail.pl script on your Web server.

- Refer to the FormMail.pl script in your Web form.

- Wait for users to visit your site, and then check your e-mail for results.

Many organizations and businesses use the FormMail script for various beneficial purposes. Some companies have made money through Web-based sales. Other sites have used the script to help charities and other worthy causes.

## Security concerns

Spam has become a concern for most Web users. Some unscrupulous individuals have taken advantage of the FormMail script because older versions could be fooled into sending e-mail to anyone. Some systems administrators still use older versions of the program. Other administrators improperly configure newer script versions, resulting in more spam on the Internet. You should use the latest version of FormMail, which has features that allow its use without inviting abuse from spammers.

*A site called the FormMail Hall of Shame contains a list of servers that still allow spam to be sent. You can visit this site at www.softwolves.pp.se/misc/formmail_hall_of_shame.*

## Other versions of FormMail

You are not limited to using the original Perl FormMail script. Alternative versions of FormMail are available for PHP (*www.dtheatre.com/scripts/formmail.php*) and ASP (*www.brainjar.com/asp/formmail*), for example.

In the following lab, you will work with the FormMail script. Suppose the Web development director asks what you think about adding a Web form to the company site, and whether you could enable such a form to process data. You profile some of the FormMail script's features and download the script. Then you discuss the potential capabilities with the director. If she decides that a form should be added to the Web site, you can program the FormMail script you downloaded to process information obtained from the Web form.

## Lab 7-1: Studying the FormMail script

OBJECTIVE
2.4.2 CGI scripts

In this lab, you will review the FormMail script and its features.

1. Open a browser and visit ***www.scriptarchive.com/formmail.html***, which is the FormMail home page. Review the description of FormMail, including the Readme file and the FAQ page.

2. Navigate to the **C:\CIW\Site_Dev\Lab Files\Lesson07** directory, and copy the **FormMail\** folder to your Desktop.

   *Note: If necessary, go to **www.scriptarchive.com/formmail.html** to visit the FormMail home page and obtain the FormMail script.*

3. Unzip the FormMail file, and extract the **Readme** and **FormMail.pl** files.

4. Open the **Readme** file in WordPad or Notepad.

5. Review the *Necessary Variables* section. This section describes the variables that you must change if you use this script with a Web server.

6. Close the **Readme** file.

7. Open the **FormMail.pl** file in WordPad or Notepad.

8. Review the script and identify the following elements of the script:

   - **$mailprog** — specifies your e-mail server program. This program could be for Windows or another operating system. Linux/UNIX servers often use Sendmail (*www.sendmail.org*) or Postfix (*www.postfix.org*).

   - **@referers** — helps control who can use the FormMail script.

   - **@valid_ENV** — allows you to specify the environment variables that will be sent with the script. Remember that FormMail is designed to send to you, via e-mail, the form information submitted by your site visitors. You can use the @valid_ENV section to get information about the host that used your script, such as the user agent (e.g., a Web browser) used to generate the request or the IP address of the user's system. The @valid_ENV element is added as a security measure so that you can learn about the submissions you receive. However, be aware that a malicious user can spoof this information.

   - **@recipients** — includes the recipient field (required) and additional optional fields that allow you to control the way that information submitted by users is processed.

9. When you are finished reviewing the FormMail script, discuss the following questions as a class:

   - Why is the FormMail script popular?

   - How could you use this script in your own situation?

In this lab, you reviewed the FormMail script.

Now that you understand the basic processes and conventions of a Web form, you can begin studying and coding individual form fields.

# Basic Tags for Creating Web Forms

You can create a user-input Web form on a Web page by placing HTML code to create various form fields in between a set of HTML <form> tags. Such forms are essential for receiving input from users and for e-commerce.

All elements of the form must be contained in the <form> element section in order for the form to function and process properly. There are many types of fields that you can place in a form, depending on the type of info you want to elicit from users. This section describes the basic HTML tags used to create a Web form. In the sections that follow, you will add a field type to your Web form with each successive lab.

## The <form> tag

The HTML <form> tag creates a user-input Web form by encompassing all the content and fields of the form on the page. The <form> tag is a container tag, so it requires both opening and closing tags. In some browsers, if you fail to supply the closing </form> tag, the form will not render. Internet Explorer displays form fields even if no <form> tag is present. However, users would be unable to submit any information because the <form> tag is required to instruct the browser where to send data.

Following is sample syntax for a <form> tag:

```
<form
    method="post"
    action="http://www.anyserver.com/cgi-bin/scriptfile">
            <input .../>
            <select> ... </select>
</form>
```

For now, ignore the <input> and <select> elements.

The <form> element has two attributes associated with it:

- *method* — specifies which method the browser will use to send form data to a Web server

- *action* — specifies the name and location of the CGI script used to process the form

These attributes are required in the <form> tag in order to process data that users submit in the form.

### The method attribute

The *method* attribute specifies the method by which the browser will send form data to a Web server. The *method* attribute takes two values:

- "get" — Form data is appended to the URL of the Web page for use in a query string. This method sends information in cleartext and is thus less secure.

- "post" — Form data is posted to the URL specified by the *action* attribute. Post is the preferred method for sending form data. It can send more characters, although sometimes post requires more processing by the CGI script.

### The action attribute

The *action* attribute specifies the name and location of the CGI script used to process the form. The contents of the form will be processed by the script and acted upon according to the instructions in the script.

## The <input>, <select> and <textarea> tags

You can use the <input>, <select> and <textarea> tags to create form fields by placing them between the <form> </form> tags.

### The <input> tag and the type attribute

The <input> tag is not a container tag; it stands alone. You use <input> to create text boxes, check boxes, radio buttons, and the Submit and Reset buttons.

The <input> element takes the *type* attribute. The value you use with the *type* attribute designates the form field type as a text box, a radio button, a Submit or Reset button, a password field or a check box. For example, to create a radio button with the <input> element, you would use the following syntax:

```
<input type="radio" name="AddToList"/>
```

You can change the value of *type* to create other buttons or fields. You can also add other attributes to customize the field's behavior. To create a password field, for example, you would use the following code:

```
Enter Your Password: <input type="password" name="Password" size="14"/>
```

You will learn more about the *name* and *value* attributes shortly.

### The <select> tag

The <select> tag is a container tag used to create single-option and multiple-option select lists. Following is an example of <select>:

```
How often do you want to be updated about Habitat For Humanity?<br/>
<select name="Frequency">
<option>Once a week</option>
<option>Once or twice a month</option>
<option>Once a month</option>
<option value="NotAtAll" >Never</option>
</select>
```

When using the <select> tag, you may want to allow users to select more than one option from the list. If so, you must use the *multiple* attribute with "multiple" as the value. For example, consider the following XHTML code:

```
<p>Which countries have you worked in?</p>
<select name="Countries" multiple="multiple" size="4">
<option>Australia</option>
<option>New Zealand</option>
<option>England</option>
<option>France</option>
<option>India</option>
<option>China</option>
</select>
```

This code allows users to select multiple countries, rather than just one.

### The <textarea> tag

The <textarea> container tag creates scrolling text area spaces. Users can enter multiple lines of text into a text area; it is larger and allows more input than a text box. Because it is a container tag, you can enter default text between the opening and closing tags, and it will appear in the text area until the user types their input into the field.

# Web Form Fields

Table 7-1 describes each type of form field discussed in this lesson.

*Table 7-1: Web form fields*

| Form Field | Description | Example |
|---|---|---|
| Text box | A text field into which a user can enter characters. | Name: |
| Radio button | Round option buttons in a group of two or more mutually exclusive options. | Do you know carpentry? ⦿ Yes ○ No |
| Check box | Square boxes in a group of two or more non-exclusive options. | Skills (check all that apply): ☑ Carpentry ☑ Cement working ☐ Medical care |
| Single-option select list | A drop-down list of two or more options from which a single selection can be made. | How often do you want to be updated about Habitat for Humanity? Once a week / Once a week / Once or twice a month / Once a month / Never |
| Multiple-option select list | An exposed list of two or more options, optionally scrollable, from which the user can make multiple selections. | Please indicate your interests (select all that apply): Swimming / Diving / Kayaking / Literature |
| Text area | A scrolling text field into which the user can enter multiple lines of text. | Comments: I am looking forward to helping! |
| Password field | A text box that visually masks the entered characters as asterisks. | Enter your password: ******** |
| File upload | A button and field that allow users to navigate to and select a local file for uploading or other purposes (for example, to validate HTML files). | Choose your file here: C:\my_application.pdf  Browse... |

*Table 7-1: Web form fields (cont'd)*

| Form Field | Description | Example |
|---|---|---|
| **Submit button** | A button that, when clicked, causes the form's action statement to process. Labeled "Submit" or "Submit Query" by default, but can display any label. | Submit |
| **Reset button** | A button that, when clicked, clears all form data and sets all form fields back to the default values for those fields. Labeled "Reset" by default, but can display any label. | Reset |

The value names for each type of form field will be discussed shortly. Figure 7-3 depicts several form fields on a Web page form.

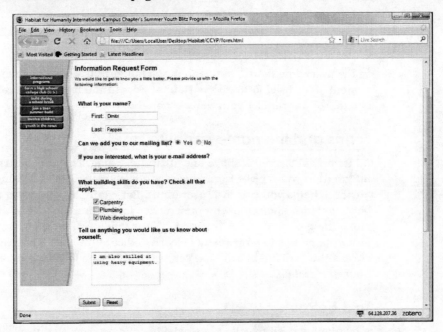

*Figure 7-3: Web form fields*

Many Web forms use form fields much more sparingly, as shown in Figure 7-4.

*Figure 7-4: Sparing use of Web form fields*

In the preceding figure, notice that a small form is embedded within other Web page content. This brief form allows Habitat For Humanity to determine if a Certificate of Title is required to transfer your vehicle donation.

## Forms and the *name* attribute

All form field elements share one attribute: *name*. The *name* attribute identifies information you receive from a user and associates it with a value you specify. The *name* attribute helps you organize user input. For example, you could use a series of check boxes to learn about a user's preferences for gardening, sailing and biking, and you could name the group of boxes "Interests." Thus when you receive information from the Web form, the names in your results clearly indicate the user's choices. That is, if the user checks the "sailing" check box, you will receive the following information: *Interests=sailing*.

## Text boxes

A text box is used to collect a single line of data from the user, such as name, e-mail or address information. The text box is the most common form field.

The syntax for creating a text box is as follows:

```
<input type="text" name="FieldName"/>
```

If you want the text box to appear with some default text inside, use the additional *value* attribute as shown:

```
<input type="text" name="FieldName" value="DefaultText"/>
```

Additionally, you can use a *size* attribute to specify the width of the text box in characters. The *size* attribute has no effect on the amount of text the user can enter; it restricts only the visual appearance of the field. Contrast this with the *maxlength* attribute. The value of *maxlength* restricts user entries to the specified number of characters; it has no effect on the display width of the field.

## File upload

You can allow your site's users to upload files to your site using a Web form. Simply use the "file" value of the *type* attribute to the <input> tag as follows:

```
Provide your resume here: <input type="file" name="UploadedFile"/>
```

This code will create a Browse button on the Web form. When a user clicks the Browse button, a Choose File dialog box will appear, which the user can use to navigate to and select a local file for uploading. An accompanying text box displays the path and file name that the user has chosen.

## Submit and Reset buttons

When you specify the <input> tag's *type* attribute value as "reset" or "submit", you create a button that performs a specific action. Clicking the Submit button sends the data from all fields in the form to be processed by the *action* specified in the <form> tag. Clicking the Reset button clears all form fields instead of submitting the data, and resets fields to their default settings. You will use these buttons in the forms you create in this lesson.

*The labs in this course provide an overview of the usage and syntax of individual form fields. The action attribute used in the <form> tag will point to an HTML test engine that provides a form response to your browser. Many test engines are available on the Internet that can be helpful for testing form code.*

In the following series of labs, you will create a Web form with a variety of form field types. Suppose the Web development director was encouraged by the information you provided her about using the FormMail script for Web form processing. She has decided that a form could be a useful addition to the Web site, and she assigns you to design a model for the Web form. The director will use your model in discussions with upper management, marketing and sales associates to gather input about the types of information that should be collected from your Web site visitors. So you consider the various form fields that you can demonstrate in your model, and the types of user information that each field is most effective for collecting.

 **Lab 7-2: Creating a simple Web form in XHTML**

**OBJECTIVE**
2.4.1 Creating HTML forms

In this lab, you will create a basic Web form using the HTML <form> and <input> tags. The *action* attribute in the <form> tag will point to a public test engine that you can use to check your form output. You would never use this URL in an actual production setting; use it only to verify that your form is functioning as expected.

1. **Editor:** From **C:\CIW\Site_Dev\Lab Files\Lesson07\Lab_7-2\**, open the file **lab_7-2.txt**.

2. **Editor:** Enter the source code indicated in bold:

```
<!DOCTYPE html
    PUBLIC "-//W3C//DTD XHTML 1.0 Transitional//EN"
    "http://www.w3.org/TR/xhtml1/DTD/xhtml1-transitional.dtd">
<html xmlns="http://www.w3.org/1999/xhtml" xml:lang="en">
<head>
<meta name="Keywords" content="CIW, Foundations, Example"/>
<meta name="Description" content="For the CIW Foundations Course"/>
<meta http-equiv="Content-Type" content="text/html; charset=utf-8"/>
<!-- <link rel="stylesheet" type="text/css" href="myform.css"
title="stylesheet"/> -->
```

```
<title>Basic Form</title>
</head>
<body>
<h1>Basic Form</h1>

<form
    method="post"
    action="http://ss1.ciwcertified.com/cgi-bin/process.pl">

Enter Your Name: <input type="text" name="Name" size="40"/>
<br/>
<br/>
Enter Your E-mail: <input type="text" name="Email" size="40"/>
<br/>
<br/>
<br/>
<input type="submit"/>
<input type="reset"/>

</form>

</body>
</html>
```

3. **Editor:** Save the file as **lab_7-2.html**.

4. **Browser:** Open the file **lab_7-2.html**. Your display should resemble Figure 7-5.

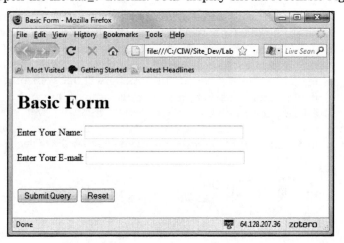

*Figure 7-5: Simple Web form*

5. **Browser:** Enter a name and an e-mail address into the text boxes, and then click the **Submit Query** button. You should see in the status bar that a server connection is being made. After a few seconds (or minutes if your connection is slow), you should see the results of your input echoed back to you on a separate page, as shown in Figure 7-6.

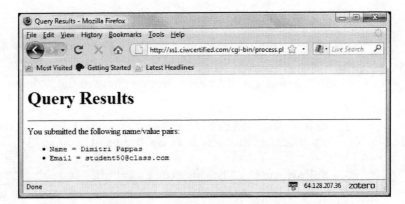

Figure 7-6: Results of submitting data to form's test engine script

6. **Browser:** Click the **Back** button in the browser to return to your Web form page.

7. **Browser:** Click the **Reset** button to clear all form data.

8. Validate your code at ***http://validator.w3.org***.

In this lab, you created a simple form, and you saw a CGI script return name=value pairs from the submitted form.

Now that you are familiar with the <input> tag, you will use it to create radio buttons and check boxes in the sections that follow.

## Radio buttons

Radio buttons are never used as stand-alone items. They are reserved for two or more mutually exclusive options. To ensure exclusivity, a group of radio buttons must share the same *name* attribute, although they will each use an individual value. The following example code shows two buttons representing mutually exclusive answers to the same question.

```
Do you know carpentry? <br/>
<input type="radio" checked="checked" name="KnowCarp" value="yes"/> Yes
<input type="radio" name="KnowCarp" value="no"/> No
```

The browser will render this code as shown in Figure 7-7.

### Do you know carpentry?
### ⦿ Yes ○ No

Figure 7-7: Radio button group

Notice that in the preceding figure, the Yes option is preselected as a default. This preselection is made possible by the *checked*="checked" attribute and value, shown in the code.

In the following lab, you will add some radio buttons to the Web form. Suppose you want the model form, which you are creating for the Web development director, to demonstrate some mutually exclusive user-input options. Radio buttons provide this capability, and they are a form field type familiar to most Web users. You also consider whether to preselect one of the radio buttons as a default. A default selection can save users time or demonstrate use of the button. However, some users may neglect to change the default selection, even if the preselected choice is not their preference. Can you use this fact to your advantage?

## Lab 7-3: Adding a radio button group to an XHTML Web form

**OBJECTIVE**
2.4.1 Creating HTML forms

In this lab, you will add a radio button group to the Web form you created in the previous lab.

1. **Editor:** From **C:\CIW\Site_Dev\Lab Files\Lesson07\Lab_7-2**, open the file **lab_7-2.html** and save it as **lab_7-3.html**.

2. **Editor:** Add the following code as indicated in bold:

```
<!DOCTYPE html
    PUBLIC "-//W3C//DTD XHTML 1.0 Transitional//EN"
    "http://www.w3.org/TR/xhtml1/DTD/xhtml1-transitional.dtd">
<html xmlns="http://www.w3.org/1999/xhtml" xml:lang="en">
<head>
<meta name="Keywords" content="CIW, Foundations, Example"/>
<meta name="Description" content="For the CIW Foundations Course"/>
<meta http-equiv="Content-Type" content="text/html; charset=utf-8"/>
<!-- <link rel="stylesheet" type="text/css" href="myform.css"
title="stylesheet"/> -->
<title>Basic Form</title>
</head>
<body>
<h1>Basic Form</h1>

<form
    method="post"
    action="http://ss1.ciwcertified.com/cgi-bin/process.pl">

Enter Your Name: <input type="text" name="Name" size="40"/>
<br/>
<br/>
Enter Your E-Mail: <input type="text" name="Email" size="40"/>
<br/>
<br/>
Should we add you to our mailing list?<br/>
<input type="radio" name="AddToList" value="yes" checked="checked"/>Yes
<input type="radio" name="AddToList" value="no"/>No
<br/>
<br/>
<input type="submit"/>
<input type="reset"/>

</form>

</body>
</html>
```

3. **Editor:** Save the **lab_7-3.html** file.

4. **Browser:** Load your file. The radio buttons should appear as they do in Figure 7-8.

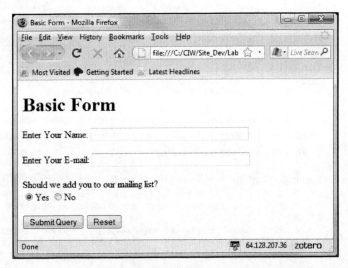

Figure 7-8: Web form after adding radio button group

5. **Browser:** Test the radio buttons by clicking the **No** button, then clicking the **Yes** button. If you can select both buttons simultaneously, you made an error in the *name* attribute for these buttons. To work properly, these buttons must use the same name for their group.

6. **Browser:** If your buttons are working, enter information into the rest of the form, then submit the form. You should see either "yes" or "no" returned for the value of the AddToList field, as shown in Figure 7-9.

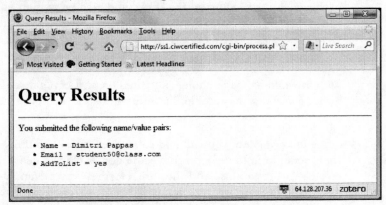

Figure 7-9: Form results with radio button group

7. **Browser:** Click the **Back** button to return to your form page.

8. Validate your code.

In this lab, you added radio buttons to a Web form.

## Check boxes

Check boxes are used for a group of non-exclusive choices. You have two options when naming check boxes, and the option you choose depends on how you plan to use the collected data. Consider the following scenario. You want a list of the user's favorite hobbies. You plan to store the user's selections in a database. Are you going to store the user's entire response, which might include multiple hobbies, in a single field? Or do you want each hobby stored in a separate field in the database? Your choice will affect how you name the fields. In the next lab, you will see the results from both options.

The syntax for creating a check box is as follows:

```
<input type="checkbox" name="groupName"/>
```

As with radio buttons, you can preselect check boxes by adding the attribute *checked*="checked" into the tag. Unlike radio buttons, however, you can preselect as many check boxes as you like because check boxes are non-exclusive.

The following code will create a check box section on a form:

```
What skills do have that can help us at Habitat for Humanity? (check all that
apply):<br/>
<input type="checkbox" name="Carpentry"/> Carpentry<br/>
<input type="checkbox" name="Plumbing"/> Plumbing<br/>
<input type="checkbox" name="Financing"/> Financing<br/>
```

This code would render as shown in Figure 7-10.

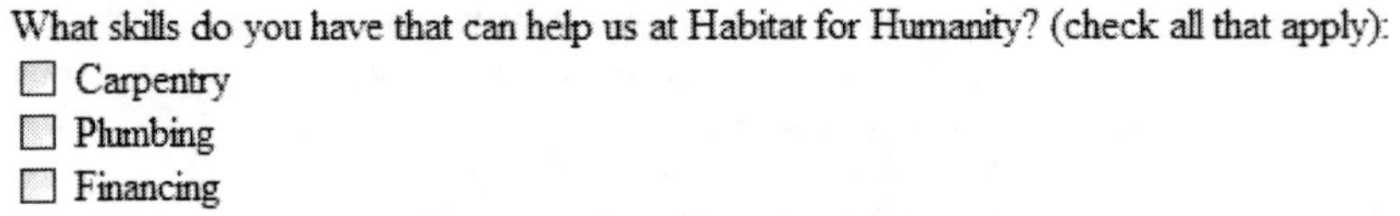

What skills do you have that can help us at Habitat for Humanity? (check all that apply):
☐ Carpentry
☐ Plumbing
☐ Financing

*Figure 7-10: Check box group*

In this check box example, the tags could also be written as follows:

```
<input type="checkbox" name="Skills"/> Carpentry<br/>
<input type="checkbox" name="Skills"/> Plumbing<br/>
<input type="checkbox" name="Skills"/> Financing<br/>
```

With this syntax, each choice is treated as part of a single database field named Skills. Either method is acceptable, but one will be more appropriate depending on how you plan to use the data.

In the following lab, you will add some check boxes to the Web form. Suppose you want your model form to demonstrate some non-exclusive user-input options. Check boxes provide this capability, and they are a form field type familiar to most Web users. You consider that your organization could benefit from learning about some of the skills that candidates possess. A group of check boxes is an effective form field for obtaining this type of information.

 **Lab 7-4: Adding check boxes to an XHTML Web form**

**OBJECTIVE**
2.4.1 Creating HTML forms

In this lab, you will add several check boxes to the Web form you have been building in the previous labs.

1. **Editor:** From **C:\CIW\Site_Dev\Lab Files\Lesson07\Lab_7-2**, open the file **lab_7-3.html** and save it as **lab_7-4.html**.

2. **Editor:** Add the following code as indicated in bold:

```
<!DOCTYPE html
    PUBLIC "-//W3C//DTD XHTML 1.0 Transitional//EN"
```

```
         "http://www.w3.org/TR/xhtml1/DTD/xhtml1-transitional.dtd">
<html xmlns="http://www.w3.org/1999/xhtml" xml:lang="en">
<head>
<meta name="Keywords" content="CIW, Foundations, Example"/>
<meta name="Description" content="For the CIW Foundations Course"/>
<meta http-equiv="Content-Type" content="text/html; charset=utf-8"/>
<!-- <link rel="stylesheet" type="text/css" href="myform.css"
title="stylesheet"/> -->
<title>Basic Form</title>
</head>
<body>
<h1>Basic Form</h1>

<form
     method="post"
     action="http://ss1.ciwcertified.com/cgi-bin/process.pl">

Enter Your Name: <input type="text" name="Name" size="40"/>
<br/>
<br/>
Enter Your E-mail: <input type="text" name="Email" size="40"/>
<br/>
<br/>
Should we add you to our mailing list?<br/>
<input type="radio" name="AddToList" value="yes" checked="checked"/>Yes
<input type="radio" name="AddToList" value="no"/>No
<br/>
<br/>

What skills do you have that can help us at Habitat for Humanity? (check all
that apply):<br/>
<input type="checkbox" name="Carpentry"/> Carpentry<br/>
<input type="checkbox" name="Plumbing"/> Plumbing<br/>
<input type="checkbox" name="Financing"/> Financing<br/>

<br/>
<br/>

<input type="submit"/>
<input type="reset"/>

</form>

</body>
</html>
```

3.  **Editor:** Save the **lab_7-4.html** file.

4.  **Browser:** Load your file. The check boxes should appear as they do in Figure 7-11.

Figure 7-11: Web form after adding check boxes

5. **Browser:** Enter information into the form. Select at least one of the check box options. Then submit the form. Your results should resemble Figure 7-12.

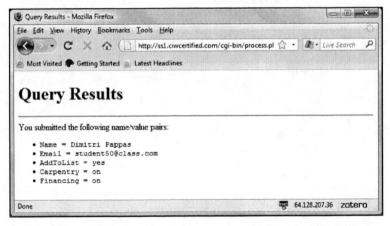

Figure 7-12: Form results with check boxes as separate data fields

6. **Editor:** Open **lab_7-4.html**, and change the check box tags as indicated in bold:

```
What skills do you have that can help us at Habitat for Humanity? (check all
that apply):<br/>
<input type="checkbox" name="Skills"/> Carpentry<br/>
<input type="checkbox" name="Skills"/> Plumbing<br/>
<input type="checkbox" name="Skills"/> Financing<br/>
```

7. **Editor:** Save the **lab_7-4.html** file.

8. **Browser:** Click the **Back** button to return to your form page.

9. **Browser:** Submit the same data again. This time you should see slightly different results, as shown in Figure 7-13.

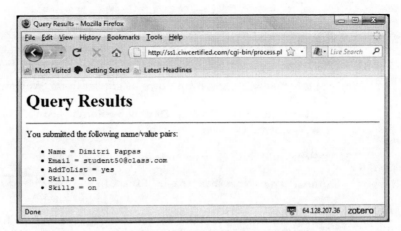

*Figure 7-13: Form results with check boxes as group data field*

**10.** Consider these results carefully. By naming all the check boxes the same, you made them function as a group. If you want to know whether candidates have at least one of the skills listed but you do not need to know which specific skills they checked, then organizing information in this way may help you create a large group to contact. You can use either method to configure your check boxes based on which best suits your needs.

**11.** Change the check box tags' *name* attribute values back to **Carpentry**, **Plumbing** and **Financing**, respectively.

**12.** Validate your code.

In this lab, you added check boxes to a Web form.

## Select lists

Select lists are drop-down lists of predetermined options. Depending on the settings, these lists can allow single or multiple selections.

### Single-option select list

The syntax for creating a drop-down single-option select list is as follows:

```
<select name="listName">
<option>Option 1 </option>
<option>Option 2 </option>
...
<option>Option n </option>
</select>
```

The value that is passed when the form is submitted is the text to the right of the <option> tag. However, if you want to pass a value different from the text that appears in the list, you can add the *value=""* attribute into any or all of the <option> tags. In the next lab, one option will be set to pass a value different from the one the user will see.

In the following lab, you will add a single-option select list to the Web form. Suppose you want your model form to demonstrate a drop-down list of choices from which users can choose one. A select list provides this capability, and it is a form field type familiar to most Web users. You consider that the marketing team will want to contact candidates via e-mail regularly, so a select list might provide an effective way to learn how often the candidates want to be contacted. How else might this type of list help the marketing team perform tasks?

## Lab 7-5: Adding a single-option drop-down list to an XHTML Web form

OBJECTIVE
2.4.1 Creating HTML
forms

In this lab, you will add a drop-down select list to the Web form you have been building.

1. **Editor:** From **C:\CIW\Site_Dev\Lab Files\Lesson07\Lab_7-2**, open the file **lab_7-4.html** and save it as **lab_7-5.html**.

2. **Editor:** Add the following code as indicated in bold:

```
<input type="checkbox" name="Financing"/> Financing<br/>

<br/>
How often would you like to receive an e-mail from Habitat for Humanity? <br/>
<select name="EmailFreq">
<option>Once a week</option>
<option>Once or twice a month </option>
<option>Once a month </option>
<option value="Remove">Never </option>
</select>
<br/>
<br/>
<br/>

<input type="submit"/>
<input type="reset"/>

</form>
```

3. **Editor:** Save the **lab_7-5.html** file.

4. **Browser:** Load the file. The select list should appear as it does in Figure 7-14.

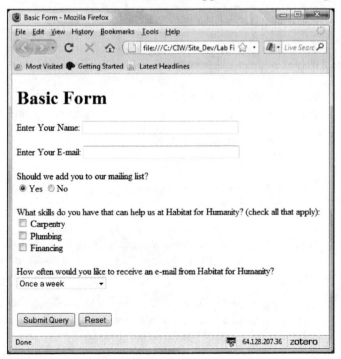

*Figure 7-14: Web form after adding select list*

5. Click and hold the arrow at the right side of the select-list box to open the drop-down list of items. Select the second list option as shown in Figure 7-15.

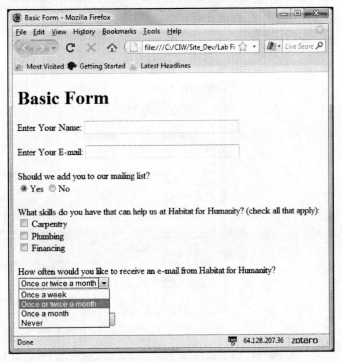

*Figure 7-15: Selecting from select list in Web form*

6. **Browser:** Fill out the rest of the form and submit it. You should see results similar to Figure 7-16.

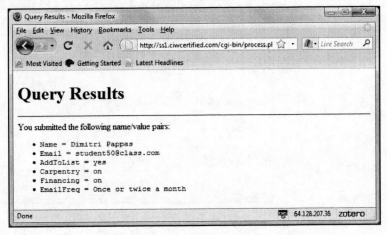

*Figure 7-16: Form results with select list*

7. **Browser:** Click the **Back** button to return to your Web form page. This time, choose the last option in the list (see Figure 7-17). This option will return a value different from the one the user sees in the form.

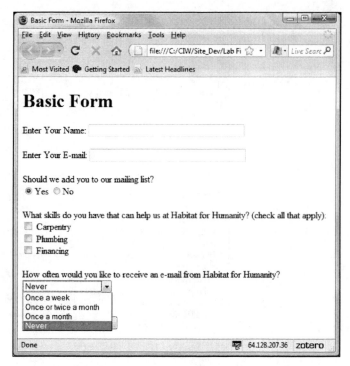

*Figure 7-17: Selecting list option with specified result value*

8. **Browser:** Submit the form. The last option in your results list should reflect the value of the *value* attribute you specified in the last <option> tag in your code. See Figure 7-18.

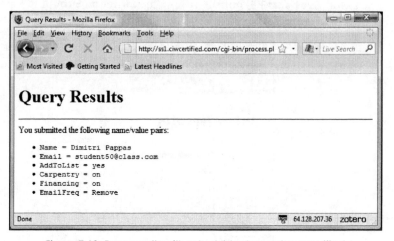

*Figure 7-18: Form results with select list return value specified*

9. Consider these results carefully. Notice that the value returned for EmailFreq is now "Remove" instead of "Never" as it appears in the user's selections. The code you entered for the *value* attribute of this <option> tag created a customized result value. This value would be useful with a CGI script that could automatically remove candidates from a mailing list if they choose the "Never" selection, yet store their e-mail information in a database for later use.

10. Validate your code.

In this lab, you created a single-option drop-down list in a Web form.

## Multiple-option select list

Within the <select> tag, you can include the *multiple* attribute as follows:

```
<select name="work" multiple="multiple" size="4">
```

The presence of this attribute automatically changes the select list to allow users to select more than one option. Because multiple selections are possible, these lists are usually presented with several, if not all, options already exposed.

The *size* attribute of the <select> tag controls the number of items that will appear in a scrolling list box. If no size is specified, the number of items that will appear by default depends on the browser.

In the following lab, you will add a multiple-option select list to the Web form. Suppose you want your model form to demonstrate a drop-down list of choices from which users can choose one or more. A select list provides this capability, and it is a form field type familiar to most Web users. You consider that Habitat For Humanity has determined several countries that require workers, so a select list might provide an effective way to learn where candidates would like to work. To facilitate scheduling, you should know all the locations that interest the candidate, instead of limiting his or her choices to just one.

### Lab 7-6: Adding a multiple-option select list to an XHTML Web form

**OBJECTIVE**
2.4.1 Creating HTML forms

In this lab, you will add a multiple-option select list to the Web form you have been building.

1. **Editor:** From **C:\CIW\Site_Dev\Lab Files\Lesson07\Lab_7-2**, open the file **lab_7-5.html** and save it as **lab_7-6.html**.

2. **Editor:** Add the following code as indicated in bold:

```
<option value="Remove">Never </option>
</select>
<br/>

<br/>
Where would you like to work? (choose all that apply):
<br/>
<select name="work" multiple="multiple" size="4">
<option>Australia</option>
<option>Japan</option>
<option>India</option>
<option>England</option>
<option>United States</option>
</select>
<br/>

<br/>
<br/>

<input type="submit"/>
<input type="reset"/>
```

3. **Editor:** Save the **lab_7-6.html** file.

4. **Browser:** Load your file. The scrolling select list box should appear as it does in Figure 7-19.

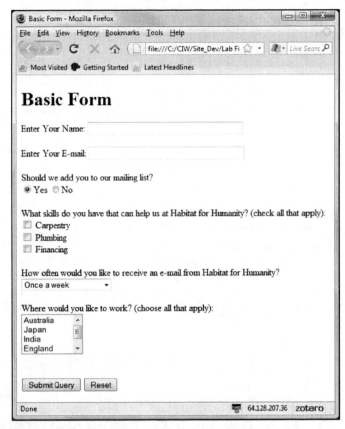

*Figure 7-19: Web form after adding multiple-option select list*

5. **Browser:** Complete all fields in the form. For the multiple-option select list, hold down the **CTRL** key while clicking to select more than one option (on Windows platforms). Then submit the form. The results should include all of your selections, as shown in Figure 7-20.

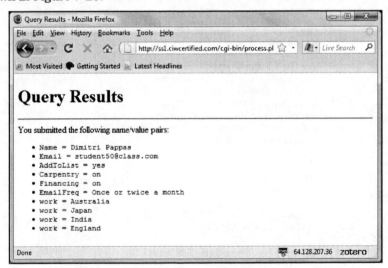

*Figure 7-20: Form results with multiple-option selection*

**6.** Use the browser **Back** button to return to your Web form page. Try choosing different selections and submitting the form again to verify that your form works correctly.

**7.** Validate your code.

In this lab, you added a multiple-option select list to a Web form.

## Scrolling text area box

You can use a text area box to gather more than one line of text from a user. The <textarea> tag provides a scrolling text box into which a user can enter a few sentences, an address, a letter to the editor or other text.

The <textarea> tag is a container tag, and the only content this tag can contain is text. Text between <textarea> tags will appear as default text within the box.

The <textarea> element has several key attributes, which you should understand and use. Table 7-2 describes these attributes and accepted values.

*Table 7-2: Attributes of <textarea> tag*

| Attribute | Description | Value |
|-----------|-------------|-------|
| **cols** | Specifies the width in characters of the scrolling text box. | Integer value (e.g., "25", "40") |
| **rows** | Specifies the number of rows of text to display in the box. | Integer value (e.g., "2", "5") |
| **wrap** | Specifies whether user-entered text can wrap to new lines in the text box. If "none" is specified, text continues on one line, so the user must scroll horizontally to read his or her entry. If "virtual" is specified, text will wrap to a new line as it approaches the box border. This line wrapping is in appearance only: The text string submitted to the script will take the form of one long line of text.<br><br>*Note: The wrap attribute is deprecated in HTML 4.01 and not allowed in XHTML 1.0. Text wrapping is now the responsibility of the user agent (i.e., browser).* | "none" or "virtual" |

In the following lab, you will add a scrolling text area box to the Web form. Suppose you want your model form to demonstrate a text box into which users can enter more than just one short line of text. A scrolling text area box provides this capability, and it is a form field type familiar to most Web users. You consider that the teams analyzing user input from your Web site's form may want to elicit general comments or questions from users. A scrolling text area box is an effective tool for inviting information and feedback that site visitors want your organization to know.

 **Lab 7-7: Adding a scrolling text area box to an XHTML Web form**

**OBJECTIVE**
2.4.1 Creating HTML forms

In this lab, you will add a scrolling text area box to the Web form you have been building.

**1. Editor:** From **C:\CIW\Site_Dev\Lab Files\Lesson07\Lab_7-2**, open the file **lab_7-6.html** and save it as **lab_7-7.html**.

2. **Editor:** Add the following code to the end of your form as indicated in bold:

```
<option>United States</option>
</select>
<br/>
<br/>
Comments:<br/>
<textarea name="comments" cols="30" rows="3">
</textarea>
<br/>
<br/>

<input type="submit"/>
<input type="reset"/>
```

3. **Editor:** Save the **lab_7-7.html** file.

4. **Browser:** Load the file. The scrolling text area box should appear as it does in Figure 7-21.

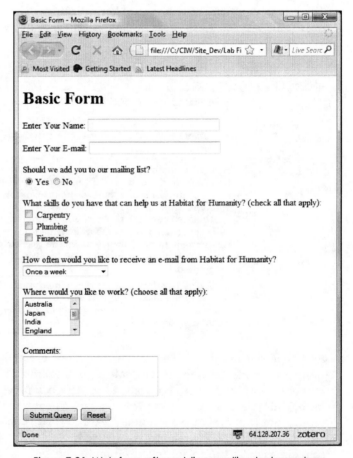

*Figure 7-21: Web form after adding scrolling text area box*

5. Type text into the scrolling text area box and submit the form. The text you typed should appear at the end of your results listing from the test engine.

6. Validate your code.

7. **When time permits:** Edit the file **lab_7-7.html** so that default text appears in the Comments field. Do this by entering text between the <textarea> </textarea> tags.

You have now worked with several XHTML form fields. When you have some time after class, you can practice your Web form-building skills. Suppose you submitted your model Web form to the Web development director as requested. The director is pleased, and so are upper management and the sales and marketing team members who reviewed it. The Web development director has gathered input from these parties, and now has directions for you to create a live Web form for the site. She has asked you to create a form that will:

- Collect a first and last name from each candidate.

- Obtain e-mail address information.

- Obtain information about the candidate's skills.

- Allow candidates to include any additional information about themselves.

This Web form page must also incorporate the look and feel, and other standard elements, of the overall site.

## Web forms and CAPTCHAs

To reduce spam submissions sent to your form, consider the use of a CAPTCHA (Completely Automated Public Turing Test to Tell Computers and Humans Apart). A CAPTCHA is a challenge-response mechanism designed to discern between a human and a "bot" in order to detect the automated systems used by spammers for registering e-mail accounts.

A CAPTCHA is an automatically generated image presented to a user who has just submitted information or made a request of a Web server. CAPTCHAs require the user to view the distorted text image, and then enter the text shown in the graphic into a form field before he or she is allowed to proceed with a transaction. The distorted image is easily recognizable by humans, but is a difficult challenge for a machine. When the user provides the correct response to a CAPTCHA, then his or her input is accepted for processing.

Many CAPTCHA services exist, including:

- Captchas.net (*http://captchas.net*)

- Captcha.cc (*www.captcha.cc*)

- Secureimage CAPTCHA (*www.phpcaptcha.org*)

## Search engine optimization (SEO) and Web forms

When conducting SEO, consider the following strategies:

- Create as simple a form as possible. Each additional field you use may reduce your score.

- Some search engines may score pages lower if a CAPTCHA is used. The problem with a CAPTCHA, or any other element that requires human input, is that a bot that encounters it will not take time to read and process all of the page. This can cause the page to be scored lower.

- Give form fields informative, descriptive labels.

- Provide a clear call to action. Do not assume that a Submit button will inform users (or search engine bots) about what they should do.

- Provide alternative text navigation.

## Case Study

# In Good Form

Lola works on the Web development team for her college. She has been assigned to create a Web form that will help the Language Department faculty plan a student trip to Europe in the summer. The faculty advisors want to use the Web page to register interested students, collect itinerary suggestions, and gather information that will help them plan the travel accommodations. Lola's form needs to collect the following information from each interested student:

- Gender

- Languages studied

- Preferred countries to visit

- Hotel room preferences

- Student limitations related to physical abilities, diet, allergies, religious practices, etc.

Lola decides to use the following form elements:

- Radio buttons to indicate gender

- Check boxes to indicate languages studied

- A scrolling text area box to indicate preferred countries

- A drop-down select list to indicate hotel room preferences

- A text box to indicate student limitations

Lola posts the Web form on the Language Department page of the college Web site. She then asks the department faculty members to review the form and let her know if they need any other information from students.

\*          \*          \*

As a class, answer the following questions:

- Did Lola use the correct form fields for the information requested? Why or why not?

- What other form fields could be used for the information requested on this form?

- What other types of information might the faculty members ask Lola to collect for this project? Which form fields would work best for each new type of information? Why?

## *Lesson Summary*

### Application project

Web forms are useless unless you can process them. Traditionally, the most popular way to process a form is through the use of a Perl-based CGI script. However, many alternatives to Perl-based CGI have emerged. Alternatives include Active Server Pages (ASP), JavaServer Pages (JSP) and PHP Hypertext Processor (PHP3).

Visit several Web sites that use forms. View the Web form source code. Can you determine where the form is processed by viewing the <form> element, and the *method* and *action* attributes?

### Skills review

In this lesson, you learned to use each of the major form field elements, and you created a functional Web form. You also saw the different form results that can be returned by setting the form action to point to a public test engine. You can test your knowledge after class by creating a form within a table in a new page.

Now that you have completed this lesson, you should be able to:

✓   2.4.1: Construct and test HTML forms.

✓   2.4.2: Identify ways that CGI scripts can parse and transmit information from a form, including e-mail, FTP, HTTP, HTTPS.

✓   2.4.3: Diagram a fundamental CGI session.

# Lesson 7 Review

1. You need to create a Web form that asks visitors to enter a password before they can access the next page. What input type would you use?

   _____

   _____

2. Which Web form tag is used to create text boxes, check boxes, radio buttons, and the Submit and Reset buttons, but not select lists?

   _____

3. Which form field allows users to enter text such as a first or last name?

   _____

4. Write the XHTML tag to create a scrolling text area box that will report input results by the name of "Feedback." The box should be 30 characters wide and five rows tall.

   _____

5. In XHTML, do form tags need to be closed? Why or why not?

   _____

   _____

   _____

# Lesson 8:
# Image Techniques

## Objectives

By the end of this lesson, you will be able to:

✎ 2.2.2: Distinguish among and identify the uses and benefits of various graphic file formats, including GIF, GIF89a, JPEG, PNG, TIFF, BMP.

✎ 2.2.4: Create and link client-side image maps.

✎ 2.2.5: Perform advanced image formatting techniques.

✎ 2.2.7: Distinguish between raster and vector graphics.

✎ 2.2.8: Scan and edit hard copy sources and images.

✎ 2.2.9: Identify steps for creating images, including resolution, format and layers.

✎ 2.2.10: Identify benefits and drawbacks of using stock photography.

✎ 2.2.11: Create a photo and portfolio management strategy, including online and offline storage, software and services (e.g., Flickr, Picasa, badongo, Google Sites).

✎ 2.10.3: Identify common proprietary Web site and page enhancement elements, including Adobe Flash and Microsoft Silverlight.

✎ 2.10.4: Evaluate the benefits and drawbacks of proprietary technologies such as Flash, Shockwave, movie formats.

# Pre-Assessment Questions

1. Which <img> attribute in XHTML and HTML indicates that an image is used as an image map?

    a. coords
    b. shape
    c. usemap
    d. map

2. Which syntax is used for defining a circle-shaped hot spot area in an image map?

    a. coords="x1,y1,x2,y2"
    b. coords="radius,y1,x1"
    c. coords="x1,y1,x2,y2,xn,yn"
    d. coords="x1,y1,radius"

3. What term is used to describe the technique of combining several GIF images in one file to create a sequence that simulates motion?

_____

# Introduction to Web Image Techniques

A primary ingredient of any successful Web page is well-placed images. You have already learned about the image file formats used on the Web. In this lesson, you will learn more about image techniques used in Web pages, including:

- Image maps.

- Image transparency.

- Interlacing.

- Animation.

You will also learn about several methods you can use to create and edit images.

## Graphic types

OBJECTIVE
2.2.2: Graphic file formats

2.2.7: Raster vs. vector graphics

Before learning about image techniques, you should understand the differences between the two types of graphical images used in Web pages:

- **Vector** — graphics that use mathematical coordinates with lines, curves and shapes to create images and specify colors. Vector graphics can be created using various tools, including Adobe Illustrator and Adobe Freehand (*www.adobe.com*). Vector graphics are generally small in file size. Their presentation size can be enlarged or shrunk (i.e., scaled) without losing image quality.

- **Bitmap** — graphics that use small dots (usually thousands) to create images and specify colors. Each dot is mapped to bits stored in a computer's memory. Bitmaps are also called raster graphics, and they include the JPEG, GIF and PNG formats. Digitized photographs are the most common type of bitmap seen on the Web. Bitmap images can be created using tools such as Paint Shop Pro (*www.corel.com*) and The GIMP (*www.gimp.org*). Making bitmap images more detailed can create large file sizes (e.g., 20 MB). Removing pixels and compressing files will decrease file size, but will also reduce image quality.

# Image Maps

OBJECTIVE
2.2.4: Client-side image maps

An image map is an image that contains clickable regions, sometimes called hot spots. Each hot spot acts as a hyperlink. You define each hot spot with a set of coordinates (indicating its position on the image) and a URL reference. Image map files originally had to be placed on the server and processed there, but now the map information can be processed on the server side or the client side. Client-side image maps use map code embedded within the HTML page.

The most difficult aspect of creating an image map is determining the coordinates of the map areas you want to use as links. After you complete this task, you simply specify the URL that corresponds to each hot spot. Many image-creation applications provide the coordinates of any position in an image as you move your cursor across it. If you do not know the coordinates for different regions of your image but you know the image's pixel height and width, you can perform mathematical calculations to determine which coordinates define which regions.

Examine the graphic shown in Figure 8-1.

Figure 8-1: Image to be used as map

Suppose you want to use this image as a set of hyperlinks that send users to other pages on your Web site. You can create an image map. Because this image consists of six visually separate sections, you could define each of the six sections as a hot spot for a link. Each hot spot can link to a different page.

For example, you could create a hot spot on the section that shows a hand. Because this area is a rectangular shape, you would define that portion of the image using four coordinates, which represent the x and y coordinates for the upper-left and lower-right corners. Coordinates depend upon the pixel size of the image. If you enlarged this image, you would have to change the coordinates. You will learn to determine the coordinates of a hot spot area shortly.

Once you define a hot spot's coordinates, you can point the hot spot to reference a URL so that when a user clicks that area of the image, the file designated by the URL is loaded. The defined hot spot area is not visible on a Web page, although when a user passes his or her cursor over a hot spot, the cursor will change into the pointing-hand icon that indicates a hyperlink.

*Applications that simplify the image map creation process are available at www.exefind.com/create-hotspot/ and www.tucows.com.*

## Defining a client-side image map

You can create either client-side or server-side image maps. Client-side image maps are more common. Server-side image maps require a CGI script, so they are not commonly used. The main advantage of a client-side map is that you can place all the code relating to the image map directly into your HTML file. The syntax for defining a client-side map for an image is as follows:

```
<map name="mapname" id="mapname">
    <area shape="shape" coords="coordinates" href="url"/>
    <area shape="shape" coords="coordinates" href="url"/>
    <area shape="shape" coords="coordinates" href="url"/>
</map>
<img src="imagemap.gif" usemap="#mapname"/>
```

Table 8-1 specifies how each element and attribute in this example is used in an image map.

Table 8-1: Image map elements and attributes

| Element / Attribute | Description |
|---|---|
| **<img> tag** | Specifies an image file in a Web page, as learned in a previous lesson. The *src* attribute specifies the image file name. |
| **<img> tag's *usemap* attribute** | Indicates that the image placed in the Web page will use an image map. Note the relationship between the <img> tag's *usemap* attribute value and the <map> tag's *name* attribute value. |
| **<map> tag** | A container tag, so it requires a closing </map> tag in both HTML and XHTML. The <map> tag encloses <area> tags. You can define your image map with the <map> tag either before or after the related <img> tag; either sequence is acceptable. |
| **<map> tag's *name* attribute** | Provides a reference name for the image map. |
| **<map> tag's *id* attribute** | Provides a reference name for the image map. In XHTML, you must also include the *id* attribute in your <map> tag, which has the same purpose as the *name* attribute. If you omit the *id* attribute, your code will not validate as any version of XHTML 1.0. |
| **<area> tags** | Stand-alone tags that define the hot spot regions of the image map. You can define as many or as few hot spot regions as you like within an image map. |
| **<area> tag's *shape* attribute** | Accepted values are:<br>- "rect" for a rectangular area (i.e., hot spot).<br>- "circle" for a circular area.<br>- "polygon" for any other shape. |
| **<area> tag's *coords* attribute** | The number and meaning of coordinates you specify with the *coords* attribute value will vary based on the *shape* attribute value:<br>- For rectangle areas: $x1,y1,x2,y2$<br>- For circle areas: $x1,y1,radius$<br>- For polygon areas: $x1,y1,x2,y2,...xn,yn$ (up to 100 pairs of coordinates) |
| **<area> tag's *href* attribute** | Value is a URL specifying the linked page that will load when the user clicks the defined hot spot area of the image map. |
| **Hash symbol (#) in the *usemap* attribute's "mapname" value** | Indicates that the "#*mapname*" value represents an image map defined within the same HTML file. If no hash symbol is present here, then the browser will look outside the HTML page for the referenced *mapname* file. |

## Defining a rectangle hot spot

Any two points can define a rectangle. Each point is represented by a horizontal ($x$) coordinate and a vertical ($y$) coordinate. Rectangles are defined by four coordinates representing the upper-left and bottom-right corners of the rectangle, as shown in Figure 8-2.

*Figure 8-2: Rectangle area defined by four coordinates*

You can define a rectangular area using the following syntax:

```
<area shape="rect" coords="x1,y1,x2,y2" href="url"/>
```

The *x1* indicates the leftmost point of the area to be defined. The *y1* indicates the topmost point of the area to be defined. The *x2* indicates the furthest point to the right in the area to be defined, and *y2* indicates the lowest point. These four coordinates will necessarily define a rectangle.

Consider the example image shown earlier in this section (see Figure 8-3).

*Figure 8-3: Image map example*

As mentioned before, coordinates depend upon the pixel size of the image. This image is 130 pixels wide and 97 pixels high. Suppose you want to define a rectangular hot spot over the hand section of this image. The coordinates that define the hand area are 1,52,33,96. If you enlarged this image, you would have to change the coordinates.

In this image, the coordinate 1 represents the distance in pixels from the left edge of the image to the left edge of the hot spot. The coordinate 1 thus represents the left edge of the image. This number is the left *x* coordinate for a rectangle. The coordinate 52 represents the distance in pixels from the top of the image to the top of the same hot spot; this is the upper *y* coordinate. The two coordinates together, 1 and 52, designate the upper-left corner of the rectangle hot spot. The coordinates 33 and 96 respectively represent the bottom-right *x* and *y* coordinates of a rectangle encompassing the hot spot. Each coordinate is measured from the top or left edge of the image.

The XHTML area definition for this image hot spot would be written as follows:

```
<area shape="rect" coords="1,52,33,96" href="hand.htm"/>
```

Figure 8-4 shows another image that can function as an image map with rectangular hot spots.

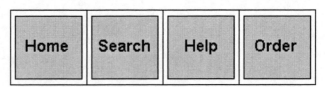

*Figure 8-4: Rectangular image with rectangular areas*

This image file is 312 pixels wide and 75 pixels high. Each square is 78 pixels wide. Using basic math, you should be able to determine the top-left and bottom-right *x* and *y* coordinates for each square area within this graphic. The code for an image map of this graphic could resemble the following:

```
<img src="buttons.gif" usemap="#ButtonMap"/>

<map name="ButtonMap" id="ButtonMap">
    <area shape="rect" coords="0,0,78,75" href="home.htm"/>
    <area shape="rect" coords="78,0,156,75" href="search.htm"/>
    <area shape="rect" coords="156,0,234,75" href="help.htm"/>
    <area shape="rect" coords="234,0,312,75" href="order.htm"/>
</map>
```

## Defining a circle hot spot

Circles are defined by two coordinates and a radius. The pair of coordinates specifies the circle's center, and the third number specifies the desired radius, or half-width, of the circle.

The syntax for defining a circle area is as follows:

```
<area shape="circle" coords="x1,y1,radius" href="url"/>
```

Figure 8-5 shows how the coordinates and radius are determined.

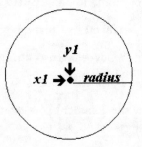

*Figure 8-5: Circle area defined by two coordinates and radius*

## Defining a polygon hot spot

When you need to define an area that is neither a circle nor a rectangle, you can use the *shape*="polygon" attribute and value, then specify coordinates for each point that defines the polygon.

Examine Figure 8-6. Note that the coordinates define the points of the polygon in sequence. For example, you could not switch the *x4* and *y4* coordinates with the *x2* and *y2* coordinates without altering the shape of the image.

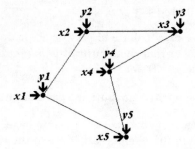

*Figure 8-6: Polygon area defined by three or more pairs of coordinates*

You can use up to 100 pairs of coordinates to define a polygon. The syntax for defining a polygon area is as follows:

```
<area shape="polygon" coords="x1,y1,x2,y2,...xn,yn" href="url"/>
```

In the next lab, you will define hot spot regions in an image. Suppose your project manager has asked you to add a new image to your Web page, and to create several hyperlinks from this image to other Web pages on the site. You review the image, and consider the areas and shapes that would work best as hyperlinks. You also consider that users may or may not use precise aim when they click an area of the image expecting to activate a certain link. You determine the coordinates for hot spot areas on the image, and write the XHTML code to create the image map on your page.

## Lab 8-1: Defining a client-side image map

OBJECTIVE
2.2.4: Client-side
image maps

In this lab, you will add an image to the Web form page and define an image map for it.

1. From the **C:\CIW\Site_Dev\Lab Files\Lesson08\** directory, copy the **Lab_8-1\** folder to your Desktop. This directory contains the file lab_8-1.html and others.

2. Open the **Lab_8-1\** folder and double-click the **lab_8-1.html** file. You will see a Habitat For Humanity page titled *Information Request Form* appear in your browser.

3. Open **lab_8-1.html** in a text editor.

4. Search for the following text string, which resides in the sidebar portion of the page:

   ```
   <!-- BEGIN IMAGE MAP CODE -->
   ```

5. Just below the comment you located, insert the following code and text to introduce the image:

   ```
   <p>
   <strong>Click anywhere on the image below
   <br/> to learn more about
   <a href="http://www.habitat.org/build"> where we build</a>.
   </strong>
   </p>
   ```

6. Below the code you just added, write the proper code to insert the **global_village_130_97.jpg** image file using the **<img>** tag. This image is 130 pixels wide and 97 pixels high. Knowing the width and height of an image is essential when calculating image map coordinates.

7. Add the ***width*** and ***height*** attributes to your <img> tag to make sure that the image is the proper size.

8. Use the ***alt*** attribute to provide some appropriate alternative text for the image. Remember that the *alt* attribute is required with images in order for your code to validate as XHTML.

9. Use the ***border*** attribute to specify that no border appears around the image.

10. The image is now inserted in your page. You are ready to begin creating the image map. Add the ***usemap*** attribute to the <img> tag to refer this image to the map instructions. Use ***"#global"*** as the attribute value.

*Note: Be sure to close your <img> tag properly.*

11. Save the file **lab_8-1.html**, and validate your code at ***http://validator.w3.org***. Although you are not finished creating the image map, you should make sure that your code validates properly before you continue.

12. Insert a **<map>** tag. Be sure to include both the ***name*** and ***id*** attributes so that your code is XHTML-compliant, and use **"global"** as the value for both.

*Note: Be sure to close your **<map>** tag properly.*

13. Using **<area>** tags, insert the image map coordinates for this rectangular image. The following table lists the coordinates that you have already determined for each hot spot in this image, as well as the associated hyperlink reference for each image map area.

*Note: Review the lesson if you do not remember the proper syntax for the <area> tag. A finished version of lab_8-1.html is provided in the C:\CIW\Site_Dev\Lab Files\Lesson08\Finished\Lab_8-1\ folder.*

| Hot Spot Coordinates | Hyperlink Reference URL |
| --- | --- |
| 0,0,32,51 | http://www.habitat.org/intl |
| 33,1,86,50 | http://www.habitat.org/wb |
| 86,1,129,50 | http://www.habitat.org/prison |
| 1,52,33,96 | http://www.habitat.org/lac |
| 34,52,86,96 | http://www.habitat.org/disaster |
| 87,52,129,96 | http://www.habitat.org/gv |

14. As you create the six **<area>** tags, be sure that you close each tag properly, and that you use the ***alt*** attribute for each <area> so that users who are using text-only browsers or settings can navigate the image map.

15. Load the page into the browser; it should resemble Figure 8-7. Each square in the new image should link to a unique URL.

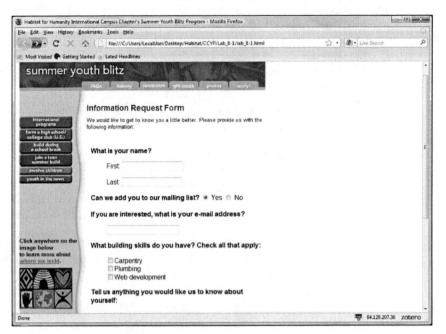

*Figure 8-7: Page with image map*

**16.** Verify that the image map functions as expected by testing each link. If the image map does not function correctly, review your code and make any necessary changes. When the image map renders and functions as expected, validate your code.

**17.** As a class, discuss the strengths and drawbacks of image maps, including:

- Their effect on users with disabilities.

- Their effect on users with text-only browsers or settings.

- Their relative worth as navigational aids.

- Their ability to improve navigation.

In this lab, you created an image map and discussed its relative benefits to a Web page.

**OBJECTIVE**
2.2.5: Advanced image formatting

# Image Transparency

An image that supports transparency provides the visual effect of blending in to the background of your Web page. In function, the page background simply shows through the transparent part of the image file. Most developers use image transparency to remove the blank image background so it appears to float on the page. However, you can make any element of an image transparent, not just its background.

The only Web-ready image file formats that support transparency are GIF 89a and PNG. The GIF 87a format does not support transparency. In Figure 8-8, you see a non-transparent PNG image rendered along the top of the page in the browser. Notice that you can see the image's white background, and that it obscures the page's background.

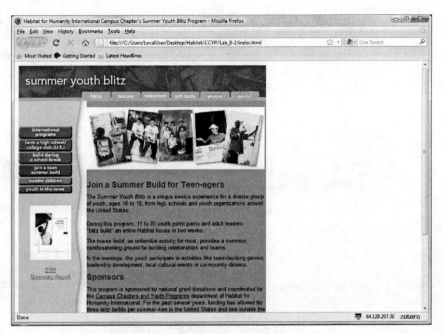

*Figure 8-8: Standard PNG image on Web page*

Although you may want an image to retain its natural background, some designs look better when the images blend with the page background. Figure 8-9 shows the same image from the previous figure now with a transparent background, allowing the page background to show through.

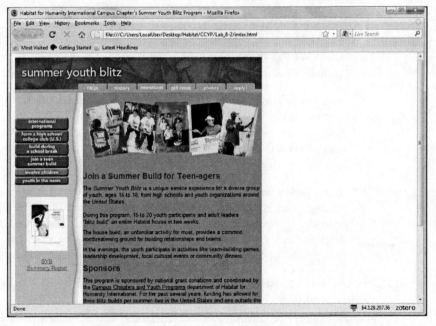

*Figure 8-9: Same image with transparent background on Web page*

Notice in this figure that you can no longer see the image's original white background; the image background is now transparent. Even if you change the Web page's background or background color, that background will appear through this image's background, making the image appear to float on the page background. Most developers refer to this type of image file as a transparent GIF, but remember that you can achieve this effect with the PNG format as well.

In the following lab, you will work with transparent GIF and PNG image files on a Web page. Suppose your project manager is pleased with the design of a Web page, but not with the graphic at the top. He and others have noted that the white background around the image is distracting, and he wants the image to blend in with other page elements. You send the original image file to a graphic artist on your development team, and she has returned PNG and GIF 89a versions of the image. You can now test both image file formats in the Web page and choose which one to use.

**Lab 8-2: Inserting transparent GIF and PNG images in a Web page**

**OBJECTIVE**
2.2.5: Advanced
image formatting

In this lab, you will insert transparent GIF 89a and transparent PNG image files into a Web page.

1.  From the **C:\CIW\Site_Dev\Lab Files\Lesson08** directory, copy the **Lab_8-2\** folder to your Desktop. This directory contains a copy of the Summer Youth Blitz page. It also contains a subfolder named Transparent\, which contains two transparent images (transSYBcollage2.gif and transSYBcollage2.png).

2.  From your Desktop, open **Lab_8-2\** and double-click the **index.html** file.

3.  You will see a version of the Summer Youth Blitz page open in your browser, this time with two images: a purple background image, and a foreground image showing youths at work on a Habitat project. Notice that the foreground image, SYBcollage2.jpg, has a white background that partially obscures the background image.

4.  Open **index.html** in an editor. Edit the **<img>** tag in this file to replace SYBcollage2.jpg with the file **transSYBcollage2.gif**, which is a transparent GIF 89a file. Save the **index.html** file, ensuring that the correct path is specified (the transSYBcollage2.gif file resides in the Transparent\ subfolder).

5.  Refresh **index.html** in your browser. You will now see the transparent image transSYBcollage2.gif in your page, if you referenced it properly in your code. This new image does not have a white background, but a transparent background that allows you to see the purple background image. Notice that the transparent image improves the look of this page.

6.  Open **index.html** in an editor, and edit the **<img>** tag so that it refers to your transparent PNG image, **transSYBcollage2.png**. Save the file **index.html** and refresh it in the browser. Notice that the PNG file also renders with a transparent background. Do you notice any differences between the two transparent image files? Which file type would you prefer to use on your Web page, and why?

In this lab, you inserted a transparent GIF image file and a transparent PNG image file into a Web page.

# Image Interlacing

**OBJECTIVE**
2.2.5: Advanced
image formatting

Interlacing is a technique that allows an image to progressively display in a browser as it downloads. The image will appear in stages over the period of downloading time. This action makes your pages more accessible to users with slower Internet connections.

Standard image formats are read from top to bottom. The top of a non-interlaced image will appear after the browser has read 50 percent of the image. The bottom half will render some time later, as shown in Figure 8-10.

*Figure 8-10: Non-interlaced image rendering in browser*

As you can see, a non-interlaced image can remain invisible or incomplete for some time to a user who is downloading the image across a slow connection.

By contrast, an interlaced image appears to fade in as it renders in the browser because it is interpreted differently. An interlaced image is repeatedly scanned from left to right. The first pass will render roughly 13 percent of the entire image. The second pass delivers 25 percent, and then continues in 25-percent increments until the image renders completely. During this process, the full image will at first appear fuzzy, but will continuously sharpen.

The only Web-ready image file formats that support interlacing are GIF and PNG. Both GIF formats, 87a and 89a, support interlacing. You can create an interlaced image by configuring an image file in a graphics-editing application and saving it as a compatible file type.

# Animation

**OBJECTIVE**
2.2.2 Graphic file formats

2.2.5: Advanced image formatting

Creating an animated image involves combining several images in a sequence that is rendered in rapid succession to simulate motion. Some image formats support animation, others do not. You can also use languages and scripts to create animation. The following sections discuss common ways to create animation using Web-based technology.

## Animated GIF and PNG

The only Web-ready image file formats that support animation are GIF 89a and PNG. Programs such as the Alchemy Mindworks GIF Construction Set (shown in Figure 8-11) allow you to incorporate several images into one file.

*Figure 8-11: GIF Construction Set*

Most animation programs allow you to control the way that images render in the browser (e.g., set the interval of appearance between images) and to create many other effects. You can obtain a copy of GIF Construction Set from Alchemy Mindworks (*www.mindworkshop.com/alchemy/gifcon.html*) or from TUCOWS (*www.tucows.com*).

You can obtain other image animation shareware programs from TUCOWS or from Download.com (*http://download.cnet.com*).

## Flash animation

OBJECTIVE
2.10.3: Proprietary
technologies

Instead of using sequences of PNG or GIF images, you can create animation using complex scripts, called macros. Adobe (*www.adobe.com*) has incorporated macros to create advanced animation capabilities using its proprietary Flash technology. Flash macros manipulate vector-based graphics to create animated sequences. Many images that appear to be animated PNGs or GIFs may actually be Flash presentations, and vice versa. Flash animations generally provide more sophisticated animation.

Flash-based animated movies are extremely popular but remain a proprietary technology. Flash movies are created using the Adobe Flash CS4 application. Animation creation applications are quite expensive. However, the Flash player, which allows you to view Flash animations, is a free browser plug-in supported by many user agents in various operating systems.

 **Tech Tip** *If you are interested in learning more about using Flash animation, it is recommended that you pursue the CIW Site Designer course series.*

## Microsoft Silverlight

OBJECTIVE
2.10.3: Proprietary
technologies

You can also create animation using another proprietary technology, Microsoft Silverlight (*www.microsoft.com/silverlight/*). Silverlight is Microsoft's response to Adobe Flash. It is compatible with multiple Web browsers (e.g., Microsoft Internet Explorer, Mozilla Firefox, Apple Safari) used on Microsoft Windows and Mac OS X operating systems.

Silverlight consists of the Silverlight application for creating Silverlight animations, and the Silverlight plug-in for viewing animations on the Web. The Silverlight plug-in needs to be launched from an HTML page via JavaScript. It is largely designed for online video playback and intense graphical interactivity.

## Java applets

Java applets can also provide animated sequences in a Web page. For the animation to render, the user agent must have a Java interpreter installed. Java animations may not render as quickly as Flash or Silverlight movies, due to the nature of the Java interpreter used. Although the Java development environment and all Java players are freely available, Java remains a proprietary technology owned by Sun.

## Scalable Vector Graphics (SVG)

You learned about vector graphics earlier in this lesson. Scalable Vector Graphics (SVG) is a W3C-recommended language developed by various vendors, including Adobe, Microsoft and Sun. SVG uses XML to describe graphics and graphical applications.

SVG allows you to create cross-platform animated movies. Not all SVG images are animated, but this application is common because SVG offers comprehensive animation support.

Unlike Java, Flash and Silverlight, SVG is an open standard. However, it provides similar features in addition to animation, including:

- **Compression** — The compression algorithms available in SVG allow you to create high-quality images and movies that are smaller in file size than other formats. SVG images have more efficient compression than JPG or GIF images.

- **Searchable text** — Text within SVG images can be indexed and searched.

- **Zooming** — You can zoom in on portions of an image without losing image quality.

SVG supports other technologies, including JPEG, GIF and Java. As with Flash, Silverlight and Java, a browser must be updated with a plug-in to render SVG data, but all major vendors incorporate support for SVG. To learn more about SVG, visit *www.w3.org/Graphics/SVG* and *www.svg.org*.

## Identifying animation techniques

There are at least two ways to learn more about an image or macro. Right-click the object and try to save it; you can then identify its properties. You can also view the source code of a Web page to see how the image or Flash/SVG/Java file was inserted into the page.

**OBJECTIVE**
2.10.4: Evaluating proprietary technologies

## Issues with animation

As you create animated images, remember the following issues:

- **Animation may seem useful and interesting, but it is frequently overused.** Animation is often used to provide entertainment rather than information. Consider the purpose of animated images on your site. If they are used to provide information, be sure to include alternative text for users who are interested only in your site's informational content.

- **Animated images can limit accessibility.** Only the oldest browsers have a problem rendering animated images. However, older browsers also cannot render any PNG images. And although relatively few people use very old browser software, consider that people who use mobile phone technology to access Web sites may have problems using animated images.

- **Animation techniques are often proprietary**, so your site visitors may need to download a plug-in. As a result, some users may choose not to visit your site. To solve this problem, you can create another version of your site to accommodate visitors without proprietary plug-ins. Remember that some browsers or users may be unable to use proprietary technologies. Creating an alternative site requires more time and resources, but ensures that your site is available to all users.

### Using non-standard images

All Web browsers capable of rendering images can process GIF, JPEG and PNG image formats by default. At times, however, you may want to use another image type. For example, an assigned project might require you to view Tagged Image File Format (TIFF) files using your browser. If you want your Web browser to render non-standard images, simply create a new MIME type for the browser.

 *When it comes to search engine optimization, using animation too heavily can cause pages to be scored lower in search engine results.*

# Creating and Managing Images

Images are essential in Web site design. Users have come to expect a visually pleasing experience that can only be achieved with the use of images. As you have seen, images can also be used for navigation in the form of image maps and graphical buttons that link to other pages or resources. On a corporate site, the organization's logo and trademarks are crucial for name recognition and branding.

There are several options you can use to obtain and manage images for use on your Web pages. You can:

- Create original images using image-creation software.

- Scan hard-copy images.

- Use stock photographs.

- Obtain photos from photo-sharing Web sites.

- Use photo management software to organize, edit and share your images.

## Creating and scanning images

**OBJECTIVE**
2.2.8: Scanning and editing images

2.2.9: Creating images

Image-creation software applications can often handle a variety of formats, such as GIF, JPEG and PNG. You can use these applications to:

- Create your own graphical images.

- Edit pictures.

- Modify digital photos.

- Create animations.

- Draw or paint images.

Popular image-creation applications include:

- Adobe Fireworks (*www.adobe.com*)

- Adobe Photoshop (*www.adobe.com*)

- Adobe Illustrator (*www.adobe.com*)

- The GIMP (*www.gimp.org*)

- Picasa (*http://picasa.google.com/*)

- Inkscape (*www.inkscape.org*)

### Image layers

When you design an image, each individual component of the image can be created on its own layer, thus allowing that component to be manipulated independently of the entire image. A series of layers will compose an entire image, and an image can have as many layers as necessary.

However, although layers are supported in the PNG file format, they are not supported by GIF or JPG formats. This means that when the image is finalized, it must be flattened into a single layer to be exported to those formats, and then the layers can no longer be manipulated. If you maintain a copy of the original layered version of the image, you can make changes easily, and other versions of the image can be exported when necessary.

### Scanning images

You can also use a scanner to scan images from a print source. The print source can be a photo, paper document, book, magazine, map or three-dimensional object (as long as it does not have a lot of depth; for example, a coin could be scanned). Unlike a photocopy machine that creates a paper hardcopy of the scanned item, a scanner creates a digital image in memory that you can save and then edit with an image-creation or photo management software application.

All digital images have certain attributes that can drastically affect quality and file size. A few of these attributes are discussed in the following sections.

### Pixels

The term "pixel" is short for "picture element." The pixel is the smallest unit displayed by a computer monitor. Pixels in a grid form the building blocks for images that a computer can display.

### Color depth

Pixels provide some amount of color information. This information, measured in bits, determines how many colors each pixel can display. For example, pixels with 4 bits of grayscale information can display up to 16 shades of gray. Eight bits of color information per pixel produces up to 256 bits of color information, and so forth. Higher bit values (also called bit depths) result in more intense or realistic colors. As the color depth increases, however, so does the file size.

### Image resolution

A user's monitor resolution determines how large onscreen images will be displayed. Screen resolution depends on the number of pixels present in a monitor's height and width. Higher screen resolutions display more pixels per inch (ppi). For example, a 17-inch monitor set to a resolution of 1024x768 will not display as many pixels per inch (ppi) as a 17-inch monitor set to 1280x960.

For printing, greater detail is achieved with higher-resolution images, and this detail is measured in dots per inch (dpi). When scanning images from a print source or importing pictures from a digital camera for use on the Web, it is generally accepted that you should set the resolution to 72 dpi in order to display the image on screen at approximately the same size as the original image.

For Web images, the dimensions of the image in pixels — rather than the dpi or ppi — are most important. When designing a Web site, you will typically resize images to the dimensions you want to use on your Web page.

The relationship between actual size and pixel size can be a bit confusing at first. To understand it, consider an image that is 128 pixels wide by 128 pixels tall. If this image is displayed on a 17-inch monitor set to 1024x768 resolution, the image will occupy one-eighth of the width and one-sixth of the height available on the monitor screen. If the monitor is set to a resolution of 1280x960, then the image will take up less space on the screen. The monitor has not increased in size, and the image is still 128 pixels by 128 pixels. What has changed is that the monitor is displaying more pixels per inch (ppi). Because monitors can be set at different resolutions, there is no way to specify that an image should be 1 inch long, for example, on a Web page. Instead, you specify image size in pixels, such as 150 pixels or 300 pixels.

## Using stock photographs

Stock photography is any group of images for which you can purchase the rights to use in printed material or on a Web site. Photographers file their images with an agency that negotiates licensing fees on the photographer's behalf. Stock photo images are then licensed from the agency.

Many modern stock photography distributors offer still photos, video and illustrations. Millions of photos are available for licensing, and all images on stock photography Web sites include embedded metadata that makes the images easily searchable by keywords.

### Licensing stock photos

To use stock images, you must purchase a license. The license is a one-time fee that allows you to use the image(s) multiple times for multiple purposes. Generally, there is no time limit on when the purchaser must use the image, but there is usually a restriction on how many times the image can be reproduced (the specified number of times is often referred to as a print run). For example, a license might allow the purchaser to print 500,000 copies of a brochure using the image.

Two types of licensing are available:

*   **Royalty-free license** — allows the buyer to use an image without having to pay a royalty each time the image is used. Royalty-free does not imply that the image is free to use without purchasing a license or that the image is in the public domain. The buyer also does not have the right to resell or transfer the image. The fee for the image is usually based on the size of the digital file. For example, a 600KB image might cost US$50 while a 10MB version of the same image might cost US$200.

- **Rights-managed license** — allows the buyer to "rent" an image through negotiation of a specific price for a specific use. Some rights-managed licenses stipulate exclusivity (i.e., the buyer may restrict similar use of the image by others for the duration of the license). Rights-managed licenses are usually more expensive than royalty-free licenses, but allow for much larger print runs. For example, a magazine with a large print run would use a rights-managed license instead of a royalty-free license. Generally, the fee charged is based on the scope of the project. For example, you might pay US$200 to use an image in a small brochure, or many thousands of dollars to use an image in a national advertising campaign.

## Advantages and disadvantages of using stock photos

When developing a Web site, there are both advantages and disadvantages to using stock photography.

Advantages include saving time and money. Image databases are quick and easy to search, licenses can be purchased online, and images can be downloaded for use immediately. In most cases, licensing fees cost much less (especially royalty-free licenses) than hiring a photographer and models, and setting up a photo shoot.

Even if you were to use internal resources for conducting a photo shoot (thereby saving the cost of the licensing fee) you must consider the time factor. Using stock photos increases project speed. Another advantage to using stock photography is that you know exactly what the finished image looks like, while an assignment photo shoot may deliver photos that require editing.

Disadvantages to using stock photography can be the cost associated with the licensing fees and a reduction in creative control. You can select only from the images that are available and you may not be able to find exactly what you want.

## Online stock photography resources

There are numerous stock photography Web sites with large databases of searchable photos and videos. These include:

- Jupiter Images (*www.jupiterimages.com*)

- Getty Images (*www.gettyimages.com*)

- Shutterstock Images (*www.shutterstock.com*)

In addition to licensing single images, many sites offer access to collections of images on a monthly or yearly subscription basis.

## Microstock photography: iStockphoto

iStockphoto (*www.istockphoto.com*) is an online microstock photography provider. Microstock photography is an offshoot of stock photography. Microstock providers deal almost exclusively over the Internet, accept photographs from amateur photographers as well as professionals, and sell their images at a very low cost (generally from US$0.20 to $10).

Image prices are based on credits. An image may cost between 1 and 20 credits, depending on size, and credits may range from US$0.95 to $1.40 each.

Contributing photographers categorize their images with keywords and upload them to the site's inspection queue, where they are reviewed for quality. Photographers receive a commission of between 20 and 40 percent of every sale. iStockphoto also sells vector graphics and raster illustrations.

Critics of iStockphoto contend that the company is devaluing the stock photography market by selling images so far below accepted price standards. The commission rate is also below the industry norm (50 percent) and based on much lower purchase fees.

### Free images

Some Web sites offer digital photos for personal and commercial use free of charge, with certain restrictions. These restrictions can include various stipulations, for example:

- The domain name of the Web site must be not be removed from the photo.

- The photos may not be resold.

- The photographer who took the photos retains the original copyright.

A few sites that offer images free of charge include:

- FreeStockPhotos.com (*www.freestockphotos.com*).

- FreeImages.co.uk (*www.freeimages.co.uk*).

- Freepixels (*www.freepixels.com*).

## Photo sharing

**OBJECTIVE**
2.2.11: Photo and portfolio management strategy

Another possible source for free images is photo-sharing Web sites, although photographs on these Web sites are copyrighted to the photographer and you must contact the photographer or owner of the photo to obtain permission to use the images.

Photo-sharing Web sites allow you upload, organize, view, share and download photos and other image files. Some sites are free, whereas others offer subscription-based services. Free sites generally rely on advertising or the selling of prints for revenue. These sites feature ads. Some sites offer subscriptions for their premium services, and a scaled-down version with fewer features as their free package.

Some photo-sharing sites require you to download an application in order to upload and manage photos. Some also support only specific platforms or browsers.

The best photo-sharing sites:

- Allow you to create private and public photo albums

- Include password-protected access

- Prevent unauthorized downloading of photos (e.g., through right-clicking and selecting a Save option)

- Provide online tools for editing photos (e.g., cropping, red-eye removal, etc.)

- Offer the ability to buy and sell prints and other gifts

- Allow you to search for photos by keyword "tags" or date.

Several sites also accept pictures taken with camera phones, and some allow you to upload and share video as well.

### History of photo sharing

The first photo-sharing sites appeared in the late 1990s offering photo finishing (e.g., touch-ups, red-eye removal, etc.) and online print ordering.

As digital cameras and camera phones became more widely used, more and more users signed up for photo-sharing services. Today, many photo-sharing sites include social networking and business elements, such as the ability to create and join communities, create private and public photo albums, and sell your personal photographs online.

Modern photo-sharing services strive to make organizing, storing and sharing digital photos convenient, safe and easy. These sites offer various ways to share pictures, including the print purchasing and creation of unique gifts (such as luggage tags, postcards, mugs, mouse pads, calendars, etc.) featuring selected photos.

Some sites are also geared to professional and semi-professional photography enthusiasts who can sell their work, or who want a forum where they can display their photos and receive feedback from other photographers around the world.

### Selecting photo-sharing services

When selecting sites and services, consumers should consider criteria such as:

- Relative ease of use.

- Tools for managing photo albums and videos.

- Tools for photo editing.

- Monthly or annual fees.

- Storage space and daily upload limits.

- Presences or absence of ads and spam.

- Ability to buy and sell prints.

- Password-protected access.

Several photo-sharing sites advertise themselves as "family-friendly," prohibiting photos or other media portraying adult content.

Popular photo-sharing sites include:

- Badongo (*www.badongo.com*).

- DotPhoto (*www.dotphoto.com*).

- Webshots (*www.webshots.com*).

- Fotki (*www.fotki.com/us/en*).

- Flickr (*www.flickr.com*).

- SmugMug (*www.smugmug.com*).

- Picasa (*http://picasa.google.com*).

- Snapfish (*www.snapfish.com*).

- Shutterfly (*www.shutterfly.com*).

- Kodak Gallery (*www.kodakgallery.com*).

## Photo management

**OBJECTIVE**
2.2.11: Photo and portfolio management strategy

You can use photo-management software to organize your portfolio. Photo-management software applications often have photo-sharing capabilities, but are designed primarily to enable you to organize, as well as edit, your photos. You can use photo-management software to:

- Scan your hard drive for pictures and create a single, digital library for them.

- Upload photos directly from your camera, scanner or memory card. You can also download photos to your camera.

- Browse, edit and share your photos from the library you create.

- Sort your photos into virtual albums.

- Add tags to photos.

- Conduct searches for photos based on specific criteria.

- Build slide shows with your photos.

- Burn pictures to CDs and DVDs.

Examples of photo management software include:

- Adobe Photoshop Lightroom (*www.adobe.com*).

- Adobe Photoshop Elements (*www.adobe.com*).

- Apple Aperture (*www.apple.com*).

- Apple iPhoto (*www.apple.com*).

- Preclick Gold (*www.preclick.com*).

- ACDSee Photo Manager (*www.acdsee.com*).

- Corel Photo Album (*www.corel.com*).

- FotoTime FotoAlbum (*www.fototime.com*).

- Roxio PhotoShow (*www.photoshow.com*).

## Search engine optimization and images

Consider the following issues in relation to search engine optimization (SEO) and images:

- The file name for an image should be as descriptive as possible. For example, consider an image of a product you want to sell on your SCUBA equipment Web site. Instead of using a name such as *product.gif* for a SCUBA regulator image file, name the image file scubapro_mk-17_regulator.gif. However, do not get carried away and create extremely long file names.

- Use the *alt* attribute in every <img> tag to provide an apt description of the image. Doing so not only improves accessibility, it also compels search engine bots to score the page better.

- Consider using keywords for image file names.

To ensure the most success, take the time to learn exactly what a search engine looks for.

## Case Study

# A Web Site's Image

Vivi works on the Web development team for a world-renowned museum in Los Angeles. She supervises the creation of image files that are posted on the site.

Vivi regularly receives new image files from the marketing department to promote exhibits, lectures and other events at the museum. She also keeps a vast catalog of image files representing the museum's offerings, grounds and most famous works. Sometimes she moves popular images to different pages of the site, where they must share space (and memory) with other related image files. She also incorporates some animated images that demonstrate preservation processes, illustrate historical timelines and recapture event highlights.

The museum Web site receives a great deal of traffic from users around the world, with the images being a popular feature of the site. Vivi has developed the following parameters for images that will be posted to the Web site:

- Images must be the best quality possible to display works of fine art.

- Images must be easily downloadable, even by clients with dial-up access (e.g., 56 Kbps or even slower).

- Images must be in formats compatible with even the oldest browsers.

Vivi receives images in various electronic and paper-based formats. She converts all image files to JPEG and GIF formats before posting them on the Web site. She also regularly reviews the visitor feedback comments submitted to the site to monitor any accessibility problems with the images.

*     *     *

As a class, discuss this scenario and answer the following questions:

- Why does Vivi use JPEG and GIF images on the site, but not PNG images?

- Is it wise for Vivi to include animated GIF images on the site? Why or why not? Are animated images useful on this Web site? What alternatives could she use for animated content?

- What accessibility challenges are inherent to Vivi's project? Are there any techniques Vivi could use to make image content on her Web site more accessible to users with limited or no image viewing capability?

- How else could Vivi use images effectively on this site?

## Lesson Summary

### Application project

This lesson discussed using image maps, transparent images, interlaced images and animated images as Web page content. Take some time to learn more about each of these techniques. Use Yahoo!, AltaVista and other search engines to conduct searches for information about each of these techniques.

Also visit Google at *www.google.com* and select the Images link. Google Image Search allows you to search images on the Web using keywords like you would for a Web page search. Experiment by entering keywords in Google Image Search, and review the image files that are returned in the search results. How does Google know which images match your search criteria? Are all of the image files returned in the search results relevant to the keywords you entered? Why or why not?

Remember to consider copyright restrictions when viewing image and animation on the Web, and posting these enhancements to your own Web pages. The images you see on the Web are the copyrighted property of the image file owner. Do not copy an image file you find on the Web and post it on your own site, or you may be subject to copyright infringement penalties. Some images are available for reuse on a copyright-free or permission-only basis. Conduct a search for Web sites providing image files that you are allowed to use for free. Can you find any useful image or animation files?

### Skills review

In this lesson, you learned about several image techniques you can use on your Web pages. You learned to create a client-side image map by determining coordinates, defining image map hot spots and linking image hot spots to other pages. You also learned about image transparency, interlacing and animation. Finally, you learned how to obtain and manage images by creating original images using image-creation software, scanning hard-copy images, using stock photographs, obtaining photos from photo-sharing Web sites, and using photo-management software to organize, edit and share your images.

Now that you have completed this lesson, you should be able to:

✓  2.2.2: Distinguish among and identify the uses and benefits of various graphic file formats, including GIF, GIF89a, JPEG, PNG, TIFF, BMP.

✓  2.2.4: Create and link client-side image maps.

✓  2.2.5: Perform advanced image formatting techniques.

✓  2.2.7: Distinguish between raster and vector graphics.

✓  2.2.8: Scan and edit hard copy sources and images.

✓  2.2.9: Identify steps for creating images, including resolution, format and layers.

✓  2.2.10: Identify benefits and drawbacks of using stock photography.

✓  2.2.11: Create a photo and portfolio management strategy, including online and offline storage, software and services (e.g., Flickr, Picasa, badongo, Google Sites).

✓  2.10.3: Identify common proprietary Web site and page enhancement elements, including Adobe Flash and Microsoft Silverlight.

✓  2.10.4: Evaluate the benefits and drawbacks of proprietary technologies such as Flash, Shockwave, movie formats.

# Lesson 8 Review

1. What is an image map "hot spot"?

   _____

2. If you do not have a graphics-editing program that shows you the coordinates of a
   given position in an image, how can you determine these coordinates?

   _____

   _____

3. Name the two coordinates used to define a point on any image shape.

   _____

4. Name two Web-ready image file formats that support transparency.

   _____

5. A non-interlaced image will begin to render after the browser has read what
   percentage of the image file?

   _____

6. Image layers are supported in which file format?

   _____

7. Why should you specify the size of your Web images in pixels?

   _____

   _____

   _____

# Lesson 9:
# HTML Frames

## *Objectives*

By the end of this lesson, you will be able to:

🖘   2.5.1: Identify the purpose of and use the <frame> and <frameset> tags.

🖘   2.5.2: Identify the purpose of and use the <noframes> tag.

🖘   2.5.3: Target HTML frames.

🖘   2.5.4: Create borderless HTML frames.

🖘   2.5.5: Identify the purpose of the <iframe> tag.

🖘   2.7.6: Evaluate the benefits of using frames in a site, and determine appropriate use.

# Pre-Assessment Questions

1.  Which HTML <a> tag attribute identifies the default frame in which all linked pages will appear?

    a.  target
    b.  href
    c.  base
    d.  frameset

2.  What attributes are used in the <frameset> tag to identify the number of rows or columns into which the frameset will divide the browser window?

    _____

3.  What <frame> tag attribute and value are used to prohibit scrollbars from appearing in a Web document?

    _____

# Introduction to XHTML Frames

**frame**
A scrollable region of a Web page in which other pages can be displayed; a single element of a frameset. Each frame has its own URL.

**frameset document**
A Web page that defines a set of adjacent frames in which other Web pages are displayed.

When designing your Web site, you may want certain information to be visible and persistent, while allowing other information to change. Both HTML and XHTML allow you to create separate panes, called **frames**, in the browser window. Each frame has its own URL, thus one frame can remain static and visible while another changes.

Today, frames are not used as often by Web designers. CSS and layers are effective alternatives. Nevertheless, in this lesson, you will work with existing sets of frames and create a new set of frames, called a frameset. A frameset is defined in a special file called a **frameset document**, which we will discuss later in this lesson.

Frames were introduced as an extension of the HTML 3.2 standard, and were first supported by the Netscape Navigator 2.0 browser. The frames technology was submitted to the W3C for consideration as an HTML standard, and is currently part of HTML 4.01 and XHTML 1.0.

Frames offer many options for Web designers and authors. Elements that site users should always see (such as navigation links, copyright notices and title graphics) can be placed in a static, individual frame. As users navigate the site, the static frame's content will persist, even though the contents of the adjoining frames may change.

**dynamic**
Always changing.

Frames are most useful when you want to combine static and **dynamic** information. Figure 9-1 shows a Web page with a table of contents in the left frame. This frame contains links that, when clicked, display the target URL's contents in the adjoining frame. The frameset document contains two separate files loaded into two frames.

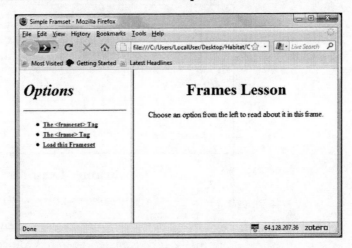

*Figure 9-1: Two frames in one Web page*

You could also add frames to a Web page form so that queries can be submitted and answered on the same page: One frame displays the query form, and the other frame presents the query results.

# The <frameset> Tag

**OBJECTIVE**
2.5.1: The <frame> and <frameset> tags

The <frameset> tag is a container tag, so it requires a closing </frameset> tag. This element allows you to define regions in your browser window and assign separate files to each region. The <frameset> tag requires a mandatory attribute of either *cols* or *rows* that designates the number and size of columns or rows as the frames that will appear in a browser window.

The frameset in the preceding figure has two frames:

- One column occupies 35 percent of the available screen width.

- The other column occupies the remaining 65 percent.

The source code for this frameset is as follows:

```
<frameset cols="35%,65%">
</frameset>
```

 *As with any other XHTML tag, you must use a closing </frameset> tag. If you are using HTML tags, the closing </frameset> is optional but highly recommended because omitting it can produce unexpected results.*

You can specify the *cols* and *rows* attributes in either of two ways:

- By percentages

- By pixels

In addition, you can use a wildcard character (*) to accommodate various user screen widths and resolutions. For example, consider the following tag:

```
<frameset rows="180,*">
</frameset>
```

This tag specifies that the first 180 pixels of the browser window are used for the top-row frame, and any remaining space is used for the bottom-row frame, as shown in Figure 9-2.

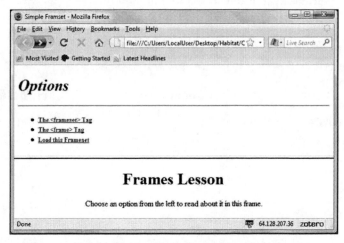

*Figure 9-2: Using frameset wildcards to allocate frame space*

OBJECTIVE
2.5.1: The <frame> and <frameset> tags

# The <frame> Tag

The <frame> tag defines the content in each frame and is placed between the <frameset> </frameset> tags. The *src* attribute (abbreviation for "source") specifies the file that will appear in the frame. The <frame> tag is not a container tag in HTML; it stands alone. In XHTML, you must close it as a non-empty tag with the closing slash ( <frame/> ) each time you use it.

In the following example, the frame source for the top frame is the file *fl-toc.html,* and the frame source for the lower frame is *fl-second.html*. The frameset defines two rows and opens the frames with the files specified in the <frame> tags.

```
<frameset rows="180,*">
    <frame src="fl-toc.html"/>
    <frame src="fl-second.html"/>
</frameset>
```

The frame source can be a local document or a URL pointing to a Web site.

# The Frameset Document

OBJECTIVE
2.5.1: The <frame>
and <frameset>
tags

The <frameset> and <frame> tags will create frames only if they are placed correctly into a file called the frameset document. In the frameset document, the <frameset> element takes the place of the <body> element.

The frameset document defines the <frameset>, <frame> and <noframes> elements. You will learn about the <noframes> element in the next section.

The following example demonstrates proper code structure for the frameset document. This XHTML source code created the frames shown in Figure 9-1 earlier in this lesson. Notice that these pages reference the XHTML 1.0 Frameset flavor in the DOCTYPE declaration.

**File name:** *fl-2frames.html*

```
<!DOCTYPE html PUBLIC "-//W3C//DTD XHTML 1.0 Frameset//EN"
    "http://www.w3.org/TR/xhtml1/DTD/xhtml1-frameset.dtd">

<html xmlns="http://www.w3.org/1999/xhtml" xml:lang="en">
<head>
<meta name="Keywords" content="CIW, Foundations, Example"/>
<meta name="Description" content="For the CIW Foundations Course"/>
<meta http-equiv="Content-Type" content="text/html; charset=utf-8"/>
<!-- <link rel="stylesheet" type="text/css" href="fl-2frames.css"
title="stylesheet"/> -->

<title>Simple Framset</title>

</head>

<frameset cols="35%,65%">

    <frame src="fl-toc.html" name="toc"/>
    <frame src="fl-second.html" name="main"/>

</frameset>
</html>
```

Remember these two key points:

- The opening <frameset> tag follows the closing </head> tag.

- The <frameset> tag must contain either the *rows* attribute or the *cols* attribute, and it may contain both. However, be careful that you do not create a Web site that is too complicated for your site visitors to read and navigate.

## Viewing source with framesets

When it is necessary to view the source code of a page with a frameset, click the frame you want to view. Then take the necessary steps for your specific browser type and version to view source (for example, select View | Source on the browser toolbar).

In the following lab, you will create a basic frameset document. Suppose your project manager wants a page on the Web site that allows a set of links to remain displayed while the pages to which they link appear in another section of the same window. Your project manager says she has seen this done on other Web sites, and she asks if you can create a model structure like this for your Web site. You tell her that you can create a frameset page that will do this, and that it could be structured in different ways. You create some sample frameset documents to demonstrate the choices to your project manager.

## Lab 9-1: Creating XHTML frames with rows and columns

In this lab, you will create a frameset document that defines two frames using the *rows* and *cols* attributes.

1. **Windows Explorer:** From the **C:\CIW\Site_Dev\Lab Files\Lesson09** directory, copy the **Lab_9-1\** folder to your Desktop.

2. **Notepad:** From the **Lab_9-1\** subfolder, open the **frameplay.html** file.

3. **Notepad:** Modify the following source code as indicated in bold:

```
<!DOCTYPE html PUBLIC "-//W3C//DTD XHTML 1.0 Frameset//EN"
    "http://www.w3.org/TR/xhtml1/DTD/xhtml1-frameset.dtd">

<html xmlns="http://www.w3.org/1999/xhtml" xml:lang="en">

<head>
<meta name="Keywords" content="CIW, Foundations, Example"/>
<meta name="Description" content="For the CIW Foundations Course"/>
<meta http-equiv="Content-Type" content="text/html; charset=utf-8"/>
<!-- <link rel="stylesheet" type="text/css" href="frameplay.css"
title="stylesheet"/> -->

<title>Frame Lesson</title>
</head>

<frameset rows="50%,*">
    <frame src="a.html"/>
    <frame src="b.html"/>
</frameset>

</html>
```

4. **Notepad:** Save your changes to **frameplay.html**.

5. **Browser:** Open the **frameplay.html** file in your browser. Your screen should resemble Figure 9-3.

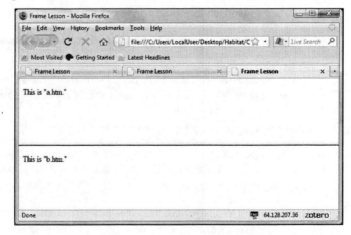

*Figure 9-3: Frameset with rows attribute*

6. **Notepad:** Open **frameplay.html**, and modify the source code as follows so that the window is divided into panes that appear vertically, rather than horizontally:

```
<frameset cols="25%,75%">
```

7. **Notepad:** Save your changes.

8. **Browser:** Open the **frameplay.html** file. Your screen should resemble Figure 9-4.

*Figure 9-4: Frameset with cols attribute*

9. If your page does not render as expected, review your code and make any necessary changes. After your page renders correctly, validate your code at **http://validator.w3.org**. Resolve any issues to ensure that your code validates to the XHTML Frameset standard.

In this lab, you created a simple frameset using both a two-row and a two-column structure.

# The <noframes> Tag

**OBJECTIVE**
2.5.2: The
<noframes> tag

Some visitors to your site may use older or alternative browsers that cannot render frames. To provide content (other than a blank screen) for these users, you can add a <noframes> tag section to your frameset document. The <noframes> tag displays alternative text or images in browsers that do not support frames. This alternative text can contain a message such as, "If you had a frames-capable browser, you would see frames here." Browsers that can display frames will ignore message specified with <noframes> tags.

The <noframes> tag is a container tag, so it requires a closing </noframes> tag. The <noframes> element is placed between the <frameset> </frameset> tags. Any text message you display with the <noframes> tag must also be enclosed within <body> </body> tags between <noframes> </noframes>.

The following example extends the XHTML and HTML source code from the previous example to accommodate users who cannot view frames. You can format the content as desired, and you can include a link to a non-frames version of your Web site.

```
<!DOCTYPE html PUBLIC "-//W3C//DTD XHTML 1.0 Frameset//EN"
    "http://www.w3.org/TR/xhtml1/DTD/xhtml1-frameset.dtd">

<html xmlns="http://www.w3.org/1999/xhtml" xml:lang="en">
<head>
<meta name="Keywords" content="CIW, Foundations, Example"/>
<meta name="Description" content="For the CIW Foundations Course"/>
<meta http-equiv="Content-Type" content="text/html; charset=utf-8"/>
<!-- <link rel="stylesheet" type="text/css" href="fl-2frames.css"
title="stylesheet"/> -->

<title>Simple Framset</title>

</head>

<frameset cols="35%,65%">
    <noframes>
<body>If you had a frames-capable browser, you would see frames here.
</body>
    </noframes>

    <frame src="fl-toc.html" name="toc"/>
    <frame src="fl-second.html" name="main"/>

</frameset>
</html>
```

*Notice that you must use the <body> tag within the <noframes> element. The <body> tag is required for page text that will appear in place of frames, or else your code will not validate (the validation error that indicates this reads, "Character data is not allowed.") Remember that the <frameset> tag replaces the <body> tag for page content in a frameset document.*

# Targeting Frames with Hyperlinks

**OBJECTIVE**
2.5.3: Target HTML
frames

In the previous examples, you could not click a link in one frame and change the content of another frame. To do this, you must target the individual frames for links. You can then click a link in one frame and open a specified file in the targeted frame.

You add the *name* attribute to each <frame> tag so you can target the frame by name. You also add the *src* attribute with a file name (or URL) to indicate the frame's default content. The syntax for targeting the <frame> tag and designating its content is as follows:

```
<frame src="url" name="framename"/>
```

You can now target the named frame in other Web documents by using the *target* attribute of the anchor tag <a>. Clicking the hyperlink created with the <a> tag causes the page specified by the *href* attribute to appear in the target frame. The syntax for this anchor tag is as follows:

```
<a href="url" target="framename"> Link Text </a>
```

For example, suppose you want to create a frame named Authors that will display a file named *james.html*. In the frameset document, you would create the following tag between the <frameset> </frameset> tags:

```
<frame src="james.html" name="authors"/>
```

You can now target the Authors frame from other Web documents by creating a link with the <a> tag and the *target* attribute. Suppose the frameset includes a page named *staffList.html*. To create a link from the Staff List page to the James page, you would enter the following code in *staffList.html*:

```
<a href="james.html" target="authors"> Visit James </a>
```

Now if you click the Visit James link on the Staff List page, the *james.html* page will appear in the frame named Authors.

Consider the following source code example again:

```
<title>Simple Framset</title>
</head>
<frameset cols="35%,65%">
    <frame src="f1-toc.html" name="toc"/>
    <frame src="f1-second.html" name="main"/>
</frameset>
</html>
```

Now study Figure 9-5, which demonstrates the targeting in this code.

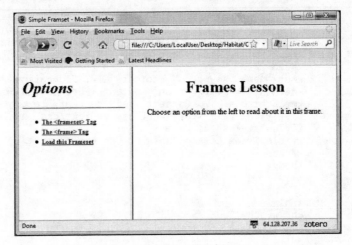

Figure 9-5: Targeting frames

To target a link from the table-of-contents or TOC frame (left) and cause the content to appear in the main (right) frame, as shown in the preceding figure, use the *target* attribute. You can specify any target named in the <frameset> tag. For example, the following code would open the Habitat home page in the frame named "main" in the frameset document:

```
<a href="http://www.habitat.org" target="main"> Visit Habitat </a>
```

Again note that the frame name specified as the *target* attribute value is the name specified with the <frame> tag *name* attribute.

If you do not specify a target, the linked content will open into the same frame as the link itself. If you specify a target name that does not match the name of any existing frame, the browser will launch a new window and open the referenced page in it. You should avoid this situation unless this specific effect is desired.

In the following lab, you will target some frames in a frameset. Suppose your project manager liked the appearance of the column-style frameset model you showed her, but she wants to see how the hyperlinks to content will work. You incorporate some content into the page and target the frames correctly to show your project manager how this type of page will function on the Web.

**Lab 9-2: Targeting XHTML frames**

In this lab, you will target the links in a table-of-contents (TOC) frame to another frame.

1. **Windows Explorer:** From the **C:\CIW\Site_Dev\Lab Files\Lesson09** directory, copy the **Lab_9-2\** folder to your Desktop.

2. **Browser:** From **Lab_9-2\**, open the file **fl-2frames.html**.

3. **Browser:** Click a link from the TOC frame. Notice that the linked file appears in the same frame as the link. To prevent this, you will re-target the links in the table of contents to point to the main (right) frame.

4. **Notepad:** From **Lab_9-2\**, open the file **fl-toc.html**. Modify the source code as indicated in bold:

```
<!DOCTYPE html
    PUBLIC "-//W3C//DTD XHTML 1.0 Transitional//EN"
    "http://www.w3.org/TR/xhtml1/DTD/xhtml1-transitional.dtd">
<html xmlns="http://www.w3.org/1999/xhtml" xml:lang="en">
<head>
<meta name="Keywords" content="CIW, Foundations, Example"/>
<meta name="Description" content="For the CIW Foundations Course"/>
<meta http-equiv="Content-Type" content="text/html; charset=utf-8"/>
<!-- <link rel="stylesheet" type="text/css" href="fl-toc.css"
title="stylesheet"/> -->
<title>Frame Lesson Table of Contents</title>
</head>
<body>
<h1>
<i>Options</i>
</h1>
<hr width="100%"/>

<ul>
<li>
<strong>
<font size="-1">
<a href="fl-frameset.html" target="main">The &lt;frameset&gt; Tag</a>
</font>
</strong>
</li>

<li>
<strong>
<font size="-1">
<a href="fl-frame.html">The &lt;frame&gt; Tag</a>
</font>
</strong>
</li>

<li>
<strong>
<font size="-1">
<a href="fl-2frames.html">Load this Frameset</a>
</font>
</strong>
</li>
</ul>

</body>
</html>
```

5. **Notepad:** Save the file **fl-toc.html**.

6. **Browser:** Reopen the file **fl-2frames.html**. Click the link that reads **The <frameset> Tag**. Your screen should resemble Figure 9-6.

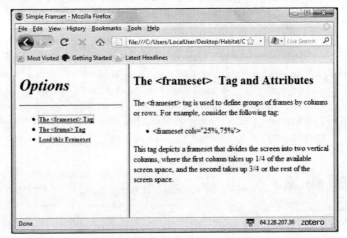

*Figure 9-6: Frame targeting*

7. Validate your code.

8. Remember that some user agents (browsers) do not render frames well. Insert the **<noframes>** tag into **fl-2frames.html** with the following message:

***If you had a frames-capable user agent, you would see frames here.***

In this lab, you targeted a frame and used the <noframes> tag.

# Specifying a Base Target

OBJECTIVE
2.5.3: Target HTML frames

From the previous lab, you can see that it could be time-consuming to manually enter a target frame for every link on the page. By specifying a base target in a frameset page, you can automatically set a default target frame for all links.

You specify a base target using a special stand-alone tag called the <base> tag. This tag allows you to specify a default *target* frame for all the links in that file. The <base> tag must be placed within the <head> section. In XHTML, this tag must be a container tag; HTML does not require you to close the <base> tag but, as usual, it is considered good practice.

For example, suppose you want all the links in the TOC frame to target the main frame. You could include the following source code in the <head> tag section of the *toc.html* page:

```
<base target="main" href="page.html"/>
```

Using this code, all links in the TOC page, when clicked, would open their corresponding files in the frame named "main" in the frameset. The *href* attribute is optional in the <base> tag.

Although the *target* attribute in the <base> tag specifies a default target for all hyperlinks on the page, you can still point any of the page's links to targets other than the default specified by <base>. If the *target* attribute is specified in an anchor tag <a>, then that target will take precedence. Only when no target is present in the <a> tag will the base target be used (if the <base> tag is present).

In the following lab, you will add a base target to your frames pages. Suppose your project manager is pleased with the frameset you demonstrated for her, so she directs you to add more links and pages to this structure. The additional pages should all open in the same frame as those you have already targeted. Your project manager asks how quickly you can complete the code to do this, because she would like you to demonstrate the frameset in a meeting later that afternoon. You consider that adding a single <base> target will save coding time, so you tell her the page will be ready in time for the meeting.

 **Lab 9-3: Adding a base target to frames**

In this lab, you will add a base target to a frames page.

1. **Notepad:** Open the file **fl-toc.html**.

2. **Notepad:** Modify the source code as indicated in bold:

```
<head>
<meta name="Keywords" content="CIW, Foundations, Example"/>
<meta name="Description" content="For the CIW Foundations Course"/>
<meta http-equiv="Content-Type" content="text/html; charset=utf-8"/>
<!-- <link rel="stylesheet" type="text/css" href="fl-toc.css"
title="stylesheet"/> -->
<title>Frame Lesson Table of Contents</title>
<base target="main"/>
</head>
```

3. **Notepad:** Save the **fl-toc.html** file.

4. **Browser:** Open **fl-2frames.html**. Click the links in the left frame. Each link should open the associated page in the right frame.

5. If your frames do not function as expected, review your code and make any necessary corrections. When the page renders and functions correctly, then validate your code.

In this lab, you added a base target to your frames pages.

# Borders, Margins and Scrolling

OBJECTIVE
2.5.4: Borderless
frames

XHTML frames support a variety of attributes that you can use to customize the appearance and function of your frames pages. Frame borders can appear or be hidden, margins between text and frames can be sized to preference, and scroll bars can added to individual panes to accommodate more content. The following sections describe each of these features in more detail.

## Borderless frames

The <frame> tag supports the *frameborder* attribute, which designates borders around each frame. A value of "0" leaves no visible borders; a value of "1" causes borders to display.

Similar to this effect in tables, invisible borders do not affect the function of your frames. Their appearance on your Web page is simply a matter a preference. You can experiment with the *frameborder* attribute on your frames pages to determine which look you prefer. Some pages look better with the visible border, and some pages look better without it.

The *frameborder* attribute is used in HTML and XHTML as follows:

```
<frame src="framehome.html" name="home" frameborder="0"/>
```

## Frame margin width and height

The <frame> tag also supports the *marginwidth* and *marginheight* attributes. The values assigned to these attributes designate the space, in pixels, between the frame's contents and the left and right margins, or top and bottom margins, respectively. A numerical value of at least "1" is required. The default space depends on the browser used to view the page.

The *marginwidth* and *marginheight* attributes are used in HTML and XHTML as follows:

```
<frame src="framehome.html" name="home" marginwidth="5" marginheight="10"/>
```

 **Tech Tip** *You can learn about additional HTML frames elements and attributes by visiting the W3C site (www.w3.org), and reading the HTML 4.01 and XHTML 1.0 specifications.*

## Scrolling frames

You can use the *scrolling* attribute of the <frame> tag to enable or disable the ability for a user to move the page up and down. Values for the *scrolling* attribute include:

- **"yes"** — enables scrolling.

- **"no"** — disables scrolling.

- **"auto"** — allows the browser to decide.

The *scrolling* attribute is used in HTML and XHTML as follows:

```
<frame src="framehome.html" name="home" frameborder="0" scrolling="no"/>
```

# Inline Frames

OBJECTIVE
2.5.5: The <iframe> tag.

Inline frames, also called floating frames, allow you to insert a separate document into an XHTML page. This creates a frame that essentially floats a page within another page. You create an inline frame using the <iframe> tag. In HTML, <iframe> is not a container tag so it does not strictly require a closing tag. In XHTML, however, you must close <iframe> as a container tag.

Following is the body of a simple XHTML page that uses an inline frame:

```
<h1>iFrame Example</h1>
<p><strong>This text is found in iframe.html</strong><p/>
<iframe src="embedded.html" scrolling="yes">
</iframe>
<p><strong>This text is also found in iframe.html. </strong></p>
```

This code is located in the file named *iframe.html*. Notice the reference to *embedded.html*. The *embedded.html* file can include any content, such as the following:

```
<h2>Embedded, Scrollable Text</h2>
<p>This text, from embedded.html, is now placed
within the file named iframe.html.<br/>
 You can scroll this text up and down to <br/>
view all of the contents of the page</p>.
```

If you were to view *iframe.html* in a Web browser, it would resemble Figure 9-7.

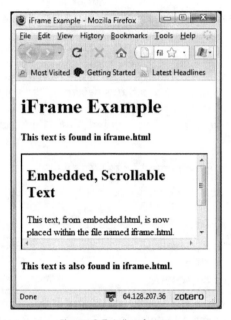

*Figure 9-7: Inline frame*

As shown in the preceding figure, you can use your mouse to scroll up and down the embedded frame. If you prefer, you can specify *scrolling="no"* in the <iframe> tag to eliminate scrolling. If you do this, however, you must make the content in the embedded frame short enough to view without scrolling.

## When to use inline frames

Inline frames are useful in the following situations:

- When all content in the Web document will remain relatively stable except in one section, such as a weekly special. The one section that changes often can be the inline frame. You can quickly modify the embedded document when necessary.

- When you want to embed a document, such as some text or a PDF, within a page instead of making it a separate page or a download.

## How inline frames are processed

If the <iframe> tag is used in a Web page, the browser identifies the referenced document, then makes a separate request for it to the server. For example, if the inline document is an XHTML file, then the Web browser generates a request to the Web server for that file. The Web server processes this request as a standard HTTP request, then downloads the file. The browser is responsible for reading the <iframe> tag and making the request.

## Support for inline frames

Inline frames are not supported in XHTML 1.0 Strict. Also, some browsers do not support inline frames, thus the inline frame simply will not appear when the page is rendered.

Because not all browsers support inline frames, you should use them sparingly. Inline frames are best restricted to situations in which you can control the browser type and version used (such as in a company intranet).

## Appropriate Use of Frames

OBJECTIVE
2.7.6: Appropriate
use of HTML frames

Frames are useful only in specific situations. You must determine whether they are appropriate for your Web site or project. Consider the following issues:

- **Function** — Frames are often used to keep certain information persistent, such as navigation links, copyright notices and title graphics. Frames work well for some types of content. For some sites, however, they may seem unnecessarily elaborate or fussy. Consider the best presentation for your content, as well as your reasons for wanting to use frames.

- **Appeal** — Frames have become less popular with users than they were in recent years. Some technologies may provide similar functionality with a simpler look. Consider whether frames might make a site seem dated.

- **Development challenges** — Creating a frameset can cause development difficulties because of the additional, rather complex code required to configure it correctly. Updating content also takes more time and care. You must ensure that you properly target frames, or visitors may not be able to use your site at all.

- **Accessibility limitations** — Although all modern graphical browsers support frames, text-based browsers become confused by them.

- **Usability** — Frames can cause problems when users click the browser's Back button. In most browsers, each frame has its own history. Clicking the Back button in a frames-enabled site will cause the browser to retrace the history of each frame in sequence. New users may not understand how the history works in their browsers, so they may become confused after reviewing several frames this way. Frustrated users who cannot find the information they seek will generally leave your site as a result.

## Frames and Search Engine Optimization

It is accepted wisdom that in general, using frames will lower your page's rank in a search engine. Many search engine spiders do not follow the frame sources from the frameset page.

For more information, consider the following resources:

- **SEO Web Design – Why Frames and SEO Don't Mix** (*www.seodesignsolutions.com/blog/search-engine-optimization/seo-web-design-why-frames-and-seo-dont-mix*)

- **SEO Issues** (*www.seo-guy.com/seo-tutorial/complicated-seo-issues.html*)

- **Frames and Search Engines** (*www.anubazaar.com/Frames_and_search_engines.htm*)

## Case Study

# Framing It Right

Lars is a freelance Web site designer. A health insurance company has contracted him to create a Web-based interface for its databases. This interface must be created using XHTML. Each page must consist of several separate sections, and each section will contain information from a company network database. Lars will probably need to update each page section on a regular basis, because the database manufacturer is upgrading the database servers. He decides to use a frameset structure for this interface.

Lars accepts another contract with a small company that sells antique books over the Internet. This company needs a series of Web pages to profile the company's more expensive books. These pages will be integrated with some existing Web site pages that do not use frames. For this project, Lars decides not to use frames, and instead to use the <div> tag to create a site with three sections.

\*     \*     \*

As a class, discuss this scenario and answer the following questions:

• Why is using a frameset a good choice for both of Lars' projects?

• What are the possible drawbacks of using frames in each of these projects?

## *Lesson Summary*

### Application project

As you use framesets to construct your Web site, remember that many older browsers do not support frames. Also remember some graphical considerations. How would your frames-enabled Web site look at 800x600 resolution? How would it look at 1280x800 resolution? View the frames pages you created in this lesson using different screen resolutions. How will these considerations affect the planning of your frames?

### Skills review

In this lesson, you learned that frames allow you to create attractive Web pages with more creative control over the user's experience. Frames also make navigation easier by allowing certain links and information to remain visible. You studied the relationship between frameset documents and individual frames, and you learned to create framesets and to target frames by name. Finally, you learned to use some <frame> element attributes to create borderless frames, adjust margin sizes and enable frame scrolling.

Now that you have completed this lesson, you should be able to:

✓   2.5.1: Identify the purpose of and use the <frame> and <frameset> tags.

✓   2.5.2: Identify the purpose of and use the <noframes> tag.

✓   2.5.3: Target HTML frames.

✓   2.5.4: Create borderless HTML frames.

✓   2.5.5: Identify the purpose of the <iframe> tag.

✓   2.7.6: Evaluate the benefits of using frames in a site, and determine appropriate use.

# Lesson 9 Review

1. What is the term for the file that defines the frames in an HTML or XHTML page?

   _____

2. Briefly describe a way in which frames can be useful in a Web site.

   _____

   _____

   _____

   _____

3. How can your frames-enabled Web site accommodate browsers that do not support frames?

   _____

   _____

4. You are targeting frames with hyperlinks so that users can click a link in one frame and change the content of another frame. If you do not specify a target, where will the linked content appear?

   _____

   _____

   _____

5. What attribute can modify the space, in pixels, between the left and right side of the frame's contents?

   _____

# Lesson 10:
# GUI HTML Editors

## Objectives

By the end of this lesson, you will be able to:

✧  2.11.1: Evaluate a GUI HTML editor according to the W3C Authoring Tool Accessibility Guidelines.

✧  2.11.2: Validate HTML code.

✧  2.11.3: Use font and page appearance options in a GUI HTML editor.

✧  2.11.4: View source code and preview Web pages in a browser.

✧  2.11.5: Create HTML tables using a GUI HTML editor.

✧  2.11.6: Publish (i.e., upload) Web pages and sites to a Web server.

# Pre-Assessment Questions

1. Which type of editing application allows Web developers to automate tasks and integrate other applications into workflow?

   a. Page editors
   b. Text editors
   c. Site management editors
   d. WYSIWYG editors

2. Which of the following features of a GUI editor offers the quickest way to create a new Web page?

   a. Templates and wizards
   b. Importing HTML pages
   c. Icon bars
   d. Table creation

3. To what extent do GUI editors generally allow developers to modify HTML or XHTML code manually?

   _____

   _____

# Introduction to GUI HTML Editors

**What You See Is What You Get (WYSIWYG)**
(pronounced whiz-ee-wig) A user-friendly editing format in which the file being edited is displayed as it will appear in the browser.

You can create Web pages using a graphical user interface (GUI) HTML editor, also called a **What You See Is What You Get (WYSIWYG)** editor. These editors allow Web authors to create Web pages without typing the requisite HTML code. Many WYSIWYG editors exist, such as Adobe Dreamweaver, Microsoft Expression Web and the open-source KompoZer (*www.kompozer.net*).

In this lesson, you will use KompoZer as your GUI editor. KompoZer complies with W3C Web standards, creates pages as HTML 4.01 Transitional and uses CSS styles. However, you can change KompoZer settings and choose to develop Web pages using Strict or Transitional DTDs and as HTML 4.01 or XHTML 1.0. KompoZer also includes a built-in HTML validator, which you can use to upload your pages to the W3C Markup Validation Service (*http://validator.w3.org*) and check for compliance.

KompoZer is used for Web page creation, not Web site management. This fact greatly simplifies the program because it focuses on the creation of one page at a time, which is similar to the way you approached HTML and XHTML coding in previous lessons. When the pages are created, you can then join them using hyperlinks. KompoZer offers no comprehensive site management tools, and site management is beyond the scope of this course.

 *To learn about site management concepts and tools, it is recommended that you pursue the CIW Site Designer series.*

This lesson will examine the basic capabilities of a GUI HTML editor, including procedures for creating text styles, icon bars, inline images, hyperlinks and tables.

# Types of GUI Editors

As mentioned, there are two types of GUI editors:

- Page editors

- Site management editors

Both are WYSIWYG programs.

## Page editors

GUI page editors allow you to create a Web page using your mouse and a toolbar. Functionality is usually limited to creating individual Web pages. Software programs that provide only page editor functionality include:

- KompoZer.

- Mozilla SeaMonkey Composer.

## Site management editors

GUI Web site management editors provide both Web page creation and site management functionality. They allow teams of designers and developers to work in an integrated environment to design, build and manage Web site and Internet applications. In addition to creating the Web pages, team members can manage the entire Web site with this type of application, both during and after development. Site management includes task automation and workflow integration with other programs (such as Microsoft Office and Web applications) in a production environment.

Software programs that provide these functions include:

- Adobe Dreamweaver.

- Adobe GoLive.

- Microsoft Expression Web.

In this lesson, you will use a GUI page editor to create pages similar to those you created using a text editor earlier in this course. First, however, you will learn about some of the features common to all GUI editors, and about accessibility guidelines for GUI editor applications.

# GUI HTML Editor Functionality

GUI HTML editors allow you to create Web pages. In most cases, you enter and edit text similar to the way you would in a word-processing application. Images, tables, links, bookmarks and so forth can be created easily because the application writes the HTML code automatically.

The following features are offered by most GUI editors:

- **Templates and Wizards** — allow you to create custom Web pages quickly by selecting from a series of choices.

- **Text Style options** — allow you to format text in different font styles, alter text size and color, and apply formats such as centering, boldface and italics. Remember that some visitors to your site may not have all the fonts installed on their systems that you want to use on your Web pages. Choose your fonts carefully, or else your page may not render as expected to some visitors.

- **Icon bars** — offer easily identifiable graphic icons to provide the same functions found in text-based menus.

- **Image features** — allow you to easily insert graphic images into a Web page.

- **Hypertext Links features** — allow you to create hypertext links to pages and files within your Web site, and to pages and files on the World Wide Web. Once the link has been created, the editor displays the target page.

- **Import HTML Pages features** — allow you to open pages from the World Wide Web and, when permissible, save them to a Web site or local file system. The editor can also import all images on a page into a Web site or file system.

OBJECTIVE
2.11.5: Tables in GUI HTML editor

- **Table Creation features** — allow you to add tables to arrange data or organize a page layout.

- **Spelling check** — Most GUI editors provide an automatic spelling checker, similar to those found in word-processing applications such as Microsoft Word and OpenOffice (*www.openoffice.org*). However, understand that a mere spelling check cannot ensure that your Web pages project the proper message. Your page content should be edited by a knowledgeable professional who understands your organization's message and the languages your site uses.

- **Publish Documents features** — allow you to click a button to post pages to a Web server. These features automatically copy files from a local hard drive to a directory on an ISP's server.

OBJECTIVE
2.11.1: W3C
Authoring Tool
Accessibility
Guidelines

# W3C Authoring Tool Accessibility Guidelines

The W3C Authoring Tool Accessibility Guidelines Recommendation outlines seven points that help determine the suitability of a GUI editor for developers with disabilities. All seven points focus on the following issues:

- The ability of the GUI editor to generate proper code

- The usability of the GUI editor by a disabled person creating a Web page

The seven points each contain checkpoints (i.e., subpoints). Each checkpoint offers specific examples of usability techniques that the GUI editor must support. You can read the W3C Authoring Tool Accessibility Guidelines Recommendation at *www.w3.org/TR/ATAG10*. Table 10-1 summarizes the major points of this Recommendation.

*Table 10-1: W3C Authoring Tool Accessibility Guidelines Recommendation summary*

| Guideline | Description | Example Technique |
|---|---|---|
| **1.0: Support accessible authoring practices** | The authoring tool must support procedures that enable the creation of accessible Web pages. In other words, if the tool does not allow you to create code that helps disabled users browse the site, then the tool is not compliant. | **1.3:** Ensure that markup generated automatically by the tool conforms to the W3C Web Content Accessibility Guidelines (WCAG) 1.0. |
| **2.0: Generate standard markup** | The tool must conform to W3C markup standards. | **2.1:** Use the latest versions of W3C Recommendations when they are available and appropriate for a task. Do not use proprietary tags (e.g., <audioscope>, <sidebar>). |
| **3.0: Support the creation of accessible content** | Content should be accessible because it is properly structured. | **3.2:** Help the author create structured content and separate information from its presentation by using style sheets. |
| **4.0: Provide ways of checking and correcting inaccessible content** | Ideally, the tool should provide its own validation engine that helps ensure code accessibility. | **4.2:** Assist authors in correcting accessibility problems. |
| **5.0: Integrate accessibility solutions into overall look and feel** | Accessibility features must be present and readily available to disabled persons. | **5.1:** Ensure that functionality related to accessible authoring practices is naturally integrated into the overall look and feel of the tool. |
| **6.0: Promote accessibility in help and documentation** | Help features in the GUI editor must be readily available and easily understood. | **6.2:** Ensure that creating accessible content is a naturally integrated part of the documentation, including examples. |
| **7.0: Ensure that the authoring tool is accessible to authors with disabilities** | All GUI editors naturally have interface elements. Due to the nature of markup, some of these interfaces can become complex. Interface complexity must be managed, and disabled users must be considered. | **7.3:** Allow the author to edit all properties of each element and object in an accessible fashion. |

As you design your Web pages, make sure that you consider the following points:

- Some users may be unable to use a mouse to navigate between links. Make sure that your pages allow users to tab to new links.

- You may need to provide larger text on your Web pages for visually impaired users.

# Creating Web Pages with a GUI Editor

The labs in this lesson will familiarize you with the toolbar, menus and functions of a GUI Web page editor, KompoZer.. Most of these features are similar in any GUI editor you use. However, the interface will differ among applications.

In the following series of labs, you will create a Web page with a GUI page editor. Suppose you want to apply for an internship with a technology training company. The company's internship requirements include beginning networking, HTML and XHTML experience. To prove your skills, you decide to create your résumé in HTML.

## Lab 10-1: Creating a Web page with a GUI editor

OBJECTIVE
2.11.3: Formatting in
GUI HTML editor

In this lab, you will create a Web page using the KompoZer GUI page editor. Similar to a résumé, this Web page will promote your skills to potential employers.

1. Create a new folder on your Desktop named **Promo**.

2. Open **Windows Explorer** and navigate to the **C:\CIW\Site_Dev\Lab Files\Lesson10\KompoZer 0.7.10\** directory. Double-click **kompozer.exe** to open the application. Close the **KompoZer Tips** dialog box that appears. You are now ready to create an HTML page in a GUI editor.

3. **KompoZer:** Select **Heading 1** from the paragraph format drop-down menu, as shown in Figure 10-1.

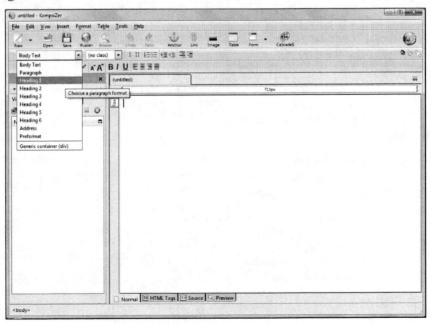

*Figure 10-1: KompoZer paragraph formatting*

**4.** Type your first, middle and last name. Select this text, and center it by selecting **Format | Align | Center** (or by clicking the **Align Center** button on the toolbar).

*Note: If you make a mistake, you can use the CTRL+Z key combination to undo your previous actions. Press CTRL+Y to redo any changes that you have undone and want to reinstate.*

**5.** Deselect your name by clicking anywhere else on the Web page.

**6.** Move the cursor to the line below your name (similar to a word processor, place the cursor at the end of your name and press the **ENTER** key). The paragraph format should return to Body Text, as displayed in the drop-down menu. If not, select **Body Text** from the paragraph format drop-down menu.

**7.** Enter the text *Internet Certified and Ready to Succeed!* Select this text and make it boldface by clicking the **Bold** button on the toolbar (or by pressing **CTRL+B**). Then, center the text.

*Note: To avoid typing, you can copy and paste the Web page text from the* **GUI_HTML_editor.txt** *file located in the* **C:\CIW\Site_Dev\Lab Files\Lesson10** *directory.*

**8.** Click the **Save** button on the KompoZer toolbar. The Page Title dialog box will appear.

**9.** In the Page Title dialog box, enter a title for your Web page. For example, enter your name, followed by — *Internet Certified*. This title will appear in the browser window title bar and the Bookmarks or Favorites folders of Web browsers. Click **OK**.

**10.** The Save Page As dialog box will appear. This dialog box allows you to name the HTML file. Name your file *default.html*, and navigate to the **Promo** directory you have just created. Then, click the **Save** button to save the file to the Promo folder.

**11.** Except for the name, your screen should closely resemble Figure 10-2.

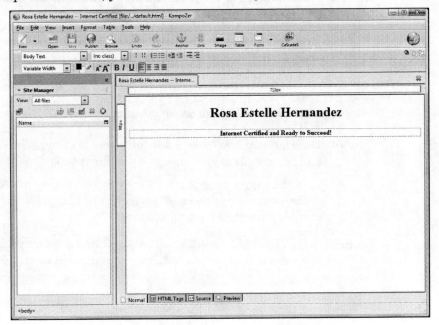

*Figure 10-2: Creating Web page using GUI HTML editor*

12. To view the Web page in a browser, click the **Browse** button on the KompoZer toolbar, or select **File | Browse Page**. In the External Protocol Request dialog box that appears, click the **Launch Application** button. Your default browser will open and display your Web page. You can now read the entire title in the browser's Title bar. When finished, close the browser window.

*Note: Make sure that you always save any changes before clicking the Browse button.*

In this lab, you began creating a résumé using a GUI Web page editor.

In the following lab, you will use a GUI page editor to modify font and background colors on a Web page. Suppose that as you are creating your résumé, you want to experiment with various color schemes. You know that color combinations can convey different moods, tones and messages. What color combinations would convey the best message for your résumé? Is a different tone appropriate when applying for an internship, rather than an entry-level position or a contract project? If you were submitting this résumé to five different companies, would you modify the résumé's look for each company?

## Lab 10-2: Changing font and background color with a GUI editor

OBJECTIVE
2.11.3: Formatting in
GUI HTML editor

In this lab, you will use the GUI page editor to change your Web page's font and background color. Continue to use the *default.html* file.

1. **KompoZer:** Select **Format | Page Colors And Background**. The Page Colors And Background dialog box will appear.

2. Select the **Use Custom Colors** radio button. Click the **Background** button, and select a color from the Block Background Color dialog box that appears.

3. Click **OK** to return to the Page Colors And Background dialog box.

4. Click the **Normal Text** button, and select a text color from the Text Color dialog box that appears. When you are satisfied with your choice, click **OK** twice to return to your page in the KompoZer window.

5. Save the **default.html** file, and view your changes in the browser.

6. As a class, discuss the following questions:

   • Thus far, you have used a few interfaces and commands. Are these interfaces and commands easy to access if you are disabled? Why or why not?

   • View the source code you have created by clicking the **Source** tab at the bottom of the KompoZer window. What type of code is being written? HTML? XHTML? Is this code standard? Which standard?

In this lab, you modified the font and background colors on your résumé. You also learned more about the type of HTML that is generated by this GUI page editor.

In the following lab, you will use a GUI page editor to add a horizontal rule to a Web page. Suppose that as you are creating your résumé, you want to experiment with graphical features on the page. You know that graphics should be used sparingly because they can distract from the important information on your page. However, you want to introduce some visual interest to the page and add an organizational element for emphasis. A horizontal rule provides a subtle graphic enhancement that will emphasize your name at the top of your résumé.

 **Lab 10-3: Adding a horizontal rule to a Web page with a GUI editor**

**OBJECTIVE**
2.11.3: Formatting in
GUI HTML editor

In this lab, you will use a GUI page editor to add a horizontal rule to a Web page. Continue to use the *default.html* file.

1. **KompoZer:** Place your cursor after the text *Internet Certified and Ready to Succeed!*, then press **ENTER** twice to create a double return (two blank lines).

2. Select **Insert | Horizontal Line** to insert a horizontal rule. After creating a horizontal line, your screen should resemble Figure 10-3.

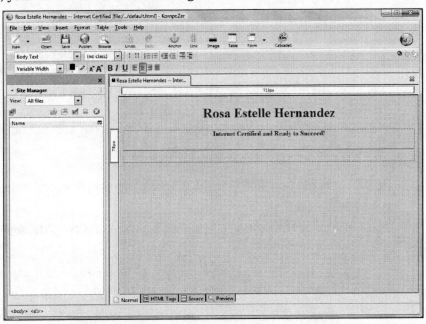

*Figure 10-3: Adding horizontal rule using GUI HTML editor*

3. Save the **default.html** file, and view your changes in the browser.

In this lab, you added a horizontal line to a Web page using a GUI page editor.

In the following lab, you will use a GUI page editor to create ordered and unordered lists on a Web page. Suppose that as you are creating your résumé, you consider that adding numbered and bulleted lists will help emphasize your achievements, as well as enhance the readability of the page. What types of information work well with numbered lists? What types of information are better as bullet points?

## Lab 10-4: Creating bulleted and numbered lists with a GUI editor

**OBJECTIVE**
2.11.3: Formatting in
GUI HTML editor

In this lab, you will use a GUI page editor to create an unordered list and an ordered list on your Web page. Continue to use the *default.html* file.

1. **KompoZer:** Place the cursor on the blank line below the horizontal rule.

2. Type the word *Certifications*, and apply bold and italic formatting.

3. Left-justify the text **Certifications** by selecting **Format | Align | Left** (or by clicking the **Align Left** button on the toolbar).

4. Press **ENTER** to create a new line beneath the text that reads **Certifications**. Your cursor should be on the new blank line.

5. Enter the following words below **Certifications** as body text, and press **ENTER** after each line of text to create separate lines:

   *CIW Associate*

   *IC3*

6. Select both new lines of text, then click the **Bulleted List** button on the toolbar to automatically insert bullet points. Alternatively, you can select the text, then select **Format | List | Bulleted**.

7. Create a new line, but make sure the new line is not bulleted. To exit the bulleted list mode, press **ENTER** and deselect the **Bulleted List** button, if necessary.

8. Left-justify the new line, if necessary.

9. On the new line, type the words *Internet Skills*, and apply bold and italic formatting.

   *Note: To avoid typing in the next step, you can copy and paste Web page text from the* **GUI_HTML_editor.txt** *file located in the* **C:\CIW\Site_Dev\Lab Files\Lesson10** *directory.*

10. Create another new line beneath **Internet Skills**. Enter the following text on separate lines as shown:

    *Web browsers, e-mail, FTP, Telnet, SSH, VNC and news clients*

    *Web page authoring in HTML, XHTML and simple Web scripts*

    *Basic networking components, protocols and server configuration*

    *Basic security concepts and virus protection*

    *Project management skills for individual and team job tasks*

11. Select the five lines of text you just entered, then click the **Numbered List** button on the toolbar to automatically insert numbering. Each line should now be numbered, and your screen should resemble Figure 10-4. Eliminate any extra space between the words **Internet Skills** and the numbered list, if necessary.

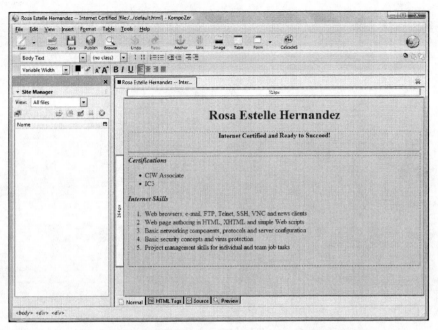

*Figure 10-4: Bulleted list and numbered list in GUI HTML editor*

**12.** Save the **default.html** file, and view your changes in the browser.

> *Note: The GUI_HTML_editor.txt file located in the \Site_Dev\Lab Files\Lesson10\ folder contains the skills list you used in this lab, which you can paste into your Web page. You will learn these skills by completing the CIW Foundations course series. You can use this list for your personal résumé when searching for a job. You can earn the CIW Associate certification by taking and passing the CIW Foundations certification exam. You can earn the IC3 certification by taking and passing the IC3 certification exams. For more information about CIW and IC3 certification exams, visit www.CIW-certified.com and www.certiport.com, respectively.*

In this lab, you created an unordered list and an ordered list on your Web page.

---

In the following lab, you will use a GUI page editor to create external hyperlinks on a Web page. Suppose that as you are creating your résumé, you consider that adding some hyperlinks to relevant Web sites could substantiate your credentials. You also consider that any sites to which you link from your résumé should be professional, reputable and relevant to your résumé information. Every reference should serve the purpose of providing useful information.

 **Lab 10-5: Creating external hyperlinks with a GUI editor**

**OBJECTIVE**
2.11.3: Formatting in GUI HTML editor

In this lab, you will use a GUI editor to create a hyperlink from your Web page to an external Web site. Continue to use the *default.html* file.

**1.** **KompoZer:** Select the words **CIW Associate** in the bulleted list.

**2.** Select **Insert | Link** (or click the **Link** button on the toolbar; or right-click the selected text and select **Create Link**) to open the Link Properties dialog box.

3.  Enter ***http://www.CIW-certified.com*** into the Link Location field, as shown in Figure 10-5.

**Link Properties**                                              ✕

┌─ Link Text ────────────────────────────────────────┐
│ CIW Associate                                       │
└─────────────────────────────────────────────────────┘
┌─ Link Location ─────────────────────────────────────┐
│ Enter a web page location, a local file, an email address, or select a Named │
│ Anchor or Heading from the popup list:              │
│ http://www.CIW-certified.com              ▼   📂     │
│ ☐ The above is an email address                     │
│ ☐ URL is relative to page location                  │
└─────────────────────────────────────────────────────┘
┌─ Target ────────────────────────────────────────────┐
│ ☐ Link is to be opened                              │
│   in a new window          ▼                         │
└─────────────────────────────────────────────────────┘

   ▼   More Properties

                                    Advanced Edit...

              OK        Cancel        Help

*Figure 10-5: Creating hyperlink in GUI HTML editor*

4.  Click **OK** to return to your Web page. Notice that the words **CIW Associate** now appear in underlined blue font, indicating that the text is a hyperlink.

    *Note: If you like, find a deep link on the CIW-certified site for the CIW Associate reference.*

5.  Highlight the text **IC3** in the bulleted list. Create a hyperlink to ***http://www.certiport.com***.

    *Note: If you like, find a deep link on the Certiport site for the IC3 reference.*

6.  Save the **default.html** file.

7.  Test the hyperlinks by viewing your page in a browser, then clicking the hyperlinks.

8.  **Browser:** When you are finished testing your hyperlinks, return to **KompoZer**.

In this lab, you created external hyperlinks in your Web page document.

---

In the following lab, you will use a GUI page editor to add an image to a Web page. Suppose you have already passed the CIW Foundations certification exam. You would then be a certified CIW Associate. CIW provides access to an official graphical logo after you earn the CIW Associate certification. As you create your résumé, you might want to include the official CIW Associate logo to tout your professional credential. Displaying this logo on your résumé adds visual interest and shows that you have industry-standard skills that employers want. The logo image you will add to your page in the next lab is similar to the one you would receive as a CIW Associate.

**Tech Tip**

*Remember that in any résumé document you submit to an organization for a professional position of any type, you should claim only skills, experience and credentials that you do in fact possess or have earned.*

### Lab 10-6: Adding an image to a Web page with a GUI editor

**OBJECTIVE**
2.11.3: Formatting in
GUI HTML editor

In this lab, you will use a GUI editor to add an image to your Web page. Continue to use the *default.html* file.

1.  **KompoZer:** Place your cursor on a blank line below the numbered list. Be sure that this new line is not numbered. If necessary, press **ENTER** to see if a new number appears. If it does, click the **Numbered List** button to stop the numbering.

    *Note: Alternatively, you can also click the **Source** tab and edit the code manually.*

2.  Add a horizontal rule. If necessary, add a blank line below the rule and place your cursor on it.

3.  **Windows Explorer:** From **C:\CIW\Site_Dev\Lab Files\Lesson10**, copy the **CIWlogo.gif** file to the **Promo\** folder on your Desktop.

4.  **KompoZer:** Select **Insert | Image** (or click the **Image** button on the toolbar) to open the Image Properties dialog box. The Location tab is selected by default.

5.  Click the **Choose File** button (the folder icon to the right of the Image Location text box). The Select Image File dialog box will appear. Navigate to the **Promo\** folder, click the **CIWlogo.gif** file, then click the **Open** button.

6.  The Image Properties dialog box will appear, with the CIWlogo.gif image you selected now entered into the **Image Location** field. Notice that the **Alternate Text** radio button is selected. The field associated with this radio button allows you to enter text that describes the image to text-only browsers, such as Lynx. Enter the words *CIW Logo* into the Alternate Text field, then click **OK** to insert the image into your document.

7.  After inserting the image, center it on the Web page.

8.  Save your changes to the **default.html** file.

9.  View your page in the browser to review your work. Your screen should resemble Figure 10-6.

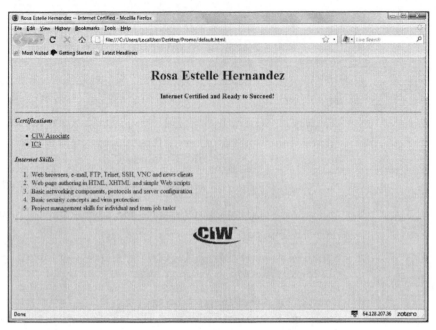

*Figure 10-6: Image displayed in Web browser*

**10.** Return to **KompoZer**.

In this lab, you added an image to your Web page document.

In the following lab, you will use a GUI page editor to create a table in a Web page. Suppose you want to add some structure to your résumé Web page. You consider that an HTML table can help organize the information on your page into a balanced, easy-to-read page design.

## Lab 10-7: Creating an HTML table with a GUI editor

OBJECTIVE
2.11.5: Tables in GUI
HTML editor

In this lab, you will use a GUI editor to create a basic table on your Web page. Continue to use the *default.html* file.

1.  **KompoZer:** Place your cursor directly before the word **Certifications** on your Web page. Press **ENTER** to create a blank line. Place your cursor on this new blank line.

2.  Select **Insert | Table** (or click the **Table** button on the toolbar). The Insert Table dialog box will appear.

3.  Click the **Precisely** tab. Verify that both the Rows and Columns fields show the value **2**. If the values are different, change them to **2**.

4.  Click the **Advanced Edit** button.

5.  Verify that the Cellspacing and Cellpadding values are both **2**. If they are not, change both values to **2**.

6.  Change the Border value to 2 by clicking the word **Border**, then entering **2** in the Value field at the bottom of the Advanced Property Editor dialog box.

7. Click **OK** to return to the Insert Table dialog box. By default, the table's Width is 100 percent of the window. The Insert Table dialog box should resemble Figure 10-7.

*Figure 10-7: Creating table using GUI HTML editor*

8. Click **OK** to insert the table.

9. Place your cursor in the table's upper-left cell. Then, right-click your mouse and select **Table Select | Row**. This action will select the first row of the table. You can now format this row as a table header.

10. With the entire first row still selected, right-click the selection and click **Table Cell Properties**. The Table Properties dialog box will appear.

11. The **Cells** tab should already be selected. Select the **Cell Style** check box, and change the style to **Header** using the drop-down menu. Click **OK**.

12. Cut the word **Certifications** from your Web page and paste it into the table's upper-left cell.

13. Cut the words **Internet Skills** from the page and paste them into the table's upper-right cell.

14. Cut the bulleted hyperlinks **CIW Associate** and **IC3**, and paste them both into the table's lower-left cell. Keep the bulleting. Ensure that both certifications occupy the same cell; do not create a new table row for each certification.

15. Cut all of the numbered list items (e.g., W*eb browsers, e-mail, FTP, Telnet,* etc.) and paste them into the table's lower-right cell. Keep the numbering. Ensure that all numbered items are placed in the same cell.

16. Place your cursor in the top-right cell of the table. Right-click and select **Table Cell Properties** to display the Table Properties dialog box.

17. In the Size section, select the **Width** check box, and enter *50* in the field. Change the value in the drop-down menu from Pixels to *% of Table*. When finished, click **OK** to return to your page. Notice that each column occupies exactly half of the table.

18. Delete all blank lines that remain above and below the table between the two horizontal rules.

*Note: When deleting extra spaces and characters, try using both the DELETE and BACKSPACE keys. Be careful not to delete the image or the horizontal rules. If you do, press CTRL+Z to undo any changes. Remember that CTRL+Y will redo any changes you undo. If you prefer using the mouse to undo and redo, select **Edit | Undo** and **Edit | Redo**.*

**19.** If you want, create additional spaces between the table data and the table borders, either by pressing the **ENTER** key or by modifying the cell padding values.

**20.** When you are finished, save the **default.html** file, then view your page in a browser. Your screen should resemble Figure 10-8.

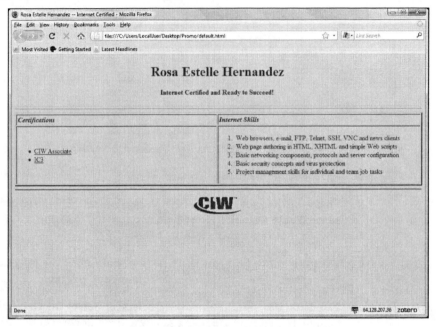

*Figure 10-8: Table displayed in Web browser*

**21.** If you want to make changes to your page, then exit the browser and return to KompoZer. Modify the page as necessary to achieve the results you want. Remember to save the file each time you change it to see an accurate representation in the Web browser.

**22.** Remove the borders from the table by opening the **Table Properties** dialog box, then selecting the **Table** tab.

*Note: Thus far, you have worked only with the Cells tab.*

**23.** In the Borders And Spacing section, change the value in the Border text box to **0**.

**24.** Click **Apply**, then **OK**. Now, save the file and view your modified page in a browser. Verify that your code renders as expected in at least one more browser.

In this lab, you created an HTML table on a Web page and formatted information in the table. The preceding series of labs introduced you to the basic features of a GUI HTML editor.

# HTML Text Editors vs. GUI Editors

The following sections describe some of the advantages and disadvantages of text editors and GUI editors. The type of editor you choose depends on your personal preferences and your specific Web project needs.

In most cases, you will use both types of HTML/XHTML editors. You can create the majority of your Web site quickly with a GUI editor, then use a text editor (most GUI editors include one) to enter scripts for advanced functionality.

## HTML text editors

Text editors such as Notepad, WordPad, Vi and Emacs present the following advantages for Web page authors:

- If you are considering learning a scripting language such as JavaScript or VBScript, you *must* learn to write code manually. If you want to add forms to your Web pages, it is also helpful to be proficient in HTML or XHTML.

- If you know HTML or XHTML code, you can maximize the benefit of GUI HTML editors by manually modifying code, independently from the editor.

- You can learn the fundamentals of HTML/XHTML and update your pages to the latest version(s).

Now consider the following drawbacks of using text editors to create Web pages:

- Typing code can be time-consuming, especially if you must learn the latest changes to code standards from the W3C.

- People with disabilities may find manual entry too time-consuming and/or too difficult.

- A text editor may require too much attention if you need only a simple page.

## GUI HTML editors

GUI HTML editors such as KompoZer, Sea Monkey Composer, Dreamweaver and Expression Web present the following advantages for Web page authors:

- GUI editors place code into files for you, which enables you to create pages quickly by simply clicking your mouse.

- Most GUI editors allow you to modify your code manually.

Now consider the following drawbacks of using GUI editors to create Web pages:

- Some GUI editors will alter or ignore any code you enter manually. For instance, you can manually add a paragraph tag <p/>, but the GUI editor may not recognize it. This situation can be frustrating if you want to format a Web page your own way.

- Many GUI editors have not kept pace with the evolution of HTML and XHTML, and thus do not provide options for using some of the recently developed tags. You must upgrade your GUI editor if you want to begin using a later version of HTML or XHTML; thus, your code may not reflect the latest (and possibly most useful) standards.

 **WARNING!** *GUI editors often simply fail to load and edit code that contains newer tags. Be careful when making changes to your pages. Make backup copies of your pages first, then test each change in the GUI editor to make sure it understands the new code.*

# Previewing Pages and Validating Code

**OBJECTIVE**
2.11.4: Source code and page previewing

You have seen in the previous labs that it is necessary to preview your pages when using a GUI editor, despite the WYSIWYG development environment. Most GUI editors make it quite easy to:

- Preview pages in a browser.

- View source code.

- Validate code using built-in validators or a site such as *http://validator.w3.org*.

Many GUI editors allow you to choose the browser you use for previewing. By not limiting you to any single browser, the GUI editor helps you to test your pages in multiple browsers, or to focus your development on your favorite or company standard browser.

## DOCTYPE options

Validation engines, such as the one provided by the W3C, first read the DOCTYPE declaration in an HTML or XHTML page before validating the code. The validation engine then examines the code according to the standards of the DTD specified in the DOCTYPE declaration. As a result, your code may fail validation with one DOCTYPE reference, but pass if you change the standard in your DOCTYPE declaration.

For example, suppose you have written code in a page to the HTML 4.01 Transitional standard, and it has validated. Then one of your team members hears that the site will be updated to XHTML in the coming months. In an effort to start the update project early, he changes the DOCTYPE on this page to refer to the XHTML 1.0 Transitional DTD. Although your page once validated as HTML 4.01 Transitional, it will no longer validate. To get the page to validate now, you can either edit the page code to conform to the XHTML Transitional standard as declared in the DOCTYPE, or you can change the DOCTYPE reference back to HTML 4.01, the standard to which the page code currently conforms.

**OBJECTIVE**
2.11.2: Validating
HTML code

## Validating HTML code

When validating code created by a GUI editor, consider the following points:

- Most GUI editors include their own native validation tools or offer menus that provide access to validators. For example, KompoZer provides the Validate HTML option, which you will use in the next lab.

- Some GUI editors have special features that help ensure accessibility in regard to validation.

In the following lab, you will validate Web page code generated by a GUI page editor. Suppose you want to ensure that your résumé page uses proper HTML code standards. You can validate your résumé page code using features in the same GUI editor you used to create the page. Validating your code is an important step, and using clean validated code in your résumé demonstrates your skill and commitment as a Web developer.

 **Lab 10-8: Validating HTML code generated by a GUI editor**

**OBJECTIVE**
2.11.2: Validating
HTML code

In this lab, you will validate the HTML code created by KompoZer.

1. **KompoZer:** Verify that you have saved all changes to your résumé document, default.html.

2. Select **Tools | Validate HTML**.

3. Load **default.html** into the validator, and perform the necessary steps to validate the code. Keep all validation values (except for your file location) at their defaults.

**4.** What results were returned from the validation process? What version of HTML or XHTML did you discover?

**5.** As a class, discuss the following questions:

- What modifications does this code need in order to validate as XHTML 1.0 Transitional?

- How long would it take to upgrade this code?

- What were the benefits of using a GUI editor to create your résumé Web page?

- What were the drawbacks?

In this lab, you validated HTML 4.01 Transitional code in a GUI editor.

# Web Site Publishing

**OBJECTIVE**
2.11.6: Publishing
Web sites

**File Transfer Protocol (FTP)**
An Internet protocol used to transfer files between computers; allows file transfer without corruption or alteration.

The final step in Web site development is publishing your site to the World Wide Web. You can publish your site in several ways, depending on the tools used to create it. Most GUI HTML editors provide a Publish feature that allows you to easily post your Web page files to your designated Web host. You can also use a **File Transfer Protocol (FTP)** client, such as Ipswitch WS_FTP Professional (*www.ipswitch.com*) or FTPx Corporation's FTP Explorer (*www.ftpx.com*).

FTP is the protocol most often used to transfer files between two computers, or a server and a computer, depending on the configuration. Transferring files over the Internet requires an FTP client to send the files and a destination FTP server to receive them. FTP can also be used to transfer files to an HTTP server, provided that the HTTP server is also running FTP. However, before you can transfer your Web site files, you must decide where your site will be hosted.

## Publishing to a test Web server

Professional Web developers post the final version of the Web site files to a test Web server before moving them to the production server for the following reasons:

- To verify that the Web server can process any CGI and database access requests.

- To locate and repair any dead links.

- To allow members of the development team and other stakeholders to preview the site. You will find that many changes are needed before your "final" code is ready for publication.

### Test server configuration

Your test server must be as nearly identical to the production server as possible. The test server should have:

- **The same operating system version** — If your production server is a Linux system or Windows Server 2008, for example, then your production system should be the same model.

- **The same type and version of Web server software** — Even if your test system uses a software type or version very similar to the production system, this test system is not adequate. For example, if your production Web server uses Apache

Server 2.2.11 and your test server is using Apache Server 2.0.63, then your testing server will not provide a true test of your site.

- **The same CGI interpreter software** — If your production server uses PHP 5.2.9, then your test server should use PHP version 5.2.9.

*Test servers are often called staging servers.*

## Publishing with KompoZer

If you want to publish files directly from KompoZer, you simply select File | Publish, then enter the appropriate information. Earlier in this course, you learned about the information required for publishing a Web site. Figure 10-9 shows example information that you might enter in the Settings tab of the Publish Page dialog box in KompoZer, such as authentication information and the name of the Web server to which you are sending the files.

*Figure 10-9: Specifying ISP and authentication information to publish Web pages*

In addition to the destination server's name (or IP address) and authentication information, you must also specify the location on the remote server that you want your files placed. In Figure 10-10, the résumé file is named default.html and will be placed in the /html/resume_files/ directory on the remote Web server.

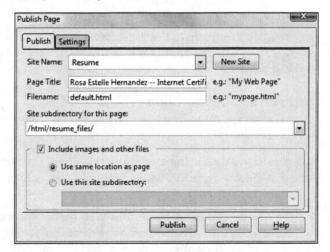

*Figure 10-10: Specifying file names and directory location for publishing*

## Case Study

# The Best GUI Editor

Patrick needs to create a Web site for a small company he is launching. He needs to develop and post the site as quickly as possible, so he decides to use a GUI Web page editor to create the site. When comparing the GUI editor applications he could use, Patrick considers the following issues:

- **The type of code that the editor creates** — Patrick must decide between HTML 4.01 and XHTML 1.0 standards, including W3C compliance. He needs a program to produce code that will validate to standards with as little manual modification as possible.

- **Accessibility** — Patrick has tendonitis and sometimes experiences difficulty using the computer's mouse. The program must accommodate his physical limitations.

- **Ability to insert customized code** — Patrick wants to include processes that require PHP and SQL statements, but he does not know those languages.

- **Publishing capabilities** — Patrick needs a program that can publish his pages to a remote Web server when he has finished creating them.

- **Cost** — Patrick wants a quality product, but he is on a tight budget because his business is young.

- **Validation features** — Patrick believes that validating Web page code to standards is important, and he plans to validate his code frequently during development.

- **Language support** — Patrick's company has an affiliate in Japan.

After considering all these issues, Patrick researches four GUI editor vendors offering various editor products. He visits the vendors' Web sites for specific information about compliance, accessibility and flexibility. He then creates a short list of GUI editors that best meet his needs.

After comparing costs, Patrick chooses an open-source GUI text editor named Rich Editor (*www.richarea.com*), which is embedded in a Web browser. The product is relatively inexpensive; is open-source technology; uses the same accessibility features as a browser (e.g., Mozilla Firefox); and supports multiple languages, including Japanese. It also allows file uploads to a remote Web server. The Rich Editor product does not offer validation support, but Patrick knows he can obtain free third-party validation tools that are current and easy to use.

*        *        *

As a class, consider the issues Patrick reviewed when choosing a GUI editor, and answer the following questions.

- Which do you think are most important features in a GUI editor product?

- Which features would you expect in a GUI editor that requires you to purchase a license, in contrast to the features you would expect from a GUI editor that is available for free? Why?

## *Lesson Summary*

### Application project

As you learned in this lesson, using a GUI HTML editor to develop Web pages can save you time. How could your company's intranet or Internet site be expanded using a GUI HTML editor? How could the GUI editor help save time and energy on these tasks? Could employees with little or no HTML experience contribute?

View the Web page you created in this lesson's labs with both Mozilla Firefox and Microsoft Internet Explorer. Does the table appear the same in each browser? How is it different? Using your HTML knowledge, how could you manually modify the table's HTML code to ensure that the table appears the same in each browser?

When time permits, create a complete Web page résumé that details your skills, associations and work experience. After you earn your CIW Associate certification, you can submit your résumé to an Internet job search company, such as Monster.com (*www.monster.com*) or Yahoo! Careers (*http://careers.yahoo.com*), or you can post it on your own Web site.

### Skills review

In this lesson, you were introduced to GUI HTML editors. You used a GUI editor to develop a Web page, and you experienced the power and control that a GUI editor provides over a development project. You explored the GUI editor's features, including text style, horizontal rules, inline images, hypertext links, table creation and code validation. Finally, you considered the advantages and disadvantages of using such a tool to develop your Web pages, and you published a page to a test Web server.

Now that you have completed this lesson, you should be able to:

✓ 2.11.1: Evaluate a GUI HTML editor according to the W3C Authoring Tool Accessibility Guidelines.

✓ 2.11.2: Validate HTML code.

✓ 2.11.3: Use font and page appearance options in a GUI HTML editor.

✓ 2.11.4: View source code and preview Web pages in a browser.

✓ 2.11.5: Create HTML tables using a GUI HTML editor.

✓ 2.11.6: Publish (i.e., upload) Web pages and sites to a Web server.

# Lesson 10 Review

1.  What is another common term for a graphical user interface (GUI) HTML editor?

    _____

2.  What two types of HTML GUI editors are available?

    _____

3.  List several HTML GUI editor applications currently available on the market.

    _____

    _____

4.  What type of application offers an interface similar to an HTML GUI editor?

    _____

5.  Name a disadvantage of creating Web pages using an HTML text editor that is resolved by using a GUI editor.

    _____

    _____

# Lesson 11: Advanced Web Technologies

## Objectives

By the end of this lesson, you will be able to:

- 2.1.6: Define the Document Object Model (DOM) and its relationship to Dynamic HTML (DHTML).

- 2.1.9: Add third-party applications to your Web page (e.g., Google gadgets for the Web).

- 2.1.10: Identify ways that a Web browser can become an application delivery platform, including strengths and weaknesses of the browser.

- 2.2.12: Create a podcast, including choosing the appropriate audio format and recording rate, specifying a quality microphone, uploading files.

- 2.8.1: Explain how to structure Web documents with CSS.

- 2.8.2: Identify ways to apply styles with CSS.

- 2.17.1: Compare popular client-side and server-side programming languages, including JavaScript, Java, PHP, Python, .Net, C, C++, Visual Basic, C#.

- 2.17.2: Define Common Gateway Interface (CGI) methods, including .Net, Django, Python, JavaServer Pages (JSP), Server-Side JavaScript (SSJS), Active Server Pages (ASP), PHP Hypertext Preprocessor (PHP), Ajax.

- 2.17.5: Identify the value of n-tier applications and associated techniques in processing online transactions.

- 2.18.1: Investigate costs associated with placing and developing your own server.

- 2.18.2: Identify costs associated with using an Application Service Provider (ASP).

- 2.18.3: Distinguish among dedicated hosting, co-location and virtual servers.

- 2.18.4: Activate features provided by managed services (e.g., CGI, forms).

- 2.18.5: Manage information relevant to a site (e.g., account information, passwords, IP addresses).

⚡ 2.19.1: Identify ways to use additional technologies to provide custom features to an end user (e.g., using JavaScript to detect Web browser type, using cookies).

⚡ 2.21.5: Identify ways to create pages for traditional and PDA-based browsers (e.g., validating code, appropriate resolutions, supported interpreters, extensive user testing).

Version 2.0

# Pre-Assessment Questions

1. How does an application created in PHP differ from an application created in JavaScript?

   a. The PHP application requires an interpreter.
   b. The PHP application requires an interpreter on a server.
   c. The PHP application requires an interpreter on a UNIX Web server.
   d. The PHP application requires an open-source interpreter.

2. Which HTML tag allows you to declare a CSS inline style in the body of an HTML document?

   a. <style>
   b. <body>
   c. <css>
   d. <inline>

3. What interpreted, cross-platform, object-based scripting language can add interactivity to a Web page?

# Extending HTML

You are not limited to XHTML and HTML when developing Web pages. In this lesson, you will learn about client-side and server-side Web technologies for extending the capabilities of your Web pages. Technologies discussed in this lesson include:

- Client-side and server-side scripting.

- Cascading Style Sheets (CSS) options.

- Dynamic HTML (DHTML).

- Developing Web pages for PDAs and smart clients.

- Web application frameworks.

- Creating aliases with TinyURL.

- Other advanced Web technologies made possible through Web 2.0 and Ajax.

This lesson will also discuss issues related to using Web service providers for site hosting and other online services.

# Server-Side and Client-Side Languages

Before you learn about specific server-side and client-side languages, it is helpful to understand some basic programming terms. Table 11-1 describes some essential concepts in programming.

*Table 11-1: Basic programming concepts*

| Concept | Description |
|---|---|
| Variable | A place in memory used to store information for later use. Variables are used in simple applications and are essential in complex ones. Variables are usually created by using the equal sign ( = ). For example, to create a variable named James, you would use the following command: James=James. Variables are often referred to as values preceded with a dollar sign ( $ ). For example, the variable named James would be referred to as $James. In many languages, variables are case-specific (e.g., the variable $James is different from the variable $james). |
| Array | A collection of variables stored in a series. Arrays are used to hold multiple values; a variable can hold only one value. |
| Function | A line of code that allows you to refer to an entire series of steps or commands. Functions are used to organize code into discrete sections. |
| Interpreter | Software used to read and process code in standard text files. Interpreters either reside on the server or are downloaded to a client. PHP, Perl and ASP are all languages that use an interpreter. Some CGI applications must explicitly specify the location of the interpreter. For example, Perl requires the first line to include a correct reference, or the script will fail. |
| Compiler | An application used to process code in standard text files into executable applications. For example, to compile a C application named james.c, you would use the gcc application: gcc james.c -o james.exe. |
| Include | A set of files called a library that you can refer to in your code. Programmers often include libraries in their code to avoid having to re-create code that has already been written. |

*Table 11-1: Basic programming concepts (cont'd)*

| Concept | Description |
|---|---|
| **Print** | A command that prints application output to a destination, often a computer screen. For example, you can create an application that prints information to a window on the screen so you can monitor the application's progress. Print is generally part of a programming language's Input/Output library, which is responsible for allowing users to input information (e.g., through a keyboard) or output information (e.g., to a monitor). |
| **Echo** | A command that repeats the input you type back to a terminal or an application window. Echo can also be used in an application to repeat input so that it can be processed or forwarded. |
| **Statement** | Logical constructs that allow you to control the way that information flows in the application. |

## Programming statements

Even relatively simple scripts must control the way that information flows within them. Sometimes, an application must determine the action it will take if a certain condition occurs or while a certain condition exists. Table 11-2 describes several programming statements that allow applications to process information.

*Table 11-2: Programming statements*

| Statement | Description |
|---|---|
| **If/then** | Executes a process only if a particular condition is true. For example, an application may contain a statement that checks whether the \tmp\ folder is present. If it is, then the application will run. Classic *if/then* statements allow only one condition to occur. Known as a conditional statement. |
| **If/then/else** | Similar to an *if/then* statement, but executes a group of additional commands if the given condition is false. For example, an *if/then/else* statement can direct the following logic: If the \tmp\ folder is not available, then check to see if the \temp\ directory is available, or else create a directory named \tmp\. Known as a conditional statement. |
| **Do while** | Runs ("do") a specified subprocess while a specified condition is true. For example, an application may continue to present an alternative window while the mouse is being right-clicked. Often used as a part of an *if/then* or *if/then/else* statement, the *do while* statement ensures that an action occurs the entire time a condition is true. Sometimes known as a *repeat until* statement. |
| **Do until** | Similar to a *do while* statement, but runs the specified subprocess until a specified number of events have occurred. For example, a calculation process may add the number 1 to the result of the previous statement until the sum reaches 100, then exit. |
| **Break** | When placed inside of a statement, allows an application to break out of an infinite loop in case of a problem. |

The following sections discuss server-side and client-side Web technologies commonly used to extend Web pages. Each of the languages discussed allows you to implement some or all of the programming statements and concepts described in the preceding tables.

# Server-Side Languages

**OBJECTIVE**
2.17.1: Programming
languages

A server-side language has the following attributes:

- Code is executed by the Web server, not by the Web browser.

- Code is generally placed into files called applications. These applications are assigned execute permissions by the Web server. In some cases, code is embedded into HTML and XHTML pages.

- Code executes because an interpreter has been installed and activated on the Web server.

Server-side scripts are used for various purposes, including:

- Browser detection.

- Database connectivity.

- Cookie creation and identification.

- Logon scripts.

- Hit counters.

- File uploading and downloading.

Common server-side languages include PHP, Perl, Active Server Pages (ASP), Visual Basic, C, C++, C# and Java. The following sections will discuss each of these languages.

## PHP Hypertext Preprocessor (PHP)

**OBJECTIVE**
2.17.2: CGI methods

PHP is an interpreted server-side scripting language for creating dynamic Web pages. It is embedded in HTML pages but is usually executed on a Web server. The following code example is a very simple PHP CGI application that creates the message "Hello, World" in XHTML, then returns a report identifying the browser used to access the Web page. This script can be placed in a Web server's CGI bin directory:

```php
<?php
$ua = $_SERVER['HTTP_USER_AGENT'];
{print"
<html>
<head>
<title>PHP Example</title>
</head>
<body>
<h1>Hello, World!</h1>
Your user agent is:<strong>{$ua}.</strong>
</body>
</html>
";}
?>
```

In this code, the syntax *<?php* begins the statement that allows code execution. Figure 11-1 shows the results of this code when viewed in a Web browser (in this case, Mozilla Firefox running on a Red Hat Linux 9.0 system using the X Window interface).

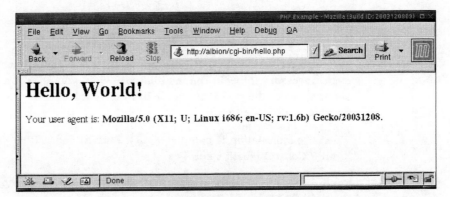

Figure 11-1: Viewing results of "Hello World" PHP script

As you can see, the PHP server-side code has detected and reported the user agent used to access it. However, you can do more with this information than simply return it to the user. You could use this information to customize a user's experience depending upon the browser used. For example, this script could direct Internet Explorer users to one version of the site, and Mozilla Firefox users to another.

In the following lab, you will perform simple browser recognition through a CGI script (in this case, PHP). Suppose your project manager wants to know if you can enable the Web site to recognize the browser type and version that visitors use to access it. This information will help the Web development team decide whether to incorporate some new technologies in the site. If many of your users are found to be using older browsers, the Web team will not incorporate some new technologies that could reduce visitor accessibility. You tell your project manager that you can experiment with a server-side CGI script to enable browser recognition.

 **Lab 11-1: Using a PHP CGI script to detect browser type**

In this lab, you will view the results of a PHP CGI script.

1. **Instructor:** From **C:\CIW\Site_Dev\Lab Files\Lesson11\Lab_11-1\XAMPP\**, copy the **xampp-win32-1.7.0-installer.exe** file to your Desktop. This file includes the following:

   - Apache Server version 2.2.11 (an open-source Web server)

   - MySQL version 5.1.30 (an open-source relational database)

   - PHP 5.2.8 (the PHP interpreter)

   - Perl version 5.8.7 (the Perl interpreter)

2. **Instructor:** Verify that your system has the following minimum requirements to install and run XAMPP:

   - At least 64 MB of RAM

   - At least 200 MB of free space on the C:\ drive

   *Note: This lab is designed for Windows Vista using the xampp-win32-1.7.0-installer.exe setup file. If you use a different operating system or version of XAMPP, then you may have to modify some steps in this lab and the labs that follow. If necessary, go to www.apachefriends.org/en/xampp.html* *to obtain the necessary installation binary. Try to use the exact same version.*

3. **Instructor:** Double-click the **xampp-win32-1.7.0-installer.exe** file and take the steps necessary to begin the installation. When you are prompted to select XAMPP options, select the check boxes for **Install Apache As Service** and **Install MySQL As Service**, then click **Install**.

4. When the installation is complete, click **Finish**. You will be prompted to start the XAMPP Control Panel. Click **Yes**.

5. Ensure that the **Apache** and **MySQL** services are running. Your XAMPP Control Panel should resemble Figure 11-2.

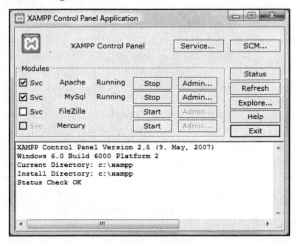

*Figure 11-2: XAMPP Control Panel with services running*

6. **Instructor:** Verify that Apache Server is running by opening a Web browser to **http://localhost**. You should see the XAMPP splash screen, verifying that Apache Server is running.

7. **Instructor:** From the **Lab_11-1\** folder, copy the **hello.php** script to the **C:\xampp\htdocs\** directory.

8. **Instructor:** Direct students to access your Web server. If your system has the IP address of 192.168.2.5, for example, have students use the URL *http://192.168.2.5/hello.php*.

9. **Students:** Access the Web server address provided by your instructor. The script will return the value of your browser type and version. In Figure 11-3, the browser and version used to access the script was Mozilla Firefox version 3.0.7, loaded from Windows Vista. (Windows NT 6.0 is the generic name for Windows Vista and Windows Server 2008.)

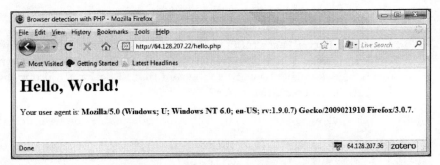

Figure 11-3: Browser recognition using PHP

10. **Students:** Close your browsers.

11. **Instructor (when time permits):** Allow students to view permissions on this file. If this system is on a standard FAT32 drive, then there will be no permissions on the file. If this system is using NTFS, then this file's permissions will be as follows:

- The file will be owned either by everyone or by the account used by Apache Server.

- The file will have execute permissions for the proper user (e.g., everyone or the account used by Apache Server).

In this lab, you viewed the results of using a simple PHP CGI script for browser recognition.

## Practical Extraction and Report Language (Perl)

Perl is a cross-platform programming language that enables users to write custom CGI programs and system management programs. Perl is a language commonly used for various purposes, including Web server processes. The following example code shows a simple Perl program that performs the same function as the PHP script profiled previously:

```perl
#!/usr/bin/perl
use CGI qw/:all/;
$cgi_object = CGI::new();

print "Content-type: text/html\n\n";
print "<html>\n<head>\n<title>\nPerl CGI
Example\n</title>\n<body>\n<h1>Hello,
World!</h1>\nYour user agent is: <b>\n";
print $cgi_object->user_agent();
print "</b>.</html>\n";
```

In this code, notice the first line that begins with the #! characters. This first line is known as the "shebang." The shebang is used in Perl applications to point to the location of the Perl interpreter. Many problems with Perl scripts originate with an improperly created shebang line.

*This code provides only a very simple example of Perl's capabilities.*

## Active Server Pages (ASP) using VBScript

OBJECTIVE
2.17.2: CGI methods

Active Server Pages (ASP) is Microsoft's original server-side scripting solution. It has largely been supplanted by .NET. You can create ASP applications using VBScript, which is quite similar to JavaScript, except that VBScript is a proprietary Microsoft language. PHP is an alternative to ASP.

The following example VBScript ASP code enables browser detection:

```
<%@ LANGUAGE=vbscript %>
<html>
<head>
<title>ASP CGI Example</title>
</head>
<body>
<h1>Hello, World!</h1>
<%
path = Request.ServerVariables("PATH_INFO")
pagename = Request.ServerVariables("HTTP_HOST")
method = Request.ServerVariables("REQUEST_METHOD")
browser = Request.ServerVariables("HTTP_USER_AGENT")
user = Request.ServerVariables("REMOTE_ADDR")
```

## C

C is a powerful compiled programming language that has served as the foundation for other languages, including C++ and Java. Although C was first developed in the late 1960s, it remains popular today. It is mostly used to develop stand-alone applications, rather than Web applications. For example, most daemons (i.e., services) are written in C.

C is a procedural language, meaning that it relies upon subprograms to accomplish a task in an application. Subprograms are contained within an application and are called by various terms depending upon the language used. In C, subprograms are called functions.

C uses standard libraries that you can include in the program. These libraries are common to any C implementation and are designed to save you coding time. Without these libraries, you would be forced into writing hundreds of lines of code each time you created an application. Many different library files exist. C has been organized as a language so that these libraries are standardized and available to everyone.

The following code demonstrates an extremely simple C program:

```
#include <stdio.h>
int main()
{
    printf("Hello, World!\n");
    return 0;
}
```

Notice that this code uses a library inclusion, called *stdio.h*. This inclusion is the standard I/O library, responsible for printing the phrase "Hello, World!" to your screen. The standard I/O library is also responsible for allowing users to input information into applications you write. However, the example code does not contain any logic that allows you to enter information into this program. All C programs must have a main function, which in C begins with the code *int main()*.

## C++

**object-oriented**
A style of programming that links data to the processes that manipulate it.

C++ is another compiled programming language. It is not a proprietary language; compilers are available from a variety of sources, including Microsoft (*www.microsoft.com*) and GNU (*www.gnu.org*). Based on C, C++ is not procedural in nature. Rather, it is an **object-oriented** language. An object-oriented language may include procedural elements, but instead of using subprograms to accomplish a task, a language such as C++ will create an object that can then be manipulated throughout the program. The primary benefit of object-oriented languages is that they allow developers to create efficient, powerful code. Table 11-3 describes common object-oriented language terms used by C++, as well as Java, Visual Basic and C#.

*Table 11-3: Object-oriented language terms*

| Term | Description |
|------|-------------|
| **Object** | A discrete portion of an application. Once an object is instantiated (i.e., created), it can then be used. All objects have specific states and behaviors that can be manipulated. An object is also known as an instance, because an object can be duplicated and then manipulated within a program. |
| **Abstraction** | The determination of all elements that make a particular object unique, separate and distinct from another instance of an object. |
| **Class** | A group of similar objects. |
| **Polymorphism** | The ability of the programming language to make an object behave differently or to take on different characteristics, depending upon its place in an application. |
| **Inheritance** | The ability for one class to share characteristics with another class. Characteristics can include an object's state, structure or behavior. |

**emulator**
A type of software that imitates a computer then allows non-native software to run in a foreign environment. Sometimes also a hardware device.

All C++ programs must be compiled to a specific computer type (e.g., IBM-compatible machines that run Windows). Once a C++ program is compiled to a specific type of host, it cannot be run on another (e.g., a Macintosh system) unless an **emulator** is used.

## Java

Java is also an object-oriented programming language. Java is a compiled language, like C and C++. Unlike C++, however, Java is designed to allow its applications to run on any operating system that has the Java interpreter installed. As a result, Java has two benefits:

- **Java is object-oriented** — It allows the creation of powerful applications.

- **Java is platform-independent** — You do not compile a Java application to a specific computer type (e.g., IBM, Macintosh or Sun Sparc). Rather, you compile a Java application to a specific Java interpreter. The Java interpreter can be installed on any system, and the Java application can be used on any system running the interpreter.

Sun Microsystems, which developed Java, coined a Java motto: "Write once, run anywhere." As with most marketing phrases, however, reality is somewhat different. Most Java developers comment that when they write a Java application, they must "write once, test everywhere" to ensure that their code runs on all operating systems.

Uncompiled text files that contain Java code often have the .java file name extension. When a file is compiled into a Java application, the file usually has the .jar extension.

*This portion of the course focuses on using Java on the server side. Java is also used to create applets, which are executed by a client's browser and are thus a client-side technology.*

### *JavaServer Pages (JSP) and Java servlets*

Java can be used to create a JavaServer Pages (JSP) API. JSP is a technology that uses Java commands embedded into XHTML and HTML code.

Java can be used to create Java servlets. A Java servlet is an application that must be installed directly onto the remote server; code from a Java servlet is not downloaded to the browser. When using Java servlets, you must perform the following steps:

• Compile the servlet.

• Place the servlet on a server that is capable of handling it.

One of the most popular Web servers that supports JSP and servlets is Apache Tomcat (*http://tomcat.apache.org/*).

 *The Microsoft implementation of Java is known as J++.*

## Visual Basic

Visual Basic (VB) is a compiled programming language developed by Microsoft Corporation. It is used for stand-alone applications and server-side Web applications. It is not often used as a client-side application in Web browsers, as is JavaScript or VBScript.

Earlier versions of Visual Basic were more procedural in nature than they were object-oriented. As of version 4, however, Visual Basic now has more object-oriented capabilities. It is often used in the Microsoft .NET CGI solution. Visual Basic is considered to be easier to use than languages such as C++ and Java, but as a result, this simplicity sometimes does not allow Visual Basic to perform all the tasks that C++ and Java can perform. For more information about Visual Basic, visit the Microsoft Visual Basic Developer Center at *http://msdn.microsoft.com/vbasic*.

## C#

C# (pronounced "C sharp") is a compiled object-oriented programming language, and is the proprietary Microsoft competitor to Java. C# was designed to be easier to use (like Visual Basic) but still powerful. C# is also sometimes known as Visual C#, the Microsoft product name. Because C# is a Microsoft-specific language, it has features that make it much easier to develop applications and interfaces for the Windows operating systems. For more information about C#, visit the Microsoft Visual C# Developer Center at *http://msdn.microsoft.com/vcsharp/*. You can access the C# language specification at *http://msdn.microsoft.com/vcsharp/aa336809.aspx*.

## Server-side includes (SSIs)

A server-side include (SSI) is an instruction within an XHTML or HTML page that directs the Web server to perform an action. SSI is considered to be an alternative to CGI because it does not use languages such as JavaScript, Visual Basic or Java. Rather, SSI instructions are written in SGML. The instruction is used to dynamically add content to a page just before it is downloaded to a user. SSI can be used to:

• Place the results of a database query into a page.

• Execute other programs.

• Indicate the last time that the displayed document was modified.

- Insert text at the bottom of a page (i.e., a footer). The footer can contain any text you want, from the current date to a customized message.

- Add the current date as a timestamp to a page.

### SSI file name extensions

A Web server that supports SSI reads each HTML page for SSI instructions, and then processes the instructions for each user request. Standard practice is for X/HTML files that use SSI to use the .shtml or .shtm file name extension, rather than simply .html or .htm. The Web server knows to look for files with these extensions.

### SSI support in Web servers

Most Web servers include SSI capability. However, the SSI feature may be disabled. For example, if you are using Apache Server, you must edit the *httpd.conf* file to enter the instructions necessary for Apache Server to process the server-side includes found in HTML pages. With Microsoft Internet Information Services (IIS), you must select features in the GUI to enable SSI.

Even though your Web server may be configured to support SSI, it may not be configured to look for the standard .shtml or .shtm file name extensions. In such cases, you can take either of two approaches:

- Find the supported extension type for SSI.

- Define a MIME type for the .shtml or .shtm extensions for the Web server.

Either solution will allow the Web server to process SSI instructions.

# Client-Side Languages

OBJECTIVE
2.17.1: Programming languages

Client-side languages run on the user's computer after the page is downloaded. Therefore, some of the processing burden can be passed from the server to the client machine. Allowing the client to do the work frees the server to perform other, more important functions and services. The following sections discuss JavaScript and VBScript, the two most popular client-side languages.

## Issues with client-side languages

Using server-side technologies is sometimes preferable because there are risks inherent in allowing the client to determine the way your Web pages render. Consider the following problems:

- Some clients do not support JavaScript or any other scripting language.

- Users can deactivate script execution in browsers that normally support it. Many companies direct their employees to disable scripting in their browsers due to security concerns. If your page relies upon client-side scripting for browser recognition and/or database connectivity, then your pages may not render as expected to some portion of your audience.

## JavaScript

JavaScript is an object-based scripting language that allows developers to add interactivity to their Web pages. JavaScript can be used on the client side or on the server side. When used on the client side, JavaScript code must reside inside HTML documents in order to run. JavaScript can add the following functionality to a Web page or site:

- Pop-up windows, such as alert, dialog and prompt boxes

- Automatic date and time changes

- Images and text that change upon mouse rollover

- Cookie creation and identification

Unlike traditional programming languages, such as C, a scripting language is used within a program to extend its capabilities. If you have ever written a macro in Microsoft Excel or used WordBasic to perform some task in a Microsoft Word document, you have already used a scripting language.

JavaScript syntax closely resembles that of C. The code is placed within your Web document so that when your browser retrieves a page that incorporates JavaScript, it runs the programs and performs the appropriate operations.

### JavaScript is object-based, not object-oriented

**object-based**
Similar to object-oriented programming languages, but does not allow for inheritance from one class to another.

JavaScript is not considered an object-oriented language because it does not support inheritance. JavaScript is an **object-based** language that has a collection of built-in objects, including:

- **Document** — allows you to obtain values from and write values to a document.

- **Navigator** — allows you to determine the type of browser accessing a Web page.

- **Array** — allows you to create a series of variables to later manipulate.

Several additional objects exist. JavaScript allows you to apply methods to all objects. For example, the *document.write* command in JavaScript allows you to write a specified value to a document. To learn more about JavaScript, enroll in the *CIW JavaScript Fundamentals* course.

### JavaScript advantages

JavaScript offers programmers several advantages, including a short development cycle, ease of learning, and platform-independence. These advantages make JavaScript a natural choice to easily and quickly extend HTML pages on the Web. Table 11-4 describes these JavaScript benefits.

*Table 11-4: JavaScript advantages*

| Advantage | Description |
|---|---|
| **Quick development** | Because JavaScript does not require time-consuming compilation, scripts can be developed in a relatively short period of time. Most of the interface features, such as forms, frames and other GUI elements, are handled by the browser and XHTML/HTML code, further shortening the development time. JavaScript programmers do not have to create or handle these elements of their applications. |
| **Easy to learn** | Although JavaScript shares many characteristics with the Java programming language, the JavaScript syntax and rules are simpler. If you know any other programming languages, it will be easy for you to learn JavaScript. |

*Table 11-4: JavaScript advantages (cont'd)*

| Advantage | Description |
|---|---|
| Platform-independence | Like XHTML and HTML, JavaScript is not specific to any operating system. The same JavaScript program can be used on any browser on any system, provided that the browser supports JavaScript. |

### Embedding JavaScript into HTML

JavaScript must reside within an HTML document. It is embedded into XHTML or HTML code using the <script> tag. Note that JavaScript placement is not restricted to the <body> element. The following example demonstrates the basic structure of an XHTML file with JavaScript.

```
<!DOCTYPE html
    PUBLIC "-//W3C//DTD XHTML 1.0 Transitional//EN"
    "http://www.w3.org/TR/xhtml1/DTD/xhtml1-transitional.dtd">
<html xmlns="http://www.w3.org/1999/xhtml" xml:lang="en">
<head>
<meta name="Keywords" content="CIW, Foundations, Example"/>
<meta name="Description" content="For the CIW Foundations Course"/>
<meta http-equiv="Content-Type" content="text/html; charset=utf-8"/>
<title>JavaScript</title>

<script>
JavaScript code goes here
</script>

</head>
<body>

<script>
JavaScript can go here too
</script>

</body>
</html>
```

In JavaScript, the Web author can communicate with the user through the *alert()* and *prompt()* functions. These functions are both properties of the *window* document. The Web author can also use the *document.write()* function to output text to the client window in sequence with an HTML or XHTML file. The *alert()* function displays an alert dialog box. The *prompt()* function requests user input in a text area within a dialog box. The *prompt()* function initiates a conversation, or dialog. The result returned by the *prompt()* can be used as an argument to another method, such as the *document.write()*.

### JavaScript and browser detection

OBJECTIVE
2.19.1: Custom site feature technologies

JavaScript can also be used to detect browser type and version. Consider the following code:

```
<!DOCTYPE html
    PUBLIC "-//W3C//DTD XHTML 1.0 Transitional//EN"
    "http://www.w3.org/TR/xhtml1/DTD/xhtml1-transitional.dtd">
<html xmlns="http://www.w3.org/1999/xhtml" xml:lang="en">
<head>
<meta name="Keywords" content="CIW, Foundations, Example"/>
<meta name="Description" content="For the CIW Foundations Course"/>
<meta http-equiv="Content-Type" content="text/html; charset=utf-8"/>
<title>Browser Detection Using JavaScript</title>
</head>
<body>
<h1> Hello, World!</h1>
<script type="text/javascript" >
```

```
document.write("Your user agent is: "+ navigator.userAgent)
document.write(".")
</script>
</body>
</html>
```

In this example, the JavaScript code uses the *write* method of the *document* object and the *userAgent* method of the *navigator* object to write the user agent information to the page. No CGI script is necessary for this code to render; you need only the JavaScript interpreter, which is included in almost all modern browsers by default.

 *User agents such as Lynx often do not support JavaScript or other forms of client-side scripting.*

Practical uses for scripts of this type include:

• Presenting different versions of a site to different browsers.

• Informing users in a corporate intranet to upgrade their browsers to a supported version.

• Ensuring accessibility to disabled users.

In the following lab, you will use JavaScript code to perform browser detection. Suppose your project manager still wants your Web pages to be able to automatically detect a user's browser type and version. However, she was not satisfied with the PHP solution you demonstrated for her previously. She asks you to demonstrate a similar solution that can be enabled on the client side.

 **Lab 11-2: Using JavaScript to detect browser type**

In this lab, you will use JavaScript in a Web page to detect the type and version of browsers being used to access the page.

1. From the **C:\CIW\Site_Dev\Lab Files\Lesson11\Lab_11-2** directory, copy the **hello.html** file to your Desktop.

2. Double-click the **hello.html** file to open it. Your screen should list the browser type and version. The example in Figure 11-4 shows that the browser is Mozilla Firefox 3.0.7 on Windows NT 6.0 (Windows Vista or Windows Server 2008).

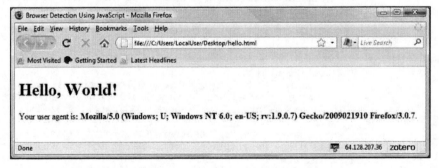

*Figure 11-4: Using JavaScript for browser detection*

3. Close your browser.

**4.** As a class, discuss the following questions:

- Is there any significant visual difference between this window generated by JavaScript and the window generated by PHP in the previous lab?

- What are the benefits of using this client-side script instead of a server-side script?

- What are the drawbacks of using this client-side script instead of a server-side script?

- What practical uses are there for this script?

**5. When time permits:** The instructor can upload this page to a Web server, then you can access this page across a network.

In this lab, you used JavaScript to detect browser type and version.

## JavaScript and cookies

**OBJECTIVE**
2.19.1: Custom site
feature
technologies

You can also use JavaScript to deposit cookies on the system hard drives of users who visit your site. Using simple JavaScript code, you can use cookies to:

- Store passwords.

- Store user preferences.

- Choose which Web pages will be displayed based on the browser version used.

JavaScript can also be used for copyright protection. A simple script can help prevent your Web site from being included in another site without proper recognition.

In the following lab, you will incorporate some simple JavaScript code into a Web page. Suppose your project manager wants a feature on the Web page that asks the user to enter his or her name, then incorporates the user input into a greeting. You can add some JavaScript code to your XHTML to create this feature.

 **Lab 11-3: Using simple JavaScript to create an interactive Web page**

In this lab, you will incorporate a simple JavaScript function into a Web page.

**1.** From **C:\CIW\Site_Dev\Lab Files\Lesson11\Lab_11-3\** directory, copy the file **lab_11-3.html** to your Desktop.

**2. Editor:** Open **lab_11-3.html**, and add the JavaScript code as indicated in bold:

```
<!DOCTYPE html
    PUBLIC "-//W3C//DTD XHTML 1.0 Transitional//EN"
    "http://www.w3.org/TR/xhtml1/DTD/xhtml1-transitional.dtd">
<html xmlns="http://www.w3.org/1999/xhtml" xml:lang="en">
<head>
<meta name="Keywords" content="CIW, Foundations, Example"/>
<meta name="Description" content="For the CIW Foundations Course"/>
<meta http-equiv="Content-Type" content="text/html; charset=utf-8"/>
<!-- <link rel="stylesheet" type="text/css" href="b.css" title="stylesheet"/>
-->
<title>Simple JavaScript</title>
</head>
<body>
```

```
<h1> Simple JavaScript </h1>
<script type="text/javascript" >

 alert("You are entering the world of JavaScript");
    document.write("Hello, ");
    document.write(prompt("What is your name?", ""));
    document.write("<br/>Welcome to JavaScript!");
</script>
</body>
</html>
```

3. **Editor:** Save the **lab_11-3.html** file.

4. **Browser:** Open **lab_11-3.html**. Your screen should resemble Figure 11-5.

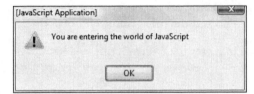

*Figure 11-5: JavaScript alert box*

5. **Browser:** Click **OK**. A dialog box will appear asking for your name. Enter your name in the text field, then click **OK**. Your screen should resemble Figure 11-6, with your name in the greeting.

*Figure 11-6: JavaScript-generated Web page*

6. Close your browser.

7. **When time permits:** Add this JavaScript code to one of the Habitat For Humanity pages from the course labs. View your page and test the script in at least one browser. After you verify that the script works, validate your code at **http://validator.w3.org**. Then answer the following question: What will happen when people with voice-recognition software and text-based browsers such as Lynx visit this page?

_____

_____

In this lab, you learned more about the capabilities of client-side JavaScript.

## VBScript

You already learned a little about VBScript in the discussion about Active Server Pages (ASP). VBScript is the Microsoft implementation of JavaScript. Like JavaScript, VBScript can be used on the client side or on the server side, and provides access to built-in documents and methods.

VBScript is proprietary, so the VBScript interpreter is installed only in Microsoft Internet Explorer. If you use VBScript on the client side, then in most cases Internet Explorer will be the only Web browser that will recognize the code you use. However, if you use VBScript on the server side, then any browser can use your pages.

VBScript syntax is quite similar to JavaScript and offers capabilities similar to JavaScript as well. To learn more about VBScript, visit *www.microsoft.com.*

# Connecting to a Database

You learned about databases and CGI earlier in this course. However, you should understand that for a database to work, you must:

- **Provide a way for the Web server and database to recognize each other** — For example, Microsoft systems use ODBC.

- **Provide permissions to the database so that it can be read and/or written to** — Most databases allow users to write to them.

## CGI and permissions

**OBJECTIVE**
2.17.2: CGI methods

2.18.4: Managed services

CGI scripts often fail to execute properly not because they are coded incorrectly, but because the Web server does not have execute permissions. Failure for CGI scripts to execute is caused by the following:

- The Web server does not have the permissions to execute files and scripts.

- The file or script used has incorrect permissions, which prohibits the server from executing the file.

In many ways, these two problems are the same issue. To solve such problems, first make sure that the Web server you are using has all of the necessary permissions. Then, modify the permissions assigned to the file so that it has only enough permissions to function. This allows the Web server to execute the file securely. Allowing a file too many permissions can cause serious security problems.

### ISPs and CGI

If you are working with an Internet Service Provider (ISP), you generally need to request the CGI services. Following are the actions you will need to request that the ISP perform:

- **Enable execute permissions on your scripts** — The ISP can assign these permissions after they receive your files.

- **Create a directory that contains available CGI scripts** — This directory is generally called the CGI bin, and is often named *cgi* or *cgi-bin.* The ISP should create this directory with your site files.

- **Provide user name and passwords with enough permissions for the system** — The ISP will usually assign the appropriate permissions. The administrative password for UNIX systems is *root.* The administrative password for Windows systems is *administrator.* However, understand that it is possible for an ISP to create new accounts that may have sufficient permissions to accomplish a task normally reserved for the *root* or *administrator* account.

OBJECTIVE
2.17.5: N-tier
applications

## N-tier applications

When discussing databases, three elements are generally involved:

- **Data** — the database file or multiple database files.

- **Business logic** — the SQL coding necessary to create relationships with the data stored in the database.

- **Presentation** — the way that data and business logic are presented on the user screen. Presentation includes Web forms created with XHTML or HTML, and application-specific interfaces such as Microsoft Access or a Web browser.

In a single-tier database, the data, business logic and presentation are all provided by one application (e.g., Microsoft Access). In a two-tier application, the client is responsible for the business logic and data presentation, and the database is stored on a separate server. In an n-tier solution, all three database elements are separated, as shown in Figure 11-7.

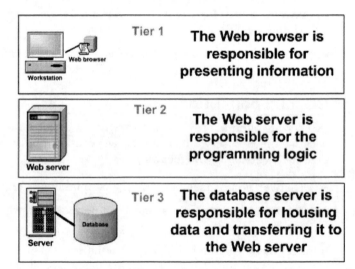

*Figure 11-7: N-tier applications*

This lesson has shown simple CGI and database communication, which is essentially a simplified n-tier solution. Table 11-5 summarizes single-tier, two-tier and n-tier computing.

*Table 11-5: Summary of single-tier, two-tier and n-tier computing*

| Model | Description | Example |
|-------|-------------|---------|
| **Single-tier** | All three layers are combined into one application or database. | A Microsoft Access database available only on a local system. A user simply opens Access, then manipulates the database. |
| **Two-tier** | The client is responsible for presentation and business logic, and a server houses only the data. Called a client-server relationship. Any change to the database requires client upgrade. | A proprietary client connects to a database server to process information. For example, using Microsoft Access to query a remote database. |

Table 11-5: Summary of single-tier, two-tier and n-tier computing (cont'd)

| Model | Description | Example |
|-------|-------------|---------|
| N-tier | The business logic, data and presentation are completely separated. An upgrade in one of the layers does not necessarily mean the others are affected. | Using a Web browser to visit a Web site that is connected to a remote database. The Web browser downloads the necessary forms and is responsible for presentation. The Web server is responsible for providing the business logic and programming. The remote database provides the data. Many times, multiple Web servers and databases are used. |

In the following lab, your instructor will demonstrate the implementation of CGI and database connectivity. Suppose your project manager has approved a version of the *syb.html* page, along with several other pages that compose much of the Habitat site. She has asked you to add a Web form to the *syb.html* page and to verify that this form can communicate with a database server. Your Web team has SQL and PHP scripts available that will allow you to test database connectivity. You can create a basic, sample database for the staging server. If your project manager likes the setup, a live database can be created for the production Web server. For now, you will connect a form to a database and test the workings of the database.

 **Lab 11-4: Implementing CGI and database connectivity *(instructor-led)***

In this lab, you will use a Web form, a MySQL database and PHP to obtain data from end users.

1. **Students:** From the **C:\CIW\Site_Dev\Lab Files\Lesson11** directory, copy the **Lab_11-4\** folder to your Desktop.

2. **Students:** Open the **Lab_11-4\** folder on your Desktop, then open the **Habitat\** subfolder.

3. **Instructor:** Review the following files with your students:

   • **Habitat\vlist.sql** — responsible for creating the database table used in this lab.

   • **Habitat\CCYP\sybinput.php** — responsible for processing all information entered into the Web form. After potential volunteers submit the form they have completed, this PHP script ensures that the information is properly placed into a database. This script contains code that authenticates with the database, then populates the database with entries. The form you will create in this lab refers to this script using the *action* attribute.

   • **Habitat\CCYP\syboutput.php** — shows the contents of the database in a formatted XHTML page with the title *Youth Blitz Signup*. The code in this file registers with the database, obtains all relevant information, then populates the XHTML page with all relevant information. This PHP script also contains authentication information. This time, the authentication information allows the script to read information in the database that will populate the XHTML page.

4.  **Students:** From **Lab_11-4\Habitat\CCYP**, open the file **syb.html** in a text editor.

5.  Find the comment that reads as follows:

    ```
    <!-- BEGIN APPLICATION FORM -->
    ```

6.  Enter the following code, shown in bold, beneath the commented phrase as shown:

    ```
    <!-- BEGIN APPLICATION FORM -->
    <form action="sybinput.php" method="post">
     <table border="0">
        <tr>
         <td>First Name</td>
         <td><input type="text" name="first" maxlength="30" size="15"/></td>
        </tr>
        <tr>
         <td>Last Name</td>
         <td><input type="text" name="last" maxlength="30" size="15"/></td>
        </tr>
        <tr>
         <td>E-Mail</td>
         <td><input type="text" name="email" maxlength="30" size="15"/></td>
        </tr>
        <tr>
         <td>Country</td>
         <td><input type="text" name="country" maxlength="30" size="15"/></td>
        </tr>
        <tr>
         <td>Skill</td>
         <td><input type="text" name="skill" maxlength="30" size="15"/></td>
        </tr>
        <tr>
         <td><input type="submit" value="Register"/></td> <td><input type="reset"
    value="Reset"/></td>
        </tr>
     </table>
    </form>

    <!-- END OF APPLICATION FORM -->
    </div>
    ```

7.  **Students:** Save **syb.html**, then view your Web page in a browser. The page, complete with the new Web form, should appear as shown in Figure 11-8.

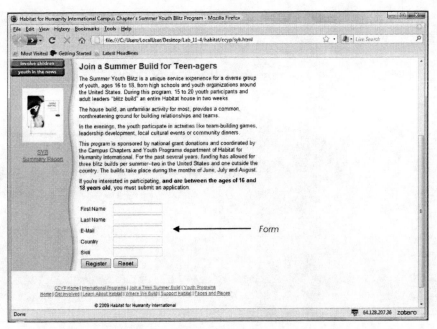

*Figure 11-8: Completed page syb.html with new form*

8. **Students:** Validate your code, then wait for your instructor.

9. **Instructor:** Install **XAMPP** if you have not done so already.

   *Note: Lab 11-1 details the steps for performing the XAMPP installation.*

10. **Instructor:** Copy the **C:\CIW\Site_Dev\Lab Files\Lesson11\Finished\Habitat\** folder and its contents to the **C:\xampp\htdocs\** directory. Make sure that you copy the **Habitat\** folder (with all of its contents) from the **Lesson11\Finished** folder. After you copy it, the Habitat\ folder and all of its contents will reside off of the C:\xampp\htdocs\ folder.

11. **Instructor:** Open your browser and go to ***http://localhost*** to display the XAMPP splash screen. Click the **English** link, if necessary, to display the XAMPP For Windows screen, shown in Figure 11-9.

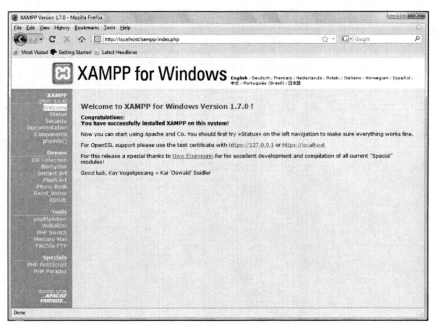

Figure 11-9: XAMPP For Windows screen

12. **Instructor:** In the left navigation bar under Tools, click the **phpMyAdmin** link to display the phpMyAdmin window.

13. **Instructor:** In the MySQL Localhost section, enter the word *Volunteers* in the Create New Database text box, then click the **Create** button.

14. **Instructor:** You will see a new page informing you that your Volunteers database has been created and is running on localhost. Click the **Import** hyperlink.

15. **Instructor:** The File To Import section will appear. Click the **Browse** button to choose a file of SQL commands for your new database. The File Upload dialog box will appear.

16. **Instructor:** Navigate to the **C:\xampp\htdocs\Habitat\** folder. Select the file **vlist.sql** by clicking it, then click the **Open** button. You have selected the SQL document that will populate the database. Click **Go** to complete this action.

17. **Instructor:** You will be informed that the import has been successfully completed and three queries have been executed.

18. **Instructor:** Obtain one of the **syb.html** pages from your students and place it in the **C:\xampp\htdocs\Habitat\CCYP\** directory.

   *Note: You may have to rename the existing syb.html page, which is present for your convenience.*

19. **Students:** Access the **syb.html** file on your instructor's system by using your Web browser to go to the instructor's system's IP address or domain name with the specific location of the resource (/habitat/ccyp/syb.html). For example, if your instructor's system has the IP address 192.168.2.2, you would enter the URL *http://192.168.2.2/habitat/ccyp/syb.html*.

20. **Students:** You will see the Web form created in an earlier lab. Enter the information requested by the form (e.g., first name, last name, e-mail, country and skill).

21. **Students:** Click the **Register** button. This action will submit the form to your instructor's database.

22. **Students:** You should see a message confirming that the variables were parsed correctly. This message means that your entry has been entered into the database that your instructor configured. Click the **View Your Entry** hyperlink to view the results.

23. **Students:** You should see several entries, including your own and those of your classmates. Your screen should resemble Figure 11-10.

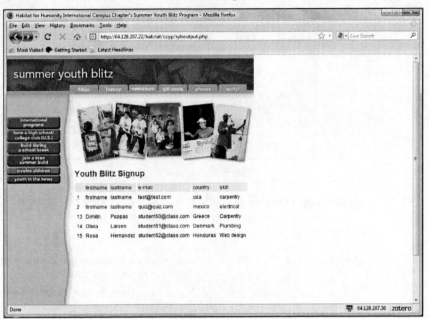

*Figure 11-10: Database entries*

24. As a class, discuss the following questions:

   • What is the purpose of storing information in a database?

   • How can this information be used by an organization such as Habitat For Humanity?

   • How can other companies use a database similar to this?

25. **Instructor:** Show students that you can manipulate the database. Navigate to the main **phpMyAdmin** page, then select the **Volunteers** database you created. Click the **Vlist** link just below the **Volunteers** link. The database should resemble Figure 11-11.

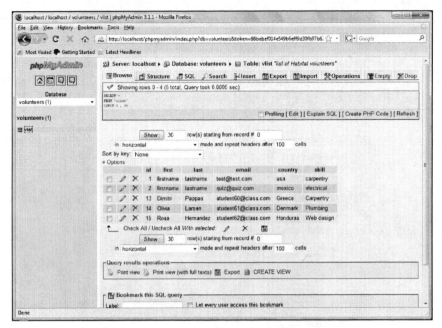

Figure 11-11: Volunteer list stored in database

26. **Instructor:** Delete the last record by clicking the **Delete** icon that appears immediately to the left of the ID number for the record. Click **OK** to confirm the deletion.

27. **Students:** View the database again by opening the **syboutput.php** script in your Web browser (e.g., *http://192.168.2.2/Habitat/CCYP/syboutput.php*). If you are already viewing this script, refresh your browser to see that a record has been removed from the database (Figure 11-12). You will see new information because the PHP script embedded in the XHTML page automatically queries the database and populates the XHTML with the latest information.

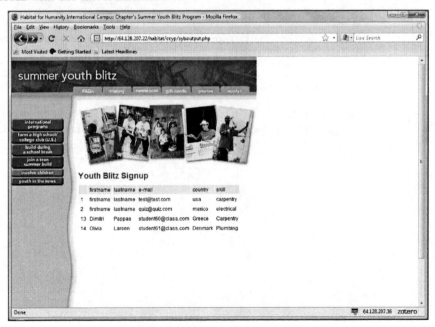

Figure 11-12: Database entries after deleting record

**28. Instructor and students:** Close all Web browsers.

In this lab, you obtained data from end users using open-source CGI and database technology.

# Styling Techniques with CSS

**OBJECTIVE**
2.8.1: Structuring
documents with CSS

Earlier in this course, you learned that Cascading Style Sheets (CSS) is a technology that allows you to apply style formatting definitions to Web page elements. You have already learned to link to external style sheets. However, you can use CSS in various other ways, as described in Table 11-6.

*Table 11-6: Using styles*

| Styling Technique | Description |
|---|---|
| **Linked** | The Web page references an external style sheet link using the XHTML <link> tag as follows:<br>`<link rel="stylesheet" type="text/css" href="syb.css" title="stylesheet"/>` |
| **Inline** | The <span> tag or style attribute is placed in the HTML page to customize either a section of content or a particular tag. |
| **Embedded** | The <style> tag is placed in the HTML page within the <head> element. Formatting instructions are specified between the <style> </style> tags instead of in a separate file. |
| **Imported** | The <style> tag is placed in the HTML page within the <head> element. An external style sheet is specified between the <style> </style> tags with the *import* statement. Code for an imported style sheet would appear as follows:<br>`<style type="text/css">`<br>`@import url(resources/habitat.css);`<br>`</style>`<br>In this statement, the *habitat.css* file that resides in the resources/ directory has been imported into the page. |

**OBJECTIVE**
2.8.2: Applying CSS
styles

The following sections discuss inline, embedded and imported styles.

## Declaring an inline style

Declaring an inline style means that you modify the tags in the body of the XHTML page. You can apply an inline style using either the <span> tag or the *style* attribute within a standard XHTML or HTML element.

 *The <style>tag ( and the <font> tag) take precedence over linked styles. The style attribute of the <span> tag also takes precedence.*

### The <span> tag

If you use the <span> tag, you need not refer to a specific element to be styled. For example, in the following code, the text *CIW Associate* will appear in black font with a red background (provided that you have not declared any other styles):

```
<span style="background: red"> CIW Associate </span>
```

Because <span> is a container tag, it will alter all text contained between it and the closing </span> tag.

### The style attribute

If you use the *style* attribute to define an inline style, you must first use standard XHTML code, as shown in Figure 11-13. You then add the *style* attribute to the tag defining the element you want to style. The value of the *style* attribute specifies the formatting for the tag element.

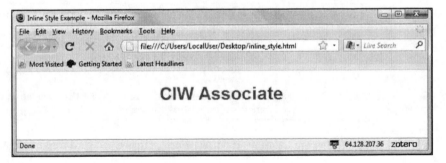

Figure 11-13: Inline style using style attribute

The style definition in this figure will remain in force until the browser encounters the closing </h1> tag. Because this *style* attribute's values define a color, a font family and a size, this definition overrides the color and font-family information normally associated with the <h1> tag. However, this style would inherit any other properties of <h1>. The code shown in the preceding figure would render as shown in Figure 11-14.

Figure 11-14: Results of inline style altering <h1> tag

Notice that the font is much larger than a standard H1 heading, and that the text is centered. It also uses the Arial font rather than Times New Roman (the standard font for the <h1> tag).

The <style> tag in CSS is meant to replace the deprecated <font> tag.

## Creating an embedded style

You can use the <style> </style> container tags within the <head> element to create an embedded style sheet, as follows:

```
<!DOCTYPE html
    PUBLIC "-//W3C//DTD XHTML 1.0 Transitional//EN"
    "http://www.w3.org/TR/xhtml1/DTD/xhtml1-transitional.dtd">
<html xmlns="http://www.w3.org/1999/xhtml" xml:lang="en">
<head>
<meta name="Keywords" content="CIW, Foundations, Example"/>
<meta name="Description" content="For the CIW Foundations Course"/>
```

```
<meta http-equiv="Content-Type" content="text/html; charset=utf-8"/>
<title> CIW Foundations </title>
<style>
h1 {color: magenta; font-family: arial; font-size: 20pt}
</style>
</head>
```

When you define an embedded style, it will remain in force until you override it with an inline style.

*Embedded styles take precedence over linked styles.*

## Using imported style sheets

Imported styles require an external file. However, the imported style sheet is different in that it contains the following code, known as the *@import* statement, at the beginning of the file:

```
@import url(filename.css)
```

See Figure 11-15 for an example of an imported style sheet file. In this example, the imported style sheet is named *import.css*.

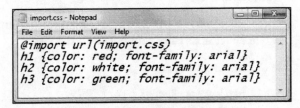

*Figure 11-15: Imported style sheet*

You must refer to the imported style sheet in your HTML document with the <style> tag and the *@import* statement, using the following syntax:

```
<!DOCTYPE html
    PUBLIC "-//W3C//DTD XHTML 1.0 Transitional//EN"
    "http://www.w3.org/TR/xhtml1/DTD/xhtml1-transitional.dtd">
<html xmlns="http://www.w3.org/1999/xhtml" xml:lang="en">
<head>
<meta name="Keywords" content="CIW, Foundations, Example"/>
<meta name="Description" content="For the CIW Foundations Course"/>
<meta http-equiv="Content-Type" content="text/html; charset=utf-8"/>
<title> CIW Foundations </title>
<style type="text/css">
@import url(import.css);
</style>
</head>
```

You can give the style sheet any file name you like, provided that you use the .css file name extension.

## Style sheets and browser compatibility

Style sheets have the potential to create consistency across a Web page or an entire site. However, a vast gulf often exists between potential and practice.

As an X/HTML developer, understand that style sheets can lead to compatibility problems because older browsers interpret style sheet commands differently. You may also encounter difficulty predicting how earlier versions of the same browser will interpret the same style sheet. Therefore, you should always test your code in as many browsers and browser versions as possible.

In the following lab, you will use CSS to customize a document. Suppose your project manager has assigned you to change the font formatting on a new Web page to match the formatting styles on the other site pages. You can do this by importing the style sheet used for the other pages into this new document. Your project manager has also requested you to customize a few elements on the new page with styles that the other pages do not use. For these elements, you can incorporate inline styles, which will take precedence over the linked styles.

 **Lab 11-5: Styling a Web page with CSS**

In this lab, you will use CSS to customize styles in a document.

1.  From the **C:\CIW\Site_Dev\Lab Files\Lesson11** directory, copy the **Lab_11-5\** folder to your Desktop.

2.  Open the **Lab_11-5\** folder on your Desktop, open **lab_11-5.html** in a Web browser, and then study its look and feel.

3.  Now, open **lab_11-5.html** in a text editor. Find the **<link>** tag. Notice that a linked style sheet is already referenced in the page.

4.  Find the following code:

    ```
    <h2>Information Request Form</h2>
    ```

5.  Comment out the code in Step 4, then create an inline style for the <h2> tag on a separate line, as shown:

    ```
    <h2 style="color: brown; font-family: arial; font-size:20pt;">Information Request Form</h2>
    ```

6.  Save the **lab_11-5.html** file.

7.  Open or refresh **lab_11-5.html** in the browser. Study your page. Notice that the font has changed: It is larger, and the color has changed from purple to brown. Notice also that this new style you created overrides the linked style sheet's instructions.

8.  Open **lab_11-5.html** in the text editor, comment out the inline style you just added, and then remove the comment from the original <h2> tag.

9.  Create an embedded style by inserting the code as shown in bold:

    ```
    <title>Habitat for Humanity International Campus Chapter's Summer Youth Blitz
    Program </title>
    <style>
    h2 {color: #996633; font-family: arial; font-size: 20pt}
    </style>
    </head>
    ```

10. Save the **lab_11-5.html** file.

11. Open or refresh **lab_11-5.html** in the browser. Study your page. You will see that the font color has changed. Also notice that this code supersedes the linked style sheet.

**12.** Review your page in at least two browsers, then validate your code.

**13.** Close all browsers and text editors.

In this lab, you used CSS to customize formatting styles in a Web document.

# Dynamic HTML (DHTML)

**Dynamic HTML (DHTML)** is an enhancement that provides animation, interactivity and dynamic updating in Web pages. With DHTML, you can create a Web page that reacts to user actions without contacting the server or downloading complex, bandwidth-consuming applications. Because it eases the burden on the server, DHTML is an effective front-end and back-end solution.

You can use DHTML to control the way in which an image will perform. For example, you can animate an image only when a mouse passes over it. Or the page can automatically scroll text headlines, similar to a Java applet or ActiveX control. Additional DHTML uses include the following:

- **Automatic adjustment of font sizes and colors** — You can use a DHTML **event handler** to animate text when a user passes a mouse over certain parts of the page.

- **Absolute positioning** — You can create text that moves to certain positions in reaction to user input.

- **New document content** — Content can be exchanged dynamically, without having to refresh the browser window.

- **Granular control over animation, audio and video** — Rather than writing page code to constantly present a video clip, you can write code to begin a sequence at a certain time or after a certain event.

DHTML is slowly becoming accepted. As an emerging technology, DHTML is imperfectly applied at present but will probably become a standard in the future.

To use DHTML, you must master three technologies:

- XHTML 1.0 or HTML 4.01

- Cascading Style Sheets (CSS1 and CSS2)

- The Document Object Model (DOM)

You have already learned about HTML and CSS. In the next section, you will learn about the DOM.

# Document Object Model (DOM)

The Document Object Model (DOM) is a standard developed by the W3C. It describes the elements, or objects, within a document rendered by a Web browser. It is a vendor-neutral, cross-platform **application programming interface (API)** that specifies how objects in a document can be referred to and manipulated through scripting languages.

The DOM is meant to be a vendor-neutral, cross-platform standard. With the DOM, you can open a new browser instance and control its functions. For example, you can determine the size of the new browser instance, the toolbars that will be open, and so forth. You can also create pop-up dialog boxes, change the font and colors used in the

**Dynamic HTML (DHTML)**
A combination of HTML, script, styles and the Document Object Model (DOM) that provides Web page interactivity.

**event handler**
A line of code that allows a language to respond to a specific event or user input.

OBJECTIVE
2.1.6: DOM and DHTML

OBJECTIVE
2.1.6: DOM and DHTML

**application programming interface (API)**
A set of universal commands, calls and functions that allows developers to communicate with an application or operating system.

current document, and alter the address bar or almost any other component of the browser.

Currently, the DOM is not as universal as expected. Most browser vendors either add their own features or do not implement all of the DOM as proposed by the W3C. You can learn more about the W3C DOM by visiting *www.w3.org/DOM/*.

## Accessing a browser's DOM

To work with the DOM for any browser, you need to use a scripting language, such as JavaScript or VBScript. JavaScript is more difficult to learn, but more universal. At present, VBScript works only with Microsoft Internet Explorer.

 *Do not confuse the DOM with the Component Object Model (COM). The DOM describes documents within a browser. The COM is a Microsoft specification for creating applications. The Distributed Component Object Model (DCOM) describes the ability to create applications that work well over network connections.*

### DOM compliance

At one time, browser and technology vendors created separate models. However, the W3C has created a standard DOM, and all future models are based on it. Browser compliance with the W3C DOM is important for the following reasons:

• Compliant browsers have all of the functionality currently needed in your workplace.

• Compliant browsers are able to offer all accessibility features advocated by the W3C.

• Compliant browsers will be able to access popular features in the future.

### Choosing a DOM-compliant browser

When choosing a browser, it is often best to use one that follows the DOM most closely. Choosing a DOM-compliant browser helps ensure that all code (e.g., XHTML and JavaScript) used by your team will be supported.

In some cases, however, a browser that is less compliant may be the best choice, because the browser may provide other features that make it the best tool for your organization. Factors that might affect browser choice include:

• **Stability and security** — Some of the more popular browsers have experienced serious security issues. Sometimes these problems occur because the code used in the browser is proprietary and therefore "closed"; it cannot be readily reviewed for problems.

• **Authentication features** — Some browsers, such as Microsoft Internet Explorer, support proprietary authentication features found in IIS. Traditionally, other browsers have not supported these features. Recently, Mozilla Firefox has supported some of Microsoft's proprietary authentication features.

• **Availability** — Most browsers are available free of charge, but some companies do not want to bother with downloading and installing a new browser when an operating system already provides one.

### Undefined object error and the DOM

You may receive an undefined object error if you visit a Web page and your browser does not support a specific DOM. In other cases, you may simply view an unformatted document in plain text. Not all versions of a browser support the same DOM. Therefore, not all objects can be defined.

If a particular DOM is not supported, another browser will usually render the Web page successfully. This relationship is common with Microsoft Internet Explorer and Mozilla Firefox.

### XHTML, the DOM and browser compatibility

Most XHTML elements and attributes are backward-compatible. However, some of the more ambitious improvements, including frames and the ability to respond to users, do not work well (or at all) with earlier browser versions. Additionally, modern browser versions interpret many XHTML commands quite differently, which means that your pages will render differently from browser to browser. Some DHTML solutions will work well in one browser but disable another. JavaScript appears slightly differently, depending on the browser.

To determine your browser's support of the W3C DOM, visit *www.w3.org/2003/02/06-dom-support.html* and read the report for your user agent.

In the following lab, you will verify your browser's compliance with the W3C DOM. Suppose some of your site users have reported difficulty using your site's frames pages. You decide to verify the Microsoft and Mozilla browsers' support of the W3C DOM to see if this could be a factor in the user difficulties.

## Lab 11-6: Verifying browser compliance with the W3C DOM

In this lab, you will learn more about browser compliance with the W3C DOM.

1.  Open **Internet Explorer**, and access ***www.w3.org/2003/02/06-dom-support.html*** to visit the W3C DOM page. Your screen should resemble Figure 11-16.

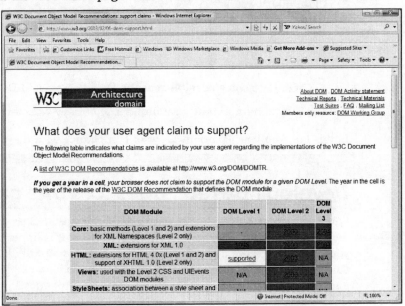

*Figure 11-16: Testing DOM compliance for Internet Explorer*

*Note: Internet Explorer may return results different from those shown in the figure if you are using a version other than 8.0.*

2. Now, open **Mozilla Firefox** and access the same W3C DOM page (***www.w3.org/2003/02/06-dom-support.html***). Your screen should resemble Figure 11-17.

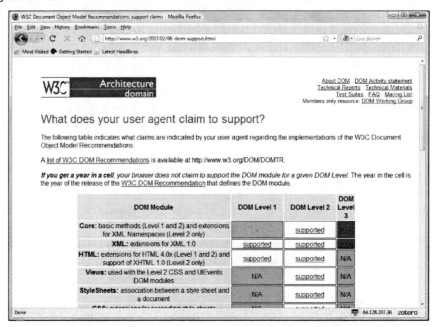

*Figure 11-17: Testing DOM compliance for Mozilla Firefox*

*Note: Mozilla Firefox may return results different from those shown in the figure if you are using a version other than 3.0.*

3. Close all browsers.

4. As a class, discuss the following questions:

   • Which browser was the most compliant?

   • What are some possible reasons for differences in DOM compliance?

   • Why is it important for a browser to comply with the W3C DOM?

In this lab, you learned about browser compliance with the W3C DOM.

# Developing Web Pages for PDAs and Smart Clients

**OBJECTIVE**
2.21.5: Designing for traditional vs. PDA-based browsers

With the increasingly widespread use of iPhones, BlackBerrys, smartphones, PDAs, mobile phones and other mobile wireless devices, it is important that you consider how your Web site (or the mobile version of your Web site) will display on these devices. As of January 2009, it is estimated that there are 3.5 billion mobile phone users worldwide, and 1 billion of them access the Internet via their phones.

There are several key points you should consider in order to optimize your Web site for viewing on mobile devices:

• **Keep your Web pages simple and uncluttered** — Mobile devices have smaller screens than desktop or laptop monitors, and Internet connectivity is often slower. It is important that your site visitors have easy access to important information without getting bogged down by unnecessary clutter. Use white space to help give the site an uncluttered look, and keep the use of images to a minimum.

- **Prioritize your content** — When users are viewing a Web site with a mobile device, they are often looking for very specific information. For example, users who are viewing a store's mobile Web site may be looking for the nearest store to their current location, as opposed to simply browsing the site. Therefore, include only content that is absolutely necessary for the viewer. For this reason, most mobile Web sites should not contain any banner ads or other types of advertisements.

- **Optimize your site to a smaller screen size** — Although screen sizes vary among mobile devices, the most common size is 240x320 pixels. Therefore, you should tailor your mobile Web site to this size to make sure your site is easily viewable by the majority of mobile device users.

As you develop a Web site designed for mobile devices, keep the following considerations in mind:

- Use clean, valid markup, and use CSS to separate the presentation from the content. Most mobile site visitors want access to content and links, and will likely have images and CSS disabled.

- Always use the *alt* attribute in your <img> tags because images may be difficult to see (or will be disabled) on mobile devices.

- Ensure that you label form fields so that they are easily identifiable.

- Use heading tags to help build the structure of the page and to style text. Use tags <h1> through <h4> only; smaller heading tags will be too difficult to see.

- Avoid using frames, layers and floats. Usually, a mobile Web site will look less awkward and be more usable if the content is stacked.

- Reduce margins and padding to give yourself more usable space in which to display content.

- Make navigation easy by providing easy-to-use navigation options and links.

- Experiment with color contrasts because colors may appear differently on mobile screens than on desktop or laptop screens. You want to ensure that your content is easy to read.

Figures 11-18 and 11-19 show the home page of the standard Web site and the mobile Web site, respectively, for Moviefone.

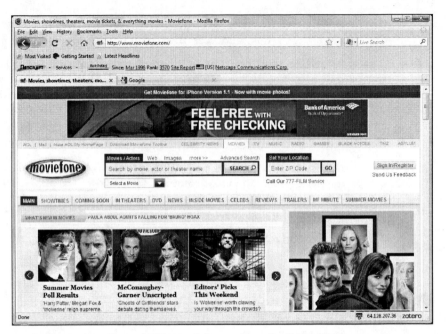

Figure 11-18: Moviefone — standard Web site

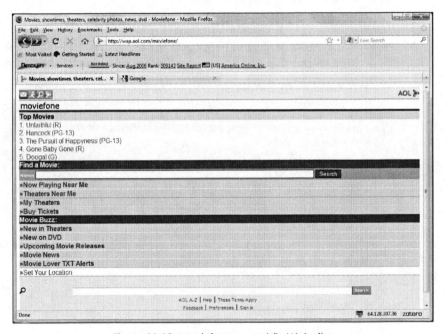

Figure 11-19: Moviefone — mobile Web site

As you can see from the two figures, the mobile version of the Web site is very simplistic compared to the standard site. What are the specific differences between the two sites?

Testing mobile Web sites on as many mobile devices as possible is critical because of the variety of devices that users will be using to access your site. It is also important to validate your markup code. Mobile browsers do not have the processor speeds or hard disk space available that desktop browsers do, and are much more prone to render incorrectly any pages that have invalid code.

Following is a list of sites that you can use to test Web pages designed for mobile devices:

- W3C mobileOK Checker (*http://validator.w3.org/mobile/*)

- Ready.mobi (*http://ready.mobi/launch.jsp*)

- dotMobi Emulator (*http://mtld.mobi/emulator.php*)

- Openwave Phone Simulator (*http://developer.openwave.com/dvl/tools_and_sdk/phone_simulator/*)

- iPhoney (*www.marketcircle.com/iphoney*)

- BlackBerry Simulators (*http://na.blackberry.com/eng/developers/resources/simulators.jsp*)

- BrowserCam (*www.browsercam.com*)

# Web Application Frameworks

**Web application framework**
A set of software tools or code that is commonly used in the creation and management of online applications.

A **Web application framework** is a software framework that enables developers to create and manage dynamic Web sites, Web applications and Web services. Software frameworks generally provide common programming code for generic functions that can be selectively overridden by the developer for specific functionality.

Web application frameworks provide software libraries that contain reusable code that developers can use to:

- Help manage the creation and maintenance of online databases.

- Provide Web page security.

- Manage data on the servers that host the Web pages.

- Provide templates that make it possible to change the background of Web pages while keeping the graphics, text and other elements of the page intact.

Two Web application frameworks that are quickly gaining favor with Web site developers are:

- Django.

- Ruby on Rails.

## Building Web pages with Django

**OBJECTIVE**
2.17.2: CGI methods

Django is an open-source Web application framework that is designed to support the development of dynamic Web sites. Django is written in Python, which is an open-source, object-oriented programming language. Python is a highly readable language that emphasizes an uncluttered visual layout by using white space as block delimiters and aaplying minimalistic syntax and semantics. If you are running a Linux or Mac OS X system, Python is probably already installed. If you are running a Windows system, you will need to install Python version 2.3 or higher (*www.python.org*) before you can install and launch Django.

Django allows developers to easily create complex, database-driven Web sites. Django emphasizes Rapid Application Development (RAD) and the Don't Repeat Yourself (DRY) principle, in which the duplication of elements is kept to an absolute minimum. With the DRY principle, modifying any single element of a system will not change logically unrelated elements, and logically related elements will change correspondingly to ensure uniformity and predictability.

To learn more about Django, visit *www.djangoproject.com.*

### Building Web pages with Ruby On Rails

OBJECTIVE
2.17.2: CGI methods

Ruby On Rails is another open-source Web application framework that also emphasizes Rapid Application Development (RAD) and the Don't Repeat Yourself (DRY) principle for rapid Web site development. Ruby On Rails (or "Rails," for short) works with a wide range of Web servers (e.g., Apache, lighttpd), databases (e.g., MySQL, Oracle, SQL Server, DB2) and operating systems (Windows, Linux, Mac OS X). Like Django, Rails emphasizes simplicity and ease-of-use so that developers can create complex Web sites quickly.

To learn more about Ruby On Rails, visit *http://rubyonrails.org/.*

# Creating Aliases with TinyURL

**TinyURL**
A free Web service that generates short aliases for long URLs.

**TinyURL** is a free Web service that provides aliases for long URLs that are short, will not break in e-mail postings and never expire.

The TinyURL home page (*http://tinyurl.com/*) includes a form in which you can enter a long URL for shortening with either of two options:

- TinyURL can create a randomly generated alias for you.

- You can create a custom alias that is more meaningful.

When users click the short URL alias, they will automatically be redirected to the long URL.

Short URL aliases are useful because they are easier to remember and type. They are also easier to use than long URLs in situations in which space may be limited.

A potential disadvantage to using TinyURLs is that they are subject to linkrot. If the URL of the original Web page changes, all URLs related to the short URL alias will become invalid.

# Working with Advanced Web Technologies

**Web 2.0**
A concept referring to the changing trends in the use of WWW technology and Web design that have led to the development of information-sharing and collaboration capabilities.

The use of advanced Web technologies has given rise to the term "Web 2.0." **Web 2.0** is a common term that refers to the changing trends in the use of World Wide Web technology and Web design since the early days of the Web when most Web pages were static, when users simply retrieved information, and when Internet connections were slow. Web use before the "bursting of the dot-com bubble" in 2001 is now referred to as "Web 1.0."

Web 2.0 is a paradigm shift in the way the Internet is used compared with the Web 1.0 day. Web 2.0 involves a more open approach to the Internet that concentrates on developing the information-sharing and collaboration capabilities of the Web. Web 2.0 has enabled users to provide a significant amount of information on the Web, and there are no longer any restrictions on what they produce.

Web 2.0 has also led to the development of Web-based communities and hosted services, such as social-networking sites, video-sharing sites, wikis, blogs, RSS feeds, podcasts and so forth. The Web is now a resource through which users have the ability to generate and distribute content, as well as to update and modify it.

**OBJECTIVE**
2.17.2: CGI methods

**Ajax**
A programming methodology that uses a number of existing technologies together and enables Web applications to make incremental updates to the user interface without the need to reload the browser page.

**XMLHttpRequest**
An application programming interface (API) that is used to transfer XML and other text data between a Web server and browser.

**cloud computing**
A computing paradigm in which users are able to access software and services over the Internet instead of from their desktops.

**Ajax** (Asynchronous JavaScript and XML ) is a Web 2.0 programming methodology that enables Web applications to interact with users in much the same way they do with desktop applications. Ajax allows you to create interactive Web applications using XHTML, CSS, the Document Object Model (DOM), JavaScript and **XMLHttpRequest**.

With the advent of Web 2.0 technologies and Ajax, you can use the Web to perform many tasks including using Web browsers as application delivery platforms, adding third-party applications to your Web page, and accessing and using Web feeds and podcasts.

 *A more detailed discussion of Web 2.0 is presented in the CIW Internet Business Foundations course.*

## Browsers as application delivery platforms

Web browsers can now serve as application delivery platforms. In other words, you can access hosted applications and services on Web sites that enable you to perform computing tasks without the need to download and install any software. Other terms used to describe this phenomenon are cloud computing and Software as a Service (SaaS).

**Cloud computing** refers to hosted applications and services offered by a third party. These hosted applications run almost entirely from one or more servers that reside on the Internet. A Web browser is the only locally installed application necessary to access these applications; no other software needs to be installed. While the applications reside on remote servers, end users can choose to store files on a local drive or on a remote system. Even though only a Web browser is used, the cloud-based applications are nevertheless meant to be as robust and as sophisticated as those installed on your local system.

 *A more detailed discussion of cloud computing is presented in the CIW Internet Business Foundations course.*

**OBJECTIVE**
2.1.10: Web browser as application delivery platform

Software as a Service (SaaS) is another term used to describe cloud computing because:

- The software responsible for providing the service cannot be downloaded and owned by the end user. It is available as a solution only on a remote basis.

- The software becomes available as a service either for free or for a fee. Many times, the service is available free for a certain period of time. Many times, two versions of a service are made available: The first version is usually a free service that is limited in some way or contains advertisements. The second version is an enhanced or "professional" service that contains no advertisements and is often full-featured. In some cases, the full-featured version is available either for a fee or in exchange for user profile information.

Meebo (*www.meebo.com*) is an example of a Web application delivery platform. Meebo is a free, Ajax-based instant messaging program that combines existing IM services onto one Web interface. Meebo supports AOL Instant Messenger, Yahoo!, MSN, Google Talk, Gmail, MySpace Instant Messenger, Facebook, Chat and others. Meebo enables users to engage in instant messaging without the need to download and install any IM software. The Meebo home page is shown in Figure 11-20.

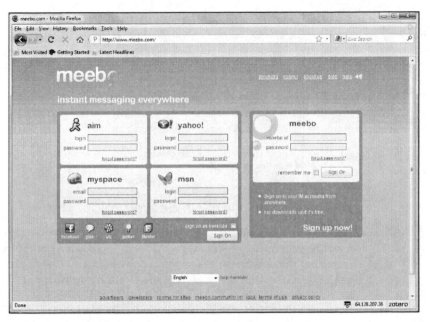

Figure 11-20: Meebo home page

Other Web environments that can serve as application delivery platforms include:

- Aptana (*www.aptana.com*).

- Bindows (*www.bindows.net*).

- Laszlo Webtop (*www.laszlosystems.com*).

- OpenLaszlo (*www.openlaszlo.org*).

### Advantages to using browsers as application delivery platforms

Following are some advantages to using browsers as application delivery platforms:

- **Flexibility** — Using powerful cloud-computing software, a single person can run a sophisticated business. Yet a large enterprise can use a very similar product as well.

- **Scalability** — As an enterprise grows, it can simply rely on its cloud-computing partner to increase capability instead of hiring additional employees and obtaining new hardware.

- **Cost reduction** — Companies that use cloud-computing software can hire fewer employees and purchase less hardware.

### Disadvantages to using browsers as application delivery platforms

Following are some drawbacks to using browsers as application delivery platforms:

- **Connectivity** — If Internet access is cut off to a particular company or division for some reason, then the cloud-based service will no longer be available. Workers would be entirely dependent upon accessing remote applications. Furthermore, if the company or end user tends to store information only on the remote servers, then this information is no longer available as well.

- **Speed** — If Internet access somehow becomes impaired, then users will not be able to use or obtain information.

- **Lockout** — If the cloud-based organization decides to limit access to its services, you may no longer be able to access information stored remotely.

## Personalizing a Web page with third-party applications

**OBJECTIVE**
2.1.9: Third-party
applications on
Web pages

You can personalize your Web pages by adding third-party applications to them. Third-party applications can dramatically increase the functionality and usability of your Web page without the need for you to create the programs yourself. However, be aware that adding such applications may slow page rendering speeds and can easily be overused.

iGoogle (*www.google.com/ig*) is an example of a service that offers many third-party applications that you can add to your Web page. This service allows you to create your own home page on iGoogle or on any other site.

In the following lab, you will add third-party applications to Web page. Suppose your project manager has asked you to customize a browser home page for each member of the project team so that they can track individual projects. You discovered iGoogle Gadgets and realized that many applications that you would like to add to enhance the pages already exist and can be easily incorporated.

**Lab 11-7: Personalizing a Web page with iGoogle Gadgets**

In this lab, you will add third-party applications to a Web page via iGoogle Gadgets.

1. Open a browser and go to **www.google.com** to display the Google home page.

2. In the upper-right corner of the page, click the **iGoogle** link. The iGoogle page will appear, as shown in Figure 11-21. You can use iGoogle to add Web feeds and Google Gadgets (mini-applications that can deliver new e-mail, weather, photos and personalized news) anywhere on a Web page.

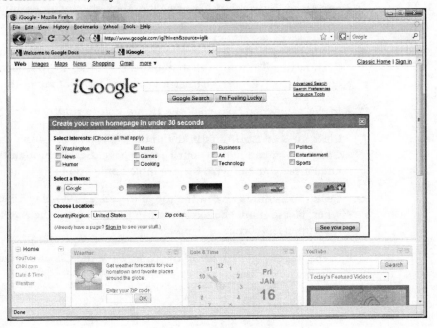

*Figure 11-21: iGoogle page*

3. Scroll through the page and notice the default Gadgets: Weather, Date & Time, YouTube and CNN.com. Links to the default Gadgets also appear in the navigation box on the left side of the screen (the area that appears under the Home link).

    

4. In the Create Your Own Homepage In Under 30 Seconds box, select several interests of your choice, enter your ZIP code, then click the **See Your Page** button. Depending on the interests you selected and location you specified, your iGoogle home page should resemble Figure 11-22.

Figure 11-22: Personalized iGoogle page

5. Scroll through the page and observe the Gadgets that were added based on your selections. Notice that the navigation box also includes links to the additional Gadgets.

6. In the navigation box, click the **Weather** link. Notice that the Weather page expands to show detailed information about the weather in your location, including an air quality chart, airport weather information and a map of the area from Google Maps.

7. In the navigation box, click the **Home** link to return to the iGoogle home page.

8. Click the **Add Stuff** link in the upper-right portion of the page to display a list of Gadgets you can add to your iGoogle page. Scroll through the list of Gadgets to familiarize yourself with the available applications.

9. Click the **Themes** link at the top of the page to display a list of available themes. When you are finished exploring the themes, click the **Back To IGoogle Home** link in the upper-left corner of the page.

10. In the upper-right corner of the page, click the **Classic Home** link to display the default Google home page.

11. Close the browser.

# Web feeds

**Web feed**
A data format for delivering Web content that is updated frequently.

A **Web feed** is a data format for delivering Web content that is updated frequently, such as blog entries and news headlines. Web feed formats allow you to view headlines and updates from your favorite Web sites without the need to open your Web browser or visit any Web sites. There are two popular feed formats:

- **RSS (Really Simple Syndication, RDF Site Summary or Rich Site Summary)** — Currently at version 2.0, RSS is the "original" family of Web feeds. RSS 2.0 has the widest acceptance of any feed format.

- **Atom** — Currently at version 1.0, Atom is a relatively recent development but is much more robust and feature-rich than RSS. Atom is designed solely for the syndication of entire news articles.

## Atom vs. RSS

Unlike RSS, Atom provides not only the document's content, but also metadata about the document:

- What it is called

- Who created it

- When it was created

- Where it is located

 *A more detailed discussion of Web feeds is presented in the CIW Internet Business Foundations course.*

# Podcasts

**podcast**
The use of audio or video digital-media files that are distributed through Web feeds to subscribed users.

A **podcast** is similar to an RSS feed in that the user can download syndicated audio or video digital-media files to computers or portable media players, such as Apple iPods. To create a podcast, you can produce your own audio files (e.g., MP3, Ogg Vorbis or WAV files) and publish them online. You can then index the files so that an RSS reader can subscribe to them. Podcasts can also consist of rebroadcasts of radio or television content, educational tutorials, and other audio content.

**OBJECTIVE**
2.2.12: Podcasts

A podcast differs from other digital formats, such as streaming media, in that the podcast files can be syndicated, subscribed to and downloaded automatically as you add new content. Users who want to subscribe to a podcast's syndicated media need to acquire feed aggregator software, such as Apple iTunes player (*www.apple.com/itunes*). Most users use MP3 players or computers that have media player software installed to listen to podcasts.

Audacity is a free digital audio editing and recording application that you can use to create podcasts. In the following lab, you will install Audacity and create and edit an audio file. Suppose you have been asked by your project manager to create an audio track to coincide with a slide presentation that she wants to present to new sales interns. You can use Audacity to easily create and edit an audio track.

**Lab 11-8: Recording audio with Audacity**

In this lab, you will install Audacity, and then create and edit an audio track. You must have a microphone or headset connected to your computer in order to complete this lab.

1. First, you will install Audacity and record speech. Copy the file **Audacity-win-1.2.6.exe** from the **C:\CIW\Site_Dev\Lab Files\Lesson11** folder to your Desktop, and install it using the default configurations.

2. Double-click the **Audacity** icon on your Desktop to launch the program and open the Audacity window.

3. You must specify the source from which Audacity will pick up sound. Select **Edit | Preferences** to display the Audacity Preferences dialog box.

4. Display the **Device** drop-down list in both the Playback and Recording sections and select the microphone or headset connected to your computer. Your Audacity Preferences dialog box should resemble Figure 11-23. Click **OK**.

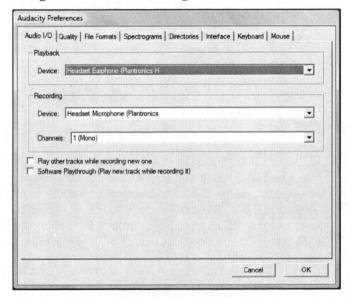

*Figure 11-23: Audacity Preferences dialog box*

5. Click the **Record** button (the red circle) to begin recording. An audio track will appear in the Audacity window.

6. Start speaking into the microphone. Notice that audio waves appear in the track as you speak. Click the **Pause** button (the blue double-vertical lines) to pause the recording.

7. When you are ready to resume speaking, click the **Pause** button again so you can continue to record.

8. When you are finished, click the **Stop** button (the yellow square). Your screen should now display an audio track of your speech, as shown in Figure 11-24.

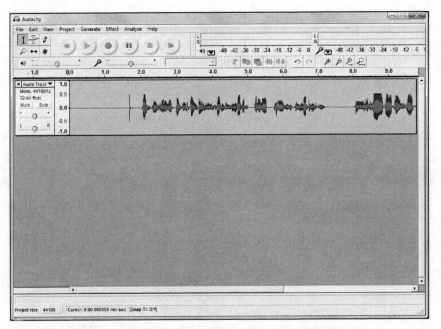

Figure 11-24: Recorded audio track — Audacity

9.  Click the **Play** button (the green right-pointing triangle) to listen to your speech.

10. Next, you will edit your speech and save it as a WAV file. The flat lines in the track represent no (or very little) sound. If you want to tighten your speech, you can remove the pauses. Click the **Skip To Start** button (the purple double left-pointing triangles) to display the beginning of your audio track.

11. Drag the mouse pointer over the portion of your speech that you want to remove, then select **Edit | Cut**. Repeat this step as necessary.

12. Click the **Play** button to listen to your speech again. Notice that the pauses have been removed.

13. Use the mouse pointer to select your entire speech, then select **Effect | Change Speed** to display the Change Speed dialog box. Enter *50.000* in the Percent Change text box, then click the **Preview** button. Notice how much faster your speech sounds. Click **Cancel**.

14. Use the mouse pointer to select your entire speech, then select **Effect | Fade In**. Play your speech again. What effect did your latest edit have?

15. You can save your file as a WAV, MP3 or Ogg Vorbis file. Select **File | Export As WAV** to display the Save WAV (Microsoft) File As dialog box. Specify a name for your file, ensure that it will be saved to your Desktop, then click the **Save** button.

16. Close the **Audacity** window without saving changes. Notice the new .wav file on your Desktop. Double-click the **.wav** icon to play your speech in your default media player.

17. When your speech has finished playing, close the media player window.

## Typosquatting

**typosquatting**
The unethical practice of registering domain names very similar to those of high-volume sites in hopes of receiving traffic from users seeking the high-volume site who mistakenly enter an incorrect URL in their browsers.

**Typosquatting** refers to an unethical practice in which the perpetrator (i.e., typosquatter) capitalizes on typing mistakes that users make when entering the URL of a Web site into a browser. Typosquatting is also known as URL hijacking. When a Web surfer accidentally enters an incorrect Web site address, he or she may end up viewing an alternative Web site owned by a typosquatter.

Typically, a typosquatter will register several possible erroneous domain names for a frequently visited Web site. The typosquatter's Web address will probably be very similar to the victim site's address; most typosquatting sites have domain names that have a one-letter difference from their victim's legitimate, trademarked domain. Typosquatters frequently use their alternative sites to distribute adware, spyware, viruses or other types of malware.

*A more detailed discussion of typosquatting is presented in the CIW Internet Business Foundations course.*

# Hosting and Web Service Providers

**OBJECTIVE**
2.18.1: In-house Web server costs

When deciding how your Web site will be hosted on the Internet, you have several options. The first decision is whether your company will host the site in-house or use some form of service provider to do the hosting for you.

Table 11-7 compares benefits and drawbacks of configuring your own hosting solution and using other providers. You will learn more about Internet Service Providers (ISPs) and Application Service Providers (ASPs) in the sections that follow.

*Table 11-7: Configuring your own server versus using service providers*

| Web Service Provision | Benefits | Drawbacks |
|---|---|---|
| **Configuring your own hosting solution** | -You have more control over your services.<br>-You have more choices. | -You must purchase and house all necessary hardware and software.<br>-Configuring your servers will take time and expertise.<br>-You must manage your own server, including security services. |
| **Using an Internet Service Provider (ISP)** | -You do not need to purchase hardware or software.<br>-The ISP will configure the server for you. | -You have fewer choices in the configuration.<br>-An ISP provides only basic services (e.g., limited CGI and small databases).<br>-You are dependent upon the ISP's management and security services. |
| **Using an Application Service Provider (ASP)** | -You do not need to purchase additional hardware or software.<br>-An ASP will do more than configure your server; it will also provide completed and finished services for your organization.<br>-The ASP will also create custom solutions. | -An ASP is usually more costly than an ISP because you must pay toward the ASP's software licenses and hardware.<br>-As with an ISP, you are dependent upon the ASP's management and security services, although an ASP's services are usually more complete and reliable. |

## Web service providers

You do not have to buy, configure and maintain your own Web server to host your site. An Internet Service Provider (ISP) can provide preconfigured servers and as much bandwidth as you are willing to pay for. Quality ISPs generally understand the needs of their customers, and they probably already provide many of the scripts and tools you need.

An Application Service Provider (ASP) may be appropriate if your company requires more complete services than an ISP provides.

### Co-location, dedicated hosting and virtual servers

**OBJECTIVE**
2.18.3: Hosting options

Table 11-8 summarizes the benefits and drawbacks of hosting solutions provided by service providers.

*Table 11-8: Service provider hosting solutions — benefits and drawbacks*

| Hosting Solution | Description | Benefits | Drawbacks |
|---|---|---|---|
| **Co-location** | The service provider allocates space for your equipment. You provide the server hardware, and the provider supplies space and necessary bandwidth for your server. | -You have complete control over your equipment.<br>-You do not have to share server resources with any other party.<br>-You have a choice over both hardware and software configuration. | -This option is more costly.<br>-If your equipment experiences problems (either hardware or software), your provider will give fee-based support because the hardware and software are yours.<br>-You may need to fix any problems yourself.<br>-You are responsible for your own security. |
| **Dedicated hosting (or co-hosting)** | The service provider gives you access to a dedicated server that it owns. | -You have less up-front cost.<br>-Your site can be launched more quickly because most providers have preconfigured servers.<br>-You do not need to purchase a server and associated software.<br>-You do not need server configuration knowledge.<br>-The service provider configures the system, then allows you to access the system and upload files. | -You are limited to the operating systems and services offered.<br>-You must inquire about the level of customer support. Many providers do not provide extensive customer service, which may lead to long wait times in case of problems.<br>-Some providers allow you total control over your dedicated host. In such cases, you (or a consultant) must secure your systems. |
| **Virtual server** | One Web server contains your site and several other sites. | -You have less up-front cost and faster deployment time.<br>-The Web service is generally running already. You simply provide your thoroughly tested code. | -You rely upon the provider's server configuration.<br>-You have no control over the server. You control only your Web files.<br>-If the provider's security is lax, then your virtual server may be easily compromised.<br>-You have less flexibility in Web server functions. |

   

### Internet Service Provider (ISP) vs. Application Service Provider (ASP)

Remember that an Internet Service Provider (ISP) provides bandwidth and possibly Web server space.

An Application Service Provider (ASP) is prepared to provide more complete services, including:

- Messaging services, such as e-mail.

- Scheduling and Personal Information Management (PIM).

- Telephony services, which might save you costs on calls.

- Advanced Web and database connectivity, including the creation of custom CGI applications.

- Enterprise resource planning (ERP), which is the ability to automate the planning and operations of your entire organization (e.g., hiring, termination, manufacturing, marketing).

### Costs of using an ASP

Costs associated with an ASP include:

- **Database connectivity** — Cost is based on the amount of database support you require.

- **Per-service costs** — Each additional service you use will increase costs.

- **Bandwidth** — In addition to increasing (or decreasing) bandwidth, you can also pay the ASP to closely monitor bandwidth usage.

- **Customer support** — An ASP can provide customer service to your company, just like an ISP. However, an ASP can also provide support to your customers, allowing you to avoid the hiring, training and maintenance costs of creating your own team.

- **Security** — Larger ASPs have their own security auditing teams.

- **Application development** — An ASP will either have its own application development team or will have relationships with remote development teams that can create custom applications for you.

### Negotiating Web services and communicating needs

When working with an ISP or an ASP, be prepared to detail your needs. Clearly provide information such as:

- Potential amount of traffic.

- Hard drive space you will need.

- Database and CGI needs.

- Additional services (e.g., custom applications).

As you contact the ASP or ISP sales representatives, obtain prices for each of the services you need. Then, negotiate your prices with service provider representatives by:

- **Indicating your present needs** — Discuss plans in which you pay full price now then negotiate lower prices later, or vice versa.

- **Asking to talk to the sales representative's manager** — The manager has the decision-making power to negotiate lower costs.

- **Asking your manager to discuss prices with the sales representative or with the representative's manager** — Escalating negotiations can enable exceptions and swifter decisions.

You may be able to negotiate lower costs based upon the nature of your organization. If your organization is not-for-profit or associated with education, for example, you may be able to obtain price discounts for services.

**OBJECTIVE**
2.18.5: Site
information
management

## Information you need from your service provider

If you use an ISP or ASP, you will need to obtain the following information from the provider:

- **Account information** — This includes user names and passwords of all accounts associated with your server. The service provider may issue you multiple user names. Write the information carefully and store it in a secure place (e.g., a locked safe).

- **IP addresses and DNS names of the server**.

- **Instructions about file and directory locations**.

- **The service provider's contact information** — Such information includes Help Desk support numbers (and possibly the names of dedicated help desk workers), e-mail and fax numbers.

## Case Study

# Choose Your CGI

Darius is the project manager of a Web development team for a mid-size corporation. The team needs to choose a CGI technology for the company's new primary Web site. Darius must write the recommendation that upper management will review in deciding whether to approve funds.

In creating a short summary of the project, Darius asked his team members to help answer the following questions:

- Do any developers in the company know common CGI technologies?

- What operating systems are currently in use in the company? (by percentage, such as 50 percent Windows, 30 percent Linux, 20 percent Solaris)

- What operating systems are ideal for this project?

- What Web servers are ideal for this project?

Darius learned that the company's computer environment was almost completely Windows-based. Also, several members of the Web development team knew how to use VBScript and had experience using Active Server Pages (ASP). Although ASP is an older Microsoft technology (.NET is newer and more versatile), the Web development team recommended ASP as the best choice.

As Darius' team made their choice, they considered the importance of using client-side technologies such as JavaScript. However, they also considered that some browsers do not support JavaScript, and that some users may deactivate JavaScript in their browsers, which could cause Web pages to render differently and disappoint some site visitors. After some deliberation, Darius and his team decided to use server-side technology (specifically ASP) for all applications.

*          *          *

As a class, consider this scenario and discuss the following points:

- Would Darius' team have chosen the same CGI technology if the computer environment had been mostly Linux? What might they have chosen instead?

- If Darius' team had chosen a client-side technology, what steps could they have taken to improve accessibility?

## Lesson Summary

### Application project

This lesson taught you more about several Web technologies, including programming languages, CSS and the W3C DOM. Visit the following sites to learn more about these technologies:

- World Wide Web Consortium (*www.w3.org*)
- W3 Schools (*www.w3schools.com*)
- PHP (*www.php.net*)
- Perl (*www.activestate.com* and *www.perl.com*)
- Active Server Pages (ASP) and .NET (*www.microsoft.com*)
- Java (*www.java.com*)

### Skills review

In this lesson, you studied Web-based technologies that extend your XHTML pages, including server-side and client-side scripts. You also learned about additional methods of applying CSS styles to your Web pages. You wrote some simple JavaScript code to make a Web page interactive, and you learned how DHTML can also add interactivity to your Web pages. You learned the purpose of the DOM and the importance of DOM Web browser support.

You also studied the issues inherent in developing Web pages for PDAs and smart clients. You learned about Web application frameworks, which contain reusable common programming code that developers can use to develop Web pages easily. You learned how to create short URL aliases using TinyURL. You also learned how browsers can be used as application delivery platforms, how to add third-party applications to Web pages, and how to incorporate Web feeds and podcasts into Web pages.

Finally, you learned more about Web site hosting, and the benefits and drawbacks of working with Internet Service Providers (ISPs) and Application Service Providers (ASPs).

Now that you have completed this lesson, you should be able to:

✓ 2.1.6: Define the Document Object Model (DOM) and its relationship to Dynamic HTML (DHTML).

✓ 2.1.9: Add third-party applications to your Web page (e.g., Google gadgets for the Web).

✓ 2.1.10: Identify ways that a Web browser can become an application delivery platform, including strengths and weaknesses of the browser.

✓ 2.2.12: Create a podcast, including choosing the appropriate audio format and recording rate, specifying a quality microphone, uploading files.

✓ 2.8.1: Explain how to structure Web documents with CSS.

✓ 2.8.2: Identify ways to apply styles with CSS.

✓ 2.17.1: Compare popular client-side and server-side programming languages, including JavaScript, Java, PHP, Python, .Net, C, C++, Visual Basic, C#.

✓  2.17.2: Define Common Gateway Interface (CGI) methods, including .Net, Django, Python, JavaServer Pages (JSP), Server-Side JavaScript (SSJS), Active Server Pages (ASP), PHP Hypertext Preprocessor (PHP), Ajax.

✓  2.17.5: Identify the value of n-tier applications and associated techniques in processing online transactions.

✓  2.18.1: Investigate costs associated with placing and developing your own server.

✓  2.18.2: Identify costs associated with using an Application Service Provider (ASP).

✓  2.18.3: Distinguish among dedicated hosting, co-location and virtual servers.

✓  2.18.4: Activate features provided by managed services (e.g., CGI, forms).

✓  2.18.5: Manage information relevant to a site (e.g., account information, passwords, IP addresses).

✓  2.19.1: Identify ways to use additional technologies to provide custom features to an end user (e.g., using JavaScript to detect Web browser type, using cookies).

✓  2.21.5: Identify ways to create pages for traditional and PDA-based browsers (e.g., validating code, appropriate resolutions, supported interpreters, extensive user testing).

# Lesson 11 Review

1. In programming, what is the term for a space of memory used to store information for later use?

   _____

2. Name the four ways in which you can apply a style sheet when implementing CSS with XHTML.

   _____

   _____

3. What programming language is platform-independent and object-oriented, and can be used to create applications called servlets?

   _____

4. What does Dynamic HTML do?

   _____

   _____

5. What is the term for the API used to standardize the way that JavaScript applications can refer to HTML and XHTML documents?

   _____

6. Name at least two ways you can optimize Web pages for viewing on mobile devices.

   _____

   _____

   _____

7. Describe a Web application framework, which developers can use to develop dynamic Web pages rapidly.

   _____

   _____

   _____

   _____

# Lesson 12:
# E-Commerce
# Practices

## Objectives

By the end of this lesson, you will be able to:

☞ 2.16.1: Define e-commerce terms and concepts, including EDI, business-to-business (B2B), business-to-consumer (B2C), Electronic Funds Transfer (EFT), Electronic Data Interchange (EDI), Open Trading Protocol (OTP), merchant systems, relationship management, customer self-service, Internet marketing, Secure Electronic Transactions (SET).

☞ 2.16.2: Compare e-commerce to traditional commerce.

☞ 2.16.3: Identify payment models used in e-commerce, including payment gateways.

☞ 2.16.4: Identify issues related to working in a global environment, including different currencies, multi-lingual issues, international shipping, supply chain, legal and regulatory issues.

☞ 2.16.5: Identify the importance of SSL/TLS to a transaction that contains sensitive information.

☞ 2.16.6: Identify the importance of online indexing and cataloging.

☞ 2.16.7: Define search engine optimization (SEO) and related key terms (e.g., Internet marketing, organic vs. non-organic [pay-per-click], Web analytics).

☞ 2.21.3: Create Web pages that rank highly for search engines that use spiders and screen readers.

# Pre-Assessment Questions

1.  Which statement best describes a payment gateway?

    a.  Software that filters packets between the merchant and the credit card vendor, and enables network address translation
    b.  Software that processes transactions between a merchant and a credit card vendor
    c.  Software that processes transactions between an ISP and a merchant
    d.  Software that filters packets between a merchant and an ASP

2.  Which of the following relies upon digital certificates embedded within a Web browser in order to authenticate hosts, encrypt transmissions and ensure data confidentiality?

    a.  SET
    b.  EDI
    c.  SSL/TLS
    d.  B2B/B2C

3.  How can Web-based technology help supply chain management?

    _____

    _____

    _____

    _____

# Traditional Commerce vs. E-Commerce

In the late 1990s, the "new economy" was said to have changed commerce. This new economy was based on "dot-com" companies that relied on investment capital and questionable business plans. Much money could be made selling software and other services that supposedly made warehouses and traditional retailers obsolete, enabling a new digital marketplace rich with business opportunities beyond the scope of traditional sellers and retailers. In many ways, however, this new model has not lived up to its promise, and in some areas this new economy has largely imploded. Many companies begun in the late 1990s no longer exist.

Nevertheless, Internet-based and Web-based technologies have remained extremely important for several reasons:

- Each year, more goods are being created, bought and sold using Internet technologies.

- Each year, more traditional businesses use Web-based technologies to work more efficiently and tap new markets.

- In some cases, opportunities still exist in the digital marketplace for those with solid business plans who can find ways to compete with traditional sellers and retailers.

If you want to do business in today's economy, you must understand the similarities and differences between traditional commerce and e-commerce, as well as the ways that both forms of commerce are used in the business environment.

**electronic commerce (e-commerce)**
The integration of communications, data management and security capabilities to allow organizations and consumers to exchange information related to the sale of good and services.

Traditional commerce and **electronic commerce (e-commerce)** share the following goals:

- Both commerce types aim to deliver a valued product or service. Sometimes, service is delivered for a profit (for example, by companies such as Amazon.com). Other times, service is delivered by a not-for-profit organization (such as Habitat For Humanity).

- Both commerce types want to serve a large audience.

- Both commerce types strive to deliver products and services as quickly as possible.

E-commerce differs from traditional commerce in the following ways:

- E-commerce customers expect shorter fulfillment times.

- E-commerce customers are expected to understand Web-based technologies, which must be learned; traditional commerce is less technologically oriented.

- E-commerce enables a company or organization to offer its goods and services to a global audience using a relatively inexpensive, digital medium.

- E-commerce customers do not need to travel or pay for telephone calls.

- E-commerce relies heavily on the Internet and encryption technologies to ensure that transmissions remain private over a public network.

- E-commerce orders are often processed without human interaction. A properly developed Web server can completely automate processes in some models. As a result, businesses can use lower-cost Internet technologies instead of costly telephone support centers. In other cases, the presence of e-commerce may necessitate telephone support centers because the organization's Internet presence generates more business.

# E-Commerce Models

OBJECTIVE
2.16.1: E-commerce terms

**business-to-consumer (B2C)**
An e-commerce model in which a Web-based business sells products and/or services to consumers or end users.

**business-to-business (B2B)**
An e-commerce model in which a Web-based business sells products and/or services to other businesses.

**consumer-to-consumer (C2C)**
An e-commerce model in which individual consumers sell their pre-owned products or personal services to other consumers.

Currently, three major e-commerce models are widely implemented:

- **Business-to-consumer (B2C)** model

- **Business-to-business (B2B)** model

- **Consumer-to-consumer (C2C)** model

Table 12-1 describes these e-commerce models.

*Table 12-1: E-commerce models*

| Model | Description | Capabilities | Examples |
|---|---|---|---|
| **Business-to-consumer (B2C)** | A Web site that targets consumers or end users, and sells products and/or services. | -Indexed catalogs of products and/or services with searching tools<br>-Sales of products and/or services to consumers<br>-Payment processing<br>-Delivery arrangements<br>-Order tracking and invoices<br>-Customer service (FAQ, e-mail, telephone contact information) | Web storefronts and reseller sites such as:<br>-Amazon.com, Barnes & Noble (books and other products)<br>-Napster and MusicNow (music downloads)<br>-NetGrocer (delivery service)<br>-1-800-Flowers.com, FTD.com (delivery of flowers and gifts)<br>-Travelzoo, Expedia (travel services and sales)<br>-Monster.com (employment services)<br>-MermaidsBath.com (small retailer of custom products) |
| **Business-to-business (B2B)** | A Web site that helps organizations to manage relationships and transactions with other businesses. | -Sales of products, raw materials and services used by businesses<br>-Payment processing<br>-Delivery arrangements<br>-Order tracking and invoices<br>-Customer service (FAQ, e-mail, telephone contact information) | Web-based operations such as:<br>-B2Bxchange (storefront creation and management)<br>-Bankserv.com, CyberCash (payment processing)<br>-Invenda Corp (formerly E-centives) (Internet coupons and promotions)<br>-Aegis Peoplesupport, ZDnet (customer service) |
| **Consumer-to-consumer (C2C)** | A Web site that helps consumers buy and sell products or services to other consumers. | Forums for consumers who want to participate:<br>-Auction sites, which allow buyers to bid the prices they pay for goods and services<br>-Web classified advertisement sites, in which consumers buy and sell products by placing and answering online classified ads | Auction sites:<br>-eBay (*www.ebay.com*)<br>-uBid (*www.ubid.com*)<br>-Bidz (*www.bidz.com*)<br>Web classified advertisement sites:<br>-Craigslist (*www.craigslist.org*)<br>-kijiji (*www.kijiji.com*)<br>-oodle (*www.oodle.com*) |

Note that a shopping portal such as The Now Mall (*www.30minutemall.com*) or Yahoo! Shopping (*http://shopping.yahoo.com/*) can introduce you to B2C outlets.

A network such as B2BToday.com (*www.b2btoday.com*) can provide leads to B2B professionals. And any search engine can help you find a business selling the product or service you need.

C2C sites generally have interfaces that are very intuitive and easy to navigate. Because the sites function as intermediaries designed to match consumers, they rely on repeat visits on a massive scale to succeed. For this reason, the sites need to be as user-friendly as possible. Consider the Craigslist home page shown in Figure 12-1.

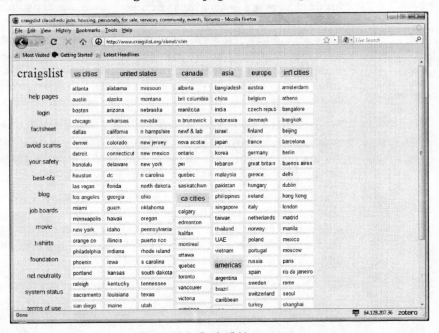

Figure 12-1: Craigslist home page

Notice that the site design is extremely basic, but you can immediately determine what links you need to click to access the classified ads for a particular city, state, country or product category.

# Business and Internet Technologies

Web-based technologies enable businesses to expand their operations and customer bases in many ways. Common business operations that use Web technologies include:

- Supply chain management.

- Enterprise resource planning (ERP).

- B2B information sharing with XML.

The following sections discuss ways that these types of businesses use Web technologies.

OBJECTIVE<br/>
2.16.4: Global<br/>
business issues

## Supply chain management (SCM)

A successful e-commerce business requires more than Internet-based technologies such as XHTML, JavaScript and server-side languages. Its operators also need a rudimentary understanding of supply chain management, which is the ability to manage the process that generates a product and distributes it to customers. Supply chain management is central to all companies, whether they are small and local, or have a global presence.

A supply chain begins with raw materials and ends with a product delivered to a consumer. The customer may be an end user who downloads a program created by your company. Your customer may expect you to provide a finished product that is ready to be used. Or the product you sell might be used as a component inside of a product manufactured and sold by your customer.

Supply chain management involves understanding the following aspects of business:

**order tracking**
The ability to determine progress on delivery of a product. Businesses often provide order-tracking support to end users via Web browsers and e-mail clients.

- **Product demand** — You must be able to estimate consumer demand for the finished product. You must determine sales volume and the frequency with which customers will demand new products. As demand fluctuates and (hopefully) increases, you must work closely with suppliers to ensure that you can meet that demand. Once you understand product demand, you can then anticipate a cycle and manage your supply chain accordingly. You can even create a chart to anticipate peaks in the cycle. This chart can help you allocate the proper resources to create your product.

- **Information flow** — You must identify the ways that you will receive and process orders, and the ways that you will inform and respond to customers. Examples of information flow include an **order tracking** service that your customers can use, as well as order tracking you can use with your suppliers.

- **Finance management** — An organization may experience high demand for a product, but may not have enough money to generate that product. Management is responsible for ensuring that the company has enough cash to meet demand. Products must occasionally be redeveloped and upgraded, which can cause a financial strain that must be managed.

Table 12-2 summarizes the most important supply chain management terms.

*Table 12-2: Supply chain management terms*

| Term | Definition |
|------|------------|
| **Upstream** | Describes suppliers to your company that provide materials for your products. |
| **Downstream** | Describes customers of your company who purchase your products. |
| **Capacity requirements plan** | Calculation of the amount of physical space and the amount of time you need to create your product. |
| **Material requirements plan** | Steps taken to anticipate demand, and the ability of your suppliers to help you meet this demand. Involves determining the individuals, capital and other resources necessary to create the product. |
| **Just In Time (JIT)** | Describes a management system that controls inventory so that raw materials arrive from upstream providers only when needed, or are stored for downstream consumption only in sellable amounts. Usually, a collection of data-tracking software. Control of inventory is essential for proper supply chain management. |
| **Material flow** | Estimate of the amount of raw material required for a product, and the amount of waste generated from the production process. |
| **Bill of materials** | List of required resources, and amount of time required to develop the resources into the product. |
| **Best practice** | A set of standards followed by an industry. Usually specifies procedures or techniques that yield proven success for common business processes or tasks. |
| **Order management** | The ability to organize requests for downstream and upstream products. Involves documenting existing inventory, and storing all orders in an accessible, stable and secure database. |

Table 12-2: Supply chain management terms (cont'd)

| Term | Definition |
|---|---|
| **Life cycle** | The amount of time a particular product will remain valid before it is necessary to upgrade it. |
| **Manufacturing resource plan** | Outline of all resources needed to create a product. Includes the capacity requirements plan, the material requirements plan and material flow estimates. |

 Supply chain management is often referred to as SCM.

Figure 12-2 illustrates the flow of a traditional supply chain.

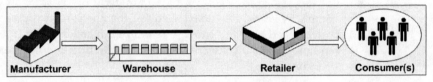

Figure 12-2: Traditional supply chain

Even though the "new economy" created by the dot-com bubble of the late 1990s has largely imploded, newer Web-based technologies have become increasingly relevant to traditional supply chains. This is because Web-based technologies can automate record keeping and inventory control. Using Web servers, databases, forms and CGI, your upstream and downstream parties can make requests and track information. This allows you to coordinate each step in the chain to increase responsiveness and create new product.

Thus, the Web interface you create may not be part of a Web storefront. The interface may instead help a company track incoming raw materials, or track the development of these raw materials into a product that your company sells.

## Enterprise resource planning (ERP)

Enterprise resource planning (ERP) involves the use of software to create an automated plan for your entire company's operations. The goal of ERP is to enhance communication among all company departments and divisions. All aspects of your organization are part of the plan, including:

- **Accounts receivable** — money that organizations and customers owe to your company.

- **Accounts payable** — money that your company owes to other organizations.

- **Research and development** — department responsible for planning and creating products.

- **Human resources** — department responsible for employee policies, hiring, termination, compensation and benefits.

- **Manufacturing** — all parts of the organization that contribute to product creation.

- **Purchasing** — department responsible for acquiring products.

- **Marketing and sales** — departments responsible for creating brands and contacting potential customers.

Increasingly, companies are using ERP software to automate execution of the company's operation plan. This software automatically monitors all purchases and transactions associated with the enterprise. ERP software automates data collection and allows management to receive real-time reports about all aspects of the business.

Companies such as SAP (*www.sap.com*), Oracle (*www.oracle.com*) and The Sage Group (*www.sage.com*) are leaders in ERP software. This software contains databases, forms and applications that allow you to track transactions. When you purchase this type of software, it is generally not ready to be used. ERP needs to be programmed and integrated with the company's existing systems. Many times, a Web development team must help integrate ERP software into the company.

Terms often used during ERP integration include:

- **Bolt-on systems** — software to aid integration of ERP software with an organization's existing systems. It is also called "off the shelf" software because it does not need to be developed or significantly customized in order to aid integration. Bolt-on systems can help the ERP software to plan manufacturing processes and warehouse storage, for example.

- **Application programming interface (API)** — a set of universal commands, calls and functions that allows developers to communicate with an application or operating system. APIs are designed to allow developers to create code more easily. Developers often need to create custom applications so that the ERP software can integrate with existing software (e.g., manufacturing systems, Web servers and databases).

- **Library** — files used to provide functionality to applications. For example, in Windows, a specific library is called a Dynamic Link Library (DLL). In UNIX/Linux, all are simply referred to as libraries.

## B2B information sharing with XML

XML has become a popular application in business because it allows information to be indexed once, then used in many different applications and companies. Once businesses agree upon using the same correct DTD, they can exchange information much more easily.

*You learned about the Document Type Definition (DTD) earlier in this course. The DTD is a set of rules (usually contained in a separate text file) that defines the structure, syntax and vocabulary used in corresponding documents. The DTD is essentially the grammar used to index content in associated documents that reference it.*

### DTD limitations

DTDs are somewhat limited in their abilities to control the types of information placed in an XML field. If both numeric and word-based information is placed in the same field, for example, then the structure of the document will not properly imitate a database entry, even though it may still be valid XHTML. This fact introduces a problem, because XML does not in and of itself guarantee that data will be properly entered and processed.

### XML schema

One way to make an XML document function more like a standard database is to use a schema, which is an addition to the XML standard. A schema controls and limits XML documents so that any data entered must follow strict rules. As a result, the information is much more searchable and can be manipulated much like information in a database. Using a schema, you can place limitations and rules on fields within a document. Once two or more parties agree upon a schema, they can exchange documents and information with confidence, knowing that their data has been described and categorized in the same way, using the same criteria.

# Internet Marketing and Search Engine Optimization (SEO)

As a member of a Web team, you must consider marketing issues because they affect the content and performance of your Web site. Internet marketing applies traditional marketing concepts to Web-based and Internet technologies. Table 12-3 discusses marketing issues and terms with which you should be familiar.

*Table 12-3: Marketing terms*

| Term | Description |
|------|-------------|
| **Branding** | The creation of a distinctive identity and place in the market for a product or organization. Allows consumers to readily identify a product and its purpose. The look and feel of your Web site is often part of a marketing department's branding. |
| **Target market** | The specific sector in a market (i.e., the audience) that a product or service addresses. The target may be broad or it may be a niche market. For example, Microsoft and Ubuntu target several markets, including the market for Web and database servers for e-commerce. |
| **Demographics** | The study of groups of people. Includes categorizing populations by interests, ethnicities, cultures and subcultures. Involves studying trends and needs associated with a particular group (for example, computer users between the ages of 18 and 49). |
| **Niche** | A smaller, specialized portion of the market. An example of a niche market in IT might be companies that provide clustering (multiple systems acting as a single host) for computer systems. Such companies service a much smaller market than computer users or Web database servers. |
| **Mind share** | The effect of marketing efforts influencing a particular target market or demographic. Mind share includes commercial phrases, catch words and sound bites that provoke recognition of the product, service or company by the public. |
| **Target date** | The projected point in time that a product or service will be released. |
| **Aggregator** | A business (usually Web-based) that markets and sells goods and services that it does not own or store. The aggregator allows other vendors to compete using its site, and then takes a percentage of the business. In essence, the site acts as a portal for an entire industry niche. |

Internet marketing consists of the following practices:

- **Search engine optimization (SEO)** — the use of specific techniques to increase a page's or site's rank on a search engine (such as Google, Yahoo! or MSN). Such techniques are said to be "organic" because they do not include paid advertisements of any kind. SEO experts edit pages and sites to enable search engines to recognize the inherent value of the content and services on the site.

- **Pay per click (PPC)** — an Internet marketing technique in which you pay for high search engine results by advertising on keywords that describe your product or service. You pay your site hosts only when your ads are clicked by the user.

- **Web analytics** — The practice of collecting data and studying user behavior in an attempt to increase market share and sales.

You will learn more about each of these practices in the sections that follow.

# Search engine optimization (SEO)

**search engine
optimization (SEO)**
The process of
improving the
volume and quality
of traffic to a Web
site by structuring
content to improve
search engine
ranking. A specific
activity of Internet
marketing.

**Search engine optimization (SEO)** involves learning how a particular search engine
ranks a Web site. You can use this knowledge to customize a site's Web pages so that the
site is ranked as highly as possible in a search engine's results. If a page is ranked highly
on search engines, that page is more likely to create situations in which potential
customers purchase goods or services.

 *SEO is a specific activity of Internet marketing.*

SEO experts must learn about and consider the factors that search engines take into
account as they rank sites, then try to create and edit Web pages accordingly. Increasing
traffic or even ranking is not enough. SEO experts are expected to lead users to a specific
result, or conversion. To do this, SEO experts can use data provided by the search engine
providers themselves.

Search engine providers, such as Google, Yahoo! and MSN, often provide search patterns
for profit. That is, the providers accumulate data on all of the searches that users
conduct on their search engines, and then determine the correlation between the
keywords used and the results found. The providers then make this data available for
sale. SEO experts can use this data to determine the most relevant keywords associated
with a particular product or service, and ensure that the keywords are used in a site's
pages.

Table 12-4 lists some of the more common SEO terms.

*Table 12-4: Common SEO terms*

| Term | Description |
|------|-------------|
| **Conversion** | The result when a customer engages significantly with a site. The most typical conversion is the purchase of a good or service. Additional examples of conversion include the capture of user information, demographic information or specific user preferences. |
| **On-page optimization** | The practice of editing Web pages so that they are ranked highly by search engines. Proper page structure and the appropriate use of keywords in the <meta> tags and in the body of each Web page (such as in the titles) is essential. |
| **Off-page optimization** | The practice of influencing factors external to Web page content so that the pages are ranked highly by search engines. The main technique to accomplish this is link building. Generally, the more that other sites link to your site, the greater the impact your site will have in a search. Also includes obtaining domain names that have existed for some time; generally, the older the domain name, the higher it is ranked in search engine results. |
| **Keywords** | Words that search engines have identified as important enough to index on their sites; used to determine page ranking. Keywords should be repeated as appropriate and should be used consistently in Web and print copy. |
| **Keyword density** | The frequency of keyword usage on a page. |
| **Click-through rate** | Measures how successful a particular campaign has been, in terms of Web hits. To obtain the click-through rate, divide the number of users who clicked on the advertisement (i.e., hits, or impressions) by the number of times the advertisement was shown. |
| **Results page** | The page returned by a search engine. Contains ranked entries, as determined by the search engine's algorithms and PPC policies. Also known as a search engine results page. |

*Table 12-4: Common SEO terms (cont'd)*

| Term | Description |
|---|---|
| **Crawlers** | Automated applications that regularly scan Web pages and search for content. Also called spiders or bots. Many SEO experts read pages using a text-only browser called Lynx, because bots see a Web page as a text-only document. |
| **Cloaking** | The practice of showing one site to crawlers and another to individuals. Used by spammers, and considered an illicit practice. Many search engines will penalize sites for this activity. |
| **Page rank** | Describes the rank of a page on a search engine results page. The term was introduced by Google. |
| **Reciprocal link** | The practice in which one site links back to another. Often lowers ranking because it is considered a quick, artificial way to increase ranking. |
| **Blackballing** | The practice in which a search engine eliminates a page or domain from consideration in search engine rankings. |
| **Black-hat SEO** | The use of techniques that are considered to be flawed or unethical by those who manage and program search engines. Includes cloaking, invisible text (wording that only crawlers can see), doorway pages (pages that are highly optimized but which redirect a user to another site) and keyword stuffing (using too many keywords on a page). |
| **Splash page** | The opening page of a site; often the page that is the most highly optimized. |

## Common SEO tactics

Entire courses have been written about SEO. In this overview, consider the following fundamental tactics that an SEO expert uses to optimize Web pages for high-ranking search engine results.

- **Using validated HTML code** — It is important to choose an HTML or XHTML standard, use it exclusively, and validate the code often.

- **Choosing appropriate keywords** — Choose relevant keywords that reflect the content of your site, then use them properly in your Web copy, as well as in all <meta>, <title> and <head> tags. Avoid overusing keywords because search engines have become very good at discerning between natural and artificial usage of words and phrases.

- **Structuring pages appropriately** — Use CSS to properly structure content on a page. Search engine crawlers will rank a properly structured page that uses CSS and the <div> tag more highly than another page that uses HTML tables.

- **Carefully evaluating the use of images and multimedia** — Flash, video and images add value to your pages. However, bots do not read this data, and a page that relies too much on multimedia can cause a site to be ranked lower. Carefully combine text with multimedia to achieve a balance.

- **Embedding text within images and using the *alt* attribute** — If you do use images, insert keywords and descriptions as meta-information inside images. Most image-creation tools allow the insertion of meta-information. Also, use the *alt* attribute of the <img> tag wisely whenever you insert an image by including a short, relevant description of the image. You can also include information that explains the image's context within the particular page it is in.

### Writing quality Web copy

Along with the SEO tactics just described, writing high-quality Web copy is very important to optimize search engine results. Following are some attributes of high-quality Web copy.

- **Brevity and conciseness** — Make the verbiage short and to the point. Make sure that your copy has a strong central idea that quickly describes your site's main purpose.

- **Proper spelling, grammar and punctuation** — Even the best copy will be ranked lowly if it is fraught with spelling and grammar errors. Use a spelling checker and a grammar checker to help verify that the copy is written correctly, although do not rely too heavily on these tools — their corrections can be flawed. It is preferable to use the services of a professional writer or editor whenever possible. Also, use formatting attributes (such as bold and italic) sparingly.

- **Appropriate use of keywords** — Make sure that your copy includes keywords, but ensure that they flow naturally with the rest of the narrative and are not overused. Use the keywords in titles to break up the content.

- **Work with trusted individuals on your team** — As you write copy, be careful not to work in isolation. Solicit input from members of the marketing and sales teams to determine the best copy. Work with a person who knows how to properly address your target audience.

## Pay per click (PPC)

**pay per click (PPC)**
An Internet marketing technique that enables you to list your site high in search engine rankings by advertising on keywords that describe your product or service.

**Pay per click (PPC)** is an Internet marketing technique that enables you to list your site high in search engine rankings by advertising on keywords that describe your product or service. Using PPC, you place your ad with established services that provide you with keywords to help your site's ranking. PPC is not considered an "organic" solution. Instead of optimizing pages to help make them appear naturally more relevant, you simply pay to have your page listed as highly as possible.

PPC is a good way to reach your target market and generate high-quality sales leads. Most Internet marketing campaigns combine SEO and PPC strategies.

## Web analytics

**Web analytics**
The practice of collecting data and studying user behavior in an attempt to increase market share and sales.

There are two types of **Web analytics**:

- **On-site analytics** — studying visitor behavior once that visitor has accessed your site

- **Off-site analytics** — determining your potential audience, and how well your site has addressed and penetrated that market

### On-site analytics

Strategies for on-site analytics include:

- **Using trend analysis software to analyze server logs** — You can use tools such as WebTrends (*www.webtrends.com*) and Webalizer (*www.webalizer.org*) to review log files and determine the number of hits (i.e., page views) your page received, the length of each stay, and demographic information about the visitors. The most useful information includes determining repeat versus new visitors, the number of impressions obtained (i.e., the number of times an advertisement appears on a screen), and the length of each session. These statistics are far more useful than merely determining the number of hits.

- **Tagging pages** — You can use a language such as JavaScript to specially mark a page and create entries that determine exactly how long a visitor used a page. The entries can also determine mouse events that could be interpreted as clicking on a shopping cart or abandoning a particular page.

### Off-site analytics

Strategies for off-site analytics include:

- **Identifying the size of your market** — You must determine the overall size of your market, including how much is spent on it per year.

- **Identifying competitors** — You must determine who your key competitors are in the market. Study their strategies and determine how you can best position your product or service. In what particular niche can your product perform well? What other factors in the market can help you better market your product?

- **Determining your market penetration** — How much of the current market are you addressing? You cannot increase your market share unless you already know how much market share you have and what has led to this success.

- **Conducting surveys** — These surveys will help you determine an audience's interest in your product or service. Determining interest level will help you choose keywords and craft your message.

- **Consulting market research sources** — Chances are that consultants such as The Gartner Group (*www.gartner.com*) have already compiled significant data about your market sector. Take the time and spend the money to learn what these resources tell you about your market. If properly consulted, these resources will help you fine-tune your message and may significantly impact the copy you write and keywords you use.

## Complete Internet marketing

Internet marketing and SEO are not isolated practices. Proper marketing and SEO involve more than creating crisp narrative text, validating your Web pages and logging in to Google Analytics. A successful marketing campaign involves:

- **A competent leader** — This individual is primarily responsible for the vision of the marketing effort, as well as coordinating team efforts. Although a team is always necessary in a marketing effort, one person will need to be responsible for instilling a sense of personal ownership for all individuals involved in the project.

- **A team effort** — Team members often include individuals from marketing, IT, sales, customer relations and product support. Each team member will have invaluable input for any marketing effort, including traditional marketing, SEO, PPC and analytics strategies.

- **Continued effort** — Successful marketing campaigns involve more than sending out a nicely worded HTML e-mail. A campaign consists of multiple, continual efforts to create and retain customers.

- **Follow-up** — Marketing professionals must work closely with sales leaders and product managers to ensure that leads are properly processed. Also, sales and marketing team members must help refine future marketing messages.

In the following lab, you will compare pay-per-click services. Suppose you want to attract targeted leads for your products and services by ensuring that visitors who conduct relevant Web searches find your site. How can you accomplish this easily at minimal cost to you?

 **Lab 12-1: Comparing pay-per-click (PPC) services**

In this lab, you will compare pay-per-click services.

1. Open a browser and visit the following pay-per-click services:

   - Google Adwords (*https://adwords.google.com*)

   - MSN AdCenter (*https://adcenter.microsoft.com*)

   - Yahoo! Search Marketing (*http://searchmarketing.yahoo.com/arp/kpsrch.php*)

   - SearchFeed (*www.searchfeed.com*)

   - Search123 (*www.search123.uk.com*)

   - Miva (*www.miva.com*)

2. Compare each of the above services by studying the pay-per-click features listed in the following table. These features will help you determine the best service for your particular needs.

| Feature | Description |
|---|---|
| **Price per keyword** | Make sure you compare prices carefully. If a particular PPC service is more effective or provides better services, paying extra may be worth it. |
| **Keyword generation service** | How does the service help you generate keywords? Does the service provide an engine, wizard or other interface for this purpose? |
| **Bidding options** | Many sites will prompt you to bid for keywords. Other sites will have fixed prices. You must determine which is appropriate for your business. |
| **Interface quality** | Ease of use is vital, because you may waste time trying to learn a difficult interface. You may also become discouraged if the interface is overly complex. |
| **Account fee** | Many sites require a fee to open an account. |
| **Monthly minimum** | Some services will charge you if you do not generate a minimum number of keyword hits per month. |
| **Software download** | Most sites are Web-based. But some services require you to install a software application. |
| **Additional features** | Write down additional features that you think will help your particular situation. These particular features might mean the difference between success and failure of your keyword campaign. |
| **Promotions** | Many PPC services have promotions that might save you money. However, make sure that these promotions do not cost you more money in the long run. |

3. Close your browser.

In this lab, you compared PPC services to determine which may be the most beneficial for your particular situation. How do the services compare with each other?

# E-Commerce Information-Formatting Technologies

**OBJECTIVE**
2.16.1: E-commerce
terms

Businesses generate various types of documents, and they format information in many ways. However, when businesses need to exchange information, they must agree upon universal information-formatting methods. These methods are used by merchants and are often called merchant systems. Information-formatting merchant systems include:

- Electronic Data Interchange (EDI).

- Open Buying on the Internet (OBI).

The following sections discuss these ways to format information in a global e-commerce environment.

## Electronic Data Interchange (EDI)

**Electronic Data Interchange (EDI)**
The inter-organization exchange of documents in a standardized electronic format directly between participating computers.

**Electronic Data Interchange (EDI)** is a universal method for formatting information so it can be transferred among organizations. Before organizations can exchange data, they must first agree on parameters and data formats. Once a standard is reached, they exchange data automatically according to this standard, without human intervention.

Information sent via a proper EDI implementation is formatted consistently and has assured data integrity. EDI has existed for at least 20 years and is used extensively by financial institutions. It provides a proven and time-honored way to exchange the following types of information:

- Invoices

- Bills

- Purchase orders

- Inventory lists

- Supply chain information

Although it is the oldest data-formatting method, EDI remains quite popular.

### EDI implementation

Until recently, EDI's overall penetration was limited to large corporations. E-commerce is generating more widespread use of EDI because agreeing on a standardized document exchange is key to e-commerce expansion. In the past few years, EDI has found a niche in certain industries, including automotive, retail, chemical, electronics, electrical, petroleum, metals, paper and office products.

The relatively recent e-commerce push has done more to standardize EDI than any initiative over the past two decades. Today, EDI messages are encoded in a standard data format governed by the American National Standards Institute (ANSI) and other specifications.

### EDI message

An EDI message contains a string of data elements, each of which represents a singular fact (such as a price, product model number, etc.) separated by delimiters. The entire string is called a data segment. One or more data segments framed by a header and trailer form a transaction set, which is the EDI unit of transmission, equivalent to a message. A transaction set often consists of information that would usually be contained in a typical business document or form. EDI messages can also be encrypted and decrypted.

### EDI drawbacks

EDI's implementation has been hampered partly because so many standardized document formats exist: Each industry uses its own "flavor" of EDI. Not only must the document formats match, but the data representation within the document must also match precisely. For example, if SKU (stock-keeping unit) is one of the elements in the data set, it must contain the same data for both organizations, otherwise the data will become corrupt.

Two organizations that exchange EDI transmissions are known as trading partners. These trading partners must agree on a standard format. Unfortunately, this format seldom is acceptable for other trading partners, resulting in multiple formats and interoperability issues.

Another limiting factor for widespread use has been the cost associated with EDI. EDI was once considered too costly to implement, but that perception seems to be changing as EDI matures and becomes a standard for e-commerce. As e-commerce becomes more important and far-reaching, EDI will play a pivotal role in binding the different elements of e-commerce together.

### EDI and XML

EDI will remain popular, especially in certain industry niches. XML is increasingly popular because it, too, is designed to organize and describe information so that it can be shared among multiple parties, regardless of the applications used to generate the information. Over the years, both EDI and XML have been used together. Combining XML and EDI will allow much more flexibility than EDI offers on its own. An additional benefit of XML is that it is both human-readable and machine-readable, whereas EDI is only machine-readable.

## Open Buying on the Internet (OBI)

**Open Buying on the Internet (OBI)**
An open-technology standard used by organizations to exchange data in a common format; an alternative to EDI.

**Open Buying on the Internet (OBI)** was designed as an alternative to EDI. OBI was developed to target high-volume, low-cost transactions, which account for almost 80 percent of most companies' purchasing activities, according to some estimates.

OBI has several corporate sponsors, including American Express, Visa, Microsoft and Dell. OBI is used by these companies and has begun to emerge as a viable method for B2B transactions.

Because OBI is based on open technologies, it does not have the incompatibility problems commonly associated with EDI. OBI supports the open technologies described in Table 12-5.

*Table 12-5: OBI support of open technologies*

| Technology | Function |
|---|---|
| HTTP and W3C-standard HTML | Content display |
| EDI X12 850 standards | Order request |
| HTTP 1.0 | Order transmission |
| SSL | Transmission security Cryptography |
| X.509 version 3 | Public-key certificates |

OBI works well for purchasing non-production items such as office supplies, cleaning products and computer equipment. Such purchases are very expensive to process with traditional methods. When an OBI system is in place, the cost of processing falls dramatically. OBI allows any approved person in an organization to buy needed products or services.

## OBI components

Following are the four components of an OBI transaction:

- **Requisitioner** — the person or software that initiates the purchase transaction

- **Buying organization** — the company that represents the requisitioner and has an OBI server

- **Selling organization** — the company that is offering the product or service for sale and has an OBI server

- **Payment authority** — the organization that acts as a neutral third party to settle the financial component of the transaction

## OBI transactions

An OBI transaction undergoes a process of validation and authorization to ensure that the purchase is authentic and approved. This process reduces the possibility of fraud and unauthorized purchases.

**Step 1:** The requisitioner needs to order office supplies, for example. This buyer accesses the selling organization's online catalog, which can be hosted on the selling company's OBI server or the buying company's OBI server.

The online catalog assigns prices specific to the buying organization. For example, one buying organization with a higher volume may be offered lower prices than other buying organizations with lower volume. This customized catalog eliminates the need for continual price negotiations and adjustments for each buyer.

The requisitioner adds products to the shopping cart and places the order with the selling organization's OBI server.

**Step 2:** The selling organization's OBI server automatically returns the order to the buying organization's OBI server for approval. Such approval involves properly identifying the requisitioning individual and ascertaining his or her spending authority. The approval process may be automatic or may require management intervention.

**Step 3:** After approval from the buying organization, the transaction is returned to the selling organization's OBI server for fulfillment.

**Step 4:** A payment authority, such as a bank or the lender's OBI server, handles the billing and money transfer.

## OBI and EDI

OBI has an additional advantage because OBI orders are formatted in ANSI EDI X12 850. This format allows companies that have already invested heavily in EDI to make their current systems OBI-compliant.

# E-Commerce Payment Technologies

Organizations need standard methods for exchanging funds just as much as they need standards for exchanging information. Several e-commerce payment technologies are in common use, either as transaction methods or as tools to secure transactions:

- Electronic Funds Transfer (EFT)

- Payment gateways

- Secure Electronic Transactions (SET)

- Open Trading Protocol (OTP)

- Secure Sockets Layer (SSL) / Transport Layer Security (TLS)

The following sections discuss these e-commerce payment technologies.

## Electronic Funds Transfer (EFT)

Electronic Funds Transfer (EFT) is a generic term that describes the ability to transfer funds using computers, rather than using paper. Banks use EFT to save time and ensure that fund exchange between individuals and businesses is as secure as possible. Other large organizations use EFT as well. EFT systems must ensure:

- **Confidentiality of payment information** — All payment information must remain completely secret. Strategies include encrypting transactions and also using certificates to authenticate users.

- **Integrity of payment information** — Payment information cannot have been altered in transit, and transaction information must be verified.

- **Merchant authentication** — All merchants involved in transactions must prove their identities. Merchant authentication includes **non-repudiation**, which helps businesses track transactions and operate securely. You can also use a **digital signature** to prove a person's identity, as well as prove that the transaction occurred.

- **Interoperability** — The model used must be widely adopted and supported. Even the slightest change will introduce incompatibilities in the model.

**non-repudiation**
The security principle of providing proof that a transaction occurred between identified parties. Repudiation occurs when one party in a transaction denies that the transaction took place.

**digital signature**
An electronic stamp added to a message that uniquely identifies its source and verifies its contents at the time of the signature.

 *EFT is also known as a wire transfer.*

### Automated Clearing House (ACH)

The Automated Clearing House (ACH) network is a nationwide batch-oriented EFT system governed in the United States by the National Automated Clearing House Association (NACHA) operating rules. These rules provide for the inter-bank clearance of electronic payments for participating financial institutions.

The American Clearing House Association, Federal Reserve, Electronic Payments Network and Visa act as ACH Operators, or central clearing facilities through which financial institutions transmit or receive ACH entries. The electronic network transfers and clears funds between banking institutions for merchants and customers.

The following parties participate in an ACH transaction:

- **Originator** — any individual, corporation or other organization that initiates entries into the ACH network.

- **Originating Depository Financial Institution (ODFI)** — a participating financial institution that originates ACH entries at the request of and by agreement with its customers and merchants. ODFIs must abide by the *NACHA Operating Rules and Guidelines.*

- **Receiving Depository Financial Institution (RDFI)** — any financial institution qualified to receive ACH entries that agrees to abide by the *NACHA Operating Rules and Guidelines.*

- **Receiver** — an individual, corporation or other organization that has authorized an originator to initiate a credit or debit entry to a transaction account held at an RDFI.

The ACH network does not have direct contact with public customers or merchants. It is the mediator between financial institutions during the transfer of funds.

A merchant establishes a merchant account to accept credit card payments or EFT payments. The merchant collects the credit card or banking information, then sends the information in batch format to the institution providing the merchant account (typically, the merchant's bank). The merchant's bank then uses the ACH network to clear the funds from the credit card issuer's bank or the customer's bank (checking account) on behalf of the merchant. The transaction is then settled.

ACH does not perform real-time processing and usually needs 24 hours to complete a transaction. ACH should not be confused with real-time credit card authorization, which verifies only card validity and available funds.

An ACH network is involved in almost every financial transaction except wire transfers. Each country has its own form of ACH, and is governed by its own laws and regulations.

## Payment gateways

**OBJECTIVE**
2.16.3: E-commerce payment models

A payment gateway is a system, either hardware-based or software-based, that mediates between a merchant (i.e., an e-commerce-enabled Web site) and an acquirer (e.g., the merchant's bank). End users do not configure their systems to become payment gateways. Once the merchant receives payment from a customer, the merchant uses the payment gateway to transmit credit card information to the bank. The gateway is responsible for several tasks, including:

- **Forwarding information to the proper parties** — When the gateway receives transaction messages, it ensures that this information is sent to the proper parties.

- **Authenticating all participants in the transaction** — Each party must prove its identity to the gateway before transactions can proceed.

- **Ensuring confidentiality** — Information must be encrypted so that it cannot be used by unauthorized parties.

- **Ensuring data integrity** — Information must be checked to ensure that it has not been altered in transit. This process also involves verifying credit card information.

Many payment gateway companies exist, including:

- VeriSign (*www.verisign.com*).

- MerchantWarehouse (*http://merchantwarehouse.com/*).

- CCAvenue (*www.ccavenue.com*).

- Authorize.Net (*www.authorizenet.com*).

- PayPoint.net (*www.paypoint.net*).

- LinkPoint (*www.firstdata.com/linkpoint/*).

- MerchantCGI.com (*http://merchantcgi.com*).

You do not have to use a third party as a payment gateway. Several companies provide dedicated payment gateway software that you can configure and administer yourself. Examples include:

- IBM Payment Gateway (*www.ibm.com*).

- SunShop Shopping Cart (*www.turnkeywebtools.com*).

## Secure Electronic Transactions (SET)

**Secure Electronic Transactions (SET)**
An Internet protocol that uses digital certificates to secure financial transactions.

Each of the parties that participates in a **Secure Electronic Transactions (SET)** payment is required to authenticate itself at some point in the payment process. SET uses both public-key (asymmetric) and private-key (symmetric) encryption techniques. It also uses the concept of enveloping for faster encryption and decryption. SET is designed to allow more complex transactions such as returning goods, obtaining a credit card, or reversing an authorization for a charge when goods cannot be shipped.

### History of SET

SET was designed to resolve an impasse that developed between two alliances. One alliance formed by MasterCard, Netscape Communications, IBM and others launched the Secure Electronic Payment Protocol (SEPP) in 1995 — only a few days after a Visa and Microsoft consortium had launched a different network payment specification called Secure Transaction Technology (STT). This timing led to an unfortunate situation in which the two major credit card companies were each backing a different electronic payment protocol.

Ultimately, good sense prevailed, and in 1996 the two protocols were merged into a unified system that would be called Secure Electronic Transactions (SET). Because it has been endorsed by companies such as American Express, Visa, MasterCard, Microsoft and others, SET has become the Internet payment standard.

### SET example

The following process describes the steps that must occur in order for an end user to use SET to purchase a product.

**Step 1:** An end user approaches an issuer bank and completes a registration form containing his or her credit card information. This information includes the user's name and billing address, the credit card account number and the expiration date. Additional information may also be required, such as security codes that may exist on the card. This session should be encrypted via a protocol such as SSL/TLS, which you will learn about shortly. All remaining sessions are encrypted by default.

**Step 2:** The issuer bank performs two steps: It first verifies the information provided by the end user. Once the information is marked valid, it then creates and signs a certificate. The issuer bank has now verified this information and becomes the trusted party. The certificate is known as a SET certificate. This type of certificate is generated via PKI. (You will learn more about certificates and PKI shortly.)

**Step 3:** The issuer bank gives the signed certificate to the end user, who can then begin shopping. However, the end user must shop at sites and stores that use SET.

**Step 4:** To serve a customer with a SET certificate, a merchant must register with the issuer bank. The merchant must provide its merchant ID number and company name to the issuer. Once the issuer registers the merchant, the issuer provides the merchant with its SET certificate. The merchant can now serve SET customers.

**Step 5:** The end user begins shopping. To make a purchase, the user presents her SET certificate to the merchant. The merchant also presents its SET certificate. Because these certificates are authenticated and signed by the issuer, the merchant and the customer can be confident that all identities are proper and secure. The transaction is also encrypted.

**Step 6:** When an end user wants to make a purchase, the merchant can verify not only the end user's identity, but can also determine whether or not the end user has sufficient funds available for the purchase.

It is important to understand that once certificates are issued, sensitive user information (e.g., user names, passwords and credit card numbers) is not transported over public networks, even in encrypted form, because the certificates perform the authentication work.

### SET vs. conventional transactions

In a conventional credit card transaction, a cardholder forwards details to the merchant, who then contacts his or her acquirer to obtain clearance for the payment. The acquirer can obtain this authorization from the institution that issued the card via a financial network operated by the card association. These private networks have existed for some time and have their own proprietary protocols operating on dedicated links with appropriate security measures. Thus, an infrastructure of links and transaction-processing computer hardware already exists to electronically authorize credit card payments. SET assumes the existence of such a facility and specifies only the subset of dialogs between the customer and merchant, and between the merchant and the payment gateway.

## Open Trading Protocol (OTP)

Open Trading Protocol (OTP) is a SET alternative being promoted by a group of corporations including AT&T, CyberCash, DigiCash, Hewlett-Packard, Oracle Corporation, Sun Microsystems, Wells Fargo Bank and the Royal Bank of Canada. It uses digital certificates to enable encryption similar to SET, but all transactions are formatted in XML, rather than in a proprietary format.

OTP defines trading protocol options, which control the way that the trade occurs. These options tell the consumer how the transaction will occur and which payment options are available. The transaction details can be handled dynamically: For example, a vendor may give a discount if a consumer uses the preferred store credit card or if a certain item is purchased in bulk.

OTP can be used for both the B2B and B2C models. The following code is an OTP example that uses XML to format a shipping address:

```
<SHIPPING>
   2677 Strawberry Fields
   Liverpool
   United Kingdom
</SHIPPING>
```

Standardized markup tags are expected for all domains. Current browsers such as Microsoft Internet Explorer and Mozilla Firefox support XML in some form, and the standards are being developed. OTP also supports EDI for transaction processing.

### OTP features

OTP has three key features:

- It provides trading protocol options to control the way that the trade occurs.

- It provides a record of the trade.

- It supports real and virtual delivery of goods and services.

OTP supports a standard, but is still a flexible method of providing offers and receipts that bind the payment to the reason that the payment occurred. This information can be used to resolve problems. Because the information is in a standard format, it facilitates the provision of automated, lower-cost customer care.

OTP supports the delivery of goods both physically and electronically. It also provides a means for linking the delivery to the offer and the payment. In this way, OTP spans the life cycle of a business transaction from terms and conditions to payment to acknowledged delivery of goods.

OTP is standardized and discussed in RFC 2802.

## Secure Sockets Layer (SSL) / Transport Layer Security (TLS)

**OBJECTIVE**
2.16.5: SSL/TLS
transactions

**Secure Sockets Layer (SSL)**
A protocol that provides authentication and encryption, used by most servers for secure exchanges over the Internet. Superseded by Transport Layer Security (TLS).

**Transport Layer Security (TLS)**
A protocol based on SSL 3.0 that provides authentication and encryption, used by most servers for secure exchanges over the Internet.

Neither SSL nor TLS are transaction methods; rather, they are tools used to secure transactions. **Secure Sockets Layer (SSL)** and **Transport Layer Security (TLS)** are methods used to encrypt data transmissions. They act as the foundation for many e-commerce protocols, including SET. SSL was developed by Netscape Corporation. Several different versions exist, including version 3.0, which was released in 1996. You can view the SSL 3.0 specification at *www.freesoft.org/CIE/Topics/ssl-draft/3-SPEC.HTM*.

TLS was developed by the IETF Network Working Group using the SSL 3.0 specification. Several RFCs extend TLS (e.g., RFC 3546) and also explain specific implementations (e.g., RFCs 3207 and 3734). TLS is quite similar to SSL, but TLS is an open standard that is updated frequently. You can read about TLS in RFC 2246. TLS has rapidly become the accepted standard, although it is often called SSL or SSL/TLS.

### Services provided by SSL/TLS

SSL and TLS are protocols that are included within transaction methods to secure transactions. SSL/TLS secures transactions through encryption. Encryption can provide the following services:

- Authentication

- Data confidentiality

- Data integrity

Many other encryption methods exist, but SSL/TLS is arguably the most universally applied.

### SSL/TLS and Public Key Infrastructure (PKI)

You need a certificate to enable host authentication before you can begin an SSL session. So before an organization can use SSL/TLS to enable encryption, it must participate in Public Key Infrastructure (PKI), which is a collection of individuals, networks and computers that together comprise the ability to authoritatively confirm the identity of a person, host or organization. PKI makes it possible for two parties that have never met each other to trust each other. Once trust is established, encryption can begin. PKI involves the following elements:

- **Digital certificate** — a signed public key that verifies a set of credentials associated with the public key of a certificate authority (CA). All SSL/TLS sessions require a valid certificate, which acts as a trusted third party to allow unknown parties to authenticate with each other and begin encryption.

- **Certificate authority (CA)** — a trusted third party that verifies the identity of the person or company that has submitted a certification request (CR). A CA is an organization that issues digital certificates and helps to ensure the identity of a person, host or process. A CA is more than just a computer that issues digital certificates; a CA is an entire organization.

- **Registration authority (RA)** — a part of the CA. The RA is used if the CA is overburdened with many requests. However, the RA only verifies credentials; the CA is the only PKI element that issues the certificates.

- **Certificate server** — contained within the CA, the computer that generates certificates. It is also known as an authentication service. The certificate server is often called a CA, although this is a misnomer.

- **Certification chain** — describes the nature of trust in PKI. A CA establishes trust by establishing itself as a trustworthy authority concerning identity. It also establishes itself as the top of a hierarchy (called a tree). The CA vouches for each entity beneath it, creating a trust pattern. If a certificate's link to the CA is placed in doubt, then this certificate is no longer valid.

- **Entity** — any host that uses, or wants to obtain and use, a certificate.

 *Many other elements exist within PKI. The elements discussed here are only the most essential.*

## Digital certificates, SSL/TLS and the X.509 standard

**X.509**
The standard used by certificate authorities (CAs) for creating digital certificates.

Digital certificates used in PKI conform to the ITU **X.509** standard. A CA creates an X.509 certificate. With certificates, two or more parties that have never met each other can trust each other indirectly, as suggested in Figure 12-3.

Encrypted, authenticated transmission across untrusted networks is now possible, because both James and the Web server trust each other indirectly through the CA.

James' Linux System

James' Linux system uses a browser that contains a certificate signed by a recognized, verifiable CA. Therefore, his browser trusts the CA.

POP3 and SMTP Server

The POP3 and SMTP Server trusts the same CA as James' browser. Therefore, it trusts James.

Certificate Authority
(CA)

*Figure 12-3: Establishing indirect trust with certificates*

Whenever a certificate is used to secure a service (e.g., to encrypt Web or POP3 traffic), a different port is used. For example, SSL/TLS-enabled Web traffic generally uses TCP Port

443, rather than the default TCP Port 80. Similarly, encrypted POP3 traffic uses TCP Port 995, rather than the standard TCP Port 110.

### Public-Key Cryptography Standards (PKCS)

Public-Key Cryptography Standards (PKCS) define 15 specific methods for securely transferring and storing certificates. When you request, store or transfer a certificate, you are using a PKCS method. Following are selected PKCS methods you should understand:

- **PKCS #1** — known as the **RSA** Cryptography Standard. Specifies the use of the RSA algorithm, as well as the format for RSA private and public keys.

- **PKCS #6** — known as the Extended-Certificate Syntax Standard. Provides extensions to the X.509 standard. Extended certificates must be signed by the same CA that issued the certificate.

- **PKCS #7** — known as the Cryptographic Message Syntax Standard. Used for S/MIME or Privacy Enhanced Mail (PEM). Used to export public keys for use in e-mail and Web clients. Also used to publish a Certificate Revocation List (CRL) or a certification chain. Used by end users to exchange public keys so they can encrypt e-mail to each other.

- **PKCS #10** — known as the Certification Request Syntax Standard. Specifies the format for a certificate request. Whenever you generate a certificate request, the resulting file will be formatted according to this standard.

- **PKCS #12** — known as the Personal Information Exchange Syntax Standard. The standard for user-based storage of private keys and certificates.

### Certificate life cycle

All certificates have a specific life span. Table 12-6 describes essential terms to understand when dealing with certificates generated through PKI.

*Table 12-6: Certificate life cycle terms*

| Term | Description |
|------|-------------|
| **Certificate policy** | Guidelines for the ways that employees in an organization should use digital certificates. |
| **Certificate Practice Statement (CPS)** | A document that explains the way that a CA verifies and manages certificates. |
| **Certificate expiration** | The invalidation of a certificate when it reaches the end of its expected life cycle. All certificates have valid beginning and end dates coded in them (e.g., October 31, 2010). Expiration occurs when a certificate is no longer valid because the end date has arrived. |
| **Certificate revocation** | The invalidation of a certificate before the end of its expected life cycle. Keys that have been revoked cannot be renewed. Reasons for revocation can include termination or reassignment of an employee, company name change, DNS name change of a server, or a compromised CA. |
| **Certificate suspension** | Temporary invalidation of a key for a specified period of time. The key can be reactivated. However, if the certificate expires during a period of suspension, a new key must be generated. |
| **Certificate renewal** | The revalidation of a key before it expires. Keys that have been revoked or have already expired cannot be renewed. |
| **Certificate destruction** | The elimination of all public and private keys; effectively, eliminating an identity from PKI. |

*Table 12-6: Certificate life cycle terms (cont'd)*

| Term | Description |
|------|-------------|
| **Certificate Revocation List (CRL)** | A list of certificates that are no longer considered valid. Users must manually download and check this list. |
| **Online Certificate Status Protocol (OCSP)** | A real-time protocol that allows users to check for revoked certificates. |

## The SSL/TLS handshake

Once a client and a server are SSL-enabled, the client and the server must negotiate a connection by using a handshake. This handshake negotiates the following:

- **The type of encryption algorithm to be used** — Encryption algorithms include RSA and DSA.

- **Authentication** — The server always authenticates with the client using a certificate. The client can optionally be forced to authenticate with the server.

- **The session key** — A symmetric key is shared between the client and the server. The session key is protected by asymmetric-key encryption. Specifically, the session key is protected by the client's public key.

## Common applications of SSL/TLS

SSL/TLS are commonly used in Web browsers, but are not limited to Web-based transactions. It is possible to use SSL/TLS to secure various types of traffic, including:

- E-mail (e.g., SMTP, POP3, IMAP and Web-based e-mail).

- FTP.

- NNTP.

- E-commerce transactions from custom-created applications.

- B2C and B2B e-commerce transactions.

## Beginning an SSL/TLS session

It is important to understand that certificates enable authentication. After authentication occurs, then encryption begins. When you begin an SSL/TLS session in your browser, the session is made possible because your browser contains the public keys of several prominent CAs. Most Web servers have certificates signed by these same CAs, and so the SSL/TLS session will begin automatically. However, if a discrepancy occurs, you will be informed. A discrepancy may be a sign of an attempted attack, or it may be caused by improper server configuration. Table 12-7 describes several common discrepancies that may lead to a warning or a failed session.

Table 12-7: SSL/TLS session discrepancies

| Discrepancy | Description |
|---|---|
| **Different host name** | The name on the server's SSL/TLS certificate is different from the name on the server. The Web browser will notice this discrepancy and issue a warning. You can choose to continue the session or cancel it. In most cases, this problem occurs due to a change in the server's configuration. In some cases, this discrepancy may be evidence that a hacker is trying to hijack your connection to steal information. |
| **Certificate expired** | The certificate being presented by the server needs to be renewed. You will receive a warning, and you can choose to cancel the transaction. |
| **Certificate date not yet valid** | The server is using a certificate before the certificate has been validated. You will receive a warning. |
| **Invalid certificate format** | The certificate contains a fatal flaw. The session cannot continue. |
| **Certificate presented by the server not signed by a recognized CA** | Browsers and other clients contain the public keys of only certain CAs. Many companies create their own certificate servers or use lesser-known CAs. You will receive a warning with options to cancel the session, accept the certificate for the current session (until the browser is closed), or install the certificate permanently, which means you will permanently recognize the CA and consider the certificate valid. |
| **Incompatible encryption settings** | Your browser is not capable of handling the encryption level required by the server. Many browsers use 40-bit encryption. If a server requires 128-bit encryption, many browsers will not be able to continue with the session. In these cases, the end user must upgrade the browser's encryption level. In some countries, using encryption higher than 40 bits is illegal. |

In the following lab, you will review an SSL/TLS session. Suppose your project manager has asked you to describe the SSL/TLS process to members of another department. They understand that it somehow enables encryption and is related to the ability to authenticate hosts. You can demonstrate an example of the way that certificates are automatically exchanged and encryption is made possible.

## Lab 12-2: Reviewing an SSL/TLS session

In this lab, you will learn how an SSL/TLS session is built using certificates.

1.  Open **Firefox** and go to *www.yahoo.com*.

2.  **Browser:** Select **Tools | Page Info** to open the Page Info window, then click the **Security** icon.

3.  Read the information in the Technical Details section. Notice that the Web page is not encrypted.

4.  Close the **Page Info** window to return to the Yahoo! home page.

5.  Go to *https://login.yahoo.com*. Notice that the URL begins with *https* rather than *http*.

6.  An alert message box may appear (depending on your browser's security settings) informing you that you have requested a secure document, which opens an SSL/TLS session. If the message appears, click **OK**.

7. When the Yahoo! sign-in Web page appears, select **Tools | Page Info** and click the **Security** icon. Notice that the information has changed due to an SSL/TLS session, as shown in Figure 12-4.

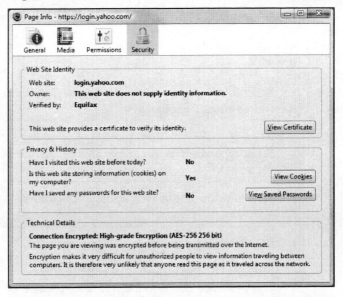

Figure 12-4: Viewing security information during SSL/TLS session

8. **Page Info:** Click the **View Certificate** button. The Certificate Viewer dialog box will appear, as shown in Figure 12-5.

Figure 12-5: Viewing certificate information

*Tech Note: The fingerprints listed in the dialog box refer to the series of bytes that make up the SHA1 and MD5 hash functions used to encrypt public keys. The SHA1 fingerprint is a 160-bit hash function, and the MD5 fingerprint is a 128-bit hash function.*

9. **Certificate Viewer:** Select the **Details** tab to learn more about the certificate.

10. Close the **Certificate Viewer** dialog box and the **Page Info** window.

11. Close **Firefox**.

12. As a class, discuss the following questions, and write your answers in the spaces provided.

- What is the term for the PKI organization that received Yahoo's credentials, then issued this certificate?

  _____

- What type of server generated this certificate? Of what is this server a part?

  _____

- How did this certificate get into the browser?

  _____

- What services does this certificate provide?

  _____

- It is assumed that you did not receive any error messages. Why were you not warned or informed about the CA that issued this certificate when your browser automatically received it?

  _____

- How can certificates help secure e-commerce transactions?

  _____

  _____

In this lab, you learned about the ways that SSL/TLS functions to secure Web-based transactions.

# Working in a Global Environment

OBJECTIVE
2.16.4: Global
business issues

Modern e-commerce technologies require you to understand global issues. Remember that by placing your business on the Web, you expand your audience to include anyone in the world with a browser and Internet access. Therefore, you must consider the level to which you will accommodate potential customers from countries outside yours. The following sections discuss the ways that businesses address issues such as:

- Currency differences.

- International shipping.

- Language concerns.

- Relationship management.

## Currency and trade

Each country (e.g., China) and economic block (e.g., European Union) uses its own currency. E-commerce sites such as eBay and global businesses such as IBM facilitate business with people in many different countries. These sites and businesses may reside in one country but do business in others all around the world. Accordingly, these businesses and organizations must be able to:

- Automatically calculate exchange rates for the day of the transaction — This practice is often called currency conversion.

- Calculate taxes and tariffs on goods — Purchases that you make may incur additional costs.

Table 12-8 describes some of the currencies used throughout the world.

*Table 12-8: Common currencies*

| Currency | Description |
|---|---|
| Euro | A currency specific to the European Union. |
| Dollar | A term used in several countries for different currencies. For example, the United States, Australia and New Zealand all use the dollar. Each of these currencies has a different value. |
| Yen | A currency specific to Japan. |
| Ruble | A currency specific to Russia. |
| Pound | A term used in several countries for different currencies. Most often associated with the United Kingdom (UK), but also used in Egypt. Egyptian pounds and UK pounds have different values. |
| Yuan | A currency specific to China. The full name of the currency is Yuan Renminbi. |

Currency values fluctuate daily, even hourly. If your e-commerce site does business in multiple currencies, you must establish, publicize and follow a policy that determines:

- When currency calculations will be made.

- When credit cards or other accounts will be updated.

## Taxes, tariffs and trade

A common misconception is that goods and services purchased over the Internet are never taxed. In some cases, products you purchase over the Internet may not be taxed. In other cases, a tax may be due to a state or government, but you might avoid paying that tax. Tax avoidance is different from untaxed purchases.

For example, suppose a person residing in Washington state in the United States purchases a computer from Dell, based in Texas, over the Internet. Dell will not collect any sales taxes on this purchase because Texas does not impose sales taxes. However, the person who purchased the computer may still be responsible for paying sales tax on this item. Some states do not enforce sales tax in this way. Some other states require Web-based businesses to charge sales tax only to customers who reside in the same state where the business is based. Be sure you understand how the laws apply in your own situation.

A tariff is a specialized form of tax levied on an item that passes across a country's border. When goods are brought into a country from another country, they are said to be imported. When goods are sent out of a country into another country, these goods are said to be exported. Another term for tariff is duty.

Table 12-9 describes essential terms to understand as you engage in global commerce.

reseller
A company that
adds some value to
an existing product
or service, then sells
it to the public or to
another company.

*Table 12-9: Global commerce terms*

| Term | Description |
|------|-------------|
| Value Added Tax (VAT) | A tax on a product or service. If a product is further processed or modified by a vendor or **reseller**, it increases in value. Each time this happens, the product may be subject to VAT. The consumer pays VAT. |
| Trade agreement | In global commerce, an agreement between individual nations that allows them to operate as a unified trading block. Examples of trade agreements include the North American Free Trade Agreement (NAFTA) and the agreements that created the European Union (EU). NAFTA allows Canada, the United States and Mexico to drop tariffs and trade barriers, and essentially act as one economic unit. Similarly, members of the European Union (e.g., France, Germany, the United Kingdom, etc.) can all benefit from such a block because their combined economies create a much larger economic entity that can compete against other trade groups. |
| Border tax adjustment | A tax or tariff is either reduced or eliminated. |

In the following lab, you will use currency-conversion tables. Suppose your Web development team is designing a B2B e-commerce solution that will allow your company to automatically receive orders and process purchases from your customer companies in Europe and the United Kingdom. Your project manager has asked you to research automatic currency-conversion tools that you could incorporate into your B2B site. You can demonstrate an example tool that allows users to easily convert currencies.

 **Lab 12-3: Converting currency values**

In this lab, you will convert currency values using a popular online tool.

1.   Open a browser and access ***www.xe.com/ucc***. You will see the Universal Currency Converter page.

2.   Convert **500 U.S. Dollars** into **U.K. Pounds**. How many pounds will you get?

3.   Convert **500 U.K. Pounds** into **Euros**. How many euros will you get?

4.   Convert **500 Euros** into **Rubles**. How many rubles will you get?

5.   Conduct additional exchanges for other currencies.

6.   Close your browser.

7.   As a class, discuss the following questions:

   •   If you ran an e-commerce site, would you want to perform these types of conversions yourself, or have them performed automatically by the site? Why?

   •   How can you adjust your prices when currency fluctuations occur?

   •   Try repeating this lab at another date. By how much have currency values changed? How would this affect your business with a European customer who is purchasing US$100 worth of product from you? What about a U.K. customer who is purchasing US$10,000 worth of product?

In this lab, you learned how to convert currency values quickly and easily using an online tool.

## International shipping

When shipping goods internationally, you must consider the following issues:

**customs**
National departments responsible for controlling items entering and leaving the country.

- **Customs** searches
- Costs incurred by customs
- Delays caused by customs
- All tariffs

### Legal and regulatory issues

As you implement an e-commerce solution, consider the following points:

- **A product you sell legally in one country may be illegal in another** — As a result, your company may become liable for breaking a law. Consult with an international lawyer before making products available.

- **A product you sell may be heavily regulated** — As a result, your company may have to pay taxes or tariffs if this product is to be sold legally.

## Language concerns

As you develop an e-commerce site, consider the following issues:

- The language(s) used by the target audience
- The characters necessary (e.g., alphanumeric, mathematical or currency symbols)

### Character sets and languages

All applications and servers use a specific character set to render text on a page. As you have already learned, it is possible to specify a character set for Web pages. You may be assigned to create a page for a language that requires a particular character set. Such languages can include Russian, Greek, Japanese, Chinese, Hebrew and Arabic. Also, certain disciplines, such as mathematics or science, require that you use non-standard characters or symbols that may not be readily available. You may have to install language packs for your GUI HTML/XHTML editor or for the Web server. If you do not specify a character set, you may not be able to create the proper symbols.

To solve this problem, specify Unicode support for all of your site's Web pages. The Unicode Technical Committee (UTC) maintains the Unicode standard. The UTC is a subcommittee of the Unicode Consortium (*www.unicode.org*). If you ever need to add support for a language or for non-standard characters, then consider obtaining Unicode support packs.

As mentioned earlier in this course, you can specify Unicode support using the <meta> tag in your XHTML pages as shown:

```
<meta http-equiv="Content-Type" content="text/html; charset=utf-8"/>
```

## Relationship management

Every business wants to establish solid relationships with all parties in its supply chain. Following are two important concepts that can help you ensure success: trust-building and customer self-service.

### Building trust

Ways to build trust include:

- **Quality customer service** — Whatever product you sell, make sure that the B2B or B2C customer feels supported. Nothing makes a customer more uncomfortable with a purchase than the perception of poor customer service.

- **Frequent contact** — Use two-way and one-way communication. Two-way communication includes sales and marketing personnel who contact customers. One-way examples include press releases and messages via an e-mail list server.

### Customer self-service

One of the best ways to build good relationships with customers is to allow them to serve themselves. Ways to enable customer self-service include:

- **Automatic order tracking** — When a product is purchased in a B2B or B2C situation, provide the ability for customers to track their orders so they can predict delivery and quickly identify any potential delivery problems.

- **Unattended choice** — Provide visitors the ability to choose products without the help of a live person. Doing so leaves visitors free to make their own choices, but makes you responsible for developing an easily navigable site.

- **Order customization** — Allow customers to add value to their purchases by specifying shipping options. Other options include gift wrapping and custom messages. Some sites give customers the chance to customize orders after the order has been placed; with this option, you must specify a cutoff date so that the order can be finalized.

## Case Study

# Customer Disservice

Maya is a marketing manager for a motorcycle supply company based in the United States. She discovered that her company's brand name was suffering because the company apparently gave the perception of poor customer service for their online business. There were several reasons for this:

- Difficulties with the online ordering process often required customers to call the company's toll-free line and talk to a person at a call center. Many calls also resulted from pricing, shipping and return policies that were not clearly explained on the site.

- Orders often took too long to fulfill, causing customers to call and ask when the order could be expected.

- Orders that were sent to other countries (e.g., Mexico and Canada) were often stalled due to customs issues.

To address these problems, Maya made the following changes:

- She worked with the Web development team to alter the site's ordering forms and pages for easier navigation. Customer calls to the help desk for assistance with orders were reduced by 64 percent.

- She posted several Customer Service pages on the Web site, complete with a Frequently Asked Questions (FAQ) page and advice about when phone calls might be necessary. Customer calls with common questions were reduced by 88 percent.

- She built an order-tracking scheme using both FedEx and UPS. Customer calls after placing orders were reduced by 95 percent.

- She directed the sales team to do some research about products that cannot be sold to international customers. Complaints about late shipment dropped 85 percent.

Maya was not able to hire any more customer service representatives, but reports of significant improvement in her company's brand name began to appear.

*          *          *

As a class, discuss this scenario and answer the following questions:

- How was Maya able to use Web-based technology to improve her company's reputation without hiring new employees?

- How was Maya able to deal with international issues?

- Maya was able to use her Web server to save the company money and improve its reputation. Consider how her Web-based solutions were cost-effective.

## Lesson Summary

### Application project

This lesson discussed several e-commerce solutions, including ways to format data using EDI and OBI, and ways to process purchases using SET, OTP and SSL/TLS. Use search engines such as Yahoo!, Google and AltaVista to conduct searches for more information about these technologies. Which technologies seem to be better known or more widely used? Which technologies seem to be available in more e-commerce solutions that you could use to implement your own site? Which technologies would you choose?

If you have used the Web to shop or make purchases, either for your personal use or your business, consider the customer service experiences you have had. Which Web businesses were easy to do business with? What made your transactions easy? Which businesses gave you problems? Are there some businesses you return to frequently because they have earned your trust as a consumer? Which ones, and why? Are there some businesses that you return to despite customer service problems you have had? Which ones, and why? How can you use these experiences to improve the customer service offered by your own e-commerce site?

### Skills review

In this lesson, you learned about the many characteristics that e-commerce and traditional commerce share, and you studied the ways that e-commerce differs from traditional commerce. This lesson also discussed Web-based technologies that can be used to improve e-commerce sites. You learned about business-to-business, business-to-consumer and consumer-to-consumer e-commerce models, and you studied their enabling technologies including EDI, OBI, SET, OTP and SSL/TLS. You also learned about Internet marketing and its associated technologies of search engine optimization (SEO), pay per click (PPC) and Web analytics. Finally, you received a brief overview of global commerce issues, and the ways that Web technologies can be used to improve customer relationships.

Now that you have completed this lesson, you should be able to:

✓ 2.16.1: Define e-commerce terms and concepts, including EDI, business-to-business (B2B), business-to-consumer (B2C), Electronic Funds Transfer (EFT), Electronic Data Interchange (EDI), Open Trading Protocol (OTP), merchant systems, relationship management, customer self-service, Internet marketing, Secure Electronic Transactions (SET).

✓ 2.16.2: Compare e-commerce to traditional commerce.

✓ 2.16.3: Identify payment models used in e-commerce, including payment gateways.

✓ 2.16.4: Identify issues related to working in a global environment, including different currencies, multi-lingual issues, international shipping, supply chain, legal and regulatory issues.

✓ 2.16.5: Identify the importance of SSL/TLS to a transaction that contains sensitive information.

✓ 2.16.6: Identify the importance of online indexing and cataloging.

✓ 2.16.7: Define search engine optimization (SEO) and related key terms (e.g., Internet marketing, organic vs. non-organic [pay-per-click], Web analytics).

✓ 2.21.3: Create Web pages that rank highly for search engines that use spiders and screen readers.

# Lesson 12 Review

1. What are the two most common e-commerce models?

   _____

2. What is a manufacturing resource plan?

   _____

   _____

   _____

3. What is Internet marketing, and of what three components does it consist?

   _____

   _____

   _____

4. What three technologies discussed in this lesson help e-commerce companies format information so that they can transfer data more easily? Which is the oldest?

   _____

5. What technologies discussed in this lesson help e-commerce companies exchange funds?

   _____

   _____

   _____

6. What is an XML schema?

   _____

   _____

   _____

7. What is a tariff?

   _____

   _____

   _____

*Version 2.0*

# Appendixes

**Appendix A:**   Objectives and Locations*
**Appendix B:**   Movies*
**Appendix C:**   Web Developer Resources*
**Appendix D:**   Works Consulted*

*Appendix found on Supplemental CD-ROM*

# CIW Foundations Glossary

**account lockout** — A legitimate practice in which a user account is automatically disabled after a certain number of failed authentication attempts.

**active partition** — A logical partition that contains the files necessary to boot an operating system. This partition is read first at boot time. If no active partition exists, or if the operating system files are corrupted or missing, the computer will report error messages.

**ActiveX** — An open set of technologies for integrating components on the Internet and within Microsoft applications.

**adapter** — A device that provides connectivity between at least two systems.

**Advanced Research Projects Agency (ARPA)** — A U.S. Department of Defense agency that created the first global computer network.

**Advanced Research Projects Agency Network (ARPANET)** — A computer network, funded by ARPA, that served as the basis for early networking research and was the backbone during the development of the Internet.

**Ajax** — A programming methodology that uses a number of existing technologies together and enables Web applications to make incremental updates to the user interface without the need to reload the browser page.

**anonymizing tools** — Internet components and application features that make the user's Internet activity untraceable.

**anti-virus software** — Software that scans disks and programs for known viruses and eliminates them.

**applets** — Small programs written in Java, which are downloaded as needed and executed within a Web page or browser.

**application programming interface (API)** — A set of universal commands, calls and functions that allows developers to communicate with an application or operating system.

**Application Service Provider (ASP)** — A company that provides applications and services (over the Internet) to individual or enterprise subscribers that would otherwise need to provide those applications and services on their own servers.

**application-level gateway** — A firewall component that inspects all packets addressed to a user-level application; uses proxies to control and filter traffic on a connection-by-connection basis. Also provides authentication.

**assignment** — The appointment of a specific resource to a specific task.

**assumption** — A factor that is considered to be real or certain for planning purposes.

**asymmetric encryption** — An encryption method in which two keys (a private key and a public key) are used to encrypt and decrypt a message. Also known as public-key encryption.

**attachment** — A file that is sent with an e-mail message.

**attenuation** — The weakening of a transmission signal as it travels farther from its source.

**AU** — Audio file format used by UNIX servers, the majority of Web servers. Most Web browsers can read AU.

**Audio Interchange File Format (AIFF)** — High-quality audio format developed by Apple Computer.

**Audio Video Interleave (AVI)** — Standard Windows file format for video files.

**authentication** — The process of verifying the identity of a user who logs on to a system, or the integrity of transmitted data.

**back end** — A series of systems that fulfill requests made by a client. Back-end systems can include mainframes and servers containing information databases.

**backbone** — The highest level in the computer network hierarchy, to which smaller networks typically connect.

**bandwidth** — The amount of information, sometimes called traffic, that can be carried on a network at one time. The total capacity of a line. Also, the rate of data transfer over a network connection; measured in bits per second.

**baseline** — A recording of network activity, obtained through documentation and monitoring, that serves as an example for comparing future network activity.

**bastion host** — A computer that houses various firewall components and services, and is connected to a public network such as the Internet.

**binary file** — A file containing data or instructions written in zeros and ones (computer language).

**BitTorrent** — A peer-to-peer file sharing protocol used for distributing large amounts of data.

**blackhole list** — A published list of IP addresses known to be sources of spam.

**block-level element** — A markup element that affects at least an entire paragraph.

**blog** — Short for "Web log." A collection of personal thoughts posted on a public Web site. Blogging is the act of adding entries to a blog.

**Bluetooth** — A standard for short-range radio signals that is used to form personal area networks (PANs).

**Boolean operator** — A symbol or word used in Internet searches to narrow search results by including or excluding certain words or phrases from the search criteria.

**bottleneck** — A point in network communication at which information is processed more slowly. Also, any element (a hard drive, I/O card or network interface card) that slows network connectivity rates.

**brand** — A concept or collection of symbols associated with a product, service or person.

**browser e-mail** — E-mail programs such as Outlook Express and Opera Mail that come bundled with a Web browser and with which they may be integrated.

**buffer** — A cache of memory used by a computer to store frequently used data. Buffers allow faster access times.

**bus** — An electronic pathway that conducts signals to connect the functional components of a computer.

**business logic** — The coding (usually in SQL) necessary to create relationships in the data stored in a database.

**business-to-business (B2B)** — An e-commerce model in which a Web-based business sells products and/or services to other businesses.

**business-to-consumer (B2C)** — An e-commerce model in which a Web-based business sells products and/or services to consumers or end users.

**byte** — A measurement of memory needed to store one 8-bit character.

**cable modem** — A device that allows computers to communicate over a network by modulating and demodulating the cable signal into a stream of data.

**call center** — A centralized office used for the purpose of processing a large volume of requests by phone.

**callback** — A process in which a remote access server returns a call to a remote client that has logged on in order to authenticate that client.

**CAPTCHA (Completely Automated Public Turing Test to Tell Computers and Humans Apart)** — A test that uses a word-verification graphic designed to differentiate humans from automated senders during online transactions.

**Carrier Sense Multiple Access/Collision Detection (CSMA/CD)** — The LAN access method used by Ethernet. Checks for network access availability with a signal.

**Cascading Style Sheets (CSS)** — A technology that allows greater style definition and formatting control of HTML elements. Formatting can be placed within the HTML or called remotely from an external style sheet.

**change management** — The process, tools and techniques that help people implement changes to achieve a desired outcome.

**character set** — The group of symbols used to render text on a page.

**client** — An individual computer connected to a network. Also, a system or application (such as a Web browser or user agent) that requests a service from another computer (the server) and is used to access files or documents.

**client-side script** — Code embedded into an HTML page and downloaded by a user; resides on the client and helps process Web form input. Common client-side scripting languages include JavaScript and VBScript.

**cloud computing** — A computing paradigm in which users are able to access software and services over the Internet instead of from their desktops.

**cluster** — A group of sectors used as the basic unit of data storage.

**coax** — Short for coaxial cable. High-capacity two-wire (signal and ground) cable; inner wire is the primary conductor, and the metal sheath serves as the ground.

**codec** — A compression/ decompression algorithm used by modern video and audio player plug-ins.

**collective intelligence** — The ability of a group to exhibit a greater degree of intelligence by solving problems collaboratively compared to the intelligence of an individual member.

**COM** — PC serial ports are referred to as numbered COM (communication) ports. COM ports have a maximum transmission speed of roughly 115 Kbps.

**common field** — A field contained in two or more database tables that forms a connection between the tables.

**Common Gateway Interface (CGI)** — A program that processes data submitted by the user. Allows a Web server to pass control to a software application, based on user request. The application receives and organizes data, then returns it in a consistent format.

**Concurrent Versions System (CVS)** — A tool that allows programmers to control different versions of the pieces of a program as those pieces are developed.

**constraint** — A factor, such as budget or time, that limits a project manager's options.

**consumer-to-consumer (C2C)** — An e-commerce model in which individual consumers sell their pre-owned products or personal services to other consumers.

**contact center** — A call center that allows consumers to contact agents via avenues other than by telephone.

**Content Management System (CMS)** — A server or series of servers that allows you to easily create, store and track all documents and information produced by an organization.

**convergence** — The integration of telephony and data technologies.

**cookie** — A text file that contains information sent between a server and a client to help maintain state and track user activities. Cookies can reside in memory or on a hard drive.

**crowdsourcing** — A problem-solving model in which a task ordinarily performed by one person is outsourced to a large group or community in order to obtain and analyze large amounts of data.

**customs** — National departments responsible for controlling items entering and leaving the country.

**cyberbullying** — Willful harm inflicted on others through the use of information and communication technologies.

**daemon** — A Linux/UNIX program that is usually initiated at startup and runs in the background until required.

**data** — Information being stored, usually in a database.

**data source name (DSN)** — A text string that is used to reference the data source by application programs.

**database** — A collection of data that can be sorted and searched using search algorithms.

**database administrator** — An individual who is responsible for the maintenance and security of an organization's database resources and data.

**database management system (DBMS)** — A program used to store, access and manipulate database information.

**dead link** — A hyperlink that, when clicked, sends a Web site visitor to a page or resource that does not exist on the server.

**decryption** — The process of converting encrypted data back to its original form.

**deep URL** — A URL that includes a path past the domain into the folder structure of a Web site.

**dictionary program** — A program specifically written to break into a password-protected system. It has a relatively large list of common password names that it repeatedly uses to gain access.

**digital certificate** — A password-protected, encrypted data file containing message encryption, user identification and message text. Used to authenticate a program or a sender's public key, or to initiate SSL sessions. Must be signed by a certificate authority (CA) to be valid.

**digital signature** — An electronic stamp added to a message that uniquely identifies its source and verifies its contents at the time of the signature.

**Digital Subscriber Line (DSL)** — A high-speed direct Internet connection that uses all-digital networks.

**Digital Video Interface (DVI)** — A video interface technology that carries uncompressed digital video data to a display.

**direct memory access (DMA)** — A process that allows devices to bypass controllers and directly access memory.

**disk cache** — Storage space on a computer hard disk used to temporarily store downloaded data.

**dithering** — The ability for a computer to approximate a color by combining the RGB values.

**document type declaration (<!DOCTYPE>)** — A declaration of document or code type embedded within an HTML, XHTML, XML or SGML document; identifies the version and nature of code used. Denoted by the <!DOCTYPE> tag at the beginning of the document.

**Document Type Definition (DTD)** — A set of rules contained in a simple text file that defines the structure, syntax and vocabulary as it relates to tags and attributes for a corresponding document.

**domain name** — An IP address represented in words.

**domain name server** — A server that resolves domain names into IP addresses.

**domain name space** — The three-level domain name hierarchy (root-level, top-level and second-level domains) that forms the Domain Name System (DNS).

**Domain Name System (DNS)** — A system that maps uniquely hierarchical names to specific Internet addresses.

**dynamic** — Always changing.

**Dynamic HTML (DHTML)** — A combination of HTML, script, styles and the Document Object Model (DOM) that provides Web page interactivity.

**e-mail client** — An e-mail program that is independent of any specific Web browser, and that you can use to send e-mail messages.

**electronic commerce (e-commerce)** — The integration of communications, data management and security capabilities to allow organizations and consumers to exchange information related to the sale of good and services.

**Electronic Data Interchange (EDI)** — The inter-organization exchange of documents in a standardized electronic format directly between participating computers.

**emoticon** — A combination of characters that, when read sideways, helps convey emotion in an e-mail message.

**emulator** — A type of software that imitates a computer then allows non-native software to run in a foreign environment. Sometimes also a hardware device.

**Encapsulated PostScript (EPS)** — File format used for importing and exporting graphics.

**encryption** — A security technique designed to prevent access to information by converting it into a scrambled (unreadable) form of text.

**end-user license agreement (EULA)** — A legal contract between the author of software and the end user that defines how the software can be used.

**event handler** — A line of code that allows a language to respond to a specific event or user input.

**event-driven** — Reacting to particular user actions or the browser's completion of a specific task.

**Extensible Hypertext Markup Language (XHTML)** — The current standard authoring language used to develop Web pages and other electronically displayed documents. XHTML requires stricter code syntax than HTML.

**Extensible Markup Language (XML)** — A markup language that describes document content instead of adding structure or formatting to document content. A simplified version of SGML.

**Extensible Stylesheet Language (XSL)** — A style language that provides formatting instructions for XML documents.

**extranet** — A network that connects enterprise intranets to the global Internet. Designed to provide access to selected external users.

**Extreme Programming (XP)** — A software development methodology that is designed to be very responsive to the customer's changing requirements.

**field** — A category of information in a database table.

**File Transfer Protocol (FTP)** — An Internet protocol used to transfer files between computers; allows file transfer without corruption or alteration.

**firewall** — A security barrier that controls the flow of information between the Internet and a private network. A firewall prevents outsiders from accessing an enterprise's internal network, which accesses the Internet indirectly through a proxy server.

**fixed-width font** — A font in which every character, including the space character, has equal width. In proportional-width fonts, letters such as I and J have less width than M or B.

**folksonomy** — The practice of categorizing online content through tags.

**foreign key** — A field in a related database table that refers to the primary key in the primary table.

**frame** — A scrollable region of a Web page in which other pages can be displayed; a single element of a frameset. Each frame has its own URL.

**frameset document** — A Web page that defines a set of adjacent frames in which other Web pages are displayed.

**front end** — A client that acts as an interface to a collection of servers (for example, mainframes or PC-based servers). A Web browser is a typical front-end client.

**fully qualified domain name (FQDN)** — The complete domain name of an Internet computer, such as www.CIW-certified.com.

**Gantt chart** — A horizontal bar chart that graphically displays project tasks and durations.

**gateway** — A node on a network that serves as a portal to other networks.

**GNU Privacy Guard (GPG)** — An open-source version of PGP, used for encrypting and decrypting e-mail messages, that does not use patented algorithms.

---

**graphical user interface (GUI)** — A program that provides visual navigation with menus and screen icons, and performs automated functions when users click command buttons.

**Graphics Interchange Format (GIF)** — A graphical image file format commonly used in HTML documents.

**greenfield** — A project that lacks any constraints imposed by prior development.

**hacker** — An unauthorized user who penetrates a host or network to access and manipulate data.

**hash** — A number generated by an algorithm from a text string. Also known as a message digest.

**hash encryption** — An encryption method in which hashes are used to verify the integrity of transmitted messages. Also known as one-way encryption

**HDMI (High-Definition Multimedia Interface)** — A compact audio/video interface for transmitting uncompressed digital data.

**header** — A block of information attached to a piece of data. The first part of a network packet. Can contain network addressing information or additional information that helps computers and applications process data.

**help desk technician** — An individual who diagnoses and resolves users' technical hardware and software problems.

**hexadecimal** — A base-16 number system that allows large numbers to be displayed by fewer characters than if the number were displayed in the regular base-10 system. In hexadecimal, the number 10 is represented as the letter A, 15 is represented as F, and 16 is represented as 10.

**home page** — The first Web page that displays when you access a domain.

**hop** — One link between two network devices; the number of hops between two devices is considered a hop count.

**host** — A computer that other computers can use to gain information; in network architecture, a host is a client or workstation.

**hosts file** — A file that contains mappings of IP addresses to host names.

**hub** — A device used to connect systems so that they can communicate with one another.

**hyperlinks** — Embedded instructions within a text file that link it to another point in the file or to a separate file.

**hypertext link** — Highlighted or underlined text in a Web page that, when clicked, links the user to another location or Web page.

**Hypertext Markup Language (HTML)** — The traditional authoring language used to develop Web pages for many applications.

**Hypertext Transfer Protocol (HTTP)** — The protocol for transporting HTML documents across the Internet.

**I/O address** — A memory location that allows resources to be allocated to a system device.

**identity theft** — Fraud committed in your name by someone else who has illicitly gained access to your personal information.

**illicit server** — An application that installs hidden services on systems. Illicit servers consist of "client" code and "server" code that enable the attacker to monitor and control the operation of the computer infected with the server code.

**image map** — A Web page image with clickable regions that are defined as "hot spot" hyperlinks to other pages or page sections.

**index** — A catalog of the contents of a database. Each entry identifies a unique database record.

**Information Technology (IT)** — The management and processing of information using computers and computer networks.

**infrared** — A spectrum of light used for communication between various network-enabled devices.

**inline images** — Images rendered in a Web page.

**instant messaging (IM)** — A computer-based method of communication in which users can type and view messages sent to one or more recipients, and view the responses immediately.

**Integrated Services Digital Network (ISDN)** — A communication standard for sending voice, video or data over digital telephone lines.

**interactive** — The characteristic of some hardware and software, such as computers, games and multimedia systems, that allows them to respond differently based on a user's actions.

**interface** — A communication channel between two components.

**Internet** — A worldwide network of interconnected networks.

**Internet Control Messaging Protocol (ICMP)** — A subset of Internet Protocol that is most often used to determine whether a computer can communicate with the rest of the network.

**Internet fraud** — Scam or other deceptive practices committed via the Internet, usually for the purpose of monetary gain or identity theft.

**Internet Message Access Protocol (IMAP)** — A protocol that resides on an incoming mail server. Similar to POP, but is more powerful. Allows sharing of mailboxes and multiple mail server access. The current version is IMAP4.

**Internet privacy** — The ability to control what information you reveal about yourself over the Internet, and to whom (or what) you reveal it.

**Internet Protocol (IP)** — The data transmission standard for the Internet. Every computer connected to the Internet has its own IP address, which enables a packet of data to be delivered to a specific computer.

**Internet Service Provider (ISP)** — An organization that maintains a gateway to the Internet and rents access to customers on a per-use or subscription basis.

**interoperability** — The ability of one computer system to communicate with another; often refers to different operating systems working together.

**interrupt request (IRQ)** — A hardware line over which devices can send interrupt signals to the processor.

**intranet** — An internal network based on TCP/IP protocols, accessible only to users within a company.

**IP address** — A unique numerical address assigned to a computer or device on a network.

**IP Security (IPsec)** — An authentication and encryption standard that provides security over the Internet. It functions at Layer 3 of the OSI/RM and can secure all packets transmitted over the network.

**Java** — An object-oriented programming language developed by Sun Microsystems that is fully cross-platform functional.

**Java Virtual Machine (JVM)** — The artificial computer that runs Java programs and allows the same code to run on different platforms.

**Joint Photographic Experts Group (JPEG)** — A graphical image file format commonly used for photographs.

**junction table** — A database table containing foreign-key fields that refer to the primary-key fields from the primary tables in a many-to-many relationship.

**Kerberos** — A proprietary key management scheme between unknown principals who want to communicate securely. Uses symmetric algorithms

and acts as a trusted third party that knows the identities of the organizations asking to communicate, but does not reveal them.

**kernel** — The essential part of an operating system; provides basic services; always resides in memory.

**key** — A variable value, such as a numeric code, that uses an algorithm to encrypt and decrypt data. Some applications encrypt and decrypt with the same key, whereas other applications use a pair of keys.

**keyword** — A word that appears on a Web page and is used by search engines to identify relevant URLs. Some words, such as "the" or "and," are too common to be used as keywords.

**Layer 2 switch** — A device that forwards traffic based on MAC addresses.

**Layer 3 switch** — A device that connects networks.

**legacy adapter board** — An older, non-Plug-And-Play adapter board.

**legacy model** — A model that, because of its age, may not support modern technologies without manipulation or upgrades.

**Lightweight Directory Access Protocol (LDAP)** — A protocol that allows a network entity to access a directory service listing.

**link rot** — The phenomenon in which hyperlinks on a Web site gradually become invalid as referenced Web page content, links and page locations change.

**list server** — A server that collects and distributes information from an authorized group of participants, called a listserve group.

**listserve group** — Users who subscribe to an e-mailing list through a list server.

**LiveScript** — The Netscape-developed scripting language that was the predecessor to JavaScript.

**local area network (LAN)** — A group of computers connected within a confined geographic area.

**lossless compression** — A type of data file compression in which all original data can be recovered when the file is decompressed.

**lossy compression** — A type of data file compression in which some file information is permanently eliminated.

**LPT** — Line printer port. PC parallel ports are referred to as numbered LPTs.

**Mail Delivery Agent (MDA)** — An e-mail server program that receives sent messages and delivers them to their proper destination mailbox.

**Mail User Agent (MUA)** — A messaging component used as a stand-alone application by the user.

**mailing list server** — An e-mail server that regularly sends e-mail messages to a specified list of users.

**malware** — Abbreviation for malicious software. Malware is software designed to harm computer systems.

**many-to-many relationship** — In databases, a relationship in which one record in Table A can relate to many matching records in Table B, and vice versa.

**markup language** — A series of commands used to format, organize and describe information on a Web page.

**mashup** — A Web page that integrates content and scripts from multiple Web sites to create new applications.

**media** — Any material that allows data to flow through it or be stored on it; includes hard and floppy disks, wire, cable, and fiber optics.

**Media Access Control (MAC) address** — The hardware address of a device connected to a network.

**Message Transfer Agent (MTA)** — A messaging component that routes, delivers and receives e-mail.

**meta search engine** — A search engine that scans Web pages for <meta> tag information.

**metalanguage** — A language used for defining other languages.

**microformat** — A data format that adds human-readable metadata to existing code so that the data can be processed by other software.

**milestone** — The end of a stage that marks the completion of a task or series of related tasks, resulting in a key deliverable.

**MIME type** — Identifies the contents of a file in the MIME encoding system using a type/subtype format; examples are image/jpg and text/plain.

**mobile computing** — A person's ability to use technology in non-stationary positions and in transit.

**modem** — Abbreviation for modulator/ demodulator. An analog device that enables computers to communicate over telephone lines by translating digital data into audio/ analog signals (on the sending computer) and then back into digital form (on the receiving computer).

**motherboard** — The main circuit board in a computer, on which the microprocessor, physical memory and support circuitry are located.

**Moving Picture Experts Group (MPEG)** — High-quality video file compression format.

**MPEG-1 Audio Layer 3 (MP3)** — Popular compression standard for audio files; retains most of the sound quality of the source.

**MPEG-2** — Current video compression standard.

**Multipurpose Internet Mail Extensions (MIME)** — A protocol that enables operating systems to map file name extensions to corresponding applications. Also used by applications to automatically process files downloaded from the Internet.

**Multistation Access Unit (MAU)** — The network device that is the central connection point for Token Ring networks.

**Musical Instrument Digital Interface (MIDI)** — A standard computer interface for creating and playing electronic music. It allows computers to re-create music in digital format for playback.

**narrowband** — A specific set of frequencies established for wireless communication (usually for voice). Communicates at lower rates than broadband.

**National Science Foundation (NSF)** — An independent agency of the U.S. government that promotes the advancement of science and engineering.

**needs analysis** — Determining a customer's needs by acquiring information, processing and evaluating the information, then creating a plan of action to address the needs.

**netbook** — A more compact, Web-oriented version of the standard laptop PC; relies on the cloud-computing model in which the Internet is used for remote access to Web applications.

**network** — A group of two or more computers connected so they can communicate with one another.

**Network Address Translation (NAT)** — The practice of hiding internal IP addresses from the external network.

**network engineer** — An individual who manages and maintains a network infrastructure.

**network interface card (NIC)** — A circuit board within a computer's central processing unit that serves as the interface enabling the computer to connect to a network.

**Network News Transfer Protocol (NNTP)** — The Internet protocol used by news servers that enables the exchange of newsgroup (Usenet) articles.

**network operating system (NOS)** — An operating system that manages network resources.

**newsgroup** — On Usenet, a subject or other topical interest group whose members exchange ideas and opinions. Participants post and receive messages via a news server.

**node** — Any entity on a network that can be managed, such as a system, repeater, router, gateway, switch or firewall. A computer or other addressable device attached to a network; a host.

**non-repudiation** — The security principle of providing proof that a transaction occurred between identified parties. Repudiation occurs when one party in a transaction denies that the transaction took place.

**object** — An element on a Web page that contains data and procedures for how that item will react when activated. On a Web page, an object is typically a multimedia presentation.

**object-based** — Similar to object-oriented programming languages, but does not allow for inheritance from one class to another.

**object-oriented** — A style of programming that links data to the processes that manipulate it.

**object-oriented programming (OOP)** — Programming concept based on objects and data and how they relate to one another, instead of logic and actions; C++ and Java are OOP languages.

**OCx** — Optical carrier levels; defines the transmission speeds used in SONET/SDH.

**Ogg Vorbis (.ogg)** — A free, open-source alternative to the MP3 compression format for audio files; creates smaller, faster downloading files.

**one-to-many relationship** — In databases, a relationship in which a record in Table A can have multiple matching records in Table B, but a record in Table B has only one matching record in Table A.

**one-to-one relationship** — In databases, a relationship in which each record in Table A can have only one matching record in Table B, and vice versa.

**online stalking** — To pursue stealthily, harass and/or prey upon another person using online venues such as chat rooms, e-mail, social networking sites, etc. The stalker may also meet the victim in an online venue and may gain his or her trust before perpetrating harassment activities.

**ontology** — The study of how a particular knowledge domain, or system, is organized. An ontology is the product of an ontological study.

**Open Buying on the Internet (OBI)** — An open-technology standard used by organizations to exchange data in a common format; an alternative to EDI.

**open source** — A peer-based development process describing organizations and products that provide free source code to the development community at large with the goal of developing better products; includes Apache Web server and Linux.

**Open Systems Interconnection (OSI) reference model** — A layered network architecture model of communication developed by the International Organization for Standardization (ISO). Defines seven layers of network functions.

**open-source license** — A "copyleft" license that removes restrictions on the use and distribution of the licensed product.

**order tracking** — The ability to determine progress on delivery of a product. Businesses often provide order-tracking support to end users via Web browsers and e-mail clients.

**P2P** — A peer-to-peer network on the Internet.

**packet** — Data processed by protocols so it can be sent across a network.

**packet sniffing** — The use of protocol analyzer software to obtain sensitive information, such as user names and passwords.

**password generator** — An algorithm that receives input from a random or pseudo-random number generator and automatically generates a password.

**password manager** — A software application you can use to store and manage multiple passwords.

**password sniffing** — A method of intercepting the transmission of a password during the authentication process. A sniffer is a program used to intercept passwords.

**patch** — Programming code that provides a temporary solution to a known problem, or bug.

**patent** — A set of exclusive rights granted to an inventor for a fixed period of time upon disclosure of the invention.

**pay per click (PPC)** — An Internet marketing technique that enables you to list your site high in search engine rankings by advertising on keywords that describe your product or service.

**PC repair technician** — An individual who installs, modifies and repairs personal computer (PC) hardware components.

**peer-to-peer network** — A network in which each computer has both server and client capabilities.

**peripheral port** — A socket on a computer into which a peripheral device is connected.

**permission bit** — A file or directory attribute that determines access. Permission bits include read, write and execute permissions.

**permissions** — Instructions given by an operating system or server (or a combination thereof) that restrict or allow access to system resources, such as files, user databases and system processes.

**Personal Digital Assistant (PDA)** — A small, handheld computer used for personal information management.

**personal information management (PIM) program** — A tool used to schedule appointments and meetings, store contact information, and manage tasks.

**planned maintenance** — Any scheduled maintenance procedures, including preventive maintenance.

**plenum** — Space between building floors; usually contains air and heating ducts, as well as communication and electrical wires.

**plug-in** — A program installed in the browser to extend its basic functionality. Allows different file formats to be viewed as part of a standard HTML document.

**podcast** — The use of audio or video digital-media files that are distributed through Web feeds to subscribed users.

**Point-to-Point Protocol (PPP)** — A protocol that allows a computer to connect to the Internet over a phone line.

**Point-to-Point Protocol over Ethernet (PPPoE)** — A protocol that implements PPP on top of the Ethernet architecture to connect an entire network to the Internet.

**Point-to-Point Tunneling Protocol (PPTP)** — A protocol that allows users and corporations to securely extend their networks over the Internet using remote access servers. Used to create VPNs.

**pop-under window** — A small browser window that appears behind the browser window you are viewing.

**pop-up window** — A small browser window that appears in front of the browser window you are viewing.

**port** — A logical opening in an operating system or protocol stack that allows the transfer of information. Not the same as a TCP or UDP port.

**Portable Document Format (PDF)** — A file format that can be transferred across platforms and retain its formatting; designated by the file name extension .pdf.

**Post Office Protocol (POP)** — A protocol that resides on an incoming mail server. The current version is POP3.

**presence** — A status indicator that conveys a person's willingness and ability to engage in communications.

**presencing** — The ability for a device to automatically track and report the user's location and availability.

**presentation responsibilities** — The forms in which the data and business logic are presented on your screen. Presentation responsibilities include XHTML and HTML forms, and application-specific interfaces such as Web browsers.

**Pretty Good Privacy (PGP)** — A method of encrypting and decrypting e-mail messages. It can also be used to encrypt a digital signature.

**primary key** — A field containing a value that uniquely identifies each record in a database table.

**print queue** — A mechanism that stores print requests until they are passed to a printing device.

**program management** — The process of managing multiple interdependent projects to improve the performance of an organization.

**project** — A sequence of tasks that must be accomplished within a certain time frame to achieve a desired result.

**project management** — The practice of applying skills and processes to activities in order to meet deadlines and achieve desired results.

**project schedule** — A document that lists the planned dates for performing tasks and meeting goals defined in a project plan.

**proprietary software** — Software that is the legal property of an entity.

**proxy server** — A server that mediates traffic between a protected network and the Internet. Translates IP addresses and filters traffic.

**PS/2-style connector** — The six-pin mini-DIN connectors introduced with the IBM PS/2.

**query** — A question posed by a user to a database to request database information. The database returns the query results based on the criteria supplied by the user in the query.

**QuickTime** — A plug-in developed by Apple Computer for storing movie and audio files in digital format.

**QuickTime Movie (MOV)** — Standard file format for Apple QuickTime; uses the .mov, .moov or .qt file name extension.

**Rapid Application Development (RAD)** — An iterative software development methodology that uses prototypes to help define customer requirements.

**record** — A collection of information in a database table consisting of one or more related fields about a specific entity, such as a person, product or event.

**relational database** — A database that contains multiple tables related through common fields.

**relationship** — A connection between two or more database tables that is based on a field that the tables have in common.

**relative URL** — A URL that gives an abbreviated path to a resource using the current page as a starting position.

**replay attack** — An attack in which packets are obtained from the network or a network host, then reused.

**Request for Comments (RFC)** — A document published by the IETF that details information about standardized Internet protocols and those in various development stages.

**reseller** — A company that adds some value to an existing product or ser vice, then sells it to the public or to another company.

**resource** — A person, department or device needed to accomplish a task.

**resource conflict** — A situation in which two or more devices share a configuration setting.

**restore point** — A snapshot of a computer's settings at a particular point in time. Also known as a system checkpoint.

**Return On Investment (ROI)** — Profit earned as a result of a project relative to the value of resources required to complete it.

**Rich Text Format (RTF)** — Portable text file format created by Microsoft that allows image insertion and text formatting; an almost universal format.

**root directory** — Topmost hard disk directory (folder).

**root-level server** — A server at the highest level of the Domain Name System.

**router** — A device that routes packets between networks based on network-layer addresses; determines the best path across a network. Also used to connect separate LANs to form a WAN.

**RSA** — A popular, proprietary public-key encryption algorithm.

**rule** — In a style sheet, a format instruction that consists of a specified selector and the properties and values applied to it. Also a line or lines; the word is related to "ruler," a tool of measurement that can be used to draw straight lines.

**sans-serif** — A font style that does not use decorative strokes at the tips of characters. Includes the Arial font family.

**scope** — The goals and tasks of a project, and the work required to complete them.

**scope creep** — Gradual increases in project scope that can undermine the success of a project.

**screen saver** — A graphic or moving image that appears on your screen when your computer is idle.

**search engine** — A powerful software program that searches Internet databases for user-specified information.

**search engine optimization (SEO)** — The process of improving the volume and quality of traffic to a Web site by structuring content to improve search engine ranking. A specific activity of Internet marketing.

**Secure Copy (SCP)** — A program used with Secure Shell (SSH) to transfer files between systems.

**Secure Electronic Transactions (SET)** — An Internet protocol that uses digital certificates to secure financial transactions.

**Secure MIME (S/MIME)** — Secure version of MIME that adds encryption to MIME data.

**Secure Shell (SSH)** — A protocol and command interface that provides secure access to a remote computer.

**Secure Sockets Layer (SSL)** — A protocol that provides authentication and encryption, used by most servers for secure exchanges over the Internet. Superseded by Transport Layer Security (TLS).

**security analyst/consultant** — An individual who examines an organization's security requirements and determines the necessary infrastructure.

**security manager** — An individual who manages the security measures used to protect electronic data.

**segment** — Part of a larger structure; common term used in networking.

**selector** — In a style sheet, any element to which designated styles are applied.

**semantic Web** — A Web 2.0 implementation by which Web data is contextualized with the addition of machine-readable metadata.

**SEO analyst** — An individual who determines the visibility of Web sites across multiple clients and search engines.

**serif** — A font style that uses characters with small decorative additions at the outermost points of the characters, called strokes. Includes the Times and Times New Roman fonts.

**server** — A computer in a network that manages the network resources and provides, or serves, information to clients.

**server administrator** — An individual who manages and maintains network servers.

**server-side script** — Code that resides on a server to help process Web form input. Server-side CGI scripts are commonly written in Perl.

**servlet** — A small Java application that runs on a server.

**shared domain** — A hosting service that allows multiple entities to share portions of the same domain name.

**shell** — A command-based interface that allows a user to issue commands.

**signature database** — In an anti-virus program, a collection of viruses, worms and illicit applications that are listed as security threats.

**Simple Mail Transfer Protocol (SMTP)** — The Internet standard protocol for transferring e-mail messages from one computer to another.

**site map** — A brief, hierarchical representation of a Web site that enables visitors to quickly identify areas of the site and navigate to them.

**Small-Screen Rendering (SSR)** — A browser technology developed for wireless devices that reformats Web pages to display on 176-pixel-wide mobile phone display screens.

**Smalltalk** — A programming language that pioneered object-oriented programming. Not popularly used in Web development.

**smart card** — A credit card that replaces the magnetic strip with an embedded chip for storing or processing data.

**smartphone** — A mobile phone that includes PC-like functionality.

**snail mail** — Slang term for the standard postal service.

**social networking** — The grouping of individuals with common interests or goals into specific groups or communities.

**socket** — The end point of a connection (either side), which usually includes the TCP or UDP port used and the IP address. Used for communication between a client and a server.

**soft phone** — A software application that enables a PC or PDA to function as a telephone using VoIP technology.

**Software as a Service (SaaS)** — A software distribution model in which the software is hosted by a service provider and licensed for use by the user.

**spam** — Unsolicited and unwanted e-mail messages; the online equivalent of junk mail.

**spam filter** — An e-mail client program that identifies and filters out spam messages before they reach the e-mail Inbox.

**spim** — Spam that is delivered through instant messaging.

**spread spectrum** — Technologies that consist of various methods for radio transmission in which frequencies or signal patterns are continuously changed.

**spyware** — A software application secretly placed on a user's system to gather information and relay it to outside parties, usually for advertising purposes.

**SSH File Transfer Protocol (S/FTP)** — A file transfer protocol that allows the encryption of transmissions using the Secure Shell (SSH) protocol.

**SSL/TLS-enabled FTP (FTPS)** — FTP that runs on an SSL/TLS-secured connection.

**stakeholder** — A person or group with an interest in a project, and with the power to exert influence (either positive or negative) over the project and affect results.

**standard** — A definition or format that has been approved by a recognized standards organization.

**Standard Generalized Markup Language (SGML)** — A metalanguage used to create other languages, including HTML and XHTML.

**Statement Of Work (SOW)** — A contract to initiate a project; the contract contains project goals and specifies how those goals will be met.

**streaming audio and video** — Audio and video files that travel over a network in real time.

**streaming media** — A continuous flow of data, usually audio or video files, that assists with the uninterrupted delivery of those files into a browser.

**Structured Query Language (SQL)** — A language used to create and maintain professional, high-performance corporate databases.

**switch** — A device that connects either individual systems or multiple networks. A Layer 1 switch connects individual systems.

**symmetric encryption** — An encryption method in which the same key is used to encrypt and decrypt a message. Also known as private-key encryption.

**Synchronous Optical Network (SONET)** — High-speed fiber-optic system used as a network and Internet backbone. The European counterpart is the Synchronous Digital Hierarchy (SDH).

**T1** — A digital carrier that transmits data at a speed of 1.544 Mbps.

**table** — A collection of data about a limited topic, organized into rows and columns in a database.

**Tagged Image File Format (TIFF)** — Commonly used graphic file format, developed by Aldus Corporation; uses the .tif or .tiff file name extension.

**tags** — Pieces of code, enclosed in angle brackets, that tell the HTML interpreter how to process or display text.

**task** — A unit of work that must be accomplished during the course of a project.

**Telnet** — The Internet standard protocol for remote terminal connection service.

**text messaging** — A method of person-to-person communication in which users type short text messages from mobile phones.

**text-level element** — A markup element that affects single characters or words.

**TinyURL** — A free Web service that generates short aliases for long URLs.

**token passing** — The LAN access method used by Token Ring networks. A data frame, or token, is passed from one node to the next around the network ring.

**top-level domain** — The group into which a domain is categorized, by common topic (company, educational institution) and/or geography (country, state).

**trace** — Thin conductive path on a circuit board, usually made of copper.

**trackback** — A method by which a blogger receives notification when other bloggers link to his or her blog entry.

**transceiver** — A device that transmits and receives digital or analog signals.

**Transmission Control Protocol/Internet Protocol (TCP/IP)** — A suite of protocols that turns data into blocks of information called packets, which are then sent across the Internet. The standard protocol used by the Internet.

**Transport Layer Security (TLS)** — A protocol based on SSL 3.0 that provides authentication and encryption, used by most servers for secure exchanges over the Internet.

**trojan** — A program disguised as a harmless application that actually produces harmful results.

**troll** — Web user who publishes negative comments or submits feedback simply to annoy or anger.

**trouble ticket** — A record of a problem related to a service provided by an ISP or ASP. Used to record receipt of a complaint and track resolution of the problem.

**tunneling protocol** — A protocol that encapsulates data packets into another packet.

**TV tuner card** — A computer component that enables television signals to be viewed on a computer monitor.

**typosquatting** — The unethical practice of registering domain names very similar to those of high-volume sites in hopes of receiving traffic from users seeking the high-volume site who mistakenly enter an incorrect URL in their browsers.

**Unicode** — A universal character set designed to support all written languages, as well as scholarly disciplines (e.g., mathematics).

**unified communications (UC)** — A business trend that seeks to simplify and integrate all forms of communication. Also, a set of technologies that enable voice to be converted into text, and vice versa.

**Uniform Resource Identifier (URI)** — A standardized method of referring to a resource using a text string.

**Uniform Resource Locator (URL)** — A text string that specifies an Internet address and the method by which the address can be accessed.

**uninterruptible power supply (UPS)** — A power supply that uses a battery to maintain power during a power outage.

**update** — A file or collection of tools that resolves system liabilities and improves software performance.

**Usenet (User Network)** — A collection of thousands of Internet computers, newsgroups and newsgroup members using Network News Transfer Protocol (NNTP) to exchange information.

**user agent** — Any application, such as a Web browser, mobile phone, PDA or help engine, that renders HTML for display to users.

**user name** — A unique name or number that identifies you when logging on to a computer system or online service. In an e-mail address, the part before the @ symbol.

**vector graphics** — Resizable images that are saved as a sequence of vector statements, which describes a series of points to be connected.

**viewer** — A scaled-down version of an application; designed to view and print files.

**virtual domain** — A hosting service that allows a company to host its domain name on a third-party ISP server.

**virtual local area network (VLAN)** — Logical subgroup within a LAN created with software instead of hardware.

**Virtual Network Computing (VNC)** — A program that allows you to control a computer at a remote location.

**Virtual Reality Modeling Language (VRML)** — A three-dimensional graphic authoring language.

**virtualization** — A software technology that enables you to run multiple virtual operating systems and applications on a single physical computer.

**virus** — A malicious program that replicates itself on computer systems, usually through executable software, and causes irreparable system damage.

**Visual Basic** — The Microsoft graphical user interface (GUI) programming language used for developing Windows applications. A modified version of the BASIC programming language.

**Visual Basic Script (VBScript)** — Scripting language from Microsoft derived from Visual Basic; used to manipulate ActiveX scripts.

**Voice over IP (VoIP)** — A technology that converts voice into data packets for transmission over a packet-switched IP network. Allows the use of the Internet for real-time voice and video traffic.

**Waterfall model** — A development process in which the development phases flow from one to the other sequentially.

**Waveform (WAV)** — Windows standard format for audio files.

**Web 2.0** — A concept referring to the changing trends in the use of WWW technology and Web design that have led to the development of information-sharing and collaboration capabilities.

**Web analytics** — The practice of collecting data and studying user behavior in an attempt to increase market share and sales.

**Web application developer** — An individual who develops primarily server-side Web applications.

**Web application framework** — A set of software tools or code that is commonly used in the creation and management of online applications.

**Web architect** — An individual who creates the overview plan of a Web site's development.

**Web browser** — A software application that enables users to access and view Web pages on the Internet.

**Web feed** — A data format for delivering Web content that is updated frequently.

**Web marketing manager** — An individual who develops and implements plans to exploit the Internet for marketing and sales opportunities.

**Web page** — An HTML document containing one or more elements (text, images, hyperlinks) that can be linked to or from other HTML pages.

**Web site** — A World Wide Web server and its content; includes multiple Web pages.

**Web site analyst** — An individual who analyzes Web site statistics to determine the site's effectiveness.

**Web site designer** — An individual who is responsible for the organization and appearance of a Web site.

**Web site manager** — An individual who manages a Web development team.

**Web-based e-mail** — Free e-mail service from a provider such as Windows Live Hotmail or Yahoo! in which you request a user name. You can access your e-mail from any computer that has access to the Internet.

**Webcast** — An audio and/or video Web event that is distributed over the Internet.

**Webinar** — An interactive Web-based seminar or training session.

**What You See Is What You Get (WYSIWYG)** — (pronounced whiz-ee-wig) A user-friendly editing format in which the file being edited is displayed as it will appear in the browser.

**wide area network (WAN)** — A group of computers connected over an expansive geographic area so their users can share files and services.

**wideband** — A large set of frequencies capable of carrying data at higher rates (for example, 1.544 Mbps). Usually carries digital signals. Includes DSL and cable Internet access.

**wiki** — A page or collection of Web pages that can be viewed and modified by anybody with a Web browser and access to the Internet.

**wireless access point (AP)** — A device that enables wireless systems to communicate with each other, provided that they are on the same network.

**Wireless Application Protocol (WAP)** — A standard protocol that wireless devices use to access the Internet.

**Wireless Markup Language (WML)** — A markup language that presents the text portions of Web pages to wireless devices.

**wizard** — A tool that assists users of an application in creating documents and/or databases based on styles and templates. Also a tool that guides users step-by-step through a software installation process.

**World Wide Web (WWW)** — A set of software programs that enables users to access resources on the Internet via hypertext documents.

**worm** — A self-replicating program or algorithm that consumes system resources.

**X.509** — The standard used by certificate authorities (CAs) for creating digital certificates.

**x.org** — A windowing system used with UNIX and all popular operating systems.

**xDSL** — Collectively, the variations of Digital Subscriber Line (DSL), which include ADSL, RADSL and HDSL.

**XMLHttpRequest** — An application programming interface (API) that is used to transfer XML and other text data between a Web server and browser.

**zone file** — A file containing a set of instructions for resolving a specific domain name into its numerical IP address. Found in DNS servers.

# Index

file naming, 1-35
file not found, 1-36
file structure of Web site, 3-11
File Transfer Protocol (FTP), 10-19
file upload button, 7-10, 7-13
file uploading and downloading, 11-6
*file* value, 7-13
finance management, 12-6
fixed-width font, 3-25
fixed-width layout, 4-24
Flash animation, 8-14
flat file database, 1-30
flavors of HTML 4.01, 2-6
flavors of XHTML, 2-10
floating frame, 9-13
font information, 4-19
font instruction, 3-30
font size, 2-5
font style elements, 3-30
form field elements, 7-10
form handling, 7-4
form, user-input, 1-8, 7-3
formatting language, 2-5
FormMail, CGI script, 7-5
forms, in supply chain, 12-7
forward slash, 5-4
forward-compatibility, writing code for, 3-35
frame margin, 9-13
frame, scrolling, 9-13
*frameborder* attribute, 9-12
frames, 9-3
frames, appropriate use, 9-15
frames, targeting, 9-8
frameset document, 9-3, 9-5
Frameset flavor of HTML, 2-6
Frameset flavor of XHTML, 2-10
Freehand, 8-3
freeware, 7-3
front-end issues, 1-12
FrontPage, 1-11
FTP, 5-4, 12-25
FTP client, 10-19
FTPx Corp. FTP Explorer, 10-19
fully qualified URL, 5-3
function, 11-4
functions, JavaScript, 11-15
fuzzy image, 8-13
Gates, Bill, 6-10, 6-15
gateway, payment, 12-19
Generalized Markup Language (GML), 2-4
generation, 2-19
get, 7-8
GIF, 1-28, 4-7, 8-3, 8-13
GIF 89a, 8-10
GIF Construction Set, 8-13
GIF, animated, 8-13
GIMP, The, 8-3
global issues, business, 12-28
glossary, creating with links, 5-12
GML, 2-4
GNU Privacy Guard (GPG), 1-28
good coding practice, 3-35
Google Chrome, 2-20
GPG, 1-28
graphic types, 8-3
graphical user interface (GUI), 1-11, 10-3
graphics, 4-5
Graphics Interchange Format (GIF), 1-28, 4-7
greater-than symbol, 4-14

grids, 6-3
GUI, 1-11
GUI editor, 1-11, 10-3, 10-16, 10-17
GUI editor, creating pages with, 10-6
GUI HTML editor features, 10-4
Habitat For Humanity, 1-37
hash symbol, 5-12, 8-5
header, table, 6-3
heading element, 3-3
heading levels, 3-22
heading style, 2-5
hearing impairment, 1-21
height, changing in table, 6-11
Hello, World, 11-6
hexadecimal code, 4-16
hidden comments, 3-36
history list, 3-10
hit counter, 11-6
horizontal portal, 1-26
horizontal rule, 4-3
horizontal rule attributes, 4-4
hosting, 11-46
hosting solution, configuring your own, 11-46
hosting solutions, 11-47
hosting, dedicated, 11-47
hot spot, 8-3
hot spot, defining, 8-5, 8-7
*href* attribute, 5-3, 5-12, 9-8
*href* attribute, <area> tag, 8-5
HTML, 1-7, 1-15, 2-4
HTML 3.2 standard, 2-5
HTML 4.01 flavors, 2-6
HTML 4.01 standard, 2-5
HTML editor, GUI, 10-4
HTML file format, 1-28
HTML interpreter, 2-5
HTML source code, 3-36
HTML tags, 3-3
HTML vs. SGML, 2-5
HTTP, 5-4, 12-16
HTTP 404 – File Not Found, 1-36
HTTP server, 1-36
HTTP server, publishing to, 10-19
HTTPS (Secure HTTP), 5-4
HyperCard, 2-4
hyperlink, 2-4, 5-3
hyperlink from image, 5-10
hyperlink, external, 5-9
hyperlink, image map, 8-3
hyperlink, internal, 5-12
hyperlink, local, 5-5
hyperlink-checking software, 5-16
hyperlinks, in frames, 9-8
hyperlinks, managing, 5-16
hyperlinks, troubleshooting, 5-4
hypermedia, 2-4
Hypertext Markup Language (HTML), 1-7, 2-4
hypertext reference (href), 5-3, 5-12
IANA, 1-27
IBM, 1-31, 2-4
IC3 certification, 10-11
icon bar, 10-4
*id* attribute, 4-22
*id* attribute, <map> tag, 8-5
*if/then* statement, 11-5
IIS, 1-36
Illustrator, Adobe, 8-3
image file formats, 4-6
image interlacing, 8-12

# Supplemental CD-ROM Contents

The *Site Development Foundations* supplemental CD-ROM contains the following files needed to complete the course labs:

## 💿 Site_Dev_Academic_Student_CD

📁 Appendix      📁 Lab Files

## 📂 Appendix

📄 Appendix_A.pdf      📄 Appendix_C.pdf
📄 Appendix_B.pdf      📄 Appendix_D.pdf

## 📂 Lab Files

📁 Lesson01    📁 Lesson06    📁 Lesson10
📁 Lesson03    📁 Lesson07    📁 Lesson11
📁 Lesson04    📁 Lesson08    📁 Resources
📁 Lesson05    📁 Lesson09

## 📂 Lab Files\Lesson01

📁 Lab_1-2

## 📂 Lab Files\Lesson03

📁 Finished     📁 Lab_3-3
📁 Lab_3-2     📁 Optional_Lab_3-1

## 📂 Lab Files\Lesson04

📁 Finished     📁 Lab_4-5
📁 Lab_4-2     📁 Lab_4-8

## 📂 Lab Files\Lesson05

📁 Finished     📁 Lab_5-4
📁 Lab_5-1

## 📂 Lab Files\Lesson06

📁 Finished
📁 Lab_6-1

## 📂 Lab Files\Lesson07

📁 Finished     📁 Lab_7-2     📁 Optional_Lab_7-1
📁 FormMail

   

## 📂 **Lab Files\Lesson08**

| | |
|---|---|
| 📁 Finished | 📁 Lab_8-2 |
| 📁 Lab_8-1 | |

## 📂 **Lab Files\Lesson09**

| | | |
|---|---|---|
| 📁 Finished | 📁 Lab_9-2 | 📁 Optional_Lab_9-2 |
| 📁 Lab_9-1 | 📁 Optional_Lab_9-1 | |

## 📂 **Lab Files\Lesson10**

| | | |
|---|---|---|
| 📁 Finished | 📁 OptLab10-1 | 📄 GUI_HTML_editor.txt |
| 📁 KompoZer 0.7.10 | 📄 CIWlogo.gif | 📄 kompozer-0.7.10-win32.zip |

## 📂 **Lab Files\Lesson11**

| | | |
|---|---|---|
| 📁 Finished | 📁 Lab_11-3 | 📁 Lab_11-5 |
| 📁 Lab_11-1 | 📁 Lab_11-4 | 📄 audacity-win-1.2.6.exe |
| 📁 Lab_11-2 | | |

## 📂 **LabFiles\Resources**

| | |
|---|---|
| 📄 216color.html | 📄 charcodes.html |